Sister Edward
from
S. E. Watkins

TO

THE CHILDREN AND GRANDCHILDREN

OF

THE BARONESS BUNSEN

THESE VOLUMES

ARE AFFECTIONATELY DEDICATED.

THE

LIFE AND LETTERS OF

FRANCES Waddington BARONESS BUNSEN

BY

AUGUSTUS John Cuthbert HARE

AUTHOR OF "MEMORIALS OF A QUIET LIFE," ETC.

"The happiest periods of history are not those of which we hear the most;
in the same manner as in the little world of man's soul, the most saintly
spirits are often existing in those who have never distinguished themselves
as authors, or left any memorial of themselves to be the theme of the world's
talk, but who have led an interior angelic life, having borne their sweet
blossoms unseen."—*Broadstone of Honour.*

IN TWO VOLUMES

VOL. I.

FOURTH EDITION

GEORGE ALLEN, SUNNYSIDE, ORPINGTON

AND

156, CHARING CROSS ROAD, LONDON

1894

CONTENTS OF VOL. I.

PREFACE.

TO write the Life and edit the Letters of the Baroness Bunsen was a task for which many members of her own family were better qualified than myself, but I gratefully undertook this labour of love in accordance with the strongly-expressed wish of her descendants, having the consciousness that, except her own children, no one could have a more tender and reverent affection for the dear and kind friend of my whole life. The story of her surroundings, of the vicissitudes through which she passed, and of her actions with their aims and endeavours, is told in her own words. With the memorials of one who wrote so much, and who always wrote what was worth reading, the only difficulty has been selection. Thousands of letters have been necessarily omitted, which nevertheless had a charm of their own. Enough, I trust, is still left, to pourtray the continuous chain of her loving and loveable life, and to lift the reader for a time into the pure and lofty atmosphere of her heart and mind.

Augustus J. C. Hare.

Holmhurst.

THE LIFE AND LETTERS OF FRANCES BARONESS BUNSEN

VOL. I.

CHAPTER I.

FAMILY INFLUENCES.

" Lives of great men all remind us
    We can make our lives sublime,
And, departing, leave behind us
    Footprints on the sands of time ;

" Footprints, that perhaps another,
    Sailing o'er life's solemn main,
A forlorn and shipwrecked brother,
    Seeing, shall take heart again."

LONGFELLOW.

ONE of the figures which excited most attention amid the multitude who thronged the terrace of Windsor Castle during the happier years of the reign of George III., was that of the venerable Mary Granville, Mrs. Delany, who resided at Windsor in her old age, as the honoured and cherished friend of the King and Queen. No one then living had more interesting recollections to relate than the beautiful old lady who, as a child, had sat on Lord Bolingbroke's knee, and had been set down as Maid of Honour by Queen Anne ; who had been intimate with the most remarkable characters of the reigns of George I. and George II., and whose sense, wit, and natural sweetness of disposition, had been wont to gather the most brilliant literary circle in Europe around her tea-table in St. James's Place. It was of her that Edmund Burke said that she was "not only a truly great woman of fashion, but the highest-bred woman in the world." "Time," says Hannah More, "took very little from her graces or her liveliness, and at eighty-eight she had still the playful charm of eighteen, honoured by all who approached her, and loved by all with whom she associated." *

Mary Granville was the elder of the two daughters of Bernard, grandson of the famous Sir Beville Granville, who, in 1643, lay dead upon the battle-field of Lansdowne Heath, with the patent of the earldom of Bath in his pocket, and a letter from Charles I. gratefully acknowledging his services and his devotion. " What would have clouded any victory," says Clarendon, " and made the loss of others less spoken of, was the death of Sir Beville Granville. . . . . A brighter courage and a gentler disposition were never married together to make the most cheerful and innocent conversation." At the Restoration, the elder son of Sir Beville became the first Earl of Bath, and his younger son Bernard, who had carried the news of the Restoration to Charles II. at Breda, was made Groom of the Bedchamber. This Bernard had two sons, George, Lord Lansdowne, celebrated for his accomplishments, and as the friend of Pope and Swift; and Bernard, who

* Memoirs of Dr. Burney, iii. 56.

married the daughter of Sir Anthony Westcombe (Consul-General of Great Britain at Cadiz), and left four children, Bernard, Beville, Mary, and Anne.

The early history of Mary Granville was a romance and a tragedy. As a child she was adopted by her father's only sister Anne, who had been Maid of Honour to Queen Mary, and after her death married Sir John Stanley,* Commissioner of Customs, and received a grant of apartments in Whitehall. Here little Mary Granville became the intimate childish friend and companion of her cousin Catherine Hyde, afterwards Duchess of Queensberry, whose father then resided over Holbein's Gate, and " whose wit, beauty, and oddities, made her from her early years, when she was Prior's ' Kitty, beautiful and young,' to the end of a long life, a general object of animadversion, censure, and admiration."

Under Lady Stanley's care Mary Granville grew up brilliant and beautiful. When she was only seventeen, while she was staying with her uncle George, Lord Lansdowne, at Longleat, he determined upon her marriage—partly to obtain a good settlement for his niece, but much more to strengthen his own political connection in Cornwall—with a Mr. Pendarves, of Roscrow, a fat, disagreeable, ugly man of sixty, of intemperate habits. It was in vain that Mary Granville remonstrated and implored mercy ; in those days marriages were seldom questions of inclination ; the

* Of Grange Gorman, Ireland, Bart.

consent of her parents was readily obtained, Lady
Stanley would not interfere, and Lord Lansdowne was
inexorable. "Never," wrote the unfortunate bride long
afterwards, "was woe dressed out in gayer colours, than
when I was led to the altar. I lost, not life indeed,
but all that makes life desirable." For some months
Lord Lansdowne attempted to reconcile his niece to
her marriage by detaining her under his roof, and endeavouring to make her believe that life was not so
much changed as she anticipated; but the time came
when she had to accompany her husband into Cornwall,
and to take up her abode in his "dark, disagreeable,
desolated castle, in which her head could not reach to
the bottom of the windows." Mr. Pendarves was almost
always intoxicated, and, when sober, indulged in fits of
violent jealousy about his beautiful wife, in spite of her
displaying perfect willingness to bury herself in utter
seclusion to satisfy him. After two years of misery,
she hailed with delight the hope of being restored to
her friends, by her husband's determination to reside
in London, but her pleasure was soon damped by finding that the house he had engaged was in Rose Street,
Soho, and that she was doomed to the constant companionship of his sister, who hated her. In London,
however, life was more endurable, for amid the many
trials which, especially in those days, lay in wait
for a lovely and neglected wife, she had the advice of
her aunt Lady Stanley and was always willing to
follow her maxim—"Avoid putting yourself in danger,

fly from temptation, for it is always odds on the tempter's side." Her willingness to give up any amusement to stay with her husband, now almost constantly confined to the house by the gout, was invariable, and he so far appreciated her dutiful submission, that seven years after his marriage he made a will in her favour, but on the morning after he made it, his wife found him dead by her side, and the will was unsigned!

Mary Pendarves was only twenty-four, when she found herself a widow. Her connection with Cornwall was broken, her husband's property having all passed away to a niece, so that she continued to reside in London. She had many admirers, but the only person who attracted her was Lord Baltimore, to whom she had nearly given her heart, when she found she had bestowed it unworthily. This disappointment, and the death of her aunt Stanley, induced her to accompany her friend Mrs. Donnellan to Ireland in 1730, on a visit which was prolonged for three years. During this time she became intimately acquainted with Swift, Dean of St. Patrick's, and with many other eminent persons, amongst them Dr. Delany, then recently married, whom she admired for his "humanity and benevolence, charity and generosity." With Swift, Mrs. Pendarves kept up a correspondence after her return to England in 1733, when she had the delight of finding in her only sister Anne Granville all that her fondest hopes could anticipate, and of cementing a lifelong friendship with Margaret, Duchess of Portland,[*] the "Grace of Graces," who was fourteen years younger than herself, and whom she had known from birth, but with whom an almost unparalleled similarity of tastes and sympathies now united her in the closest bonds of intimacy. In 1740 she witnessed the happy marriage of her sister Anne with Mr. Dewes, of Wellesbourne, after which she found her principal interests in the house of the Duke and Duchess of Portland, till Dr. Delany, then a widower, made her an offer of marriage. This proposal, though opposed by her brother and many of her other friends, she was induced to accept after having been nineteen years a widow, by her high estimation of Dr. Delany, and she was married in 1743. In the following year her husband was made Dean of Down, and she accompanied him to Ireland, where their principal residence was at Delville near Dublin.

In accepting Dr. Delany as her husband, Mrs. Pendarves had stipulated to be as little separated as possible from Mrs. Dewes, the beloved " sister of her heart." Accordingly, every third year was spent in England, chiefly between Wellesbourne and Bulstrode, and from 1744 to 1746, the sisters were almost constantly in each other's society, enjoying what they called " days snatched out of the shade " of the rest of their lives. Even when in the most thorough enjoyment of her

* Margaret Cavendish Harley, born 1714, wife of William, second Duke of Portland, was the only child and heiress of Edward, second Earl of Oxford, by his wife Henrietta Cavendish Holles, only child and heiress of John, Duke of Newcastle.

husband's companionship, and of his beautiful property of Delville, Mrs. Delany felt a void in the absence of her sister.

"How often," she wrote in 1750, "do I delude myself with agreeable visions. We walk together from room to room, I show you all my stores of every kind; you are most pleased with my workroom and the library within it; the Dean hurries us into the garden, there you are more pleased than with anything in the house; the fine prospect, the variety of walks, the shades, the seats, the flowers, and the deer, all take your fancy; and all our pleasures are heightened by the dear little Mary's running and bounding as we go along, but alas! the vision is vanished, a cloud is come over it for the present, and instead of enjoying your presence I am addressing a letter to you that must go, by sea and land, hundreds of miles before it kisses your hands."

Yet these were the golden years of Mrs. Delany's life, and when her husband was frequently spoken of as the probable recipient of a vacant bishopric, she only dreaded an honour which must remove her from her beloved Delville, and break up a present of which the happiness was assured, for an uncertain future.

"I have often," she wrote in 1752, "thought of late my lot most singularly happy, more so than is generally met with in this world of woe : a husband of infinite merit, and deservedly most dear to me; a sister whose delicate and uncommon friendship makes me the envy of all other sisters; a brother of worth and honour; and a friend in the Duchess of Portland not to be equalled, besides so many other friends, that altogether make up the sum of my happiness."

In Ireland also, Mrs. Delany had much pleasure in the society of her goddaughter, "Sally Chapone," sister-in-law of the Hester Chapone, who was the authoress of the well-known "Letters on the Improvement of the Mind." This Sarah Chapone was married at Delville to Daniel Sandford, of Sandford Hall in Shropshire; her second son, born at Delville, was Daniel Sandford, afterwards Bishop of Edinburgh, in whom Mrs. Delany always retained an almost maternal interest.

In 1760 the happiness of Mrs Delany became overshadowed by the failing health of her idolised sister. She joined her in England with the Dean, and accompanied her to Bristol hot-wells, where she had the anguish of seeing her fade day by day, till her peaceful death in the following June. Mr. Dewes was compelled to be absent from his wife's death-bed with his boys at Wellesbourne: so that their only daughter, Mary Dewes, was alone with her mother and aunt at the time, and to her in her desolation Mrs. Delany seemed at once to transfer all the boundless affection she had felt for the sister she had lost. Henceforward the education and the happiness of her niece Mary was the chief object of her life.

The loss of Mrs. Delany's sister was followed in

1768, at Bath, by that of her husband, the Dean of Down, to whom she had been tenderly attached. The then widowed Duchess of Portland immediately joined her sorrowing friend, and accompanied her to Calwich in Staffordshire, the residence of her brother, where she was joined by her beloved niece. In her elder and only surviving brother,* Bernard Granville, Mrs. Delany found little sympathy. He was a high-bred and accomplished person, but stern, unloving, and unloved. He had lived longer than was good for him in the society of Rousseau and others at Paris, and, after his return to England, a disappointment in love had induced him to dispose of that part of the Granville property which he had inherited in Cornwall, and to purchase the estate of Calwich, where he established himself wholly amongst strangers, breaking off all family habits, and caring little henceforward to see any of his relations, except the children of his sister, Mrs. Dewes, who were dreadfully afraid of him. His most constant associate in the neighbourhood was Rousseau, who came into the country, attracted by the society of Mr. Granville, but refused to take up his residence at Calwich, preferring to live in the empty mansion of Mr. Davenport—Wootton Hall on Wever Hill, just above the rich pastures and woods where the monastery of Calwich had once occupied a sunny slope near a small river flowing towards the Dove.

* Beville Granville, second brother of Mrs. Delany, had died in Jamaica (without children) in 1736.

To young Mary Dewes the presence of "Monsieur
Rousseau," who used to write notes to her—"à ma belle
voisine," had been a relief in her long visits to her
formidable uncle, and her partiality for him rather
shocked Mrs. Delany, who wrote to her,—"I always
take alarm when virtue in general terms is the idol,
without the support of *religion*, the only foundation
that can be our security to build upon." Another
constant visitor at Calwich had been Handel, who used
to play for hours upon the organ there. A manuscript
collection of Handel's music in thirty-eight volumes,
was written for Mr. Granville under the direction of
the great composer himself. On Mr. Granville's death,
in 1775, he left his property of Calwich to John Dewes,
the youngest son of his sister Anne. Mrs. Delany
was at that time resident at Windsor, and on her
presenting her nephew to the King, he desired that
Mr. Dewes should thenceforth take the name of
Granville. This is the Mr. Granville, brother of Mary
Dewes, who is frequently mentioned afterwards in
these volumes.*

Mrs. Delany purchased a house in St. James's Place,
where, in winter, the Dowager Duchess of Portland

* John Dewes or D'Ewes who assumed the name of Granville, married Harriet Joan, second daughter and co-heiress of John De la Bere,
of Southam near Cheltenham, and died 1826. The death of his only son
John Granville, in 1800, is described in these memoirs. He was succeeded in his estates by his nephew Court (son of his elder brother
Bernard D'Ewes and Anne eldest daughter of the above John De la
Bere of Southam) who sold the property of Calwich.

spent every evening with her, many other friends
dropping in around the hospitable tea-table. The
summers were spent with the Duchess at Bulstrode,
whither Mary Dewes generally accompanied Mrs.
Delany; indeed the Duchess became almost as fond
of "our Mary" as Mrs. Delany herself, and from
Bulstrode Miss Dewes was married at Upton Church
in December, 1770, to Mr. Port of Ilam in Derbyshire, who had changed his name from that of Sparrow
on succeeding to the property of a maternal uncle. In
the following year, their eldest daughter, Georgina
Mary Ann, was born, and obtained her first name by
being goddaughter, as her mother was before her, to
their cousin Georgina Spencer (afterwards Countess
Cowper) daughter of John, Earl Granville, and her
second and third names from her aunt and mother. Mary
Dewes had many other children afterwards,* but none
were so dear to Mrs. Delany as the eldest-born, who
was almost equally beloved by the Duchess of Portland

* John, born March 15, 1773, godson of the Duchess of Portland.
George Rowe, born August 18, 1774, called by Mrs. Delany from his
beauty "my little Vandyke:" who entered the navy under Admiral
Jervis, and died at Antigua of yellow fever on board H.M.S. *Reprisal*.
Bernard, born March 7, 1776, who succeeded to the family living of Ilam,
being the last relic of the family estates in Derbyshire, where he was
greatly beloved, and died in 1854. Louisa, born April 7, 1778, who
married Mr. Brownlow Villiers Layard, afterwards Rector of Uffington
in Lincolnshire. Beville, born January 22, 1780, who entered Lord
Howe's regiment of 19th Light Dragoons, and died at Bungalore in the
East Indies, July 6, 1801, of a wound received in action. Harriet,
born June 15, 1781, who died unmarried. Frances Anne, born April 18,
1783, who married Mr. Ram, of Clonolten, Co. Wexford.

—" our little Portia " or " our little lamb," the two
old ladies called her—and the Duchess gave her an ivory
box, on the lid of which was worked in hair on satin
a little lamb sheltered by two old trees, intended to be
emblematic of the child and her aged protectresses.
When she was six years old, Mrs. Delany, fearing
that she might not live to see her great niece grow up,
wrote an " Essay on Propriety " for the future formation of her manners.   In the following year the extravagance of Mr. Port obliged him to let Ilam, and the
" sweet bird " of seven years old came to live altogether
as a daughter with her old aunt of seventy-eight.   It
made the sunshine of her life.   " She is everybody's
delight," wrote Mrs. Delany to Mrs. Port, " so no wonder she should wind about my heart, being attached to
it by the double tie of being the child of my dearest
Mary, and I could carry this chain at least a link
higher." *   The education of her adopted child was
henceforward Mrs. Delany's chief occupation, and it is
touching to read of the stately old lady having procured a master " to teach *us* to walk and curtsy."   Both
Mrs. Delany and the Duchess found delight in instructing her in botany and conchology, which were their
own favourite pursuits, for the collection of precious
stones, shells, flowers, and rare animals at Bulstrode
was already celebrated all over Europe : the birth of
a new flower was an event of life in the circle of the

* That to her own sister Anne Granville, grandmother of the little
" Portia."

Duchess, and her correspondence is filled with minute questions on botany and natural history. It was a marked day at Bulstrode, when the Duchess, coming into her friend's room, found her surrounded by paper chips, and asked Mrs. Delany "what she was doing with that geranium," when, taking up the beautiful flower lying on the table which had attracted her notice, she found that it was a paper imitation from the hand of her friend. This, executed in her seventy-second year, was the first specimen of the wonderful Flora of paper which was the principal recreation of the latter years of Mrs. Delany, and which is still the marvel of all who behold it.*

The letters of Mrs. Delany to her niece have become important as memorials of the personal history of George III. and his family. Their visits to Bulstrode were constant. Sometimes the King rode over alone attended by a single equerry. Sometimes the Queen and Princesses arrived in two coaches and six, accompanied by the King and a number of gentlemen on horseback. To Mrs. Delany the royal personages were ever full of kindness and courtesy. One day the King brought her " a gold knotting-shuttle," and the

* Horace Walpole in his "Anecdotes of Painters," mentions Mrs. Delany, who "at the age of seventy-four *invented* the art of paper mosaic, with which material (coloured) she executed, in eight years, within 20 of 1,000 various flowers and flowering shrubs with a precision and truth unparalleled." Sir Joseph Banks used to say that Mrs. Delany's mosaic flowers were the only representations of nature from which he could venture to describe a plant botani-cally without the least fear of committing an error.

Queen a frame for weaving fringe upon. They were
gratified with the pleasure which she showed in the
royal children, and when the Queen remarked that she
had not yet seen all of them, the King said, " That is a
fault which is easily rectified," and desired that a day
might be fixed for Mrs. Delany to come with the Duchess
to drink tea at Windsor Castle. On this her first visit,
as on many others, the old lady was led about by
the little Princes and Princesses. Soon afterwards the
Queen was so gracious as to take a lesson from Mrs.
Delany on her spinning-wheel at Bulstrode, and to
accept from her the present of a spinning-wheel : Mrs.
Delany said that she " forgot her infirmities in the cordial of royal kindness." As an instance of the charming
manners which characterised the royal children she
mentions the little Princess Mary (afterwards Duchess
of Gloucester) in " cherry-coloured tabby with silver
leading strings," having forgotten her name, and coming up to her with —" How do you do, Duchess of Portland's friend, and how does your little niece do ? I
wish you had brought her."

In July, 1785, the tender friendship of a lifetime was
broken by the death of the Duchess of Portland. Mrs.
Delany was then in her eighty-fifth year, and bitterly
felt the blow. Her great niece, the little " Portia,"
was immediately sent to meet her on her return from
Bulstrode to her own house in London. All her friends
vied in showing her sympathy, but that which touched
her most was the conduct of George III. and Queen

Charlotte, who said that they availed themselves of the circumstance that she might miss her summer visits at Bulstrode to present her with a house at Windsor, and to desire that she would always move there when the court moved. At the same time, with that delicate attention which marked their whole conduct towards her, the King presented her with £300 a year, that she might not suffer by the expense of an additional establishment; while to prevent even the appearance of a pension, as well as the possibility of the sum being diminished by taxation, the Queen used regularly to bring the half-year's amount in a pocket-book when she made her a visit. A touching instance of the extreme kindness of heart shown by Queen Charlotte at this time is narrated in a letter from Mrs. Preston to Mrs. F. Hamilton—"As soon as the Duchess of Portland died, Mrs. Delany got into the chaise to go to her own house, the Duke followed her, begging to know what she would accept that had belonged to his mother. Mrs. Delany recollected a bird that the Duchess always fed and kept in her own room, and desired to have it, and felt towards it, as you must suppose! In a few days, Mrs. Delany got a bad fever, and the bird died; but for some hours she was too ill even to recollect her bird. The Queen had one of the same sort which she valued extremely (a weaver bird); she took it with her own hands, and while Mrs. Delany slept she had the cage brought, and put her own bird into it, charging every one not to let it go so near Mrs.

Delany, that she could perceive the change, till she was enough recovered, better to bear the loss of her first favourite."

When Mrs. Delany was about to move to Windsor, the Queen sent to desire that her "dearest Mrs. Delany" would bring herself and her niece, clothes and attendants, but stores of every kind would be laid in for her, and on reaching her new home she was received and welcomed by the King himself.

The garden of Mrs. Delany's house joined that of the Queen's Lodge. On the morning after her arrival Her Majesty sent one of her ladies to know "how she had rested," and "whether her coming would not be troublesome." Writing to Mrs. Hamilton afterwards, Mrs. Delany says, "Her Majesty came up-stairs. Our meeting was mutually affecting. She repeated in the strongest terms her wish, and the King's, that I should be as easy and as happy as they could possibly make me; that they waived all ceremony, and desired to come to me like *friends!*" Henceforward Mrs. Delany usually spent two or three evenings at the Queen's Lodge, visits which were frequently returned without any ceremony by the royal family. The King would lead her about leaning on his arm: the Queen would come, unannounced, to dine with her "on veal cutlets and orange pudding:" she was permitted to have a share in all their sorrows and anxieties, and of their domestic happiness her journals and letters give the most delightful pictures.

" *November* 9, 1785.—I have been several evenings at the Queen's Lodge, with no other company but their own most lovely family. They sit round a large table, on which are books, work, pencils, and paper. The Queen has the goodness to make me sit down next to her; and delights me with her conversation, whilst the younger part of the family are drawing and working, the beautiful babe, Princess Amelia, bearing her part in the entertainment, sometimes in one of her sister's laps, sometimes playing with the King on the carpet; which altogether, exhibits such a delightful scene, as would require an Addison's pen, or a Vandyke's pencil, to do justice to it. In the next room is the band of music, which plays from eight o'clock till ten. The King directs them what pieces of music to play, chiefly Handel. Here I must stop and return to my own house. On the 28th their Majesties, the five princesses, and the youngest princes, came at seven o'clock in the evening to drink tea with me. All the princes and princesses had a commerce table,—Miss Emily Clayton, daughter to Lady Louisa Clayton, and Miss Port, did the honours of it."

" *August* 11, 1787.—At this time of year the evenings are devoted by my royal friends to the terrace till eight o'clock, when they return to the Lodge to their tea and concert of music, and happy are those that are admitted to that circle ! The Queen has had the goodness to command me to come whenever it is quite easy for me to do it, without sending particularly for me, lest it should embarrass me to refuse ; so that most evenings at half an hour past seven I go to Miss Burney's apartment, and when the royal family return from the terrace, the King, or one of the princesses (generally the youngest, Princess Amelia, just four years old), come into the room, take me by the hand, and lead me into the drawing-room, where there is a chair ready for me by the Queen's left hand. The three eldest princesses sit round the table, and the ladies in waiting, Lady Charlotte Finch and Lady Elizabeth Walde-grave. A vacant chair is left for the King, whenever he pleases to sit down in it. *Everyone* is employed with their pencil, needle, or knotting. Between the pieces of music the conversation is easy and pleasant; and, for an hour before the conclusion of the whole, the King plays at back-gammon with one of his equerries."

These were happy days for the little "Portia," who was frequently allowed the companionship of the younger princesses, Mary and Sophia, while with Miss Emilia Clayton* she made an intimate friendship, which was broken by her first great sorrow, in the death of that young lady of a rapid decline in 1787. Queen Charlotte took a personal interest in the writing lessons of Mrs. Delany's niece, and taught her to imitate her own beautiful handwriting, which is known to have been singularly perfect. The Queen also desired that Miss Port should have drawing lessons from the same master as the Princesses, lessons always given between the hours of divine service on a Sunday, which was considered a proper day for a quiet and interesting occupation which was neither labour nor dissipation.

* Daughter of Lady Louisa Clayton, Lady of the Bedchamber to Princess Amelia, second daughter of George II.

An amusing adventure is narrated in a letter of 1787,* of which Miss Port was the heroine. The royal family were absent at Kew, and as they did not like to live a day without seeing Mrs. Delany, they took her with them. On one of the days of their absence, the King went over to Windsor, and while he was walking on the terrace, thought he would go into Mrs. Delany's, and knocked at a room door. A young lady was sitting in the room, and said, "Who is there?" A voice replied "*It is me*," then said she "*Me* may stay where he is." Again there was a knock, and she again said, "Who is there?" The voice answered "*It is me*," then said she "*Me* is impertinent, and may go about his business." Upon the knocking being repeated a third time, some person who was with her advised her to open the door, and *see* who it could be; when, to her great astonishment, who should it be but the King himself! All she could utter was, "What *shall* I say?" "Nothing at all," said his Majesty, "you were very right to be cautious who you admitted."

Surrounded to the last by an atmosphere of affectionate reverence, Mrs. Delany died in her house in St. James's Place on the 15th April, 1788, aged eighty-eight. Miss Port was then only seventeen, and the blow was almost overwhelming to her. Not only did she lose her second mother, the wise and loving companion of her life, but her life itself, in all its surroundings and associations, was necessarily changed hence-

* Mrs Mee to Mrs. Anne Viney.

forward.* In her passionate devotion to her aunt, she
had imbibed her tastes, and was capable of drawing
just comparisons, and of measuring others by the standard of her who had trained her mind from infancy.
She had lived in an atmosphere of extreme refinement,
as well as of virtue, and although not old enough to
be formally presented at Court, she was known to all
who belonged to it, and was in the habit of daily intercourse with the different members of the Royal Family.
The days she looked back upon had been passed in the
most perfect happiness. With the comfort and security
of home, she had enjoyed the society of all the great and
good who met in Mrs. Delany's house, and though she
had never entered the dissipation of the world, she had
lived in the constant enjoyment of all the best things
the world had to bestow.

In looking forward to the desolate future of her
niece, and in entrusting her to the guardianship of Mr.
Court D'Ewes, of Wellesbourne, the eldest son of her
beloved sister Anne, Mrs. Delany had entirely miscal-
culated his future conduct. As is too often the case,
she fancied that because to *her* he was all respect and
attention, he must feel exactly as she did towards his
niece. It never seems to have entered into her contemplation that he would not carry out all her desires and
wishes, whether expressed or not. In fact she thought

* For almost all the particulars given here of Mrs. Delany, the
editor is indebted to Lady Llanover's " Life and Correspondence of
Mrs. Delany."

that there was but one mind between them, and that, for his own sake, he would be, not only the guardian, but the father, and the sympathising counsellor and protector of her adopted child, whose dazzling beauty and remarkable intellectual qualities, Mrs. Delany believed that she placed in the tenderest as well as the safest hands, when she entrusted her to her uncle, and left everything of importance to his decision. But events were very different to her anticipations. Mr. D'Ewes had naturally a cold and ungenial nature, and, from the moment of Mrs. Delany's death, her cherished child had not only reason to feel that she was neither loved or understood, but was treated by her uncle with positive coldness and harshness, as well as with neglect of her worldly interests.

It does not appear that Mrs. Delany was ever as partial to her nephew Granville of Calwich, or as intimate with him, as she was with his brother of Wellesbourne, an estrangement which might naturally arise from her having been herself once looked upon as the heiress of her brother Granville; and having been disinherited in favour of this nephew, probably in consequence of her brother's annoyance at her marriage with Dr. Delany, who was not her equal in birth. Young Granville of Calwich was, however, of a very different disposition to his brother. Full of kindness and geniality, he vied in acts of liberality and benevolence with his wife Harriet Joan De la Bere, who was peculiarly dignified and high-bred,

though her reserve generally caused young persons to
stand in awe of her.   Thus, in her deep sorrow, Miss
Port was thankful when she was allowed to leave Wellesbourne and take refuge with her younger uncle and
aunt, and Mrs. Granville, usually so undemonstrative,
was soon won by her rare qualities, to regard her with
warm affection.   She took her to Bath, where, as was
then the fashion, it was considered necessary for health
to spend some weeks or months every year, and where
Mr. Granville had a house of his own : and here, though
Miss Port had never been " out " in the common accep-
tation of the term, she could not accompany her uncle
and aunt in their walks and drives, without seeing and
being seen.

It is not known that Miss Port ever spoke to the
gentleman she afterwards married, before he proposed
for her to Mr. and Mrs. Granville, according to the
practice then in vogue.   There could not have been the
slightest intimacy (if any acquaintance) between Mr.
Waddington and herself, and the first idea she had of
a proposal from him was through some words accidentally dropped by her uncle and aunt to each other,
when they were unconscious or unobservant that she
was in the room.   The effect upon her was electrical.
Sensitive and impulsive by nature to the highest
degree, the impression made was that her relations
could not have her real interests at heart if for a
moment they could even recognise the possibility of
such a marriage, while the consciousness that the

gentleman in question must disinterestedly care for her to think of it, suddenly determined her to accept his proposal if it was made. Thus, when her uncle considered it his duty to make a formal announcement of the offer she had received, and to request her decision, he was astonished by her immediate acceptance of it. She was entirely engrossed by the torturing idea that those she was beginning to love did not love her. She thought nothing of a disparity of age of between twenty and thirty years—nothing of anything, but that an individual, said to be unexceptionable in character, valued her, she knew not why. Since the death of Mrs. Delany, the world had been a blank to her. She believed it would always remain so, and meantime she would endeavour to make one person happy, though she never expected to be so herself. She married at eighteen in the same state of mind in which a nun takes the black veil, except that there are few nuns who believe none are left to care for them outside the walls of their prison.

Mr. Waddington had a good fortune, and his family was of very ancient origin, though at that time it had fallen into insignificance. Walter de Waddington was lord of Waddington in Lincolnshire, and had a daughter, who in the thirteenth century married Sir Roger Tempest, Knt., of Bracewell. In the eighteenth century there are records of inter-marriages with the families of Beckwith of Aldborough, Tyrwhitt of Stamfield, and Cradock of Hartforth in Yorkshire.

In 1740, the Rev. Joshua Waddington, Vicar of Harworth and Walkeringham in Nottinghamshire, married Ann, daughter of the Rev. Thomas Ferrand, Vicar of Bingley. Ann Ferrand was ultimately the heiress of Towes in Lincolnshire, which devolved through her to her son Thomas. Her son Benjamin Waddington married Miss Port.

Upon his marriage, Mr. Waddington rented Dunston Park in Berkshire, but merely as a temporary residence. There, his eldest daughter Harriet was born (1790), who survived only a few months. Her birth was followed, on the 4th of March, 1791, by that of Frances, afterwards Baroness Bunsen. Soon after this Mr. Waddington removed to Llanover, an estate he had purchased in South Wales, where his beautiful wife consented to reside for the next eleven years in perfect seclusion, without even visiting London; where she not only educated her daughter but herself, while accommodating herself to the life which she felt it her duty not only to endure but to learn to enjoy. Her delight in Nature was her greatest consolation in this total isolation from all the friends, associates, and companions of her former existence, and she cultivated this taste to the uttermost, and imparted it to her children.

There were perhaps only two points of resemblance in the disposition of the father and mother of the Baroness Bunsen, and these were generosity in their actions and a scrupulous regard to truth. Being exceedingly phlegmatic, Mr. Waddington was without

the slightest particle of imagination. He was a remarkable instance of a great reader, who had no
preference with regard to subject and who kept no
particular object in view. He would steadily read
for hours with the most perfect satisfaction, and never
appeared to skip a single page. Whatever work he
began he regularly finished, and he seldom made
the slightest comment upon it. Travels, biographies,
and also works of fiction, were perused with the same
patient attention. If the weather was fine and he
could take his accustomed long walks and rides, he
was much out of doors, but if the weather prevented
this, he would seat himself in his great chair in
his own room and read from breakfast-time—8 or
8.30 till 1 o'clock, and again from 2 or 3 till 5
o'clock, which was his regular dinner-hour. He never
seemed to know the meaning of the word *ennui :*
punctual as a machine in all his habits, he pursued
his various occupations like clock-work, and their
monotony never seemed to weary him. A good deal
of his time was taken up by the business of a magistrate, which was then transacted by each country
gentleman in his own room. It has been said that
many of them had butlers who were expected to read
up the law and answer to certain points when referred
to, but it is not believed that Mr. Waddington's well-
known butler " Abraham " ever did more than acquaint
himself with the persons and circumstances of those
who came to seek justice from his master.

Mr. Waddington's time for conversation was after his dinner, when his wife would keep him company, and hear anything that had occurred during the day either to interest or annoy him. If any unforeseen event in or out of the establishment happened to disturb him, he instantly went to her, and she possessed great influence over him, though his routine of life was not in the slightest degree altered by her society. For some time he troubled and worried himself with farming, but finding that it did not increase his happiness and very much interfered with his comfort to see everything going wrong, he gradually put his agricultural affairs into the hands of his wife, who amongst other useful arts had acquired a practical knowledge of the subject, and soon succeeded in establishing order and neatness in the farming department.

Mrs. Waddington was an excellent judge of horses, seeming to inherit the gift of her family in her judgment of those animals, and without ever having been a hard rider or being accustomed to follow the hounds, she was always perfectly at home on horseback—an accomplishment she had been taught by her father at a very early age. As long as her health permitted, one of her greatest pleasures was taking rides in the beautiful country by which she was surrounded. One of her favourite expeditions was to the residence of her old friend and neighbour Admiral Gell, near Crickhowel, whither her little daughter Frances accompanied her when old enough—and often afterwards recurred with delight to those summer evening rides amid the singing of nightingales.

There was no country paper of any kind published within forty miles of Llanover, and the chief dependence for news was upon the arrival from London of the *Morning Chronicle*, which came in the evening. But, as there was no post-delivery, Mr. Waddington would never accustom himself to look forward to the arrival of letters or newspapers, and unless there was any reason to *expect* letters, the newspapers were never considered of sufficient importance for any one to be sent four miles on purpose to fetch them. Although few men have been more truly, though secretly, a father of the fatherless, or have lent large sums with greater generosity to assist friends in distress, yet he had a peculiar aversion to the expenditure of any avoidable small sum, and he did not conceal that the payment of turnpikes was an object of consideration which often turned the balance against sending to the post office.* His old servants and workmen were, however, much attached to him, and although his temper was very choleric when provoked, he was substantially so benevolent and just a master that this warmth of temper, which was quickly over, was regarded by them more as a peculiarity than a fault.

* On one occasion he lost several thousand pounds which he had lent to a friend, from his determination to save the postage of a letter of inquiry as to the payment of the policy of insurance. The friend died suddenly, the policy was not paid, and the whole sum was forfeited.

The susceptibility of Mr. Waddington to small things in money matters was by no means shared by his wife, who combined equal generosity with liberality on all subjects. To her servants she was a friend as well as a mistress, and she took a personal interest in the welfare of each and all of her poorer neighbours. During the period of her quiet life at Llanover she suffered great affliction in the death of two infant daughters—Matilda and Mary Ann. The latter died of small-pox (1792), at the age of one year and seven months, and her mother could never allude to her death without anguish. The child had been innoculated for the small-pox (vaccination being then unknown), and she was attended night and day by her mother, upon whom the effect lasted for life of seeing her expire under that grievous disease (which had been produced artificially) upon a being previously in perfect health. It is probable that the deaths of these infants and the loss of her eldest child, which she attributed to the ignorance of a professed nurse when she herself was utterly inexperienced, was the direct cause of the extraordinary care as well as knowledge for which she was eminently distinguished in later life as regarded the treatment of children and invalids. She applied her powerful intellect to the subject; and although she neither wrote books nor tormented others with advice, she taught herself by observation to discriminate between good and evil, and became the instructress as well as the mistress of her nurses.

CHAPTER II.

RECOLLECTIONS OF CHILDHOOD.

"Think nought a trifle, though it small appear,
  Small sands the mountain, moments make the year,
  And trifles life."
                                        YOUNG.

  "Il n'y a pas de petites choses dans ce monde, attendu
que Dieu se mêle de toutes."—MADAME SWETCHINE.

ABOUT four miles from Abergavenny, where the
green meadows are divided by the river Usk, nine
crystal springs bursting side by side from a rock, beneath a wooded hill, form the holy fountain of Gofer,
the hermit whose memory gives a name to Llanover,
or the Church of Gofer.* On the left, the thickly
wooded valley is girt by the Blawreng, or the "grey
ridge:" on the right, above the nearer hills, rises the
quaint form of Pen-y-val, or the Sugar-loaf: while,
behind Abergavenny, is Scyrryd Vawr, or "the Holy
Mountain," which, like Monserrat in Spain and La
Vernia in Italy, is supposed to have been rent asunder

---

* Gofer is one of the three uncanonized saints of Gwent, Henwg
and Gwareg being the two others.

at the Crucifixion, and which still bears on its summit
the ruins of a chapel of St. Michael, whither Roman
Catholic peasants ascend on Michelmas Eve, and bring
away its sacred earth to place in the coffins of their
dead, or to throw into graves to keep evil spirits at a
distance.

In the midst of the valley, embosomed in trees,
stands the White House of Llanover, roomy, simple,
and old-fashioned, and surrounded by large shrubberies.
A brook rushes rapidly through the garden, forming
pools, cascades, and islets charming to children, and
imparting a constant freshness to the green depths
around. The planting of larches (then a new tree)
around Llanover was one of the favourite occupations
of Mr. Waddington's life: in 1799 no less than 120,000
larch-trees were brought from Glasgow for this purpose.

At Llanover, four daughters were born to Mr. and
Mrs. Waddington, of whom only two—Emilia, born
February 3rd, 1794, and Augusta, born March 21st,
1802—lived to grow up.

In her eighty-third year, the Baroness Bunsen, at the
solicitation of her daughters and grand-daughters, committed to writing some *ricordi* of her childhood, from
which the following notes are extracted.

" The first event in my life of which I have a distinct
recollection was sitting for the portrait painted of me,
with my sister Emilia, by Mr. Roche, a deaf and dumb
miniature-painter at Bath, where my parents staid for

a short time in 1796. My beautiful aunt, Louisa Port was then with us, the charming and lively companion of my mother, of whose presence I was always glad. I remember many walks at Bath with my mother and her sister Louisa, and have indistinct visions of their dress—especially of a purple silk which my aunt called her 'dignified dress,' and which was made in the then-beginning fashion of 'a round gown,' that is, an entire skirt, not open in front and parting to show the under-petticoat. Short sleeves, morning as well as evening, were then universal, and my mother had long gloves of York tan (as they were called), yellow, and reaching to the elbow, sewed into a cuff of green satin which was pinned on the sleeve: her cloak was of black silk trimmed with black lace, very narrow, and hanging down long in front. I remember a bonnet like that worn by the peasants of the Canton du Valais, black satin with yellow satin bows set all round the rather lengthy crown.

"One day I walked with my mother and aunt to the Sydney Gardens, as they were called. In one part were swings, and one in particular called a Merlin swing, in which the swingers sat two and two, opposite; those at the corners pulling ropes alternately by which the swing was set in motion. Two gentlemen, who had joined us in our walk, acceded to the desire of the ladies in mounting the swing. My little sister and I remained on the gravel walk with the maid, and saw one of these gentlemen become paler and paler, till he almost fainted, and was helped out of the swing by the gardener. This was M. Lajand de Cherval, an emigrant, and a man of brilliant conversation, who had been in the intimacy of

Talleyrand when he was in his ecclesiastical splendour. I saw him once many years later, a specimen of that high-bred old French society which will hardly be found to survive now. I observed his name as one of the intimates of Talleyrand during the visit of Mr. Pitt on that early occasion of his travelling in France before the Revolution ; and as having asked a question as to the quarter from whence Mr. Pitt would most apprehend alteration and danger to the English constituted authority as then exist-ing ; when Mr. Pitt replied, ' From the democratic power, which is steadily increasing.' This opinion, contrasted with the Resolution fresh in memory, proposed in Parlia-ment by Mr. Fox, that ' the royal authority had increased, was increasing, and ought to be diminished,' will hardly have failed to impress the mind of the highly-gifted ques-tioner as to the specific gravity of the young man before him, whom as yet the world knew not.

" The birth of my sister Matilda (23rd September, 1797) is the first event of which I have a clear consciousness both as to joy and sorrow : to see the baby and touch it, caused a sensation which still thrills through me ; and her death (7th October) was a terrible new idea, and caused bitter tears. That morning my father entered the room in tears, and when I begged to know the reason, I heard him speak, but only distinguished the words—' Poor Matilda ! ' which I supposed meant only that he had found her ill, for I knew that she had been so the day before ; and it was not till I had come with my little sister Emily to breakfast with my father, that I understood the awful fact, from hearing him give orders to Rosser the carpenter for the coffin ! I caught directions for the letters to be inscribed upon it, which caused me a burst of crying hard to get the better of—which was the duty of the moment, for 'to cry is naughty,' in nursery law. I was pained that little Emily could not understand what was the matter, and nowhere did I meet with a demonstration of sympathy : so I had a lesson, often repeated in my early life, that sorrow must be borne alone. My mother was too ill to be visited, and not till long after had I the new pleasure of seeing her up and dressed, and again able to hear me read and do lessons. I can see her now in mind, as I first saw her again then, in a dress of printed calico, with tight sleeves reaching to the elbow, and brown leathern mittens.

"A great event in my early life was a journey made in 1797 to visit a number of relations. Our first station was Derby, where my grandfather Mr. Port had a house, after he was obliged to leave his beautiful residence of Ilam, from the embarrassment of his pecuniary circumstances. My grandfather was a handsome old gentleman, very kind to children. His daughter Louisa was at the head of his household, and a younger daughter Harriet was a piece of still life in the house, overflowing with kindness and devotedness to everybody ; but, as the only plain member of the family, not regarded as her qualities deserved. My aunt Harriet is the person in my life's experience to whom I have felt most bound to bear affection, for she deserved it of me by her unfailing kindness. My youngest aunt, Fanny (afterwards Mrs. Ram) lived entirely with her parents by adoption, my great uncle and aunt, Mr. and Mrs. Granville of Calwich.

"From Derby we went to Tuxford in Nottinghamshire,

the dwelling of my father's brother George—a clergyman,
who had been tutor to Prince William, afterwards Duke
of Clarence and subsequently King—a most uncompromising Liberal, not to say Radical, who had much influence over the opinions of his relations.   At York, we were
received at the Deanery by the Dean and his daughter,
Miss Fountayne.   The Deanery was very striking to me,
in its antiquated dignity and gloom.   The Cathedral is
still fresh in my memory !   How I have longed to see it
again, but that has never happened ; only I think I have
renewed the very early, but deep and sincere tribute of
heart-beating admiration and solemn awe, then called
forth, every time that I have seen a Gothic cathedral since.
From York we proceeded to Pocklington, where Mr.
Baskett, the husband of my father's youngest sister, was
the clergyman.   I liked the time spent in that curious
old house of Pocklington, and remember the party as very
lively and sociable, and delighted with my mother.   Here
too I saw old Mrs. Waddington, my father's mother (who
died at the age of 93), on a visit to her daughter.   In returning, my parents paused for a few hours at Ludlow in
Herefordshire, and I first remember having been excited
to strong emotion by scenery, in exploring its old castle
and its beautiful river and bridge.

"In the following year, when I was again at Bath with
my parents and Aunt Louisa, one of the events was a
morning-visit to my mother, on account of old acquaintance from her Windsor-life with Mrs. Delany, from the
Prince Ernest, afterwards Duke of Cumberland, later King
of Hanover.   I was placed with little Emily, to stand in a
corner by the window, and ordered to look out—but rather

I looked the other way, greatly curious as to what a Prince might be like, and I believe was disappointed to see him appear much like the gentlemen that accompanied him, very tall, fair, freckled, and flaxen-haired: such is my impression. Another frequent visitor was Tom Sheridan, who interested me far more than the Prince, and the image of his fine face and figure, and the charm of his animated conversation, remain distinct in my memory, though I probably understood very little of the subject of the fun which entertained me: only I know that he teased my mother and aunt by describing how they had tripped over the miry streets with drapery held up, and that he imitated the inevitable hop, skip, and jump : and he blamed himself for out-staying the hour when they ought to have been at dinner, assuring them that the mutton would be over-roasted, the potatoes boiled to rags, and that their plates would scorch their fingers—repeating that they ought to turn him out of the house, but still staying on and making them laugh, as I did in a corner. This was the father of the three beautiful ladies whom later I admired in London and gazed at with an interest independent of their rare perfections.* Later than the date of this vision, so bright to my young eyes, as well as to those of my elders, it was told in my hearing that Tom Sheridan had married a Miss Calendar : and still later came the tidings that Tom Sheridan, in hopeless consumption, had gone to try the effect of a milder climate, at the Cape of Good Hope—where the scene soon closed in death. I hope and believe that he

* The Duchess of Somerset; Lady Dufferin, afterwards Lady Gifford; and the Hon. Mrs. Norton, afterwards Lady Stirling Maxwell.

was happy in the love of his wife, and thus may have known something of the best that life can afford. Could I but remember right, the lines in Crabbe's Gipsy—

> " ' Though abused and driven astray
> Thou hast travelled far and wandered long;
> Thy God hath seen thee all the way,
> And every turn that led thee wrong.'

"In 1799 my father became Sheriff for the county. There was a general invitation of neighbours of various classes to breakfast, on the morning when he was to drive with four horses and servants in new liveries, to meet and escort the Judges coming to Monmouth. I well remember the unusual bustle, the tables set out, and the farmers' wives and daughters invited in and seated at the breakfast tables, served and attended to by my mother after the cavalcade had departed. The hill-field and its steep ascent gave opportunity for seeing the javelin-men, consisting of my father's servants, labourers and other neighbours, all in his livery and on horseback, who trotted in the best order they could manage, preceding the carriage. My father had picked out the men to whom the handsome new clothing was sure to be the most desirable. He had said, ' I told Neddy the blacksmith that he should be one of the javelin-men, if he would but wash his face '—which rare operation was accordingly performed : and the suit of clothes then given formed Neddy's regular Sunday-attire, as long as I remember him. This was perhaps the first occasion in my life when I had a reason to observe upon my father. I had taken my parents entirely as a matter of fact, and compared them neither with existences or ideals. I now perceived that my father acted characteristically in the case of selection of javelin-men, on a high motive rather than a meaner one ; although there was temptation on the score of appearance and personal effect, to have thought it due to himself to make a first public appearance with a showy troop of men well-grown and matched.

"This year of my father's shrievalty was marked by the attempt to assassinate the King (George III.) in the Theatre, and the strong revulsion of feeling produced by the King's noble and manly bearing, standing firm without starting or withdrawing at the report of the pistol which failed to strike him, and bowing graciously to the audience, as though considering (and justly) the act as single, and not the result of conspiracy. The moment was favourable to Royalty, for a burst of rejoicing and congratulation followed, and my father was called upon to convey a loyal address from the county to the King. His journey to London caused anxiety, for the murder of a Mr. Mellish by foot-pads on Hounslow Heath was a recent event, and the roads about London were considered very unsafe : but the mail-coach, where there was a guard in a red uniform with a blunderbuss, was thought less liable to attack than a simple carriage, as in the case of Mr. Mellish.

"During the (very unusual) absence of my father, it was settled that my mother should go to her father at Derby. Much did I like that visit. I slept in my Aunt Louisa's room, and of the pretty things in it, she had many stories to tell me, for they came from her dear old home at Ilam. Her father's embarrassments had obliged him to let his beautiful inheritance to the Bateman family. I was taken to see it while they lived there, in the picturesque old family house of the Ports, so much

more suited to the scenery than the overgrown castel-
lated building, constructed by Mr. Watts Russell, who
became the purchaser, when my uncle John Port succeeded to the entailed property in 1807.

"Many circumstances marked the bright time spent at
Derby. First there was the Battle of the Nile, and the
great popular delight, and general illumination, every
female of all ranks wearing a bow or cockade of sky-blue
ribbon, considered the loyal, ministerial colour. Mrs.
Feilding happened to be at Derby, consulting Dr. Darwin
for her daughter, and she dined that day at my grandfather's, and was rallied on having forgotten to put on a
cockade, which was zealously provided for her. My mother
called upon Mrs. Darwin, and thus I saw the three beautiful daughters, whose appearance is still distinct in my
recollection. I always delighted to look upon beauty, but
took care not to explain why I stared at the objects of my
admiration, because I was always reminded of the solemn
truth that 'beauty is of no value.' The daughters of Dr.
Darwin had a right to the inheritance of beauty from their
mother, formerly Mrs. Pole of Redburn. In the long course
of subsequent years, I have heard with cordial interest that
the three lovely girls adorned in life the families into which
they married, by merit equal to their beauty.

"At Derby I saw two persons who fixed themselves in
my memory as the first French emigrants I had seen. My
Aunt Louisa one rainy day looking out of the window
exclaimed, 'There they are, under their umbrella, perhaps
they would come in and drink tea with us.' My Uncle
Bernard accordingly went out, and respectfully made the
invitation, and re-entered with an oldish gentleman and a

very young lady, pretty, graceful, and of most refined appearance and manners, whose slightly foreign accent seemed to me a decoration. I heard my Aunt Louisa's account another time of the neatness of the small dwelling in which she had visited this lady, finding her in the whitest cornette tied under the chin, and a white jacket over her dark petticoat, busied in sweeping the house, as (she observed) she 'kept no maid,' and to my aunt's knowledge, performed every kind of household work with delicate hands not used to such labour. My mother met her cordially, and had some further communication with her, and a letter in consequence, with the signature 'Praslin du Pont.' The sight and consciousness of this lady, laid an early foundation for the impression I have retained through life of the merit and charm of the ideal of French womanhood.

" Soon after our return home, we received intelligence of the birth of a second son to my Uncle George, at Tuxford, to whom the name of Horatio* was given, in reference to the admired hero of the day—Horatio Nelson. The close of 1799 was marked by the failure of harvest, which brought on a deplorable scarcity, for the relief of which my father's best efforts and continual exertions were employed. He wrote to his brother Joshua at New York, with a commission to send him a quantity of wheat-flour, which he sold in small quantities at cost price to the poor, establishing himself in the servants' hall, seeing the applicants individually, and taking all measures to prevent the approach of such as wished to buy cheap in order to

* Horace Waddington, Permanent Under-Secretary to the Home Office.

sell dear. My father's example was followed, and much more American flour imported. Well do I remember that everybody was exhorted to consume as little bread as possible at daily meals, bread was cut in pieces for each member of the dinner-party, and contrivances were tried to make the flour go farther by adding rice or boiled potatoes in making bread, which was not found to answer, as either of those additions had the effect of increasing appetite and consumption.

"The year 1799 closed in a manner very distasteful to me, in a removal very late in the season, in the gloomiest of weather, to Clifton near Bristol. Here my mother and my sister Emily were always ill, which I had a firm conviction was owing to the daily visits of Dr. Beddoes,* and the prescriptions he sent. At this time John and William Lambton were staying in the house of Dr. Beddoes, and had lessons in French, as I did, from M. d'Estrade. The elder of these brothers acquired an honoured and historical name as Lord Durham, the younger entered the Guards and was at Rome in my time with a beautiful young wife. During this winter also a young genius from the Land's End, Humphrey Davy, since so celebrated, arrived in Dr. Beddoes' intimate circle; and as stories were told in my hearing of his companionship with Beddoes in scientific experiments, I fancied his small person (with a very wide mouth) with King the surgeon, as catching rats with tongs, and subjecting them in receivers to the effects of various vapours, while Dr. Beddoes was counting seconds

---

* Dr. Thomas Beddoes, 1760—1808, of great learning and linguistic attainments, author of the Hygëia, and founder of the Pneumatic Institution.

on the stop-watch, which I had seen him use when feeling pulses. Much were the various gases talked of in my hearing, and many persons amused themselves with being subjected to 'laughing gas,' of which I have heard as of an old acquaintance after the lapse of seventy years! long after the death of Dr. Beddoes, who had hoped much in gases as a means of medical relief.

"The 'Anti-Jacobin,' with Canning's wit, was a great means of animation in the house, in which we children took a full share, repeating the name of 'Matilda Pottingen,' and the 'University of Gottingen,' and lines from the 'Voyage of the Learned to the North Pole.' Once, and once only, have I named the 'Anti-Jacobin' since those early days! for it would have been an unwelcome subject among Germans, even though the absurdities which Canning made fun of, are quite as odious to Germans as to any other nation.

"A matter of life-long interest during this stay at Clifton, was my being allowed to see the inside of a theatre, and the acting of Mrs. Siddons. I then felt my way into the strongest current of sensation independent of reality, which life has ever made to me. I know of no excitement of feeling so absorbing as that produced by the combination of all the fine arts, which brings into actual existence, living and breathing before us, the varieties of human fate and feeling, in more or less gracefulness of form and grouping, more or less of truth and melody of voice and expression. At that date Mrs. Siddons fully preserved her symmetry of figure and perfection of features, her brilliancy of eye and power of expression: I did not see her again till many years later, when increase of flesh had spoiled the general effect, though the talent remained undiminished.

"It was in the June of this year that the startling news one day arrived of the sudden death of John Granville, the only child of the Uncle and Aunt Granville who fill a great place in my early recollections. In the previous summer he had spent a few days at Llanover, and was as engaging to us children as to all older members of society —beautiful in person, intelligent in mind, everywhere showered upon with 'golden opinions,' commended at school, adored at home, having just entered upon his twenty-first year, so that the whole mass of our relations were full of the anticipations of his coming of age. He had gone to Clifton with a cough to have recourse to the two nostrums of the Hot-Wells and Dr. Carrick. His mother was watchful, but not anxious ; when in a moment, before her eyes, the precious life was closed to all earthly consciousness. Immediately on receiving the grievous news, my mother went to Clifton, and brought back the bereaved parents to Llanover. I remember how she would walk up and down the gravel in front of the house with her uncle, who was soothed by the tones of her voice, and for whom she always seemed to find conversation by the hour, alternating with long sittings in the little morning-room with Aunt Granville, whose calm and patient endurance of her lot inspired deeper sympathy than the more aggressive grief of her husband. Before the fine season ended, the family of my mother's Uncle Dewes, the elder brother of Uncle Granville, also came on a visit. The lady was a second wife, Judith Beresford before her marriage, who ruled all around her with the absolute power usually exercised by second wives. I remember with great pleasure her charming singing, and her duets with her lovely step-daughter, Anne Dewes.* This cousin ' Nanny Dewes ' was most attractive in my eyes, and not in mine only, for she was the admired of all beholders, and the darling of her elder relations, while her contemporaries could not help forgiving the homage she received, from the absence of all pretension on her part. Her countenance and demeanour were the effusion of the purest and most perfect feminine modesty, without shyness: she seemed not to fear or mistrust her fellow-creatures, any more than to presume over them. Her voice, in speaking as in singing, seemed to pour forth the melody of the whole being, and each syllable dropped from the lips and the pearls within, as if the purpose of speaking was to show their perfection. Her look seemed to ask everybody to be kind to her, without making demands as of a right. This much-prized daughter, and her brother, Court Dewes, were the only children left of the admired first wife of my Uncle Dewes, who was the sister of Aunt Granville. They were De la Beres, of an ancient family, whose curious old-fashioned residence near Cheltenham was purchased by Lord Ellenborough, after his return from his government of India. The first Mrs. Dewes was very beautiful, in a higher style than her sister (although dear Aunt Granville continued a pretty woman even to old age), yet her features were rather to

* Anne, only daughter of Bernard D'Ewes and his first wife Anne de la Bere, born, 1778, married G. F. Stratton, Esq., of Tew Park, Oxfordshire, and died Jan. 20, 1861, having to the last fulfilled the bright promise of her youth.

be traced in her son than in her far more beautiful
daughter. By the death of John Granville, this son,
Court Dewes, became the heir of his uncle's property of
Calwich, as well as of his father's estate of Wellesbourne
in Warwickshire.

"The year 1801 was not far advanced before Clifton
again attracted the family for six weeks. Aunt Louisa
was again the cherished inmate, with whom I was happy
to walk; yet I often was out on the broad sunny pave-
ment of 'the Mall' alone with my skipping-rope, and
looking with longing eyes upon the six daughters of Lady
Eleanor Dundas, who lived next door, and also came out
with skipping-ropes, and with whom I should have been
glad to have associated. Two or three seemed older than
myself—those who in after years were Lady Carmichael,
Mrs. Bruce, and Mrs. Harford Battersby*: the others
were younger. I remember now for the first time fre-
quenting with Aunt Louisa the beautiful path along the
Avon, under the rocks and woods, which at every subsequent period of viewing them, my expanding faculties
have perceived to be more beautiful than before, whereas
I fancy in fact their original effect must have been the
finest, before many a fine tree was cut away, and many a
mass of rock blown up for burning into lime, or other
purposes of utility. By-and-by I perceived that we were
often joined in these walks by one of Aunt Louisa's
partners at balls, by name Brownlow Villiers Layard, a
son of the Dean of Bristol, wearing the uniform of a

* Mother of my beloved son-in-law, John Battersby Harford, and
of my dear daughter-in-law, Mary Louisa de Bunsen.—*Note by the
writer.*

regiment quartered on the Downs. I retain much more of the attendant circumstances of the intimacy which led to my Aunt Louisa's marriage, and to my losing her altogether as an ingredient in my life, than I shall care to write down; but the outward parts are so far curious, as belonging to conditions of the times which I believe have altered for the better. The Dean of Bristol was considered a fair specimen of a dignified clergyman, but his advancement in clerical rank and emoluments was attributed to the influence of his sister, then Duchess of Ancaster, though she had passed to that condition through the lower state of governess to the Duke's young sister, whom she had attended when accompanying her brother in shooting expeditions, an over-exercise which hastened her early death. With the dates of these events I am unacquainted, and they are immaterial; but, in 1801, soon after the engagement of Aunt Louisa was concluded with Mr. Layard, under protest of all relations, the Dean of Bristol died, and it was feared that no means of subsistence would remain for his family. Mourning for the Dean was redoubled by the death of the Duchess of Ancaster, which seemed to close all prospects for the future, when some worldly-wise persons suggested that the rich living of Uffington, which had been enjoyed by the Dean, might be bestowed upon his son, were the Duke but so graciously inclined. It was only necessary for young Layard to throw off his regimentals, put on a black coat, go through a short preparation at Oxford, and be ordained, if only some bishop would ordain him. It would have been in vain to ask Archbishop Prettyman (tutor to Mr. Pitt), at the head of the diocese in which

Uffington was situated, for he was strict; but Bishop Horsley made no objection, and the thing was done: the MS. sermons of the Dean were secured to his son, and at the end of 1803 or beginning of the next year the pair were married. They declared themselves aggrieved at the opposition my parents had made to their union—all intercourse ceased, except by occasional letters; and the intimate connection, which had seemed one of heart and life, was broken. I saw my Aunt Louisa but once again, after many years. Fourteen years of married life were granted to her, and seven sons born; a few days after the birth of the last she expired of total exhaustion of vital powers, on the 3rd of July, 1817, just after my marriage.

"The autumn of 1801 was a very quiet time at Llanover, when my mother was too unwell to leave her sofa, and I wrote all her letters to her dictation, which was a great advantage to me as to the formation of style and language. The winter was to me a happy one, undisturbed by strangers and visitors, so that nothing was in the way to prevent my being constantly with my mother, reading to her, or in one way or other employed by her, and for her; only it was sorrowful to me to see her so ill, and it was not till a light began to break upon me as to the cause that I was told by my mother that she 'hoped I should soon have another sister.' This was not long before the birth of Augusta,* on the 21st March, 1802. I cannot express the joy and delight with which I hailed the baby, which seemed to make me amends for the ever-present first sorrow of my life: those who have felt the charm which belongs to infant-life from its very beginning, can

* Now Lady Llanover.

judge how the constant interest of watching such an expanding intelligence filled and animated my every hour.

"The following summer was spent by my father's sister,
Mrs. Monk,* at Llanover. Great was the interest of all
we could hear about that which was seen and done, by
those who ventured over to Paris after the preliminaries of
a treaty of peace had been signed at Amiens! We heard
too of the striking appearance of Madame Recamier in
London, in the spring of the year, drawing attention not
only by the freshness of a beauty which was destined to
outlive youth and prosperity, but by the first appearance
of a style of dress soon imitated, in which the clothing was
as far as possible from a covering, and the wearer, on
issuing forth from her door, threw over her head a trans-
parent veil of white muslin, reaching to the knees. The
reports of Paris, and of the English who flocked thither,
were many and various, and due comment was made on
Mr. Fox's sedulous attendance at the *levée* of the First
Consul, on the morning of one of the week days besides
the occasions of invitation. Of the conversations that
took place, which seemed much sought by the ruling
personage, I remember one specimen, which most probably came from Mr. Fox's own communications. Napoleon observed that he was much taken up by the
formation of a 'Constitution for the Swiss' :—upon which
Fox remarked to his hearers 'that he was surprised at
such a pretension on the part of Napoleon,' for 'he must
know sufficiently what was meant by a Constitution, to be

* Mrs. Monk, eldest sister of Mr. Waddington, lived to the age of
102. She was mother of the learned James Henry Monk, afterwards
Bishop of Gloucester and Bristol.

aware that no individual could be able to construct one, or
judge of one, for another nation.'

" Early in the year 1803 we received the melancholy
intelligence of the death of Beville Port, my mother's
youngest brother, at Bungalore in the Mysore Country,
where he had been quartered with his regiment. His
appointment to a cornetcy, and being ordered to India,
had made him very happy in 1801; and he owed it to an
application by letter from my mother to Prince Ernest,
encouraged by the proof of friendly remembrance that he
had given her by his visit at Bath in 1798. I remember
well having been allowed to read the letter, which my
mind's eye still beholds, in her beautiful handwriting:
and I also saw the Prince's obliging reply, in which he
informed her that he had lost no time ' in requesting his
brother the Duke of York to consider the matter, and that
he was happy to announce having obtained the nomination of Mr. Beville Port to the desired cornetcy.' All
accounts that could be obtained from brother-officers
proved Beville Port to have been as beloved in that distant
land where his young life was so speedily closed, as he
was in his own family. The case of the younger sons of
my grandfather Port was truly distressing, his broken
circumstances never allowing of their being furthered on
their way by the advantages of education to which their
birth and the position of the families to which they
belonged, would have given them a right. Bernard could
be supported at Brasenose College, Oxford, because one of
his ancestors had contributed to its foundation, and the
vicarage of Ilam was in prospect for his life-provision,
but for George Port, the third son, and Beville the fourth,

nothing was apparently to be had but scrivener-work at an attorney's-office in a country town. From this repulsive slavery George had run away and taken refuge on board ship, where, after much endurance of hardship of body, and family reproach and unforgivingness, he worked his way in his profession by merit alone, and distinguished himself so much at the taking of Port au Prince, as to receive public commendation, and promotion : but only two days later he was laid low by yellow-fever, and consigned to an untimely grave. This sad winding-up of all that life, and hope, and good gifts could promise, took place before my infant life had ripened into consciousness : but I knew that my mother grieved over the fate of George, and was thus steeled in mind to overcome a just aversion to making an application to Prince Ernest for the sake of Beville.

" The year 1803 was a marked date in my life on account of my being then for the first time in London, where my parents spent May and June. I recall with surprise how gradually and imperceptibly the fact oozed out, that the dream of peace was over, and the horrors of war had recommenced. But young soldiers and sailors hailed the prospect of activity, and however vexatious the idea of new and increased expenditure in a conflict which too many considered to be as hopeless as it would be ruinous, the insolence of Buonaparte and of the French newspapers failed not to arouse the spirit in the nation, which held out so long under reverses and apprehensions : and a great help to this Anti-Gallican excitement among women and children and the ignorant, was the threat of immediate invasion, which I remember in the following autumn to have reverberated from the Camp at Boulogne over the Channel, into every English cottage and servants-hall and nursery.

"In London I was taken to see the collection of Mr. Townley, which formed afterwards the nucleus of the antique marbles of the British Museum. It was the first time of my seeing antique statues, though the antique was familiar to me through the designs of Flaxman from the Iliad and Odyssey and Æschylus. Of the objects in the Townley collection, now admired elsewhere, I only remember individually the female bust of such surpassing beauty, apparently springing from a flower, evidently a portrait, but the person unknown. I saw too some of the first paintings which were purchased to form the National Gallery, and which were then in the collection of Mr. Angerstein, whose house was in Pall Mall, the windows of the large room which contained the 'Raising of Lazarus' by Sebastian del Piombo, opening towards Carlton Gardens.

"I was taken to see 'The Tempest' at Drury Lane Theatre, when Kemble filled the part of Prospero, and that of Miranda was represented by the very pretty Miss Brunton, afterwards Lady Craven. One evening also I was taken to Vauxhall, and it seemed to be expected of me to be greatly struck with the effect of the general illumination by coloured lamps, but I had a very mean impression of the evening. A pretended waterfall and the poor performances of songs intended to be humorous, did not meet my pre-estimation of the amusements of a place, which was said to be often visited by this, that, and the other person, who might, I thought, have used better their freedom of choice. Why not go to the theatre? I thought: for the stage was ever to me intensely interesting, and I could not comprehend the want of enthusiasm for a 'play,' which many persons professed. It was much later suggested to me, that this very real and not fancied idiosyncrasy of a great part of the pleasure-seeking world, is to be accounted for by the general longing to be individually part of the show, to be considered worth seeing or worth hearing, or in short capable of taking part in what occupied all.

"At this time my Uncle William Waddington * was residing in a large house with a garden, called Crescent House, Brompton, and I remember having been surprised at the insight and knowledge he showed in respect to gardening, making a point of having the finest flowers. I heard much of the journey to S. Remy in Normandy, which he and Mrs. William Waddington had made to visit her parents Mr. and Mrs. Sykes: † and she had brought from Paris many things new and admired; I remember a French gauze *fichu* twisted round her head and pinned to good effect. Her health was utterly undisturbed by the rapid production and nursing of her numerous family, to whom she was an indefatigably careful mother, doing by each and all what she judged wisest and best. I am moved to record this last impression I retain of her, although I probably saw her many times later, for although some years of the raging war against Napoleon, stood in the way of

* Grandfather of William Henry, Minister for Public Instruction and Foreign Affairs in France, and of Madame Charles de Bunsen.

† They were still in receipt of a pension, granted to a maternal ancestor, "Trusty Richard," the Penderell who assisted the escape of Charles II. after the Battle of Worcester.

the transplanting of the family into France, the urgency
of Mr. Sykes was well known as to the necessity of establishing the incomparable energy and intelligence of his
son-in-law upon the property which was to be the inheritance of his children.

"I saw many persons who were new to me this time in
London, but have no impression of having been especially
interested in anyone, except on the occasion of a visit paid
to my mother by Reginald Heber and his elder brother.
Reginald Heber was then about to set out on his tour, to
such parts of Europe as continued open to the English
traveller ; and his elder brother was still at that height of
public estimation, which lasted over the well-remembered
Dedication to Heber by Walter Scott, of one of the portions
of his poem of Marmion. There had been a university
friendship between Reginald Heber and my Uncle Bernard, which on retrospect I somewhat wonder at,—so
different do the two appear at this distance of time. Uncle
Bernard was not only a kind friend to children, but altogether a worthy man, intelligent, high-minded, and not
merely proud of his family connexions, but worthy of his
place in society. He was a gentleman all over, but though
he passed blamelessly through life, he never followed up
any of its noblest objects. Though at Oxford he was
never entangled in any offence against the moral law, he
probably allowed himself liberty to infringe many a college rule. On one such occasion, re-entering the quadrangle from a country expedition in which he had driven
four-in-hand, he recklessly retained in his grasp his long-
lashed riding whip, and made it smack, when one of the
authorities coming out, noticing the misdeed more un-

l, endeavoured to
1and. Much did
ey laugh, on this
re, in writing a
he displayed in
ble to those who
e case. This MS.
ard,* and added,
her gave him an

June to proceed
erbyshire border,
d looked forward
desire for further
but found to my
equent occasions)
re of England is
iy travelling, and
es, with which I

een widened by
arance of a lake,
the Italian-villa
ose of concealing
am, and keeping
ral building con-
tained a picture-gallery and music-room, in which my
Uncle Granville would occasionally practise the violon-
cello, both he and his brother Dewes having fortunately

* The popularity of Mr. Bernard Port and his remarkable talent for
versification is still well remembered in Derbyshire and Staffordshire.

attained the consciousness (so rare amongst dilettanti) that their life-long passion for music was, as related to performance, unfortunate, and thus best exercised out of hearing. The older part of the house was of bachelor dimensions: the library, very spacious, sunny, and sheltered, showed dark rows of venerable books, little used by the modern world since the death of Mr. Bernard Granville, who had been a man of studious habits, and containing besides, a collection of the MS. works of Händel, who often passed his summer leisure at Calwich, and played on the organ in the dining-room, upon which his bust was erected. My Uncle Granville had added much to make the house complete as a residence and I believe with much taste. He had just finished his improvements, which were to be all ready for his beloved son's coming of age, when in June, 1800, the desolated dwelling opened to receive the funeral procession on its way to Ellaston Church, and my cousin, Court Dewes, who inherited at the death of my Uncle Granville, after a few years' possession, sold the last Granville relics, retaining only his paternal Dewes property of Wellesbourne, not far from Stratford-on-Avon in Warwickshire. Calwich has since been sold to the Dean of York, pulled down, and rebuilt on a higher level, in my remembrance occupied by stables and farm-buildings, and by an ancient walled garden, which dated from the time of the monastery. I am unacquainted with the present aspect of things in this once well-known and admired spot, where many memories are buried, besides mine, but most of those who would have dwelt on them as I do, are now buried also. At the melancholy sale of Calwich, a grand landscape by Rem-

brandt, the gift, or legacy, of Händel, was purchased by
Mr. Davenport Bromley.

" I delighted in the woods and waters and meadows of
Calwich. Everything within and without was strange and
new, and far superior in effect to anything I had yet seen.
The afflicted chiefs of the family had resumed the old
routine of receiving comers and goers with kind hospitality, and keeping the machine of life in motion, though
the mainspring was broken. After dinner (which was
considered to be very late at five o'clock), the gentlemen
(in silk stockings and shorts) played at bowls in the
spacious bowling-green, in sight of which sat the ladies.
Before rising, however, from the dinner-table, my Uncle
Granville used to ask for a song from whatever ladies
were capable of singing, and at this time Mrs. Dewes
and the beloved Nanny were there to gratify him. After
the song the ladies retired, but speedily reassembled
on the broad gravel-walk, for the rest of the summer
evening, unless a walk was undertaken, in which I was
always glad to follow Aunt Granville. Every flower
and tree were then objects of delight. I hope the walk
to Cabin Knowle continues as charming as it was to me
—a rock partially overgrown with the plants which flou-
rish in limestone clefts, and overshadowed by trees growing up the slope, while an abundant spring gushed up
underneath from a still pool, and found its way to the
river.

" A custom prevailed then, that after the company had
parted, with a general ' Good night,' the ladies went up-
stairs together, and in two's and three's adjourned with
renewed animation to a confidential talking-over of persons

or things. Is this fashion perennial, or has it become obsolete? At least let it be hoped that persons no longer adjourn to a room where children are said to be 'in their soundest sleep,' as happened to me, who, though tall of my age, was reckoned among 'the children.' A bright light was near my bed, and an animated conversation was begun, of which I heard nothing but the murmur, till my own name was mentioned, and then I started and turned. The movement caused the interlocutors to depart, but I had heard words enough to be engraved for ever; and it was not a renewal of sleep, but a burst of bitter tears, which followed upon the removal of light, and close of conversation. The trace of the tears had vanished next morning: but the internal 'battle of life and fate' was durably aggravated.

"At this time the family were just rejoicing in the engagement of my Aunt Fanny to Mr. Abel John Ram, whose family (from the south of Ireland) was one of those who had sadly experienced the ill-usage then fresh in memory, from Roman-Catholic fanaticism in the rebellion —when the old coachman who had served the family during two generations, at the bidding of his associates, drove off his master's four fine carriage-horses, to draw the artillery collected to war against law and government. Many were the causes of grievance which drove Colonel Ram from his ancestral home, and forced him to bring his family to England, where they hired a beautiful house and garden near Ashbourne, the property of Sir Brook Boothby, who had given up his country residence in despair after the death of an only child, Penelope, of whose infant loveliness, short life, and fine intelligence, Aunt Louisa used to tell me so much and so feelingly, that I feel as if I had known her.

"Colonel Ram had with him two sons, of whom the eldest and heir attached himself to my Aunt Fanny from the very first time of meeting: the second son was in the navy, and fell little more than a year later, at the battle of Trafalgar. My Aunt Fanny rises before me at this time as one of the rare combinations of feminine excellence that I have had opportunity of knowing as being such, in the course of my life, and I find it hard to give a just view of the degree of merit of which I became gradually conscious. Her true humility and self-abnegation were more especially to be prized in one who had been a favourite, praised and admired on all sides, from her earliest years. She was a beauty without doubt, but I could only acknowledge without admiring the complex of external advantages. Her skin was of exquisite whiteness; her small figure of perfect proportion and faultless modelling; her hands and arms, throat and bust, defied criticism. Devoted through life, to her adopted parents, to her husband, to her children, to every fellow-creature whose needs or sufferings seemed to create a claim upon her, she lived up to her convictions as a Christian, with a fulness of force in acting and suffering, such as is everywhere uncommon. Her husband was an amiable man, and loved her in an idolising manner; he accepted to the full his wife's estimate of duty, in its height and depth and width and universality, as far as words, and acts of devotion could go, but he had not her powers of self-denial, and followed family habits of expenditure without due calculation of the means remaining to him after the action of various causes of diminution. I have altogether seen but little of my aunt: and she will have been far from guessing how highly I rated her.

"In returning homewards from Calwich, a visit was made at Wellesbourne, where I saw a garden adorned with all the luxury of showy plants then attainable, grouped in pots to the best effect; for in those days the discovery had not been made of planting fuchsias and geraniums in the open ground. Then too I saw Warwick Castle, of which the vivid impression remains to this moment: for when I had a second glimpse in 1849, the scene appeared as familiar to me, as the reverberation of a well-known melody. The well-preserved, not over-built entrance: the long gallery from the hall, at the extremity of which the Vandyke portrait of Charles I., with his horse, and his spaniel, and the splendid figure of the richly coloured palefrenier, are lighted from the unseen end of a cross-gallery: and thirdly the view from the windows towards the river, showing the broken arch of a bridge now superseded; these are all bright visions which I can at any moment recall from the long past.

"It must have been in this same autumn of 1803, that I heard in the conversation of the Ultra Opposition who occasionally came to my father's house, a testimony which might well be trusted to the insight and energy with which Mr. Pitt (then out of office and residing within the Cinque-Ports) watched over the improvement of works of defence along the coast, and the exercising of the volunteers, in the prospect of the threatened invasion of the French; when the communication concluded with the observation, that 'Pitt might have proved a great military commander, had his faculties been directed accordingly.'

"The excitement against the French which made the public mind roll and roar like a troubled sea, extended even to the usually quiet neighbourhood of Llanover: and we heard families named who had their horses harnessed every night, to be ready for escape at any hour—whither? might be asked. The terror, however, did not last long; for the seeming arbiter of war suddenly directed his legions to remove from Boulogne to the high plains of Central Germany, and the surrender of Ulm and of a gallant army commenced the course of calamity which ended in Austerlitz and the ruin of Austria, and finally (in January, 1804) in the death of Mr. Pitt: the battle of Trafalgar and the death of Nelson, having, to the British mind, removed to a distance of comparative indifference the yet more awful concussions of Europe. My father had an interest in the navy and in Lord Nelson which seemed hard to explain. I believe it was in him a reflection from the powerful mind of his brother George, who had sailed much about the high-seas in attendance upon his pupil Prince William, Duke of Clarence, and was much more calculated to distinguish himself in the naval than the clerical profession. I well remember my father's coming in with big tears swelling from his eyes, to tell us of the death of Nelson and the accompanying victory.

"The spring of 1804, spent at Clifton, was marked by a vision of the Napiers. Colonel and Lady Sarah Napier, the parents of that distinguished family, had come to Clifton in hopes of renovating the shattered health of Colonel Napier, whose death, somewhat later, took place there, where he is buried at Redland Chapel on the Downs. Two of the sons, both very young, belonged to that portion of the army (then reckoned raw, but afterwards so famous) which Sir John Moore was training into due discipline, in a camp near Dover. They were allowed leave of absence to visit their father, whose illness was known to be serious, although not recognised as mortal, for Charles and William Napier called more than once upon my mother, and their appearance and conversation were very striking to me. I had never seen anything like them before, and little have I seen since to compare with them. I was brought to their notice in a manner very trying to my great natural shyness, for I was commanded to recite the poem by Mr. Soame upon Bunbury (elder brother of Sir Henry Bunbury) who had died young in India : but their engaging manners made this exposure less bitter to me than on other similar occasions. They both expressed unbounded admiration of their general Sir John Moore, which they said was not gained by indulgence, for he was very strict with young officers, whom he used to send to drill, to their great surprise, after they had supposed themselves perfect in the military exercise.

" It was in 1804 that an event very material to myself took place, in my being taken by my parents to the triennial musical festival at Hereford : the first occasion of my becoming acquainted with any performance of music beyond a single song, or a wandering band or barrelorgan : which perhaps explains the tender feeling I retain towards the latter, out of gratitude for the rare pleasure they gave me, when at Clifton they were accidentally called upon to stop before the windows : I never could comprehend the customary fury expressed against them, as ' disturbers of the peace of the neighbourhood,' when I felt, without finding words to express, that they thrilled through the emptiness of the common atmosphere, with a memento of thought or of passion, of absent and distant joy or woe. The oratorio of Sampson, on the first evening at Hereford, and the Messiah on the last morning, are fixed in grateful remembrance. Mrs. Billington was the soprano-singer, and Harrison and Bartleman were the tenor and bass : and did I but possess the musical power, coveted in vain all my life, I could now pour forth from the treasure of song then laid in faithful memory, the strains of the first-named, in ' Let the bright Seraphim,' and in ' I know that my Redeemer liveth,' and the deep and mellow tones of Bartleman seem to be still reproduced when I think of them. After the evening performances, a ball took place, which was to me a new sight. The daughters of Sir George Cornewall, most of them still unmarried, occupied my attention. Miss Fanny Cornewall became soon after Lady Hereford, and Miss Harriet became Mrs. Lewis (later the mother of two much distinguished sons, of whom the younger was Sir George Cornewall Lewis). Miss Caroline Cornewall married not long after, and was slightly known to me later as Lady Duff Gordon. Mr. Price (later Sir Uvedale Price) and his fine park of Foxley, are very distinct in my Hereford recollection. The work of Mr. Price on the Picturesque I knew well, having read it aloud to my mother, both of us taking it in *con amore*.

" ' Youth looks out upon life, as a distant prospect sun-gilt,' is a remark made by Johnson on a very hacknied

subject, which must present itself to every human being
under one or another aspect.   With me, the 'sun-gilding'
had soon passed away; and only while that lasted, can I
discern spots which tempt me to delineation, or tracks
which guided to scenes or objects of interest.   I was, in a
grave and dispirited family, the only piece of health and
activity and comparative cheerfulness, and I had to contend against becoming accustomed to the habit of dwelling upon evil whether present or prospective.   Four lines
(which I believe form part of a sonnet of Miss Seward's)
may be taken as the text of most of my unspoken meditations, or reveries—

> 'Come, bright Imagination! come, relume
> Thine orient lamp! with renovating ray
> Shine on the mind, and pierce its gathering gloom
> With all the fires of intellectual day!' "

CHAPTER III.

HOME LIFE AT LLANOVER.

" Le bonheur se trouvait pour elle dans un grand développement de ses facultés, elle résidait dans l'application."—MADAME ROLAND.

IN the extreme quiet of her life at Llanover, Mrs. Waddington found all-sufficient interest in the education of her daughters Frances and Emilia. But while Emilia Waddington touched all the tenderest chords of her mother's heart by her patient and cheerful endurance of suffering, the vigorous constitution and more advanced age of her elder child rendered her every day an increasingly valuable companion to the parent, whose peculiar system of tuition was certainly eminently successful. She never overloaded her daughter with tasks, but from the earliest age she interested her by reading aloud or by recounting what she herself had read, repeating such parts as she considered would make a beneficial impression. " Whatever you do, do it with all your might," was a maxim from which she never departed. A great deal of rest was insisted upon, and a great deal of air and exercise,

but when employed, no half attention was allowed or
even endured. Idle hands and listless looks were never
permitted for an instant. The moment attention
flagged, the book was closed and put away, and a habit
of self-examination and reflection was engendered,
which in general is too much neglected.

In after years, the Baroness Bunsen, when referring
to her child-life at Llanover, often spoke of the way in
which her early habits of absolute self-dependence were
engendered. On seeing how in many families it is
supposed that children must be " watched " from morning till night, she used to describe how different was
her up-bringing, left entirely without any guidance
except her mother's directions, from which she never
thought of deviating, as to the employment of her
time ; without any regular lesson-hours, yet, when in
the house, expected to be always busy with one thing
or other, and that, not in any solitary retreat, but in
her mother's sitting-room, exposed to constant interruptions, and therefore trained to pin down attention
to the utmost.

Frances Waddington never was placed under a
governess, and till she was fourteen, almost the only
instruction she received except that of her mother, was
from a female artist (Miss Palmer), who was remarkable for her admirable style of sketching from nature.
Before she was six years old the young Frances used to
accompany this lady, watching her at work, and very
soon beginning to take the same view. Her improve-

ment was extraordinarily rapid, and encouraged by her mother, whose exquisite taste and accurate eye detected the slightest fault in drawing or colouring, she made such progress as very soon to outstrip her early instructress. Mrs. Waddington encouraged her little daughter in the practice of drawing everything that came in her way, whether it was a landscape, a building, a figure, an animal, or a table with a pair of candlesticks upon it. There are volumes of her drawings from nature before she was six years old. She was advised, on looking at any object, to think of how she would draw it, and how the lights and shades fell, and to be able to give a reason for every line she made. Especially remarkable as evidence of her artistic skill, and thorough knowledge of form at this time, are her many cuttings out in black paper—an art now almost forgotten, but which was then greatly admired.

The extreme truthfulness, remembered as characteristic of both her father and mother, is so quaintly evinced in the following letter of their little Frances, written at four years old, that it claims insertion :—

"My dear Aunt Harriet,—Mamma desires me to write to you, and she told me to write to my grandpapa, or else I should not think of sending you letters, as I do not remember either of you. My aunts Louisa and Fanny I do remember, and love very much. My grandmamma Waddington has given Emily and me three guineas. I cannot tell what else to say.—F. WADDINGTON."

Being encouraged, as early as 1802, to keep a journal of her inner life, Frances Waddington inscribed upon the first page the precept of Dr. Johnson, " The great thing to be recorded is the state of your own mind; and you should write down everything that you remember, for you cannot judge at first what is good or bad ; and write immediately while the impression is fresh, for it will not be the same thing a week afterwards."

A great reader, and interested on all subjects which exercised the understanding, Mrs. Waddington possessed unusual powers of expression both in writing and conversation, and had a peculiarly musical voice, which combined harmony with power and flexibility of intonation and was without the least affectation. There are many instances on record of the electrical effect which her voice produced, and one is remembered of her suddenly speaking to a post-boy, who was beating his horse cruelly, in tones which seemed to strike him motionless. Her reading aloud was a special gift. Whatever she read—the Bible, or poetry, or the plays of Shakspeare, her voice and manner were exactly suited to the subject. She encouraged the power of recitation in her daughter Frances, who used from an early age to learn many poems by heart for her own pleasure and that of her mother : this was merely resorted to as a recreation, her retentive memory prevented its being a labour. She also frequently wrote to the dictation of her mother, and they read together continually.

Already in childhood, Emilia Waddington had become the confirmed invalid which she continued through
life, and was able to have little share in her sisters'
employments, so that, till her fourteenth year, the life
of Frances, except for her mother, would have been
singularly lonely and monotonous. At that time, she
was allowed to have occasional lessons in music and
dancing. Amongst the few persons whom she was in
the habit of seeing from time to time, were the Allens
of Cresselly, who, being natives and residents of South
Wales, had frequent opportunities of coming to Llanover on their journies to and from London. The
Allen of Cresselly of that time married the daughter
of Lord Robert Seymour (then of Taliarris). His
only brother, Baugh Allen (afterwards appointed by
Mr. Waddington's will trustee for Madame de Bunsen's fortune), was for many years Master of Dulwich
College, an office which he resigned on his marriage
with the niece of Sir Samuel Romilly. Their sisters,
though not celebrated by poets or biographers, were
perhaps more worthy of public record than many of
their contemporaries whose lives have been written.
They were remarkable in many ways. Of eight daughters the greater number were exceedingly handsome,
and there was not one who did not excel in conver-
sational powers, or who had not a talent for writing,
which though confined, as far as is known, to intimate
correspondence, might have been employed on literary
productions with advantage to the world. The eldest

married Sir James Mackintosh : another married M. de
Sismondi : two married the well-known brothers, John
and Josiah Wedgewood ; another the Rev. Matthew
Surtees, brother-in-law of the Lord Chancellor Eldon ;
and another (mentioned later in these volumes) married the Rev. E. Drewe, Rector of Broad-Hambury, in
Devonshire, and was mother of the late Lady Gifford
and Lady Alderson.

During the many years of her early married life,
spent in the centre of Welsh cottages and Welsh cottagers, Mrs. Waddington did not think of acquiring
knowledge of the Welsh language, which had a large
share in her occupations, when, after the marriage of
her elder daughters, she was only occupied by the care
of her youngest child, who from childhood exhibited
a passionate attachment for everything connected with
the country of her birth. The interest in the ancient
language of Britain which her daughter Augusta
awakened in Mrs. Waddington was afterwards much
increased by conversation with Baron Bunsen and his
learned countrymen Professor Lepsius and Dr. Meyer,
who proved to her the value of Welsh with reference
to philology as well as to historical and antiquarian
subjects.

In her fifteenth year Frances Waddington spent
some time in London, when her mother, who had
been accustomed to all that was best in the society of
Windsor and St. James's in her youth, but who had
looked upon herself as a kind of pariah from society in

her Welsh seclusion, and imagined herself forgotten by her former associates, was equally surprised and grati-fied by the warmth with which she was greeted. Espe-cially cordial was her reception by the daughters of Thomas Earl of Pomfret—Lady Charlotte Finch, Lady Juliana Penn, and Lady Louisa Clayton, who had been amongst the most intimate friends of Mrs. Delany. Her interview with the Royal Family on the occasion of her first visit to London is described in a letter from Frances Waddington to her aunt Miss Harriet Port.

"*June* 5, 1805.—I must begin by telling you that yester-day the Princesses, and afterwards the Queen, on hearing that mamma was with the Miss Fieldings,* sent for her, Emily, Augusta, and me; and, after having given you so great a piece of news, I will tell you the whole story methodically. Mamma went to Lady C. Finch's to see Miss Augusta Fielding's and Miss Finch's dresses, and was a good deal surprised at finding Miss Fielding in full dress, though she was not to go to court, and, on inquiring the reason, understood that she was going to the Princesses, to stay with them till they were sent for by the Queen. After having given mamma this piece of information, Miss Fielding whispered to her sister, and then said, ' I have no doubt they would send for you if they knew you were here.' She ran out of the room, and coming back in a few minutes, said that the Princesses desired we would

* Daughters of Captain Fielding, R.N., by Sophia, daughter of Lady Charlotte Finch, who was governess to the princesses.

all come up. Miss Fielding then got for mamma a purple
cap and feathers of her sister's and a white muslin gown
of her own, which she helped her to put on, while Miss
Augusta fastened the feathers in mamma's head, which
you, who know what it is to have to dress in a hurry, particularly for Court, where she was forced to go early, will
acknowledge to have been excessively good-natured. All
this time Miss Fielding's maid trimmed me out in a coral
necklace and a worked muslin gown of her mistress's,
with a long train. Emily unluckily had left her cap at
home and came only in a hat, so Miss Fielding formed the
expedient of tying a blue Barcelona handkerchief round
her head, and a necklace round her throat, and then, our
borrowed feathers having been properly adjusted, we went
to their Royal Highnesses, all of us, as you may believe,
in a pretty good fright, except Augusta, who was perfectly
at her ease. We came into a very little room, which the
Princesses, with their hoops, almost exclusively occupied.
I guessed at once which was Princess Augusta by her
kindness to mamma, Princess Elizabeth by her size, and
Princess Mary by her beauty. Princess Amelia was not
there, and Princess Sophia I did not much look at, as I
was occupied in admiring Princess Mary's headdress, which
was a large plume of white ostrich feathers, and a very
small plume of black feathers placed before the white
ones : her hair was drawn up quite smooth to the top of
her head, with one large curl hanging from thence almost
down to her throat. Her petticoat was white and silver,
and the drapery and body, as well as I can recollect, were
of purple silk, covered with spangles, and a border and
fringe of silver. Princess Elizabeth had eleven immense

yellow ostrich feathers in her head, which you may imagine had not a very good effect. We had been in the room five minutes, during which time Princess Elizabeth took a great deal of notice of Augusta (who says that ' the lady in a blue gown and hoop took her to the window and kissed her') when Princess Charlotte of Wales came in, dressed in a pale pink frock covered with lace and wearing a beautiful pearl necklace and bracelets and a diamond cross. She is a very pretty and delicate-looking child, and has light brown hair, which curls all over her head. Princess Elizabeth took her by the hand. The Queen then sent for the Princesses, and if they had been anyone else, I must have laughed at seeing them sidle out of the room, holding their hoops with both hands. We were moving towards Miss Fielding's room, when mamma was told that Princess Elizabeth wanted her; so we all followed mamma and Miss Fielding into a room, where we saw Her Majesty with all the Princesses, and Mrs. Fielding and a great many more ladies. Emily and I stood outside the door till Princess Elizabeth called us in, and the Queen made some remarks on mamma's having two such great girls, and she spoke very graciously to mamma, and made inquiries after Madame d'Arblay.* Then she said she would not detain us any longer, so we walked off, and had just put on our own clothes, when Mrs. Fielding came and made us dress again, to go to the Princess Charlotte, who was to remain with Lady C. Finch for some time. We went and

* Because the pension of Madame d'Arblay, which had ceased on her marriage and residence in France, had been restored on the representation and personal influence of Mrs. Waddington, who made known her reduced circumstances to Queen Charlotte.

staid with her Royal Highness for about an hour, who played as good-naturedly as possible with Augusta, who was never better pleased in her life. The Princess said in the prettiest manner imaginable 'Would not Mrs. Waddington sit down?' and in short has quite the manners of a little queen, though she is as natural as possible."

A few days later Frances Waddington was present at the trial of Lord Melville, impeached for having connived at a system of peculation while Treasurer of the Navy.

FRANCES WADDINGTON *to* MISS HARRIET PORT.

"11 *June*, 1805.—Mamma received, through Lady Albinia Cumberland,* an order from Lady Willoughby for two tickets for the Great Chamberlain's box for the last day of Lord Melville's trial, whenever that should be. We only knew late on Wednesday afternoon that it was fixed for Thursday, when I got up at five, as we were told many people would go at that time, but my aunt Fanny† did not call for me till seven. The doors were not opened till nine, but during the interval Colonel Ram took us into the Houses of Lords and Commons. I never could have imagined what a real squeeze was until I found myself in the passage leading to the Great Chamberlain's box; however, we were soon safely seated, and were exactly in front of the throne. At twelve the procession of peers commenced, the Masters in Chancery in long wigs—some in purple and

* Daughter of George, third Earl of Buckinghamshire.
† Then Mrs. Ram.

gold, some scarlet and gold, and some in black and gold
robes; then the Lord Chancellor, the barons, bishops,
viscounts, and so on—those of least rank walking first,
and the procession ending with the Royal Dukes. Then a
man bearing a sceptre, having commanded silence in the
King's name on *pain of imprisonment*, the trial began, which
certainly was not amusing, as it consisted solely of Lord
Erskine's asking the opinion of each peer on the ten
different articles of impeachment, and the peer got up in
his place and answered 'guilty' or 'not guilty,' putting
his hand on his heart. Not one gave the answer really
well and gracefully except the Duke of Cumberland; but
the Royal Dukes all spoke audibly, which I am sure the
peers did not. We did not get home till five o'clock, so I
had been twelve hours without eating anything but some
sea biscuits.

Dr. Burney dined with us, and at twelve P.M. mamma
went to Lady Lansdowne's masquerade dressed as a pilgrim.
There were some incomparable masks, especially Sir Walter
Raleigh by Mr. W. Lyttleton, who lugged about his History
of the World, and began reading it aloud to Queen Elizabeth. The Duke of Clarence, dressed as a woman, walked
about all night with Mrs. Jordan, and the Duke of Sussex
with Grassini, whose delightful acting in 'Camilla' I have
not yet told you of."

The kindness of her reception in the preceding year
induced Mrs. Waddington to return to London in 1806,
when she visited Windsor with her children and Mr.
and Mrs. Ram; the King, who was then in his sixty-
seventh year, being already virtually under sentence of

blindness, a cataract having formed over one of his
eyes, and a second being in process.

FRANCES WADDINGTON *to* MISS HARRIET PORT.

"30 *June*, 1806.—Yesterday mamma, Emily, Augusta
and I went to Windsor, and staid from six till almost eight
with Lady Albinia Cumberland, who told mamma that she
had a most warm friend in Princess Elizabeth, and that
she had been speaking of her in the highest terms that
very day at dinner. We drank tea with Lady Albinia, and
then went on the terrace, where the King, all the Princesses
except Princess Mary, and the Duke of Cambridge were
walking. The first time they passed by, Princess Augusta
and one of the others turned out of the line, and came up
to mamma, saying 'How do you do? I am so glad to see
you.' The next time they all stopped for more than a
quarter of an hour. The King said to mamma, 'I did not
know you at first, I am grown quite blind lately;' so
mamma answered, 'But your Majesty looks well.'—'Yes,
I am in perfect health, I have no right to complain.' The
King then stooped to Augusta—'And who is this little
thing?' Upon which Princess Augusta said, 'Oh, that is
a very beautiful little thing!' and mamma lifted Augusta
up, and the King looked at her and praised her, and Princess
Elizabeth kissed her, and then said, 'These are the two
others,' and she took me by the arm, and put me close to
the King, who looked at me through his glass, and said,
'You are a very undutiful daughter to grow taller than
your mother' (a proof of the badness of his eyes), and he
asked me how long we had been in town. Emily was then
shown to him, and he asked mamma after Uncle Dewes,

and said, 'Well, and how do you think the old walls look?' and laughed at her expressing her delight at hearing the chimes; and Princess Elizabeth said to me, 'I have such a beautiful drawing of yours.'"

To the SAME.

"23 *June*, 1806.—I must tell my aunt Harriet and my grandpapa that Pamela, a Frenchwoman, the daughter and éleve of Madame de Genlis, is one of the very sweetest creatures I ever had the pleasure of beholding. Last night we went to Lady Sarah Napier, when she ran into the room looking not more than six and twenty. After Lord Edward Fitzgerald's death she married an American merchant named Pitcairne. Her gown was of printed calico, but only came over her shoulders, with two short sleeves: all that was seen in front was a white body and petticoat. On her head was a little black Oxonian's cap, made of black crape and beads which she pulled off to Lady Sarah. Her black eyes are in perpetual motion; she has not a morsel of rouge, and she laughed at the beautiful Dowager Duchess of Rutland for wearing so much, saying 'When I am a grandmother, I will have a clean face, that I may not daub my little grandchildren's noses with rouge when I kiss them.'

"We have been with Lady Stuart and Miss Hobart to see Lord Stafford's pictures. They give tickets for people to see them every Wednesday, when the rooms are crowded like the Royal Academy Exhibition. The pictures are extremely fine, but it is quite ridiculous to observe out of the numbers that came into the room, how few thought it necessary even to *look* at them. I stood very near Mrs.

Siddons for some time, to hear what she said. At length she picked out a painting of some Dutch fishwomen, the last thing upon earth you could call interesting, and 'what a sweet composition is that!' was pronounced in her deepest tragedy tones."

In the following year the Windsor visit was repeated.

FRANCES WADDINGTON *to* MISS PORT.

"13 *July*, 1807. — Yesterday we went to Windsor. The crowd on the Terrace was amazing and the heat intense. The first time the Royal Family passed, only Princess Elizabeth spoke to mamma and shook hands with her. The next time they all stopped, and Princess Elizabeth kindly took a great deal of trouble to get the Queen to make out mamma, which she did at last, with some difficulty, and then, to make amends, told her that ' she was not much altered since she saw her last.' Then Princess Elizabeth said twice 'This is Mrs. Waddington's daughter,' and the Queen commented on my looking so much stouter than mamma, then she asked after mamma's health and mamma told her she was very much troubled with headaches. ' Oh,' said the Queen, 'that is like me, I have very bad headaches.' Then the Queen turned to my aunt Fanny and Mr. Ram, and Princess Mary spoke most kindly to mamma, and so did the Duke of Cambridge. The King spoke to mamma, but did not say anything particular : he looked grave, and stood staring at her for near five minutes, but I am afraid he could not see her. The Queen is grown so enormous that she looks as if she carried all the fifteen Princes and Princesses before her."

In the summer of 1808, the family passed a longer time in London, for Frances Waddington was now seventeen, though from her mother's frequent and severe headaches she did not go out very much, and then only under the chaperonage of some trusted friend.

FRANCES WADDINGTON *to* MISS HARRIET PORT.

"6 *July*, 1808. — I must now tell you of yesterday. We were dressed and with Miss Fielding by half-past twelve. We were called in first to see Princess Mary and Princess Charlotte, then to Princess Sophia. The Queen and the other Princesses were so hurried they could not come, but promised to come if possible after the drawing-room. Those two Princesses were very kind to mamma, particularly Princess Sophia, but they both looked sadly ill, and though very smiling and good-natured, I think there is a striking appearance of melancholy in their countenances. Princess Sophia was beautifully dressed in pink and silver tissue covered with blonde lace and wreaths of silver flowers. Princess Mary was very magnificent in white and silver. Princess Charlotte's dress was blue and silver tissue with a white lace frock, a diamond necklace and cross, her hair (which grows beautifully about her forehead) curled in front, and done up behind in curls with a diamond arrow, diamond brooches on her sleeves. The Duchess of Brunswick is quite a vulgar-looking old woman, dressed in white crape, being in deep mourning for her daughter. The Dukes of Kent, Cumberland, and Cambridge, were in magnificent field-marshal's uniforms. When the Queen and the Princesses went into the drawing-room, Princess Charlotte came back to Miss Fielding, and staid till half-past four, as kind as possible to Augusta, whom she knew at first sight, and seemed to like much better than the other children. Nothing can be more perfect than her manners, her figure and carriage are charming, with a pretty animated countenance, and nothing like pride about her, suffering Lady Robert Fitzgerald's children to take liberties with her, without even *looking* displeased. She is very much to be pitied, for the only amusement she has in the year is coming to Lady Charlotte Finch's, on the King and Queen's birthday; and she does nothing from morning till night but learn lessons which she hears Lady de Clifford say are unnecessary. Mamma spoke to her of Miss Hunt, and she answered with emotion, ' O, I was very naughty when Miss Hunt was with me,' and then mentioned what mamma knew before, that Miss Hunt wrote to her on her birthday. The Bishop of Salisbury, Princess Charlotte's *preceptor*, as they call him, said to mamma—' I wish to God we could have Miss Hunt back again, she cannot be replaced.' "

In 1809 Frances Waddington was dangerously ill at Llanover from typhus fever. In the following November, partly for the advantage of masters, she went with her father, mother, and sisters to spend the winter in Edinburgh—a winter of great enjoyment, as affording that mental stimulus which she so greatly missed at home. It was a pleasure to Mrs. Waddington to recall many old associations in the society of Mrs. Delany's favourite godson, Dr. Daniel Sandford, then Bishop of Edinburgh, and to her daughter his friendship was of the greatest advantage, as he was able to enter into the many difficulties on religious subjects which presented themselves to her active mind, and to show her how—not to turn away from, but to solve them. His children also were pronounced by Frances Waddington the most agreeable she ever saw. The society of Sir Walter Scott, of Mr. Alison, Mr. Jeffrey, and of the charming Lady Louisa Stuart (granddaughter of Lady Mary Wortley Montagu) —the life-long friend of Mrs. Waddington, also combined to render the winter most enjoyable. Another delight was the incomparable acting of Mrs. Siddons, who was in Edinburgh at this time. It was during this winter that the attention they excited in others awakened Mrs. Waddington to the superiority of her daughter's intellectual gifts. After her return to Llanover she wrote to her nephew, James Monk, afterwards Bishop of Gloucester.—

" 3 *July*, 1810.—I was very much gratified by my six months in Edinburgh. Mr. Waddington certainly was tired of the place, but Fanny was delighted, and had extraordinary reasons for being so,—for never was greater justice done to her talents and acquirements. Professor Playfair said in a mixed company that he never had met with so well-balanced or so elegantly cultivated a mind as Miss Waddington's, and many more similar speeches inevitably travelled to me, made by other men about her. I say *men* only, for I kept all the boys aloof, not allowing one to enter the house, excepting Lord Glenbervie's son, Mr. Douglas, Mr. G. Rich, and Lord John Russell, who, bye the bye, is the only English young man of any promise at Edinburgh."

Great was the pleasure of a few days spent with the Fergussons of Raith, and the enjoyment of its fine library, its collections of prints, and casts of antique gems. On returning to Llanover, Miss Waddington attended to her various studies with fresh energy, as well as to the education of her younger sisters. She says in her diary :—

" 10 *June*, 1810.—Our books having at last arrived from Edinburgh, I have my Greek. Latin, Spanish, and Italian, Euclid, and Smith's *Wealth of Nations* to go on with, besides drawing, practising, and working, hearing Emily read Italian and seeing her embroider, and watching over Augusta in her mathematics, her drawing, and her music, and doing geography with her. I cannot always contrive all these things in one day, but I endeavour to make up the second day for what I omit in the first."

In July Professor Monk came to Llanover on a long visit, when Frances Waddington took the opportunity of " going on with mathematics and Latin, to the exclusion of most other things." The friendship which began with her cousin over mathematical lessons, led to a correspondence of many years. In Mr. Monk, both mother and daughter, during the monotony of their Llanover life, found one who was capable of entering into the books which formed almost their sole interest, and who was always willing to discuss them and advise upon them. The appearance of the successive novels of Walter Scott were at this time the chief excitements of many an English home, but at Llanover were scarcely more of events than the publication of the different works of Madame de Staël, for whose character and writings Mrs. Waddington had conceived the most boundless admiration. "Le talent de Madame de Staël agit comme une sensation," wrote Mrs. Waddington, borrowing the authoress's own words as applied to Claudius, a novel-writer. The appearance of *L'Allemagne* especially excited the most violent enthusiasm. Mrs. Waddington could not find words to give an idea of the "maraviglia, ed amore, la riverenza, mille affetti insieme, tutti raccolti al cor," excited by the first and second volumes. Meanwhile, in the society around Llanover, neither mother nor daughter found anything perfectly congenial.—"Fanny and I see too many people *qui occupent le même gradin que nous*," wrote Mrs. Waddington to Professor Monk.

FRANCES WADDINGTON *to the* REV. J. II. MONK.

"*Llanover*, 15 *March*, 1813.—I make an opportunity, a thing never to be found ready made, to write to you. . . . As I think you will like to hear of the persons that most interested us at Bath, I will begin with Mrs. Frances

Bowdler, sister to Mrs. Harriet Bowdler, who published Miss Smith's Fragments, and who is still more known as the queen of a coterie of ladies at Bath. The two sisters differ so completely in character and taste, that they have for years lived separately, though on perfectly good terms. Mrs. Frances has lived in, and enjoyed, the most desirable society in her own country, and has enlarged her ideas and quickened her perceptions, by a long residence abroad; while Mrs. Harriet has remained fixed like an oyster to her rock, receiving, as Bishop Warburton says, foul water or fresh, just as it happened to flow towards her. The consequence has been, that the former has retained the originality of her character, and the acuteness of her understanding, while the excellent talents of the latter have not preserved her from sinking into the insipidity which must ever result from indiscriminate intercourse with the herd of ordinary mortals. Mrs. F. Bowdler's favourite topic of conversation was one particularly interesting to me—the modern inhabitants and literature of that country, which was in ancient days fruitful perhaps beyond all others in worth and genius.

"We have lately been reading Mrs. Hannah More's new work, 'Christian Morals,' with great pleasure, though we must ever prefer the writings which established her reputation, to those which she has published since it was established, the former having been executed by faculties in their prime, improved by a long residence in the house of Garrick and amongst his associates, and by intimate friendship and correspondence with Lord Orford; whereas the latter have been the production of advanced years, decayed health, and taste vitiated by the society of sectaries, and of Mrs. Patty and Mrs. Prue (or whatever may be their names), her sisters. All this being considered, it is only wonderful that she should still be able in the highest degree to 'come with power into the conscience,' and to reiterate truths long since familiar, not only with fervour ever increasing, but with unceasing variety: however, at the same time that we are grateful to Mrs. Hannah More for the publication of this work, it is impossible not to feel indignant at the depravity of taste which has induced her to interlard her most animating passages with offensive allusions, degrading similes, and pedantic words, by which she lessens the effect of her exhortations. Another thing that distressed me in this work was the false reasoning, as I considered it, respecting Providence: for it has always appeared to me that the belief in particular interpositions of the Divine Hand interferes with that fundamental principle of religion which teaches us that 'God works by means, not miracles;' that he sets at work causes, which produce the system of things and course of events we behold; wherefore, in the very effect of those causes, we may with truth say we discern the hand of God, but then it is *mediately*, not *immediately* ; a 'special interference' of God would be an interference with his own moral government. Surely the very word ' *interposition* ' denotes the fallacy of the doctrine; from what should God *interpose* to save us ? from another power ? But we know that ' all power is of God;' otherwise we should be admitting the *good* and *evil principle* of the ancient Persians. As to the consolation which it is urged may be derived from the doctrine of a particular Providence, surely nothing more can be required than the declaration, so solemnly reiterated, in different words, that 'all things shall *work together* for good to them that love God.' "

Mrs. Waddington *to* Rev. Professor Monk.

"I spent the last evening of being in town with Madame de Staël, but in such a state of suffering that nothing but my most ardent desire for years to hear and see the most wonderful woman of her age, could have induced me to struggle thro'. Still, as I went with 'the man in Europe she most admires' (her own words), she thought I must be worth cultivating, and, therefore, in the most engaging manner bid me 'not forget her,' but 'when I could, come again.' In my life I never was so highly gratified by conversation. Her speaking is quite equal to her writing. Indeed Sir J. Mackintosh told me that, except Burke *sometimes*, he never heard anything at all approaching to her dazzling eloquence. Fanny spent several hours on Monday night listening to Madame de Staël, Sir J. Mackintosh, Dumont, and Mr. W. Smith, and on her return home sat on my bed two hours, repeating the very words of many of the sentences of Madame de Staël, and also the admirable and acute comments of the men who drew her out."

" 8 *December,* 1813.—Do not think that I am insensible to public events, because I have said nothing about the astonishing reverses. The altered countenance of Napoleon in the print in Colnaghi's shop convinced me, in July, that he would no longer ' unassailable hold on his course unshaken of motion.' That fat, enervated countenance, so unlike the Buonaparte by Appiani after the Battle of Marengo, was not made to govern the world. Still I firmly believe within my life he will be again the greatest potentate on earth.

"Poor Emily is much worse. Alas, alas! how exactly does a sentence of Madame de Staël's paint her situation— 'Terminée comme évènement, mais qui subsiste encore comme souffrance,' and this at nineteen."

FRANCES WADDINGTON *to* PROFESSOR MONK.

"17 *April*, 1814.—My Mother bids me say that you have conferred the greatest of all possible obligations on her, by having excited for one moment the slightest interest in Madame de Staël for her. For years Madame de Staël has been literally 'l'objet de son rêve;' and both my mother and myself felt to so great a degree the irresistible enchantment of her last work, that we both addressed her; but we had not courage to send the effusions of our hearts, every word that we could use seemed so dull, so dead, so inexpressive of the sense we entertained of the inestimable benefit of *De l'Allemagne;* even though she herself has said in her preface to the *Lettres sur Rousseau,* 'Que le sentiment de sa faiblesse même ne doit pas empêcher d'offrir son hommage à un génie supérieur.' But one must have her talent to speak of her as she deserves, though happily this is not necessary for understanding and admiring her!—As the Brahmin said to Sir William Jones, 'The night-blowing Ceres beholds but one moon; but the moon sheds her cheering light on many a night-blowing Ceres.'

"Every word you say about the most extraordinary of all revolutions. the restoration of the Bourbons, we entirely subscribe to; all that is now to be hoped is that the representative system may atone for the folly of re-calling *ces imbéciles*, who were the first, twenty years ago, to desert their country, their brother, and their king, not-withstanding his supplications to them to remain in France. My mother and I felt so much for the French prisoners at Abergavenny on this occasion, that we went over on Monday to see them; amongst our particular acquaintance, the dejection and indignation is extreme. General Rey, late Governor of St. Sebastian, desired the Vicar of Abergavenny to write to Lord Bathurst for an official certificate respecting the events that have taken place, in order that the prisoners may assemble and declare by a public act their adherence to the decrees of the Con-servative Senate."

MRS. WADDINGTON *to* REV. PROFESSOR MONK.

"*August* 26, 1814.—We have had for almost a month the master who taught me French and Italian to perfect Fanny in those languages. She could not write a line in Italian when Moyon came, and her translations now would sur-prise you, most particularly the spelling, which she scarcely ever errs in, from her extraordinary attention in reading, never having learnt a word by rote in her life. Moyon says, that excepting the youngest sister of Lord Howick, he never saw a girl at all to compare with Fanny."

FRANCES WADDINGTON *to the* REV. PROFESSOR MONK.

"*Llanover, Jan.* 25, 1815.—We have just finished ' Wa-verley.' It is not surprising to us now that you should have requested *not to be informed, if we did not like* ' *Waverley* '

—that you should have wished to be spared the painful
sensation consequent upon discovering your friends to be
incapable alike of the noblest and of the commonest sympathies of human nature. I have thought, and said, that
I could never like the person who did not feel like myself
about two other works, namely, 'Corinne' and 'Delphine:'
but in those two instances, the unsoundness of the moral
principle forms a ground of objection so highly to be
respected, as to preclude a very close scrutiny as to the
degree of native insensibility which must combine with it
to prevent the strong sensations of delight and admiration
that I experience. But to the case of 'Waverley' this
observation does not apply, for wherever our minds can for
an instant turn away from the consideration of the gay
fancy; the sound reason; the sterling humour; the powers
of reflection and condensation; the feeling, acute, profound,
tender, yet chastened; the very soul and spirit of poetry;
the stores of information, the accuracy of observation,
which every page of this work summons us to attribute to
its author,—we are called upon to admit, that the noblest
principles of moral rectitude are throughout inculcated;
that they are not merely interwoven into the contexture of
the work, but that every feeling that is excited, every impression that is left by it, is of the most salutary nature;
the reader is forcibly led by the author to condemn every
defect in character, every error in conduct, though combined
with the most interesting qualities, though tending to the
most desirable results. That our enjoyment might be perfect and entire, wanting nothing, every part of 'Waverley'
impressed upon our minds the conviction that we owe it to
Walter Scott. When first it came out, we were told posi-

tively that he had written it, afterwards positively that he had not; but now, nothing can do away the certainty we feel on the subject—every perfection that shines forth in full splendour in this novel, is discernible in a degree in his conversation.

"We have not yet seen the *Edinburgh Review* of 'Waverley,' and I know not when I shall venture to read it, certainly not till I have enjoyed some time longer the exalting sensation of unmixed admiration. The *Review* will probably point out some fault, which I may be compelled to admit, though I have not been able to detect it. How many faults, supposing they existed, might be covered by the single merit of having delineated two female characters so perfect, gentle, calm, *enduring*, yet enthusiastic in sentiment, firm in principle, resolute in action! Ambiguous excellence, though under different lineaments, is, I think, to be found in Dr. Moore's *Laura*, and Godwin's *Marguerite;* but in the works of the most distinguished female novel writers there is nothing with which I am acquainted, equal to these masculine conceptions of female perfection.

"But to go on describing the different effects produced upon us by different parts of this book, to tell you how it has made us laugh, how it has made us weep, how incessantly the scenes it describes dwell before my mother's and my imagination, is out of the question; therefore I will break off from the subject, after saying that we continually and devoutly rejoice not to have lived in the times when the scene of 'Waverley' is laid; for to say nothing of the strong temptation to be led into error with the erring minority, in opinion at least, no sensation excited by public

events in these days, can enable us to form an adequate
conception of the actual suffering that must have been
occasioned by witnessing the infliction of the heaviest
punishments, however justly incurred, on noble and interesting characters, for a mistake in judgment, induced by
feelings, often amiable, ever pardonable.

"I cannot yet quit the subject of 'Waverley' without
commenting upon what appears to me a striking peculiarity in those closing scenes of anguish,—that so very
few words are spoken, that in the course of those few
words, the sufferers barely mention a few of the torturing
circumstances of their situation, and then quickly revert to
other subjects, as if dreading yet more to agonize and
unnerve themselves and their auditor. It has ever been
observed that such is the conduct natural to superior minds
in deep distress; but every other writer that I can remember has departed from nature in this respect, for the sake
of harrowing up to a greater degree the feelings of the
reader, and has contrived in some manner, either by means
of the principal characters, or of bystanders, to analyse
and explain all the causes of misery, lest they should not
be fully understood and entered into."

"*Llanover, August* 19, 1815.—To your question whether
we have any schemes for the Continent, I answer that we
can at present only think of going to St. Helena. On the
subject connected with that favoured island I know not
how to go on, as by your not mentioning it, I perceive it
has sunk with you into total insignificance, and I cannot
solicit your bare approbation of particulars of conduct and
demeanour that we admire and applaud. I have always
been of opinion that the best justification of Napoleon

might be made by a dispassionate comparison of the
actions and circumstances of his life with those of other
rulers of nations, contemporary and deceased; and in the
lately discovered scheme of our ministry for kidnapping
Napoleon, and conveying him from Elba to St. Helena, in
defiance of treaties, at the moment that he, in anticipation
of his opponents, made his escape into France, I find an
additional proof of what I had long believed, that individuals called upon to govern their fellow-men, and consequently raised by their situation above those fears which
keep the majority of human beings within the bounds of
morality, are, with very few exceptions, arbitrary and
iniquitous as far as they have the power of being so."

In 1816, Mr. and Mrs. Waddington decided on spending the winter in Italy. They left England sufficiently
late in the autumn to make it desirable to pass by Paris
on the outside of the barriers, and not to enter the town
for fear of being detained, the delicate health of Mrs.
Waddington and her daughter Emilia, and the necessity of passing the Simplon making it imperative to
proceed south with as little delay as possible. The
father, mother, and their daughter Emilia, occupied
one carriage; in a second their eldest daughter took
charge of her sister Augusta. By Frances Waddington the journey was hailed with rapture as the opening
of a new life; but, when she parted from her home at
Llanover, she little imagined that three and twenty
years would pass, before she saw it again!

CHAPTER IV.

BUNSEN.

"Let no man out of a weak conceit of sobriety, or an ill-applied moderation, think or maintain that a man can search too far, or be too well studied in the book of God's word, or in the book of God's works, divinity or philosophy, but rather let men endeavour at endless progress or proficience in both."
—BACON, *Advancement of Learning*.

" L'homme s'agite, et Dieu le mène."
FENELON.

AT the end of the last century, on one side of a quiet street of the old town of Corbach, in the little principality of Waldeck, stood a low thatched house of humble aspect. Here, on summer evenings, a little aged man was wont to sit by the window, a picture of peaceful contentment, as he placidly smoked his pipe, and watched the movements of his cocks and hens in the adjoining poultry-yard. His strongly marked features, his resolute penetrating eyes and shaggy eyebrows, indicated a hot-tempered yet kindly spirit within, which despised all distinctions of rank, and measured men only by what they were in themselves. Constantly busied in household cares, his fragile, deli-

cate wife lingered ever and anon to give a glance of
respectful attention to each word of her husband,
reserving her looks of love for a beautiful, fair-
complexioned, curly-haired boy, with bright eyes and
finely chiselled features, who seemed out of place in
the sombre framework, which was nevertheless illuminated by his presence.

Christian Carl Josias was the son of Heinrich Christian Bunsen's old age, the unexpected gift of God
after his marriage in 1790 with Johannette Eleanore
Brocken, who was then advanced in life. Heinrich
Bunsen was the descendant of a family, who had lived
for centuries at Corbach, and filled posts of confidence
in the municipal hierarchy of that ancient town. Yet,
though one of its members is spoken of as an author,
another as a poet, the family generally had never risen
above the rank of agriculturists, a calling indicated
by the three ears of wheat upon their escutcheon, as
it is by the name, for Bunse means yeoman in old
Teutonic language. In his youth Heinrich Bunsen
had not been fortunate. He had been induced, by the
promise of rapid military advancement, to enlist in a
regiment of natives of Waldeck engaged in the service
of Holland. But when he returned after twenty-nine
years of exile, he found his hopes of fortune restricted
to a small retiring pension, and to the produce of a few
paternal acres, with the pittance he could earn by
making copies of legal documents. During his ex-
patriation he had married his first wife, who died in

1782, leaving two daughters, Christiana and Helene. These children, in the first hours of desolation, he had the anguish of seeing deprived, not only of maternal care, but of the comforts of life, which his scanty means, hitherto eked out by a mother's solicitude, could no longer afford them. But his sister, Helene Stricker, came to the rescue, and received the children into her house at Amsterdam, and Heinrich Bunsen returned alone to Corbach in 1789.

In the following year he married again with Johannette Brocken, who had lived for fifteen years in the Palace of Bergheim, a valued dependant in the household of Christine, Countess of Waldeck. Their only child was born on the 25th of August, 1791, and received his first name Christian from the Countess of Waldeck; his second Carl from her daughter, Countess Caroline of Limburg-Gaildorf; his third, Josias, from Count Josias of Waldeck; all three members of the house of Waldeck officiating as his god-parents. At seven years old, little Christian Bunsen was .sent to the Gymnasium, or Latin School of Corbach, but continued to reside at his parents' house, which about this time received a visit from his half-sister Christiana, nineteen years older than himself, who " had the power of interesting and attaching her young brother more than any other person, impressing upon his mind the conclusions of her powerful and independent understanding." Bunsen remained at the Corbach school till he was sixteen, " seizing upon information offered as a

property to which he had a natural claim, achieving
tasks with power and certainty, as though he already
possessed by intuition the knowledge he was acquiring." His voracity for books was insatiable, and having soon exhausted all the small libraries of his parents
and neighbours, he used to spend any stray moments in
assisting his father in the copying of law-papers, that
he might earn some small coins towards their acquire-
ment. It is a proof of his aptitude for languages that
as the pastor of a distant village possessed the treasure
of Glover's "Leonidas," and a few other English books,
he was able while still a boy to teach himself English
by their diligent study.

Many pleasant glimpses of Bunsen's boyhood are
derived from the recollections of his friend Wolrad
Schumacher, who at an early age was sent to the
Corbach school from his paternal home in the neighbouring town of Arolsen.

" I left Arolsen," he says, " with extreme sorrow, which
was not diminished by the gloomy aspect of my new abode
and my new teacher. But my heart did not break nor
harden ; all at once I found myself sitting beside Christian
Bunsen, in the dwelling of his parents, kindly received by
them as well as by their son. How this happened I have
no remembrance, so suddenly and rapidly did all the late
occurrences drag me along with them ; but all at once I
found myself spending whole winter evenings in that
house. The father read the newspaper or a book, the
mother sat by him knitting, a female servant was spinning

in the corner behind the stove, Christian and I sat on a bench under the window towards the street, somewhat in the shade. Little do I recall of what was spoken, when suddenly we start up at the sound of a bell which summons me home ; the leave-taking at the house-door extended to some length; then he accompanies me to my home; I follow him back to his own; till at last parting becomes unavoidable.

"The dwelling of the family was in a side street; the thatched roof, the threshold at the entrance, the stable on your right hand after entering, reminded you of the arrangement of the abode of a Westphalian yeoman : there was besides a flight of stairs to the upper story on the right, and on the left the outlet to a small garden. The dwelling-chamber, roomy and light, was on the left from the house-door. Christian Bunsen's own small room was in the upper story, towards the garden. Here, during my Corbach school-years, did I go in and out, finding my friend never otherwise than occupied, full of zeal and earnestness over his books. In the morning he was up with the sun, which shone straight into his window, look-ing towards the east. During the summer evenings, when I came in the twilight to fetch him to walk, he was read-ing or writing, but ever turned from his occupation to receive me with bright kindness. Throughout the school, he was admired as a genius. In knowledge and compre-hension, no individual could measure with him in any degree, and his laboriousness cast all the rest into the shade."

When he was sixteen, Bunsen had reached the high-

est form in the school at Corbach, and he was then
sent to Marburg University, Heinrich Bunsen having
made it possible by excessive industry and economy
during his son's residence at home, to meet the expense
of giving him a college education.   But the University
of Marburg was then rapidly declining, and in the
following year Bunsen removed to Göttingen, whither
the fame of his scholarship had preceded him, and
where he was most warmly welcomed by Heyne, then
the leading classical scholar of Germany, who soon
perceived for himself that he had to do with a student
of uncommon gifts, and rendered his future more easy
and hopeful by procuring him the work and salary of
an extra teacher at the Gymnasium.   A few months
later, Bunsen's position was further assured by his
appointment as private tutor to William Backhouse
Astor, son of the famous American merchant.

   The years spent at Göttingen were amongst the
happiest of Bunsen's life.   The ardour displayed in all
he undertook was shown in nothing more than in his
friendships.   The two youths with whom he had lodg-
ings in common were Lachmann, afterwards celebrated
as a philological writer, and from his edition of the
New Testament ; and Lücke, afterwards well known
as a theological teacher, and from his critical edition of
the Gospel of St. John.   Bunsen's room was the largest,
and there a noble band of friends was wont to gather,
whose bond of affection remained unbroken, till it was
severed by death.

"The instinctive discernment of differences of character," says Schumacher, "of mental gifts and qualities
of the heart, for which Bunsen was ever remarkable, his
faculty of meeting without artifice or dissimulation every
variety of mind, influentially or sympathetically,—was,
perhaps, never so powerfully called forth, so brought into
living action, as among his friends at Göttingen ; Reinhard
Bunsen, Thienemann, Ernst Schulze, Ludwig Abeken, and
many others, might be named as seeming to correspond to
various portions of his intellectual being, and being met
by him accordingly. The last-mentioned, in whom the
germ of early death was fast developing, was an object of
his peculiar affection and attention. How would he carry
on discussion with the worthy intelligent friend Agricola!
and hold argument, as in the atmosphere of Pericles,
with the refined Greek scholar Dissen! With the caustic
spirit of Lachmann he hit upon the right stimulus by
which to lead him into disputation : to the learned
ungentle Dr. Reck he would listen with the patience of
an anchorite, ending with proposing to him a humorous
toast. In short, he read men as he did books; but,
before all things should be noted of him that, having a
heart himself, he never failed to do justice to the heart of
another.

"Often did he in the evening drop asleep like a child on
his seat : but in the morning he rose in summer at four, in
winter at five o'clock, and, after a rapid but not negligent
toilet, hastened forth with a face of joyous thought to his
books and the desk in his study.

"'*Plus ultra*' was Bunsen's motto during the time at
Göttingen ; afterwards, he chose ' *In silentio et spe.*' "

We have a later picture of the student band at Göttingen from the pen of Ernst Schulze, the poet, after his return from active service during the campaign against the French in 1813.

"My isolation led me back to my friends. By the untiring efforts of Bunsen our whole circle, consisting of Lachmann, Lücke, Reck, Bunsen, and myself, and further widened by the addition of the admirable Brandis—also in intimacy less close, by that of Brandis's brother, of Jacobs, Klenze, and Ulrich—was brought together again. A spirit of zealous but friendly emulation arose amongst us; and on a certain cheerful evening, at my suggestion, we made a vow, each to each other and to all, that we would effect something great in our lives. It was a noble circle, in which an oppressed heart could expand and breathe again. Bunsen, the man of kingly and all-ruling spirit, considering all branches of knowledge, all forms of mental exertion, but as means to accomplish a single great object, —who, open at all times to every sort of impression, could with indescribable power appropriate and make his own all that seemed in nature most opposite; who, with the keenest, and at times appalling clearness of intellectual perception, united a depth of sympathising feeling, and who, with an energy, ceaselessly diverted into a multitude of channels, never lost sight of his object;—Brandis, whose cheerful faithful heart beamed from his countenance, and in whom much learning and keen intelligence had not lessened the power of pleasing, and being pleased; —Lachmann, fine-grained, critical, satirical and witty, but with the vague longings of a heart that knew not its will

or way, of irritable fibre, and almost feverish tempera-
ment;—Lücke, in all the radiance of prosperous love and of
religious enthusiasm, upright, firm, earnestly endeavouring
after a sphere of active usefulness, yet deeply meditative,
and inclined to mysticism; — lastly, the unimpassioned
Reck, ever taking care of his friends, ever provided with
good advice for everyone, having a clear and intelligent
but always politic view of life, and making amends to his
associates by zeal and faithful attachment for his want of
susceptibility of the beautiful, and for the absence of polish
and refinement. The bond which united us was at this
time riveted for ever." *

Academic honours continued to crown the exertions
of Bunsen. In 1812 he was appointed teacher of
Hebrew to the highest, and of Greek to the second
form of the Göttingen school. In the same year he
gained the prize for an "Essay on the Athenian Law
of Inheritance," which attracted so much attention,
that the University of Jena soon afterwards presented
him unsolicited with the diploma of a Doctor of Philosophy. Meantime his relations with William Astor were
of the happiest nature, and with him in 1813 he made
a tour to Vienna, Munich, Switzerland, and Northern
Italy. In 1814, Astor returned to America, promising
to come back and meet Bunsen again in Europe in
two years' time. Bunsen at once took advantage of the
opportunity for a journey to Holland to visit his sister

* These paragraphs, from the recollections of Schumacher and
Schulze, have already appeared in the "Memoirs of Baron Bunsen."

Christiana, with whom, as he wrote to Brandis—"a few days filled up the long chasm of eight years' separation." It was then for the first time that he learnt the sad story of his sister's life. The death of her aunt Helene Stricker had deprived her at fifteen of the only protector to whom her independent nature could attach itself, and for many years she had fulfilled the arduous task of companion to an aged invalid lady, who provided for her at her death. Meantime, she had become acquainted with a young officer of good family named Faber, who inspired her with a devoted attachment, and who endeavoured to make her promise to marry him, as soon as his circumstances allowed of it. But when she made his proposal known to her father, he, having been in some manner entrusted with the guardianship of Faber by his family, felt himself bound to put a positive prohibition upon any engagement between the young officer and his portionless daughter, and harshly forbade her ever seeing him or writing to him. Faber was sent away on distant service but, through two and twenty years of absence, remained faithful to his love for Christiana. Then he traced her to Amsterdam, and a meeting took place ; but " in the pallid and emaciated woman of thirty-nine he could find nothing of the girl of seventeen, whom he had left in bloom and freshness." He urged her, however, to fulfil an engagement, which, though never formally made, had been faithfully kept by both, and she promised to marry him as soon as he should return from the Russian expedition, for which the vast army was then collecting. Faber never returned; he fell in Russia. At the same time, the failure of banks swallowed up the whole of the funds from which Christiana had derived her maintenance, and she was left to subsist upon a pittance gained by fine needle-work. Then her eyesight gave way, her health failed, and she would have perished from want of care and comforts, but for the charity of two Dutch ladies, who discovered her destitution.

The broken health and sad disclosures of Christiana were an unexpected shock to her brother, but he, who never in after life shrank from a responsibility, at once determined to undertake the cost of her maintenance, and insisted upon reconducting her to his father's home at Corbach, till he should be appointed to a professorship, and be enabled to offer to share with her a home of his own.

In the following year (1815), the desire of acquiring the Danish language and of studying Icelandic, induced Bunsen to accompany his friend Brandis to Copenhagen, where he was received by Dr. Brandis (Physician to the King of Denmark) with paternal love and kindness, an affection ever after returned with filial warmth and recollection. The two young friends settled in the town for the sake of more uninterrupted leisure for study, but daily resorted to the country-house of Dr. Brandis for dinner, and remained there till just before the closing of the city gates at midnight. Many

were the Danish notabilities who at this time eagerly
met the acquaintance of Bunsen, and he greatly enjoyed
the time spent amongst them. He also crossed the sea to
the Swedish coast, and visited the university of Lund.
A fortnight passed in the companionship of Chamisso
was greatly valued, and left a deep impression of the
rare gifts of the poet.* Meantime, Bunsen devoted
himself with great success to the study of Danish, and
also received lessons from a learned Icelander, with
whom he read Snurro Sturlesen and the Edda, &c., in
the original.

In the beginning of November, the friends crossed
to Swinemünde, and proceeded to Berlin. Here
Bunsen continued his linguistic studies, and became
acquainted with Schleiermacher, Solger, Buttmann, Sa-
vigny, but above all with Niebuhr, who was then
crushed to the earth by the death of his wife, but
roused himself to receive the young students, with the
kindness which he was ever ready to show to those
who were truly seeking after knowledge and truth.
Bunsen at once found his way to his heart, and the
relation of master and disciple was then established,
which continued through life. " Other visits demand
notice," wrote Bunsen to Lücke, soon after his arrival
at Berlin, " but I can now only speak of those to
Niebuhr. It would be hard to describe my astonishment at his command over the entire domain of know-

* A French refugee, who never spoke German fluently and yet
wrote admirable verses that ensured him lasting fame.

ledge. All that can be known seems to be within his grasp, and everything known to him to be at hand, as if held by a thread."

The number of men whom Bunsen found at Berlin with the intention and energy to carry out great plans, and the reception he met with from them, strengthened the wish he already felt to become a Prussian subject. He was encouraged by the advice of Niebuhr, before whom he laid a detailed plan of intellectual labour, in his determination to devote his life to historical, philological, and philosophical research, for which purpose he at that time intended to follow up his study of the northern languages, by a course of Persian at Paris and Sanscrit at Oxford, to be followed by a three years' residence at Calcutta for the investigation of Oriental history and languages.

Bunsen remained at Berlin till the spring of 1816, when he went to Paris to join Mr. Astor. Soon after, Astor departed with some friends for a three months' tour in Italy, leaving Bunsen to rejoin him at the end of that time and spend the interval much to his satisfaction in the study of Persian, under the auspices of Silvestre de Sacy, reckoned the greatest Oriental scholar in Europe. As he found it impossible to understand the writings of the best Persian poets without a knowledge of Arabic, he began to attend lectures in Arabic also. "I work with *fury* and delight," he wrote to Brandis, "because I must get on, and I do get on." "I am perfectly well," he informed his

sister, "and arrange my day as I like; work from six
in the morning till four in the afternoon, only in the
course of that time having a walk in the garden of the
Luxembourg, where I also often study; from four to
six I dine and walk, from six to seven sleep; from
seven to eleven work again. In that manner I can
make it possible to work in the evening, which I otherwise never could."

With July came the necessity for proceeding to
Florence to rejoin Mr. Astor. But Astor was already
on the eve of departure, having just received a summons from his father for his immediate return to
America. Thither he urgently pressed Bunsen to accompany him, but found him obdurately determined to
remain in Europe, till he should be prepared for his
Oriental journey. Still, the departure of Astor, and
the consequent revulsion of all his plans was a great
blow to Bunsen. He often narrated afterwards how in
the first shock of solitude—without prospects, he sate
down "an unprovided wanderer" in the Loggia
de' Lanzi,—where, after a time, he took courage again,
and proceeded onwards, from a condition utterly desolate, to success and happiness in life. Sunshine first
came in the shape of a young Englishman, Mr. Cathcart, who undertook to assist him in the execution of
his Indian plans, on condition of his sparing three
hours daily for his instruction in French, and becoming his guide amid the treasures of Florence and
Rome.

The connection with Mr. Cathcart was one which to the end continued to give Bunsen complete satisfaction. But greater happiness was in store for him at Florence, in the arrival of Niebuhr, who had been appointed Prussian Envoy at Rome, and who was accompanied by Brandis as Secretary of Legation. With these congenial spirits Bunsen drank in the full enjoyment of the art-treasures of Florence, and when he arrived at Rome with Mr. Cathcart, he found Niebuhr and Brandis established there. "There is but one Rome and one Niebuhr," he wrote to his sister Christiana, and again—"Niebuhr is equally sole of his kind with Rome; him alone will I acknowledge as my lord and master; his instructions, and his personal excellence in every respect, as well as in that of learning, stand highest in estimation among all the men I know; he is essentially the person to form me into a thorough man and citizen of my country; moreover, as regards the realisation of my plans to become a Prussian, he is equally the man."

Thus when, on his return to England, Mr. Cathcart wished to have taken Bunsen with him, believing that he might be able, by introductions, to further his Indian projects; Bunsen's strong longing after the East had been subdued by conversations with Niebuhr, who was inclined to think that the same ends of study might be attained within the limits of Europe, combined with which Bunsen felt that an eastern journey must separate him from Niebuhr, from whom, he wrote, "as a man and a scholar I can learn more than from all other persons put together."

Amid the varied enjoyments of Rome, that which Bunsen most appreciated was the leisure for taking in and digesting the fruit of his former labours. At first he entered little into society, and shrunk from making acquaintances, dreading the uncongeniality of those who seek to renew in Rome the frivolities of the London season. But it so happened that amongst the first people to whom he was introduced, were Mrs. Waddington and her daughters, then occupying the first-floor of the Palazzo Gavotti. Here, while Mr. Waddington pursued the even tenour of his home life, reading or writing in a nook screened off in one of the apartments, and retiring to bed at his usual early hour, all that was best in English, Italian, and German society gathered around his wife, whose noble type of beauty was almost more remarkable than in her first youth, and whose intellectual charm was equally felt by men of all nationalities. At her receptions in the ' prima sera ' Bunsen was a welcome and an unfailing guest, rejoicing that he found there few except those who were capable of taking something more than a surface-interest in the scenes around them. The young Emily Waddington, whose whole life had hitherto been clouded by ill-health, had benefited greatly from the Italian climate, and was enjoying a transient happiness in her engagement with Colonel Manley. This circumstance, and a congeniality of interests, combined to throw Bunsen completely into the society of her elder sister, when he accompanied them to visit the temples and towers of Rome and the Campagna. Already in April, 1817, he had written to his sister Christiana that he was permitted to read German with Miss Wadding-ton, but that he " was a little in love," and that there-fore, as a penniless student who could not think of aspiring to the hand of a girl of fortune, he should "no longer go continually to visit the family." Yet Mrs. Waddington so little suspected the possibility of an attachment on the part of her idolised daughter, that she continued to encourage the visits of one whose society and information gave an additional charm to the interests of Rome, and thus, when on the last morning of May, her eyes were suddenly opened by Bunsen's own revelation of his love for her child and his agony at their impending separation, she felt that—while she had every confidence in the man who asked her for the greatest blessing she had to bestow—she could not undo her own work. Mr. Waddington was much startled and appealed to Niebuhr, in the unexpected turn affairs had taken ; but Niebuhr only answered— " The talents, abilities, and character of Bunsen are a capital more safely to be reckoned upon than any other, however securely invested ; and had I a daughter my-self, to such a man I would gladly consign her." That evening, having received the consent of her parents,—on the steps of the cross, which for centuries marked the site of Christian martyrdoms in the centre

of the Coliseum,—Bunsen asked Frances Waddington to become his wife.

MRS. WADDINGTON *to the* REV. PROFESSOR MONK.

" . . . I will own to you that my spirits have had
a *shake,* and that nothing but presenting to myself the
agony of my death-bed, had I left Fanny without a protector, without a person to be to her what I had been,
brings my mind into the state of thankfulness and cheerfulness, that it ought to be in, from the consciousness of
her being as happy as it is possible for a human being to
be : for some bitter must be mixed with the sweet, and
she herself says that she should fear that her present enjoyments were too great to last, did not the loss of me,
and the banishment from England, cost such pangs, as
make her confidently hope to preserve all the blessings
that her union with the exclusive choice of her heart, with
the object of her utmost admiration and love, has put her
in possession of. It is only doing justice to the best of
daughters and one of the most perfect of human beings, to
tell you that at any moment one word from me would have
prevented my dearest Fanny's marriage, and that without
a murmur she would have given Bunsen up. But after I
had for almost six months afforded every facility for her to
attach herself, after I was myself convinced that excepting
in fortune and in his being a foreigner he was in every
way completely qualified to make her happy, I should
have been a monster from selfish considerations to have
destroyed my own work. How it was my own work, and
yet unintentionally, I have to recount. Bunsen's astonishing
self-command had prevented his voice from betraying him,

and the innumerable multiplicity of objects in Rome that we almost daily were together engaged in contemplating, had furnished such an unceasing flow of conversation, that there literally was not time for sentiment to be displayed: while his respect for me, caused him so constantly to offer me his arm, to place himself by my side, that there was no marked attention towards Fanny, though the most unfeigned admiration. The great strength of Bunsen's expressions of astonishment and delight, in Fanny's *mine* of mind and knowledge, I attributed in some part to his never having before met with a well-educated Englishwoman, and the rest, *I quietly took as her due,* having too long been accustomed to her being valued just in proportion to the discernment, virtue, and talents, of the individual with whom she conversed. Security was still further lulled by knowing Bunsen's plans, that to Calcutta, for the purposes of study (the laws, language, and philosophy of the Hindoos being one of the subjects to which he is most devoted, as subservient to the great object to which his mind ever since eighteen has been bent—the affinity of languages), he was resolved within two years to set off, and to obtain some previous information he had given me two letters, which Lord Lansdowne at Mr. Niebuhr's request was to present, that I might correct the German idiom . . . . But I must not say more about Bunsen, and about Fanny only give the substance, that she declared to me—and *her word is truth,* that till Bunsen proposed to her, she did not know she was attached to him:—that she had delighted in floating on in her present existence, that each moment was filled to her heart's content, and that she never asked herself, how large or how small a share

Bunsen had individually in her enjoyments; that she felt with so sad a sensation that she was going very soon to quit Rome and Emily, that from principle she always drove the thought from her mind, knowing that a calamity is always the better borne, from not being previously dwelt upon; that she never analysed her regrets, and therefore never ascertained the component parts, and that so far from concealing from me her inmost thoughts, she did not know of their existence, till on Saturday, the 31st May, in the Coliseum by moonlight at eleven o'clock at night (having on that very morning asked my permission to speak for himself), Bunsen presented to her view what he should suffer from a separation, how he should be blessed by a union: when every nerve vibrated to the touch, and she was aware that her life would lose half its charm if not spent with him."

CHAPTER V.

MARRIAGE.

"Felices ter et amplius,
  Quos irrupta tenet copula, nec malis
Divulsus querimoniis
  Suprema citius solvet amor die."

HORACE.

"Nothing is sweeter than Love, nothing more courageous, nothing higher, nothing wider, nothing more pleasant, nothing fuller nor better in heaven and earth ; because Love is born of God, and cannot rest but in God, above all created things."—THOMAS À KEMPIS.

ON the 1st of July, 1817, Frances Waddington was married to Bunsen, in the ancient chapel of the old Palazzo Savelli, which rises upon the ruins of the Theatre of Marcellus, and which was then inhabited by Niebuhr. Only her parents and youngest sister, Niebuhr, Brandis, and Mr. Clifford—an old family friend, were present. Bunsen's first gift to his wife was his father's wedding-ring. " It is nothing very beautiful," he said, " but I hope you will let me see it sometimes on your hand—it was given me with my father's blessing, and I transfer that to you with it—it is a good blessing." The wedded pair drove immediately after the ceremony to Frascati, where rooms were ready for them in the Casino Accorambuoni, one of those charming flower-hidden residences, half stately-villa, half primitive farm-house, which are only to be found in Italy, and only to be found in perfection on the Alban hills. "In the carriage we spoke not a word at first," wrote Bunsen, soon afterwards, to his sister Christiana, "but as we passed the Coliseum and looked towards the Cross at the foot of which we had sat, when we exchanged the important words,—we pressed each other's hands."

It is quaintly characteristic of the hospitalities which were such a leading feature in the family life of Bunsen and his wife, and which were equally continued in all places and under all circumstances, that they should have begun immediately after their marriage. A day or two were scarcely suffered to elapse before Carl August Brandis, Bunsen's dearest friend, came to share his happiness at Frascati. With him, the Bunsens spent the long bright days of the late summer in full enjoyment of the glorious wooded hills which look down upon Campagna, and of the two blue lakes which are set like gems in their midst; together they passed the mornings in the large cool rooms, or in the little garden with its two fountains, in a common reading of Milton, Dante, or Bacon; and together, in the evenings, they went forth on long excursions, lingering till the splendours of sunset had tinged the plain and the distant city with crimson and gold, and returning by the light of the fire-flies.

The glorious subjects in the Alban Hills and at Rome, as it was in those days long ago, gave constant employment to the artistic powers of Madame Bunsen. Thorwaldsen said of her sepia sketches of Rome and its environs that he " knew no artist, whether professional or amateur, who then equalled her in exact representation, from her power of choosing a view which made a complete picture, without adding or abstracting from the reality before her."

From Frascati, Bunsen wrote to his sister, begging her to tranquillise his friends in Holland as to his purposes in life. " When they hear that I have given up my journey to India and am married, they may, like many of my acquaintances (not my intimate friends) in Germany, apprehend that all my undertakings are given up. But my journey to India was only to be a means to an end; and even though it may sound presumptuous that I hope to succeed in forming a clear view of the earliest life of the Oriental nations, without crossing the line—yet do I make that declaration without misgiving." In the autumn, however, Bunsen's tie to Rome was riveted, for Brandis, who had been acting as diplomatic secretary to Niebuhr since his arrival in Rome, was obliged by ill-health to resign and to return to Germany; when Niebuhr invited Bunsen to succeed to the vacant office of Secretary of Legation.

Emily Waddington had been married a few days before her sister to Colonel Manley, who had an appointment from the Pope, which compelled him to fix his residence at Rome or in the Alban Hills; and in both places the sisters, who in earlier life had not been congenial to one another, met affectionately and often. The trial of separation from their mother was equally severe to both and drew them closer to each other, for a few days after the marriage of her eldest daughter, Mrs. Waddington had set out on her return to England with her husband and her youngest daughter Augusta —feeling that the necessary wrench from her elder children would be the more difficult, the longer it was delayed.

" Only fifteen days after my marriage," wrote Madame Bunsen to Bishop Sandford, " I parted from her, who has been not only the guide and protectress of my existence, but in such a degree the principal, as to seem almost the sole object of my thoughts and affections—who has been to me far more than any words can express. In the peculiarly close connection that subsisted between my mother and myself, if she had had the shadow of a wish that I should have remained with her till death parted us, it would have been a natural and necessary consequence that no circumstances of unqualified esteem and attachment to another person could have caused me to leave her, even though she had *consented* and *acquiesced*. She who had been 'my fate, alone could speak my doom,'—and it required her decided will and desire to dissolve the tie that bound us. Her entire approval of Mr. Bunsen will be sufficient to satisfy you, my dear sir, and you will believe that every month, and every day, strengthens the confidence in his principles and in his affection with which I at first consigned myself to his protection. That he should not be an Englishman—and that, consequently, a great portion of my life must be spent out of England, and separated from my mother—will occasion the admixture of so much positive evil amongst the blessings I enjoy, as almost to be a security to me that I may *hope* for a continuance of that abundant share of good which has been bestowed upon me. Had every circumstance attending my change of condition been exactly as I could have wished, it would have been fearful—for in the natural course of things, some blow utterly destructive of my happiness must have been expected to follow. My life had hitherto been so blest—I had been so nourished on tenderness, so accustomed to talents, understanding, and cultivation, as well as to high religious principle, that the number of essential requisites to enable me to lead anything more than a mere vegetative existence was great, and I never anticipated the possibility of finding them united. For having thus found them, I never cease to be thankful, although I feel that I can never be thankful enough."

The close tie which had existed between mother and daughter was never weakened by absence, and at the end of twelve years' separation the mother found in her child the same heart-confidence as when they parted. But she found in her also one of the noblest types of wedded love that any country has produced, showing how entirely a woman can fulfil to the utmost the duties of wife and mother, without ever failing in the least degree to be the intellectual and spiritual companion of her husband.

MADAME BUNSEN *to her* MOTHER.

"15 *July*, 1817.—I lay still, and shed a very few more tears, talking to Charles at intervals about my Mother, and her journey, for some time after she left me. Then I went to sleep, and Charles slept too, leaning against my pillow, for he would not leave me. . . . . Some few times since, it is true, the tears have risen to my eyes, but they have been driven away; for my Mother's parting words, though I never have trusted myself to think them over, have literally vibrated in my ears, and 'lain like a cordial in my heart, sending forth spirits to recruit my strength.'

"I never could have believed, my own Mother, that I could have borne your departure so well, because I could not have known thoroughly, without this trial, how much Charles was to me. He sympathises in my feelings to the exact degree that does me good. It will not do to think and recollect that my Mother has nothing to soothe *her*—but her own reflections."

"*Frascati*, 20 *July*, 1817, *Monday*.—Yesterday I read with Charles most comfortably and satisfactorily. After we had finished the prayers, we read different chapters of the Bible, comparing the German and English; and when M. Brandis came, an hour and a half before dinner, to read with Charles, I read to myself in 'Self-Knowledge.'* After dinner Charles and I read a good deal in Milton and Dante, then walked out, and sat down in the Villa Belvedere, where M. Brandis joined us. We walked to the top

* Mason's Self-Knowledge, 1786.

of that hill, where the view was most beautiful. . . . . As
to my spirits—I never could have realised that I should
have borne the parting from my Mother so well, for I never
could have imagined in what a degree Charles would cheer
and support me, how accurately he would observe by my
face when my thoughts needed to be diverted, and how well
he would succeed in turning the current of my ideas. I
know the effect of salutary occupation, but still I am not
attributing too much to Charles, because I also know that
fulness of employment avails little without the sensation of
security of dependence, and animation of mind, such as the
consciousness of his presence gives.

"Since I parted with my Mother, some lines of Dante,
often remembered before, but never before in sorrow, have
often occurred to me—

> ' Era già l'ora che volge 'l desio
> Ai naviganti, e intenerisce il cuore,
> Lo di ch' han detto a' dolci amici addio ;
>   E che lo novo peregrin d'amore
> Punge, se odi squilla di lontano,
> Che paja il giorno pianger che si muore.' "
>
> (Purg. cto. viii.)

"*Frascati, August* 7, 1817.—At three o'clock I set off on
an ass with the Guardaroba and his wife to see their Vigna,
two miles distant, along a beautiful road. The people were
very much pleased at my going with them, and talked
à l'envie to entertain me and themselves, and did the honours
of their belongings with the ease that we observe in Welsh
cottagers. The Vigna is a beautiful sheltered spot, with a
great many fruit trees, besides the vines and crop of canes,
and a well in the rock, in which they put some of the pears

they had gathered for me to *rinfrescare*. I brought back a great many almonds and pears, and a few peaches. They told me their corn-field had yielded tenfold this year. I returned home at six o'clock, and drew till it was dark, and then read to myself. Charles did not come home till after ten. He brought me from Rome Verstappen's picture from Thorwaldsen and various stores and treasures; among others, Voss's translation of the Iliad and Odyssey, and the work by Neander on the character of Julian, which he had borrowed from Thorwaldsen, who, he says, will come soon and bring some clay with him: he had been working extremely hard lately, and has made two statues as large as life since he finished the Ballatrice—a Ganymede, and a Shepherd with his Dog.

"Charles brought back M. Overbeck with him from Rome, who is with us still, and I hope we shall keep him longer, for he seems to enjoy being here, and he is a very agreeable inmate, thankful for every attention, and constantly afraid of being troublesome; interested in conversation, but nevertheless quite happy to employ himself independently for many hours in the day, either in painting or walking out. He brought his easel and a beautiful little picture of the Virgin and Child, which he is finishing. I have a great wish to attempt copying it, and yesterday morning while he was out I began and half finished the outline, with which he was very much surprised, and told me he could not make such clean and true strokes himself!

"I must mention a letter which has given me great pleasure, from M. Brandis's father.* It is everything I could wish, and gives so pleasing an impression of the

* Dr. Brandis, Physician to the King of Denmark.

writer that it furnishes additional evidence that we may trust to the pledge afforded by M. Brandis's own character, that *good* must necessarily be annexed to his name and blood. The letter begins with an assurance, that he will always hold me in particular regard, as being the first person who has given him the pleasure of knowing he has a daughter-in-law, and that whenever *another* of *his sons* brings him another, he hopes she will have won his son's heart in an equally worthy manner. He says he loves Charles as well as his own sons, but will not praise him, because there is no use in that, as the matter is concluded, —and will only say that it is not merely natural to him to seek after all that is excellent, but that he can only exist in clinging to it. He says that it is difficult to refuse our invitation to Frascati, but that it would be impossible to him to take such a journey : however that he will send one of his sons, who must put on a wig to look as like him as possible,—but he promises me, if I will come to see him at Copenhagen, to take his wig off, and represent his son. He concludes by giving me his blessing."

" *Frascati*, 14 *August*, 1817.—How intense is the heat ! I almost gasp for a tramontana, for even the coolness of the morning is only relief by comparison. However I have nothing to complain of, but the weakness occasioned by the climate. Charles is ever the same, —and if I wanted reviving—which I do not in mind, though I do in body—it would be sufficient for that purpose to behold a being in such full enjoyment of existence — so uninterruptedly gay, busy, animated—and to feel that he loves me every day more and takes greater delight in my presence, and *admits to himself* that he does so. He is very busy all morning, studying and writing; and reads Plato with Mr. Brandis for the last half-hour before dinner. I always sit drawing, or writing, or reading in his room, but we do not interrupt each other. I have nearly finished my copy of Overbeck's Madonna, and it is a great pleasure to think that my Mother will some time see it."

"19 *Sept.*, 1817. — I can truly assure my Mother, that my mind settles daily to a more full and steady enjoyment of existence. I use that phrase, as implying much more to my Mother who knows me, than if I had merely said I was *happy*—because it proves that the composure of entire satisfaction is my habitual state. I feel continually convinced of being more and more beloved, and in a manner that has fallen to the lot of few human beings, of being prized for *anything* and *everything* that has a pretension to be good in me,—and I have the consciousness of giving pleasure even by my silent presence, and by every word and action. O my Mother, the only risk is that I should be quite spoiled!—it is *too* good for any human creature not to have *unreasonableness* to contend with, and my occupations too are very much what I like, except that I find, as usual, time to do but little of what I wish to do.

"I hope we may perhaps go to Naples next summer It is curious that the danger as to robbers is not near Naples, but within the Papal frontier, where at present nearly the whole population consists of banditti, very savage in their practices, taking captives, and often murdering them, if not ransomed very speedily. Many of the troops the Pope has sent against them, or rather the Monsignore at the head of the Pope's War Office, have deserted to the robbers: the present state of things therefore is so nearly desperate, that I think there is some ground for hoping an amendment,—possibly the poor Pope may die in next Advent's fast, and then the Austrians may establish *some* government,—if it was only a military rule, that would be better than *no* government."

" 25 *Sept.*—I will here assure my Mother, that *never* in any way has my privilege to employ myself *as I please, without criticism*, been infringed: and I can safely promise her, that as far as time and strength allow, nothing shall be lost that she has taken pleasure in seeing me acquire. . . . . When Charles and I sit together, we neither interrupt or constrain each other. The only thing in which my time is ever spent, in exclusive compliance with a fancy of Charles and Mr. Brandis, is in reading the dialogues of Plato, two or three evenings in the week, for an hour. I read aloud the German translation, and they look at the Greek the while. For this book I confess I have as yet acquired no taste, but it is a very fine practice, not only in reading German, but in fixing attention: and the representation is most curious, not only of the enlightened opinions of two individuals, Plato and Socrates, but of the total want of all fixed principles of belief, on the commonest points of religion and morality, amongst the rest of the Athenians of their time: also, the talent with which the dialogues are conducted is admirable; and if the work did not possess so many merits, the interest that Charles and Mr. Brandis take in helping me to understand it, by giving explanatory particulars as to numberless points on which I am uninformed, would be reason sufficient to prefer continuing to read it.

" On Charles's birthday,* my dearest Mother, I showed him Patrick † for the first time, putting a mark in the prayer 'On the day of one's Birth.' He was very much pleased, and the next morning before breakfast proposed that we should read a prayer together, which we have done many times since, and we often before breakfast read some chapters in the Bible. I have constantly more satisfaction, and I feel that he has also, in our regular Sunday readings.

" We are beginning to experience the inconveniences of a mere summer-house. From the smallness of the rooms, we are either in want of fresh air, or exposed to draughts of wind : still we ought not to complain of Casino Accorambuoni, for it has not let in the rain upon us, that is to say—only a little : but I look forward with pleasure to inhabiting large rooms with large windows. Next Monday Charles will go to Rome, and take Laura to superintend cleaning and to take care of furniture till we come to inhabit. Last Monday we went to Monte Compatri, setting off at eight o'clock, and returning at three to dinner. Mr. Brandis and Mr. Platner went with us, and we took a basket with fruit and cold ham and bread. It rained when we reached Monte Compatri, but we got under shelter, and Mr. Brandis read aloud part of *Götz von Berlichingen :* the views were most exquisite, and I enjoy the thoughts of going the same road again to Palestrina."

* 25th August.
† The Devotional Works of Symon Patrick, Bishop of Chichester, afterwards of Ely (1626—1707).

"*Frascati*, 2 *Oct.*, 1817.—On Monday morning Charles went to Rome, and in the course of that day, I packed everything. Mr. Brandis came and managed the carrettieri for me, about loading the luggage, and though their delays caused him to lose three hours of a fine morning, he almost reproached me for having given him 'nothing to do' to help me, according to his own wish and Charles's charge—but I explained that had I been ever so well inclined to give him more trouble than could be avoided, I could not well have contrived to give him either my gowns and petticoats, or the sheets and tablecloths to pack. Indeed, my own dearest Mother, I have so many plagues saved me, of all sorts and kinds, that it is only almost alarming. I have had a long note from Charles each day since he went away, and I have written to him each day: and these four days that I have been alone, I have not been lonely, for I have been well enough to be constantly busy, have taken three sketches; drawn some dogtooth violets, which are now in full autumnal blow; copied some Handel; and read Machiavel and several chapters in regular progress through Job and Ezekiel. The reason that caused me to begin the latter, was hearing from Charles a comment Mr. Niebuhr had made on the thoroughly Judaic spirit, and narrowness of mind of Ezekiel, as contrasted with Isaiah. I think very likely the observation is just, but I believe the reason I have always felt, and my Mother has always felt, so much delight in reading Isaiah, is that in speaking of the future Redeemer, his soul seems filled with his actual presence, and he has almost imbibed beforehand the spirit of Christianity—he is not a mere passive medium for the transmission of Divine oracles. One of the plans that Charles has made for the winter, is to read the book of Job in the Hebrew, with a countryman of his of the name of Wolfe, a converted Jew, who is at present in the Roman college, and has made great progress in the Oriental languages."

"6 *Oct.*, 1817.—Mr. Charles Brandis speaks with great animation of the effect that the young Napoleon produced upon him. He said that the child spoke to him, asking him different questions, where he had been, where he was going—'like a little Prince;' that he had a marked character of countenance as well as manner, and that his features were *not like his father's;* that he had beautiful flaxen hair in great abundance. The only anecdote he told me of him was curious. The two young lions that the Princess of Wales sent to the Emperor of Austria, were conveyed to Schönbrunn, where the young Napoleon resides, and he became very fond of them, and quite familiar with them. When the Emperor came to see these lions, the child thought some signs of apprehension were to be perceived in his countenance; he ran, and clasped one of the lions round the neck, exclaiming, 'Now, grandpapa, you may come near, he shan't touch you.' He can speak both German and French, but sometimes does not choose to speak the former. It is most entertaining to hear that the eldest son of the Emperor mimics the deportment of the young Napoleon, making the clumsiest imitations of gestures, that in the other are graceful, because easy and natural.

"Particulars of the death of Madame de Staël will have reached my Mother from other quarters, but I will mention that though she suffered terribly in body and mind till within a few minutes of her death, she expired as if falling asleep. She desired her daughter to declare her marriage with Rocca as soon as she was dead, but not to mention it before. Therefore the Duchesse de Broglie collected all her friends around her mother's coffin, the night before it was removed from Paris, informed them of the duty imposed upon her, and then fainted. Madame de Staël has left Rocca and her child one third of her property."

"*Palazzo Astalli, Rome*, 11 *Oct.*—We profited by the cessation of rain on Tuesday evening to come *home*, and have ever since been unpacking and settling. I have had some trouble, my own Mother, but no *plague*. I was quite surprised to find how much was done, the rooms painted, all fresh and clean, carpet laid down, and a sufficient number of chairs and tables and other necessaries, to begin with. I have never ceased to be sensible of the freshness and cleanliness, and space, and light and air of these rooms since I came into them. I have got my Mother's picture : sometimes I am hard enough not to trust myself to look at it! Oh it is very like—almost too like ! "

" 18 *Oct.*, 1817.—Charles is just gone to Mr. Niebuhr's, who has asked several of his favourites to meet at his house in commemoration of the Battle of Leipzig—and, before I go to bed, I may treat myself in expressing to my Mother the continually renewed thankfulness I feel towards her for that all but living image of herself, which now occupies the room I inhabit, receives me whenever I return to it, and—looks so much as if it were going to speak to me— that for a minute together I cannot look at it, but a hundred glances in the course of the day I *can* take without doing any mischief.

"I have called upon Mr. and Mrs. Niebuhr since their return to Rome, when they were both very gracious. I had only an opportunity of exchanging a few words with Mr. Niebuhr, and very much doubt whether I shall ever *get on* with him, but my Mother will agree with me that ' l'on peut très bien *attendre*,' and that it is not a matter to make violent efforts in."

"30 *Oct.*, 1817.—Yesterday morning Charles and I walked over the Capitol to the Coliseum directly after breakfast, and yesterday evening we took the same walk, returning as the Ave-Maria was sounding. I therefore observed the equestrian statue of Marcus Aurelius in the same day receiving the first sunbeams, and displaying its fine outline in a mass of darkness against the clear sky after the sun was set.

"I would give the world that my words should sufficiently prove to my Mother how happy I am. I feel myself continually more beloved, more highly valued, more delighted in,—and have an hourly consciousness of the truth of an assurance Charles made to me the other day in these words—' I feel what you are in every fibre of my heart.' "

"11 *Nov.*, 1817.—We have removed to Palazzo Caffarelli, on the Capitol, and how I wish I could send my Mother a sketch of the inside of my room, but still more that I could send the view from the windows, which is a never-failing delight, in all changes of atmosphere.

"I must give my Mother an account of a business that has occupied a good deal of Charles's time latterly, when he was not busy house arranging. Mr. Brandis and he had long talked of contriving some manner in which the Jubilee of the Reformation should not pass unmarked amongst the German Protestants collected at Rome, as it was appointed to be celebrated throughout Protestant Germany on the 2nd of November, the day on which, in 1517, Luther publicly burnt the papal bull that had been issued to condemn his doctrines, thereby declaring for the first time a positive separation from the Church of Rome. For this purpose, it was to be wished that a religious service could be performed. Charles proposed to translate the service of the Church of England, which was approved by Mr. Niebuhr, and he set to work, and soon finished. Wherever a Biblical phrase was to be observed, he referred to Luther's translation of the Bible, and made use of the original words. In this part of the work I helped him to some degree, as I could generally, though not always, find the place in the English Bible, where a similar phrase was employed, and then the parallel passage in the German Bible was easily found. When this was done, Mr. Niebuhr scrupled having the meeting take place in his own house, because he could not exclude any individual, and there might be some who would write a misrepresentation of the matter, or who at any rate would declare that he had taken a decided part in favour of the English liturgy, which he had rather not appear to do, as the adoption of some general form of worship is a matter of great contention at present in Germany, where nothing is yet established, but every clergyman reads as much or as little as he pleases : but it is, as I understand, the particular wish of the King of Prussia, that something as near as possible to the English liturgy should be adopted, because he was so struck with it when in England. Mr. Niebuhr therefore expressed a wish that all should assemble in our house, which accordingly took place on Sunday the 9th of November, on account of Mr. Brandis's having been too ill to move the Sunday before. Mr. and Mrs. Niebuhr came, and Madame de Humboldt* and her daughter, and a great many men, in all nearly forty persons. Charles and Mr. Brandis read the translation between them, and their selection did extremely well, for they thought themselves obliged to omit some things, lest the length of the service should frighten a set of people, most of whom were not accustomed to think going to church at all necessary. Mrs. Niebuhr was blooming and gracious, and asked us to come the following evening. I have reason to think that all the trouble I have at different times taken to talk to her is not thrown away, for in her manner there is now something so like cordiality, that I feel *as far as it goes* she rather likes me, and is pleased to see me. Mr. Niebuhr gave me one of his bows and two of his smiles, but nothing more." †

"25 *Nov.*, 1817.—Last Sunday I had the very disagreeable interruption of a visit from Mr. Niebuhr, his wife and child, the last the most pleasing of my visitors, for he was lively and good-humoured. During the whole time Mr. Niebuhr was in the house, he walked the rooms, with Charles and two other men, or stood with them on the

* The highly-gifted wife of William Humboldt, the great statesman and philologer,—"la première intelligence de l'Europe," as Madame de Stael described him at the time of the Congress of Vienna.

† It will be seen how steadily the feeling of Madame Bunsen for Madame Niebuhr strengthened and deepened into a true friendship, and how differently she afterwards regarded Niebuhr himself. Madame Niebuhr was his second wife, Margaret Hensler—"Gretchen" —the niece and adopted daughter of his first wife's sister, Madame Hensler.

loggia—never sat down, or came near me. At last, at the usual *speaking* time, when his wife was fidgetting away, and he was fidgetting after her, he supposed I was going to go into mourning for the Princess Charlotte. I replied with strong expression of regret for her loss. He was pleased to draw an inference from my words that I was a *Tory* and had no confidence for the country's welfare, but in royalty. I denied the inference, as undauntedly as my Mother could have wished, on a ground that I knew he could not object to, that the character of the late King had been a circumstance of great value to his subjects, and that his granddaughter being so young, it had not been forbidden to hope that much might be expected from her."

"19 *Feb.*, 1818.—I have long omitted to tell what my Mother will be pleased to learn, that Thorwaldsen has received an order to execute the bassi-relievi of the Entry of Alexander into Babylon, in marble. The order has been given by the Marchese Somariva, a very rich Milanese, who was a commissary, I believe, for the French army : he has a palace at Milan, another near the lake of Como, and another at Paris. Thorwaldsen is now going to form a succession of designs from the Iliad and Odyssey, for bassi-relievi, for the Crown Prince of Bavaria, who when he passed through Rome originally expressed a wish that Thorwaldsen would make designs from the New Testament, for a frieze to be placed along the top of a double row of columns, to lead up to the high-altar of a church that the Prince intends to build at Munich. From the time this was talked of, it was observed that poor Thorwaldsen was quite dispirited at the thoughts of it, his *soul* did not enter into the idea of the design, and it was an additionally discouraging circumstance, that his works were to be placed at a height of twenty feet. It is believed that some of Thorwaldsen's friends mentioned this state of his mind to the Prince on his return, and that he has in consequence changed the order,—which I think is very fortunate, for there can be little doubt from the two specimens of *Priam at the feet of Achilles* and the *Departure of Briseis*, that Thorwaldsen will enter into the spirit of Homer. Thorwaldsen has been very busy, and therefore very happy lately, not in consequence of the number of orders he has received, but because his whole mind has been absorbed in a statue of Hope, not quite finished yet, which I think one of his most beautiful works. I do not know anything to compare it with; the figure is standing still, and firm on both feet, but just ready to move: she holds up her drapery with one hand, by which means the form of her limbs is as well to be perceived as if she were not completely covered; the hair is arranged in a manner that appears to me quite original—a quantity of curls brought from behind over the forehead, but supported from falling over the face by a band or diadem, the rest of the hair hanging in curls in the neck. The countenance I think most remarkable: Thorwaldsen said himself he thought 'the expression of Hope ought to be perfect repose,' and such he has made it, but the most *animated repose*."

On the 2nd of April, 1818, a letter from Bunsen to Mrs. Waddington headed "Fanny is well—Henry sends you his love"—announced the birth of his eldest born.

"As to godfathers, I have followed the idea, which I

always had before I was married, and therefore shall first ask my own dear father, whose name the child is to have, viz. Henry or Heinrich; then he who has received me, and treated me, and continues to love me as a father, old Mr. Brandis, whom his son will represent as I shall my father; and lastly, Mr. Niebuhr, because there is no man living to whom, besides the other two, I have more obligation."

MADAME BUNSEN *to her* MOTHER.

"18 *April*, 1818.—O my Mother, I need not ask you to bless God for me, and pray to Him to make me thankful: I feel that I can never be thankful enough. My treasure is now asleep in his crib. . . . Angelina's* behaviour has been quite perfect: I could not by any person have been served with more intelligence, activity, and unwearied good humour. My Mother will more easily guess, without being told, what the conduct of friends has been towards me:—in what a degree I feel the tie drawn closer between myself and my dear Emily by the unceasing acts of kindness she has performed, and all the trouble she has taken for me:—how I am bound for life to Mrs. Drewe,† for the tenderness and zeal with which she has attended to me:—how far dearer than ever Charles has become to me, as I feel that I am also become to him."

"22 *April*, 1818.—The day three weeks that my child was born, I was out for a long time. I went first for a

* The faithful Angelina, frequently mentioned in these memoirs, is still living (1878) in the Palazzo Caffarelli, with a small pension from the Baroness Bunsen, and receiving much kindness from the present Prussian ambassador, as from his predecessors.

† Born Allen of Cresselly, a very old family friend. See ch. iii.

few minutes to Mrs. Niebuhr, who has latterly shown me so many attentions, with so much appearance of interest, that I am confirmed in the belief that as far as she has any feeling towards me, it is a feeling of unmixed goodwill and complacency. Then I fetched Emily, who went with me to the Villa Borghese, which is in the beauty of purple blossomed Judas trees and laburnum. My baby was with me too and slept the whole journey.

" On Thursday we went to Thorwaldsen's, and saw a fine Mercury upon which he is now working with great delight, and which keeps his spirits in some degree from sinking under the weight of the Crown Prince's commission: the single specimen he has made of that frieze, the three Mary's at the tomb, is quite detestable, and I am sure he looks at it with as little patience as anybody else—they are absolutely theatrical figures."

" 1 *July*, 1818.—Donna Christina Bonaparte is married to Count Posse—a Swede, and Donna Anna to the Prince Ercolani of Bologna. The latter is said to be a great match: the former displeased Madame Mère and the Princess Borghese so much, that they would not be present when the contract was signed; it was reported that they grounded their objections upon the circumstance of the Swede's being *a subject of a subject of their family.*

' The day before yesterday poor Fohr* was drowned in the Tiber! I cannot describe the shock which this accident has produced, for Fohr's life was of value to many. . . . . He was walking near the Ponte Molle with three

---

* Carl Philip Fohr, a young painter of much promise. His townsmen at Heidelberg have done honour to his memory by naming a beautiful walk over the hills " Fohr's Weg."

friends. One of them, named Bahrdt, being a good swimmer, resolved to cross an eddy, so well known to be dangerous, that the soldiers stationed near the bridge have orders to warn bathers not to venture near it. Fohr knew but little how to swim, but insisted upon following Bahrdt, though urged by all three to refrain. Bahrdt had nearly reached the other side, when he heard an outcry from the two who remained on the bank, and turning round, saw Fohr struggling in the eddy; he seized him by the hair, but the strength of the stream forced it from his grasp—he then swam below the place of danger, and came up again against the current, in the hope of catching him. He was able to reach Fohr's hand, but life was already fled, the hand dropped from his grasp, the body sank, and has not been found again. Fohr's poor dog had four days before been nearly drowned in the same spot, and therefore dared not venture after his master, but ran howling along the bank, and could by no efforts be brought away, till his master's clothes were shewn him, and then he followed the clothes home.

"Mr. Overbeck is going to be married to Mademoiselle Hirtel, the daughter of an Austrian baron, with whom Wilhelm Schlegel was a few years ago so much in love, that he wanted to have proposed to her, but Madame de Staël would not let him. I saw Mademoiselle Hirtel for the first time at Genzano, where she is settled for the summer, with Madame Herz, Frederic Schlegel, and two German misses— altogether a curious coterie, which I should be much entertained to see more of, if we could go again to Genzano. Mdlle. Hirtel is a thorough gentlewoman, very pretty, with a countenance full of feeling and animation, and she certainly can only be induced to marry Overbeck by being attached to him."

"4 *July*, 1818.—Last night the remains of poor Fohr were deposited near the pyramid of Caius Cestius. The night before they had been found by a fisherman a mile below San Paolo fuori le Mura. There being no German clergyman in Rome, Charles translated and read the burial-service of the Church of England : afterwards he and Mr. Niebuhr read alternately, at Mr. N.'s suggestion, a fine funeral hymn, contained in a collection of ancient German sacred poetry, and intended to be sung by two choirs responsively. In conclusion, Charles spoke a few sentences relative to the character of the deceased and the feelings of survivors. I wish I could give my Mother an idea of how well this *ever-difficult* duty was performed. . . . . A great number of people formed a circle round the grave—the friends and associates of Fohr, the people who carried torches and had conveyed the coffin, and the guard which is always stationed at the Protestant burying-place. The Italians all stood in perfect stillness and fixed attention : it was a dark, but gloriously starlight night, and the flashes of lightning without cloud or storm were frequent."

"8 *July*, 1818.—My dear Emily has been here. She had just received my Mother's letter containing a summons to England. I cannot describe the spring *that* gave me—the unmixed pleasure. I could not feel disappointed it was not myself that was summoned, having such a fixed conviction of the impossibility of moving; and the loss to myself of Emily's presence did not occur to me as matter of regret, nor does it yet,—though I shall miss her dear face.

"The other night, when we were looking at the view in the light of the full moon, Charles longed for my Mother's presence—a summer night is the time when he wishes for her. The time when I wish for her most of all is when I look at my child: I cannot write anything to give an image of him, and I cannot draw him to my satisfaction."

"1 *Sept.*, 1818.—Charles will look for a lodging at Genzano, that we may go into the country when Emily goes away. My Mother will be glad to hear that we are to have dear Mr. Brandis in the house with us. Charles has *begged him* of Mr. Niebuhr on the plea that in the present low state of his spirits, he ought not to spend so many hours alone as he was accustomed to do in Mr. Niebuhr's house, and that he has long formed habits of living day after day and hour after hour with Charles, as a brother."

"4 *Sept.*, 1818.—I trust my Mother will have made out from my late letters in what perfect comfort and enjoyment I have passed this summer, having had health and strength enough to pass my time as I liked, and being free from interruptions. I shall take care not to forget that some trouble must be taken for society, but that society must be good indeed, which I could feel to be otherwise than an intrusion. There is no conversation from which I receive so many ideas, no mind that communicates to mine such an impulse, as that of my dear Charles: and I have the blessing of feeling that I am constantly more and more prized by him, and that he is more happy in my presence. I am also indescribably thankful to be conscious how much closer the bond has been drawn between me and my dear Emily in these fourteen months that we have spent as it were together, since my Mother left us. I feel her affection towards me as much increased as mine towards her, and I have received from her little kindnesses and little services innumerable."

After Madame Bunsen parted with her sister at Rome, they never met again. Mrs. Manley, whilst she had pleased her husband by making his house agreeable to his numerous Italian friends, had been exerting herself beyond her feeble powers. Though her affection for him was unaltered, she could not evade an inner consciousness which she never allowed to appear till she lay upon her death-bed, that her marriage had been a mistake. Her early life had been devoted to strong religious impressions of that class which are none the less real because they frequently raise external trifles to the rank of spiritual duties; and, though her husband never interfered with her conduct on subjects of faith, or attempted to influence her belief, she felt ere long that the fact of his being a Roman Catholic, and evading all subjects connected with religion, created a barrier between them on the matters nearest her heart. She had long discovered also that his fortune was far from being that which it had been represented to be before her marriage was allowed by her parents, which she suffered from chiefly because she dreaded the effect of the disclosure upon their minds. When the hour of departure for England was fixed, she concealed from her sister that she knew she was returning to her own country to die.

The fatigues of the journey increased her malady, and when her mother welcomed her at the door of Llanover, it was to hear her conviction that she was dying fast, but that God had heard her prayer, not to be parted from her mother and family during her last days. She expressed herself as being joyful in spirit for almost the first time for the last two years — " in which she had lived as under a mask." She wished only that two requests might be granted—one, that her husband might not be informed of the certainty of her approaching death, but that he might continue to indulge his present hopes of her recovery; the other, that in the prayers offered in her presence, not a word of petition for recovery might be uttered, as she had not strength to endure so terrible a thought. From this time she lay tranquil and resigned, but could seldom speak: all symptoms showed the entire break-up of nature, although she had still strength to endure much pain, and for a longer time than the physician had deemed possible. " I pray for the happiness of my husband," she said; " he loves me, and has ever cared for me to the utmost of his power; but that is now past; all ties are broken, except that which binds me to my Mother, by whom I was taught the knowledge of God."* Mrs. Manley died on the 12th April, 1819. There are few cases in which one may venture to say as positively as in this, that according to human wisdom and perception there was no other way

* Letter of Bunsen to his sister Christiana.

but by the release of nature, for escaping from a really
tragical combination of circumstances, not one of which
could have been thought of without despair.* Meantime life continued to glide happily by with the Bunsens
at Rome—their only clouds arising from this sorrow,
and from their separation from Brandis, who left
Rome so ill, and at the same time "so heavenly-
minded in benevolence, inward peace and clearness, and
so convinced of the near approach of his end," that his
friends, when they parted, could not but fear they had
seen him for the last time, though he lived to a good
old age.† Long and affectionately remembered were
the last afternoons passed by the Bunsens with this
brother-like friend, chiefly in the turfy avenues with
their glorious mountain-views, which extend from the
steps of St. John Lateran to the old basilica of Santa
Croce.

MADAME BUNSEN *to her* MOTHER.

"16 *March*, 1819.—Mr. Hinds and Mr. Thirlwall are
here. . . . . My Mother, I know, has sometimes suspected
that a man's abilities are to be judged of in an *inverse ratio*
to his Cambridge honours,—but I believe that rule is
really not without exception, for Mr. Thirlwall‡ is cer-

---

* See Letter of Bunsen to Mrs. Waddington, in the Memoirs of
Baron Bunsen.

† Professor Brandis outlived Bunsen himself. He died at Bonn, where
he filled the chair of Professor of Moral Philosophy, in July, 1867.

‡ Connop Thirlwall, afterwards Historian of Greece and Bishop of
St. David's, died 1875.

tainly no dunce, although, as I have been informed, he
attained high honours at Cambridge at an earlier age than
anybody, except, I believe, Porson. In the course of their
first interview, Charles heard enough from him to induce
him to believe that Mr. Thirlwall had studied Greek and
Hebrew in good earnest, not merely for *prizes ;* also, that
he had read Mr. Niebuhr's Roman History proved him to
possess no trifling knowledge of German,* and as he expressed a wish to improve himself in the language, Charles
ventured to invite him to come to us on a Tuesday evening, whenever he was not otherwise engaged, seeing that
many Germans were in the habit of calling on that day,
and making the necessary explanations, that a regular
assembly was not to be expected, for that I was unable to
send formal invitations, on account of being so frequently
laid up : and Mr. Thirlwall has never missed any Tuesday
evening since, except the *moccoli* night, and one other when
it rained dogs and cats. He comes at eight o'clock, and
never stirs to go away till everybody else has wished good-
night, often at almost twelve o'clock. It is impossible for
any one to behave more like a man of sense and a gentleman, than he has always done,—ready and eager to converse with anybody that is at leisure to speak to him, but
never looking fidgety when by necessity left to himself;
always seeming animated and attentive, whether listening
to music, or trying to make out what people say in German, or looking at one of Göthe's songs in the book,
while it is sung ; and so there are a great many reasons
for our being *very much* pleased with Mr. Thirlwall, yet I

* Seven years after this, Thirlwall joined his friend Julius Hare in
translation of Niebuhr's History of Rome.

rather suspect him of being very cold, and very dry—and although he seeks, and seeks with general success, to understand everything, and in every possible way increase his stock of ideas, I doubt the possibility of his understanding anything that is to be *felt* rather than *explained*, and that cannot be reduced to a system. I was led to this result by some most extraordinary questions that he asked Charles about Faust (which he had borrowed of us, and which he greatly admired nevertheless, attempting a translation of one of my favourite passages, which however I had not pointed out to him as being such),—and also by his great fondness for the poems of Wordsworth, two volumes of which he insisted upon lending Charles, containing stuff, to my perceptions, yet more contemptible than the contents of that enormous quarto (the eighth section of the second part of an intended poem, I believe) which my Mother and I once attempted to read. These books he accompanied with a note, in which he laid great stress upon the necessity of reading the author's *prose essays on his own poems*, in order to be enabled to relish the latter. Yet Mr. Thirlwall speaks of Dante in a manner that would seem to prove a thorough taste for his poetry, as well as that he has really and truly studied it; for he said to me that he thought no person who had taken the trouble to understand the whole of the ' Divina Commedia ' would doubt about preferring the Paradiso to the two preceding parts; an opinion in which I thoroughly agree—but nobody can understand it, without having obtained a knowledge of the history of the times, and the systems of theology and philosophy (which were present to the mind of Dante) by means of studying the commentators, or being *assisted*, as I was, by the studies of others.

"As Mr. Thirlwall can speak French sufficiently well to make himself understood, and as he has *something to say*, Charles found it very practicable to make him and Professor Bekker acquainted—though Professor Bekker has usually the great defect of *never* speaking but when he is prompted by his own inclination, and of never being *inclined to speak* except to persons whom he has long known, that is, to whose faces and manners he has become accustomed, and whose understanding or character he respects or likes.* . . . . In conclusion, I must say about Mr. Thirlwall, that I was prepossessed in his favour by his having made up in a marked manner to Charles, rather than to myself. I had no difficulty in getting on with him, but I had all the advances to make : and I can never think the worse of a young man, just fresh from college, and unused to the society of women, for not being at his ease with them at first."

"22 *June*, 1819.—All that my Augusta tells me of Calwich has given me a great deal of pleasure. It reminds me of the time when I was there at twelve years old, when my Augusta was only a month older than my Henry is now, when the weather, the flower-garden, the water, the verdure, were all bright and beautiful, and when I very much enjoyed myself.

* Niebuhr said of the extraordinary linguist and philologist Bekker that he was " silent in seven languages " (schweigt in sieben Sprachen). In a letter from Berlin of September, 1857, Bunsen speaks of Professor Bekker's peculiarities as still the same—" Madame Grimm told me that she had made Bekker not only speak, but laugh." Bekker once said—" This is the first time I have spoken these three years.'

"How I thank my Mother for her gifts to Mrs. Niebuhr, whose behaviour to me has indeed been all that I could wish, invariably—and it is difficult for me to find any means of making a return of any sort, except having made her some *minced-pie meat* at Christmas, and a candle-screen in the autumn, which last has proved very useful, on account of the state her eyes have been in for some time. . . . . I must not say anything, and indeed I hardly wish to do so, about my Mother's extravagance, because I know it pleases her to be extravagant for my sake.

"A few evenings ago I walked with Charles over Ponte Sisto to Palazzo Corsini, for the purpose of seeing the gallery. The custode was not at home, so we went on to Santa Maria in Trastevere, to look at some ancient mosaics, and returned to the Corsini garden, where I have so often been with my Mother. After sitting down a little while, we set off home, but by way of Piazza Sciarra in the Corso, to eat ices. When we had ascended our own dear hill, we found the sweetest boy in the world, greeting us with such joy—well-pleased to be taken in my arms, and afterwards upon his father's back, and very soon equally well-pleased to be undressed and go to bed, it being Ave Maria, the usual time for dropping asleep. The Campo Vaccino is the place for my Henry when he is out. There he trots and stops, and looks at the oxen lying by the side of the carts, and the flocks of sheep and goats, and the asses."

"28 *June*, 1819.—In the course of last week a Lutheran clergyman arrived, as chaplain to the Prussian Embassy, in consequence of Mr. Niebuhr's representations to the King

of Prussia of the great need in which the numerous colony
of German Protestants at Rome stood of having a person
among them whose office it should be to keep alive a sense
of religion, and counteract the influence of Catholic priests,
by which so many conversions have been effected: and
service was for the first time performed yesterday at Mr.
Niebuhr's, to a congregation of seventy persons, which
was more than was expected could have been so soon collected, as many people are gone into different parts of the
country for the summer. I have seldom in my life been
so deeply struck by a sermon as by that which the chaplain delivered, and I wish I had space to give such an
account of his selection of matter, and of his manner of
treating it, as might enable my Mother to form an idea of
the strength of understanding, the justness of feeling, and
the knowledge of the doctrines and spirit of Christianity
which he proved himself to possess;—she would rejoice for
me and for Charles in the first place, and for a number of
unknown creatures in the next, that such an individual
should have been induced to come here. The service consisted of prayers and hymns, and two chapters from the
New Testament, one of which, containing the parable of
the Prodigal Son, was explained and commented upon in
the sermon. It has always been allowed to the clergymen
in Germany to make what selections they pleased from a
vast quantity of materials for forming a Liturgy—a liberty
which has been to a fatal degree abused, but which in the
present instance was used in the most admirable manner.
The prayers were those of Luther, with some additions to
suit the circumstances of the congregation. The hymns
were all belonging to the period of the Reformation, both

words and music, and one was composed by Luther himself."

"15 *July*, 1819.—It is a very pretty sight when Henry
is with the little Niebuhr's, they have such delight in
seeing each other, and the little Amelia and my Henry are
so animated and Marcus so quiet, in the manner of showing satisfaction.   Marcus smiles at Henry, puts his hands
gently on his shoulders, and kisses him on the cheek, as
he has been taught to do to his little sister.   The little
girl is engaging, but not pretty, but Marcus has a really
beautiful head, and an expression of deep thought and
fixed attention that is still more striking and uncommon
than his features.

"The great heat of the weather has so much weakened
me latterly, that for a fortnight I have not been out of the
house, except on a Sunday to attend the service which is
regularly performed at Mr. Niebuhr's, and one glorious
night when I drove with Mr. and Mrs. Niebuhr to the
Coliseum.

"It is my most particular advice to A. not to allow the
young Baron de Hügel to come to Italy, as he is only just
come from Eton,—he had much better be sent to Oxford,
and perhaps after eight or ten years, when he has learnt a
great deal at home, and has become well fixed in English
habits and tastes, he may travel, without the certainty of
being contaminated by all the evil of the Continent, and
confirmed in all that he brought with him from England.
It is not that I mean to say there is nothing to be learnt in
Italy : on the contrary, the longer I remain, the more I
am aware of the abundance of ideas that may be acquired,
and the depths of knowledge that may be penetrated here,

—but with no good can anybody come in contact, but by scrutiny into *the past*, of which boys of eighteen have no notion,—they see nothing in Italy but the paltry frippery of its present state, and generally confound in their feelings the noble relics of its ancient and modern greatness, with the *antique Immondezzaji* through which it is necessary to wade in order to get at them.

"Amongst the many subjects on which I wish to comment to my Mother, Schmieder (the chaplain) is one of the principal. I am so sure of the pleasure she would have in hearing of a character of so high and rare a description, as his more and more appears to me, the more it is unfolded. He has now been here four weeks, I have seen a great deal of him, and Charles still more—but I have seen nothing that disturbs or alters the first impression." *

On the 13th of August Mrs. Waddington was informed of the birth of her second grandson, called Ernest Christian Louis, the first name being after his father's boy-friend, the poet Ernst Schulze, of whose death he had heard in the first weeks of his married life.

Madame Bunsen *to her* Mother.

"21 *Sept.*, 1819.—If I could but describe how daily more and more engaging my Ernest becomes!—what a pair of blue eyes he opens! His hair is dark, but light

---

* Dr. Schmieder still lives (1878)—the venerable Provost of the Preacher's Seminary at Wittenberg, a place of residence and tuition for a limited number of candidates for holy orders.

hair is reckoned such a beauty, that the nurses, in short every Italian who has seen him, has endeavoured to console me with the assurance that he will be 'biondo come il fratello'—which amuses me very much, because I have no doubt they know as well as myself that hair is much more apt to become darker than lighter.

"On Sunday the 19th September, my Ernest was christened at Mr. Niebuhr's, after the service—in consequence of Dr. Schmieder's having expressed a wish that the christening should take place in the place of public worship, rather than at home;—as he considered it more consonant to the design of baptism that it should be performed so far publicly, as that the congregation should be enabled to witness it if they chose, and thereby have an additional chance of being reminded of their own obligations. The prayers he read were those of Luther, composing altogether a service not quite so long as ours, but in every respect similar. I was thankful again to be able to attend the service, and to hear Dr. Schmieder preach. During the long interval in which I have not stirred from home, Charles has given me every Sunday a detailed account of the sermon, which always contains an explanation of the Epistle or Gospel for the day, but every time I miss hearing one of his sermons, I feel I have missed an opportunity of real advantage. It is known to Dr. Schmieder's friends that he writes down in the course of the week, sometimes in two or three different ways, his thoughts on the subject on which he intends to preach, but he preaches extempore, without any reference to notes, which certainly gives great additional effect to the words he utters. Every Wednesday evening, he gives explanations of Isaiah, and reads prayers, to any persons, few or many, that choose to attend."

"8 *Nov.*, 1819.—I must tell my Mother the usual employments of our evenings. On Sunday we read in the Bible, with Dr. Schmieder, of whose soundness of belief, and rectitude of feeling, I am the more convinced, the more I hear of his explanations and comments. The other persons present include three painters. One my Mother will find in the catalogue as *Giulio Schnorr di Carolsfeld.* It is difficult to make an intelligible description of Schnorr, and to depict his power of making such keen, dry, penetrating observations on character, that had circumstances destined him for a fine man of the world, he would have been a consummate *persifleur.* The names of *Olivier* and *Rhebenitz* my Mother will also find in the catalogue.

"On Wednesday evenings, at the Ave Maria, we go to a room at Mr. Niebuhr's where the congregation assemble, to which Schmieder has lately begun to give explanations of the articles of the confession of Augsburg. On Thursday evening we generally go to Mr. Niebuhr's, and I am always glad when I am not prevented from going by any accidental circumstance, for Mr. Niebuhr has been for a long time in a sufficiently good state of health to be infinitely animated and conversible, and when that is the case, I can imagine no greater intellectual gratification than to hear him talk, let the subject be what it may. I have heard him converse on many subjects, but he has such a power of diversifying everything by the originality of his conceptions, and the liveliness of his imagination, that I should think it impossible for the most ignorant listener to consider any topic dry upon which he touched. On Monday evening we hope soon to contrive at least once a fortnight to enjoy again a treat which we had once a week five weeks last summer—of hearing some of the Motetts of Palestrina executed in the right manner, without instruments, at home. We had long tried to get together some dilettanti acquaintances, who knew how to sing other music, to execute them, with the help of a simple accompaniment; but at length finding that no dependence could be placed on dilettanti, we committed the extravagance of calling in professional aid—and yet no great extravagance, for to our one singer from the Papal chapel we gave 6 pauls a night—or 2s. 9d. sterling, for singing in six pieces: our contralto, the Maestro Giovannini, was satisfied with an occasional *regalo*, of a few pounds of chocolate, or bottles of wine: our tenor was a Dane, named Bai, late Consul at Algiers, with a most exquisite voice, and great knowledge of music: and for the bass we were rich enough in Sardi, but sometimes Maldura came also. Bai, alas, has now left Rome, therefore we shall have the tenor to seek and to pay whenever we get our musicians together again— for which reason we mean to be economical, and not have the indulgence every week. Charles has often given utterance to the wish that my Mother could be present, when we have been listening to these Motetts. I am sure if anything on earth can give an idea of the angelic choir, it must be the music of Palestrina! and yet I do not forget the glorious effect of Händel—but all music to which instruments contribute, must be a degree more earthly, than that in which human voices are alone to themselves sufficient, where nothing mechanical is needed.

"I have never been able to tell that my Henry can now

pronounce *nonna** most distinctly. He now asks of his own accord to kiss my Mother's picture and he never sees any of his new clothes or shoes without saying 'nonna' and generally ' grazie ' afterwards. To-day, I gave him a bit of pear, and after he had bowed his dear head, waved his hand, and said ' grazie ' to me, he said ' nonna ' and ' grazie '—you may be sure without being bidden, so fixed is his association between *nonna* and things that please him.

" Thank you, my Mother, a thousand, thousand times, for your letter to Charles. I cannot express the joy it is to me, or rather, the foundation of happiness, to perceive that you believe, what I have long been aware of, that it is impossible you and Charles should differ in opinion, if only opportunity is given to make known the grounds of your respective decisions.

" In one of my Mother's letters to me some time ago, she expresses her belief that the image of my departed sister would present itself with peculiar distinctness, and with a saddening effect, when my child was born—that I should then more strongly recall the idea of her care of myself, her love for my first child, and most truly so it was—but yet I was not saddened, for there is no moment of her life, the recollection of which can possibly excite a wish to recall her—not even those moments of comparative enjoyment in which she held my Henry in her arms. Alas! he cannot recollect her, but her love to him, if I can help it, shall not have been thrown away."

" 5 *Jan.*, 1820.—Alas, my Mother, this Christmas and New Year will have been saddened to you by many a vision of sorrow !—to me they have been more solemn than usual;

* Grandmother.

and to Charles they have been clouded by the tidings of
the death of his mother, whose vital powers failed on
the 27th of November. . . . . My dear Charles does not
think it possible that his father can long survive the
death of his wife. He is in his seventy-seventh year,
and the happiness of his life has for so great a length
of time entirely consisted in seeing her, speaking to
her, and feeling her to be near him, that it is scarcely
possible he should physically sustain the shock of her
removal. He is sure to be carefully attended to by
Charles's youngest sister, who lives very near him, and
who had wished to prevail upon him to come into her
house, that she might have him hourly under her eyes :
but he objected with vehemence, and said he would never
be conveyed from the house he had inhabited with his wife
so many years, except to be buried. Their union had been
most perfect, and the affections of their hearts had only
seemed to strengthen, in proportion as bodily and mental
powers became enfeebled.

"I think that the letter I sent to my Mother about this
time last year, was so interrupted that I could not give any
account of the Christmas tree that was made, to Henry's
great delight, by Charles and Mr. Brandis. This year
we made him a still finer tree. . . . . Henry was brought
in by Angelina. At first he stared, and could not understand what it all meant, but after a minute he made an
exclamation of delight, which was continually renewed
with increasing animation as he spied the various treasures
in detail. Ernest opened his two eyes at the sight,
stretched out his fat arms, and jumped and smiled. . . . .
On Christmas Eve I put Henry to sleep, that I might let

Angelina go to her supper, for as a strange specimen of
Italian taste, the servants had not chosen to eat any dinner,
that they might have the full enjoyment of a 'cena di
Natale'—which I should have understood better, if they
had put off the supper till after midnight, because *then* it
would have been lawful to eat *grasso*, but as their supper
took place at 8 o'clock, they were as much obliged to eat
magro as at any other part of the day. Henry was not the
only person who received Christmas-boxes—his mother too
had from Rhebenitz* a drawing of Henry with his nurse,
from Olivier a drawing of Ernest with his nurse, and from
Schnorr a drawing of Ruth and Naomi. These three
artists lodge over us. After our labours were ended, we
were very glad of our *cena*, as well as the servants. We
had rice-milk, cold ham, anchovies and bread and butter,
apples, oranges, and dried figs; the only person present
besides those already mentioned was Platner; we should
have been glad to have invited Dr. Schmieder and his wife,
but they were gone to help to make a tree for Marcus and
Amelia."

"21 *Jan.*, 1820.—On Monday the weather was so bright,
and I was so well and strong, that I walked to Santa
Maria Maggiore, to see, or rather to let the nurse see, the
benediction of the animals before the church of Sant'
Antonio, and I helped part of the way to carry my heavy
Ernest, while Charles helped the maid to carry Henry.

"I have never told my Mother that I have for some time
had in hand the 'History of the Council of Trent,' by
Father Paul Sarpi, which extremely interests me. It is

---

* Theodore Rhebenitz, of Lübeck, who, quitting his university
studies, had come to study painting in Rome.

one of the books forbidden by the Church of Rome, and with much reason, for every line breathes the spirit of Protestantism. Father Paul Sarpi never professed himself a Protestant, because he hoped the Venetian Government, in which he had great influence, would in time be induced to declare against the Pope, and establish the Reformation throughout their states—an event which was very near taking place, but which was prevented by the unfortunate issue of the battle on the Weissen Berge in Bohemia,* in which the Protestant army was overthrown by the Imperialists. Father Paul was so well known as the declared enemy of the Court of Rome, that many attempts were made by his enemies to assassinate him. His work contains a view of all characters and circumstances which had influence, whether propitious or adverse, on the cause of religion at the time;—the style is clear, concise, simple, and forcible, although the language is very nearly the same with that which the modern Italians so wretchedly misuse, and consequently in itself less energetic than that of earlier Italian writers,—but the mind of the author bestows vigour upon it, and his occasional summing up of the distinguishing characteristics of Popes and their favourites, contains instances of keen and at the same time dispassionate dignified satire, to which I know no parallel. I often recollect with surprise, how often I have been asked, in England and out of England, about books in classical Italian prose, which were worth reading on account of the subject, and never could get any information. Cardinal Bentivoglio's very dry 'Guerra di Fiandra' was the only not-trashy work in Italian prose

* 8 Nov., 1620.

of which I could even procure the title. At last I have learnt, that there is no modern language so rich in historical works of intrinsic excellence, as Italian, and that some of the early historians of Florence approach nearer to the excellence of the Greek and Roman models, than the historians of any other country, or, more precisely speaking, than Hume or Gibbon, whom Mr. Niebuhr rates far above any of the historical writers of France or Germany,—but Gibbon he considers as greatly superior to Hume, in diligence of searching after, and honesty in stating, the truth of facts, except in a very few instances, in which his judgment was warped by his anti-Christian spirit. Varchi, and the elder Villani, are the two Florentine historians whom Mr. Niebuhr considers of the most distinguished excellence, in particular the former. I will mention a passage of Göthe, and of Novalis,—as my Mother says that a word often gives her much matter for meditation:—Göthe says, 'The history of a man is his character:'—and Novalis says, 'The mind, and the fate, of an individual, are but different words for the same conception.'

"Of all the books I have, which both my Mother and I know, Patrick's 'Pilgrim' is that which gains upon me the most. It appears to me the only piece of what Dr. Johnson calls 'hortatory theology,' with which I am acquainted, that does not occasionally fall into the error, *in fact*, however denied *in words*, of admitting a species of *dualism* into the definition of that which is needful to salvation—that is to say, annexing at one time a specific value to certain outward acts, although insisting at another time upon inefficiency of anything and everything but faith—faith in the real, the original sense of the word; too often used to signify *belief*, the assent of the understanding to the dogmas of religion (in which we have no more merit, than in beholding the light by means of the organ which was granted us for the power of discerning it), and it is only when used in this sense (*i.e.* of belief), that it can be said that *faith alone is insufficient.* That faith which is defined by Patrick, which breathes through every line of his book, is a living and active principle, which stimulates all those in whom it subsists to strive against the corruptions of their moral nature, which rouses the best affections of the heart, and diffuses them over all fellow-partakers in the body of sin and death, fellow-heirs of the mercy of God through Christ."

"7 *Feb.*, 1820.—Yesterday, after church, we walked to Santa Sabba on the Aventine, formerly a monastery, whence there is a very fine view, but we did not this time find anybody at home to let us in; we had, however, a delightful walk, in as utter stillness and solitude as if we had been a hundred miles from a great town, and I gathered some wild violets in the lane. During this time my sweet boys had been in the garden belonging to Palazzo Caffarelli. I made coffee in the same garden after dinner for Charles, and Rhebenitz, and Olivier, who accompanied us, and Henry enjoyed himself, running about, scratching the earth with a stick, and rolling an orange. We saw the glorious sunset, and remained till after Venus was visible; then I set myself to play on the pianoforte, and afterwards cut the bread and butter for tea, and then we had our accustomed Sunday readings, with the usual set. I mention all these successive occupations, to show my Mother that I can do a great deal in the course of the day without being knocked up, and I must also mention that a good part of the morning before we went to church was spent in carrying about my sweet Ernest, during the time the nurse dressed herself and went to mass."

"12 *Feb.*, 1820.—Charles has had a second, and a severer shock, in the intelligence of the death of his father, who survived his wife only six weeks. He was in his seventy-seventh year, but retained all his faculties to the last. When the first three or four days elapsed after the death of his wife, he became more composed, but continually grieved after her, always concluding his expressions of lamentation with the words—' She will soon fetch me.' Charles had repeatedly expressed his conviction that the next letter he received from home would contain information of his father's death—but still, it is impossible to be prepared for such an event, and he has deeply grieved, though he has struggled to employ himself as usual."

"3 *March*, 1820.—O! if I could describe how dear and engaging my Ernest becomes! I wish I could draw him as he is at this moment—playing with a great orange, which he holds between his two fat hands, and tries to put into his mouth. Yesterday Henry walked between his papa and mamma all the way to the Coliseum. Ernest followed, calling after me, and crowing at my red shawl: when we arrived, we sat down upon a stone, while Henry ran about, gathering daisies : he walked about a quarter of the way home, and then petitioned to be taken ' *in braccia, a mama,*' and his father carried him."

" 11 *March*, 1820.—Two days ago, my Mother, I was at sunset in the garden of the Passionisti, behind the Coliseum, where women cannot enter except by express permission from the Pope. It is where Oswald * heard the Ave Maria. O how glorious were the views at that hour. I know no spot so beautiful in Rome. I wish the Pope would give a standing permission for so harmless a person as myself, that I might go daily, it is such an easy distance.

" On the festival of the Conversion of St. Paul, I walked to San Paolo fuori le Mura. The weather was glorious and I enjoyed the walk extremely. It was sad to observe how few individuals made that day the same pilgrimage with ourselves—for if the Roman Catholics in Italy believe *anything* with reference to religion, they believe that *time* and place add much to the efficacy of devotion. I find that the general effect of the Church of San Paolo always gains upon me, although never to such a degree as to make me cease to feel how defective the basilica form is for a church, when compared to the mode of construction in Gothic churches. I believe the state of neglect in which San Paolo has been left for centuries, contributes much to its effect, for the absence of the tinselly and variegated decorations with which every other Italian church is disfigured, leaves the eye undisturbed in contemplating the magnitude and simplicity of the design of the building, and the real magnificence of its granite and marble columns. I had an additional interest in examining every part of the church this time, from having lately heard a description of the ancient church of St. Peter's, which Platner has been compiling for the work on which he is engaged: the

* In Madame de Staël's " Corinne."

design of both buildings must have been precisely the same, and they were erected at the same period, the foundations having been in all probability laid by Constantine; in particular, by seeing the front of San Paolo, a perfect idea may be formed of the appearance of St. Peter's;— that front, my dearest Mother never saw, for when we were at the church together, we had nobody to tell us that we ought to have a door opened at the opposite extremity to the present entrance. At the real entrance are gates of bronze, the work of Greek artists of the time of Gregory VII., which are very curious, though most assuredly not beautiful: and above the portico on the outside are very ancient mosaics, the greater part of which are in good preservation. This point is to be seen in the distant view that I made for my Mother, with a reach of the Tiber in front. It was taken—with Emily! I have never been at the spot since, and for some time, did not like to think of going, but I mean to go again soon: it is a beautiful spot, and although

'When the Spring
Comes forth her work of gladness to renew,
With all her reckless birds upon the wing,
I may turn from all she bears to *that* she cannot bring,'

—still, I shall be thankful, that she is not *here*, not in Rome!—that body, which when I last contemplated San Paolo from the bank of the Tiber, shrank with pain from the September breeze of Italy, is no longer susceptible of suffering—and that spirit, which was animated with the hope of being restored to her home, and to her mother, now dwells in the eternal home, with Him, in whom is life!"

"23 *March*, 1820.—Within these ten days I have been to St. Peter's, to the underground church, into which women cannot enter, unless by express permission, except on Whit-Monday, on which day men are excluded. We took Henry with us, of course leaving him in the light of the sun while we went underground. It was the first time he had ever been in St. Peter's, and he was extremely delighted, and called out so loud at the sight of the great white statues, that his voice echoed to the other end of the church. He took great notice of the colossal cherubs that support the holy-water, and said, ' Mama, puppo casca '—Puppo means a little child, and he thought the cherub would fall; he stroked its foot, but complained that it was dirty—' Piedino grasso,—cacca.' On seeing one of the statues with his hand stretched out, he imitated it, and said, ' Zitto tutti '—having often been told by his father, to his great amusement, that his old friend Marcus Aurelius on the Capitol stretches out his hand and says, ' Zitto tutti— Roma è mia! ' He was very happy at the Villa Pamfili, and it has made a great impression—the tall pines (the poor child has never seen trees anywhere else), the ane-mones and violets, the fountains, and the soft grass upon which he fell so often without hurting himself—many a time has he mentioned some of the things that he saw and did there, looking up eagerly to have the rest enumerated to him."

"12 *April*, 1820.—On Easter Sunday, my sweet Henry's birthday, I had wished to have taken him to St. Peter's, for it is very unlikely I shall again see the benediction given by the present Pope: but after having been at church early, I was too much tired to go out again. My

Henry however had a great deal of amusement, for little Marcus and Amelia Niebuhr came to see him, and brought him a cake, with a long taper stuck in the middle and three shorter stuck round. It is a German custom to give such cakes on birthdays: the taper in the centre represents the flame of life, and round the cake are placed as many other tapers as the person is years old, with one for the year that is just coming, and the cake is covered with flowers, or sugar-plums, or dried fruits. Then Henry's three friends, Igo, and Doro, and Giu (Federigo, Teodoro, and Giulio *), who lodge over us, brought him a waggon drawn by painted grey oxen, containing flowers and oranges and a piping man and a tumbling man. St. Peter's was illuminated in the evening, which was a great delight to Henry, who stayed up to see the change from lanterns to flambeaux, although just before it he became so sleepy, that he put his arms round his own mother's neck, and his cheek against her cheek, and dropped off.

"I have reason to be greatly obliged to Mr. and Mrs. Niebuhr for continued and increasing kindness in word, deed, and manner."

"15 *June*, 1820.—On Sunday the 7th we went to Frascati, and next morning drove to the Villa Mondragone. The prospect seemed more magnificent than ever. My Mother will remember how the row of pines, and the avenue of cypresses, and the olive-grounds, appeared from the terrace. On our return we went to our old Casino Accorambuoni, and found the house, and the terrace and the view, looking as they used to look. We dined, and I had a fine sleep after dinner, and we afterwards drove through the

* Olivier, Rhebenitz, and Schnorr.

Villa Bracciano and the beautiful wood to Grotta Ferrata, went into the church, and saw the Domenichino chapel, which pleased Henry very much, but my Ernest not less, and he did nothing but laugh loud, and call after the painted figures on the walls. Next morning very early, we drove to Monte Compatri, which is beyond Monte Porzio, and higher on the mountain, from whence the nurse was delighted to be able to discern Zagarola, and even, as she said, her own vineyard! Often did she assure us it was only five miles further—and we should have been almost as pleased as herself to have indulged her with driving there, if Zagarola was not in a very unsafe quarter as to robbers. After having rested ourselves and our horses during the heat of the day, and had our dinner, we went through Marino, Castello, Albano and L'Ariccia, to Genzano. The drive was most beautiful, and the wood, and the fountain, and the old tower at Marino, in the evening sun, produced their most magnificent effect. On Wednesday morning I sat out a long time, first in a garden in sight of the lake, afterwards in a shady avenue which leads towards L'Ariccia, in which my sweet boys enjoyed themselves extremely ; and Charles read aloud to me. Thursday was the octave of the fête of Corpus Domini, which is the occasion of a festival peculiar to Genzano that I had long wished to see, and the effect greatly surpassed my expectations. My Mother will remember the arrangement of flowers in patterns, on the steps leading to the underground church of St. Peter's, on the octave of Corpus Domini three years ago, and that will give her an idea in some degree of what is done on a great scale at Genzano the length of two streets, along which the procession passes an hour before dark. The streets are on the steep declivity of the hill, and at the bottom is another wider street, where there is a fountain. At the top of one street, terminating the vista, is the church, at the top of the other an altar erected for the occasion, under a high pavilion. Between the church and the altar is an avenue. A narrow space is left on each side the street for foot passengers, and the centre is parted off by what I can only call *columns of foliage*—thin wooden posts about three feet high, with branches of box, rosemary, or myrtle, tied so thick over them, that the wood is not to be seen, and at the top of each, either a flower-pot full of carnations, or a great nosegay of lilies, embosomed in green. The centre of the streets between these two rows is first covered thick with box, rosemary, sage, and sweet herbs, and then divided into compartments, strewed with flowers of all colours in various devices, the possessor of every house taking care to ornament the compartment before his dwelling. It would take too much time and space to enumerate even a part of the devices, but the flowers principally made use of were the yellow Spanish broom, the white matricula, the scarlet wild poppy, and the purple and lilac wild Venus's looking-glass; roses and lilies and carnations, being greater scarcities, were only introduced occasionally, to form wreaths. The procession moved from the church along the avenue, and then *over the flowers* the whole length of both streets back to the church: the crowd which followed it of course trampled and confounded everything, but closed in and concealed the devastation. We saw the procession from our windows, and my Henry sung 'Evviva la Croce' as loud as he could, every time a cross or crucifix was carried by. I went along the streets to see the *infiorata* as soon as it was finished; Charles carried Henry, and Ernest was carried by his nurse; both were very happy, but the joy of Ernest at seeing so many people and so many flowers, was the most apparent: he laughed and crowed the whole way, and was much noticed and admired. Often did I hear—'Ma, Dio la benedica! che bella creatura!'"

On the 22nd of July, the birth of her eldest grand-daughter was announced to Mrs. Waddington.

MADAME BUNSEN *to her* MOTHER.

"10 *August*, 1820.—Oh! it is such a happiness to have my little girl, and hold her, and touch her, and look at her, that I sometimes fancy I must have been unjust to her darling brothers, and that I could not have loved them so much when they were as little, and yet I *did* certainly. . . . . I have looked and gazed and examined my sweet girl, till I am convinced she will be like my Mother."

"6 *Sept.*, 1820.—My Mother, I for ever grudge myself the delight my children give me, when I think that you have been for so long a time without an enjoyment that you would live upon—feed upon—I know you would. This feeling more especially occurs to me when I see my Henry's eyes, as they were fixed upon me yesterday morning at breakfast, when he came running to me 'Mama, Righetto * rotto un bicchiere'—in a whisper, not to inter-

* The Italian nurse-word for Enrico.

rupt papa, who was reading the newspaper. . . . . And I long particularly for my mother to see my Ernest, when he embraces his own mother. He has the most touching manner of clinging round my neck, and pressing his soft face against me. I have not been able for a long, long time to do anything for that poor child, except love him, for he is too heavy for me to carry,—but he is most aware how well I love him, or he would not love me so much. Yesterday I drove out for the first time, with my three treasures. I went along the Tiber, beyond Porta Portese, and afterwards to Villa Borghese. Last Sunday I was at church, and my little angel was christened—*Mary Frances*. I must *call* my girl Mary, the name that I love so much. I could almost fancy I had heard my Mother called by it, which I never did."

" 24 *Sept.*, 1820.—Yesterday I attended the christening of Mrs. Niebuhr's little girl, born eighteen days after my Mary, to whom I had been much gratified by being asked to be godmother."

" 3 *Dec.*, 1820.—Alas! I shall never see Bishop Sandford * again in this world !—may I be worthy to be recognised by him in another."

" *Christmas Day*, 1820.—Before we went to church to receive the Sacrament, Charles and I read together the 13th and 14th chapters of the Gospel of St. John, and I was struck particularly with the words of our Saviour—'What I do thou knowest not now, but thou shalt know hereafter.' It is true that without this assurance, we ought to be equally satisfied that all the circumstances of life, as ordained by

---

* Bishop of Edinburgh. The old family friendship with his mother " Sally Chapone " is mentioned early in the volume.

God, must be for our good—but the promise of future explanation, probably even in this world, might well operate to tranquillise us, on points the most inexplicable in appearance.

"I can say nothing of my Mary, except that she is always well—what other words could I use to give an idea of how lovely she is? The fact is according to Charles's words the other day—'We ought to pray God that we may not quite worship her, lest she should be taken from us as a punishment.' "

CHAPTER VI.

SHADOWS.

" The mother gave, in tears and pain,
    The flowers she most did love ;
Sbe knew she should find them all again
    In the fields of light above.

" O, not in cruelty, not in wrath
    The Reaper came that day ;
'Twas an angel visited the green earth,
    And took the flowers away."
                                        LONGFELLOW.

IN the year 1821, Bunsen's mind was chiefly occupied
with the hope of bringing about the establishment
of a common form of worship throughout Protestant
Germany, as a means of drawing its various churches
into Christian communion and fellowship. With this
view, he devoted himself to his *Gebetbuch*, on a plan
indicated, but not carried out, by Luther : and to his
Gesangbuch, a collection of hymns chiefly chosen from
the works of the more ancient hymn-writers. Not less
was he anxious for the improvement of hymn-music in
Germany, and for this object was assisted by his young
friend Reisiger in selecting or reforming versions of

the finest chorales. The complete success of some concerts of sacred music which were given by the Niebuhrs in honour of Baron Stein* and Prince Hardenberg, also induced Bunsen to persuade the director of the Papal Choir to allow some of its members to sing on fixed evenings during the winter months at the Palazzo Caffarelli, when his family and their intimate circle of friends had such an enjoyment of the masterpieces of ancient music as is seldom attainable.

Next to the Niebuhrs, the most valued friend of the Bunsens at this time resident in Rome was Augustus Kestner, the Hanoverian Secretary of Legation, "of whose worth and merit," wrote Madame Bunsen, quoting Göthe, "a detailed biography alone can be competent to measure and estimate the full circumference." † Most intimate also, and greatly valued in their house was the fresco-painter, Julius Schnorr von Carolsfeld, who lived above them in the Palazzo Caffarelli,‡ and in a less degree Augustus Grahl, the

---

* Carl, Baron von Stein, the minister of Frederick William III. It was he who introduced the measures which transformed the old into the modern Prussia by advocating the reform of those abuses which had led to the great Revolution in France. After the Battle of Jena, Napoleon insisted upon his dismissal, and he spent some time at the Russian court, where he prepared the way for that understanding between Russia, Austria, and Prussia which caused the coalition fatal to Napoleon. His latter years were spent in retirement on his estates near Nassau, where a monument was erected in his memory by public subscription in 1872.

† Kestner died in 1853, having kept up his faithful friendship for the Bunsens to the last.

‡ He left Rome in 1825.

miniature painter, who inhabited rooms in the left wing of the palace.*

The month of March was clouded by the sudden death, from an infectious fever, of William Waddington, a cousin of Madame Bunsen, who had come to Rome to visit the antiquities. On this occasion the disinterested character of Bunsen was vividly shown in his making no opposition to his wife's strong wish—fearless of the risk for herself—to minister to her dying relative, " dreading nothing," as Mrs. Waddington afterwards wrote to Professor Monk, and "intent alone on robbing death of its terrors, and winning a soul to Heaven."

In May, Bunsen and his wife paid a visit at Albano to the Niebuhrs, who had already removed thither for the summer *villeggiatura*, and they then engaged the apartments, to which Madame Bunsen removed with her children at the end of June. The business of the legation still detained Bunsen in Rome, but change of air had become especially desirable for the precious infant Mary, whose health and animation had flagged with the summer heat. Her mother soon beheld with anguish that she did not amend. On her birthday, the 22nd of July, Bunsen drove out to visit his family, filled with the pleasant tidings of the happy engagement of his dear friend Brandis to the object of six years' attachment. He walked, as usual, up the long hill which leads from the Campagna to the town. Outside the gates of Albano his wife met him, and he

* He left Rome in 1830.

saw in her eyes, what she strove to tell with composure—"She is with God."*

Little Mary had scarcely been laid in the beautiful burial-ground under the shadow of the Pyramid of Caius Cestius, when Henry became alarmingly ill. Then Madame Bunsen herself, worn with nursing her children, fell sick of tertian fever, and, on the 25th of August, Bunsen, coming out from Rome to his sick family, arrived "like a stone," a state which was soon changed to one of burning fever. Five days afterwards, he was in such extreme danger, that he gave his wife what he believed to be his dying directions, his dying benediction; but one of the rapid transitions, frequent in that country, which has as great a power of curing as of endangering, allowed of his removal to his own house at Rome, and by the end of September he began to amend.

MADAME BUNSEN *to her* MOTHER.

"1 *Jan.*, 1821.—The old year has closed brightly upon me, my Mother, to the mind's eye, and the body's eye— and the new year came forth under a glowing firmament. Clouds might perhaps be perceived in the distant horizon, or rather mists, which render all indistinct and uncertain; but those which I see or fancy, may evaporate before they approach, and should they condense in rain, I trust and believe I shall have, as I have always had, a sheltering roof;—and should they burst in thunder, and the lightning-stroke, I shall know that no hand can have guided it

* Bunsen to his sister Christiana.

but the hand of God. Do not alarm yourself, my Mother, with the supposition that these words contain any especial allusion : I foresee no evil—except that I may be detained yet longer from my Mother. That is evil enough, but perhaps the event may yet be better than I anticipate."

" 7 *Feb.*, 1821.—To show how far we have been from feeling in any degree the cold of which my Mother speaks, I have had two pots of heliotrope flowering before my windows the whole winter, the almond trees were in blossom at the end of January, and a few lemon buds have expanded within the last week. We had, I think, three-and-twenty days of uninterrupted tramontana, with the finest warm sun, and the clearest sky, since which we have been shrinking from a keen north-east wind which has frozen the ground, and hung the lioness-fountains at the foot of the Capitol round with icicles, to the great surprise of Henry.

"I have passed a week of such dissipation and disturb-ance, that it is with some difficulty I can collect my thoughts to give an account of it. First of all, last Friday Mr. Niebuhr gave a great fête. My Mother will wonder, as all Rome has wondered, at such an event, and has conjectured in vain what could be the reason. *We* know it was given in honour of Baron Stein, and not of the princes and ambassadors who were invited besides : a selection of the music of Palestrina, consisting of the celebrated 'Missa di Papa Marcello,' and the Motett—'Tu es Petrus,'—and afterwards the 'Dies Iræ' of Pittoni, were performed by the singers of the Papal Chapel, who were stationed at the further end of the long gallery. The effect of the music is not to be described,—often as I have been in the Papal Chapel, I never heard anything equal to it,—for the singers not having any reason for hurrying, were induced to give every note its due value ; and the complication of sound was of that subduing nature, as to make you draw your breath, or lift up your eyes, lest some other object or sensation should divide your attention, and cause you to lose a particle. Oh thus, thus only can the angels sing ! Had but my Mother heard it too !

"But I know not how it happens that I have never wished for my Mother more, than when looking at Thérèse de Stein, Baron Stein's second daughter.* I know my mother would feast upon her face, she possesses what my Mother would call the ' dignity of beauty,' of which I had heard much more than I had ever seen in life, till I saw her—but I must not digress upon this inviting subject.

"On Sunday, after church, I went into the garden, but had scarcely entered it, when Charles called to me from a window to come in immediately. He had been at Mr. Niebuhr's, and brought the intelligence (which I will mention beforehand, turned out to be false, however credited by Consalvi himself) that a counter-revolution had broken out in Naples, and that the carbonari troops, in despair, were advancing through Tivoli to plunder Rome with all speed before the arrival of the Austrians :—consequently that I must pack up, and be ready to set off at an hour's notice, whenever we should hear that the Pope had commenced his journey to Civita Vecchia. My Mother will easily

* Afterwards Countess Kielmannsegge. Her grandson, Graf Gröben, is now the only representative of Stein.

believe that I had not much appetite for my dinner, which at that moment was brought on the table. It was then about three o'clock, and till eight o'clock in the evening I never sat down, but continued running about the house, collecting things together, and giving directions. About ten, it was ascertained that no counter-revolution had occurred, and that there was no immediate danger of the approach of the Neapolitans, consequently we went to bed, and slept in peace, and I was so fresh again the next day, that I went to a great ball given by Madame Appony* on account of the Emperor's birthday, which was the finest fête I ever saw.

"How little I have said of my darling children. They are well, and merry, and good, and engaging : whichever of the three I look at, I always imagine it is *that* child in particular that I wish most to show to my Mother."

" 14 *Feb.*, 1821.—The glorious weather lately has occasioned my being much in the garden with my dear children, weeding, and hoeing, and teaching my lazy boy to carry away the weeds in his wheelbarrow. Then when I have gathered oranges for my boys, and given them to the maid to peel, I sit down in the sun, and read. My darling Mary is happy in the house, and happy in the garden, and thinks nothing so great amusement as being jumped by her own mother, while the nurse plays with her."

" 9 *March*, 1821.—I must try to give my Mother some account of people that I have seen this winter. The family of the Baron de Redent† have been here a year and

* Austrian ambassadress in Rome.
† Hanoverian Minister.

a half. We were introduced to them soon after their arrival, and as they had regular evenings for receiving company, we ought to have gone to their house, but I was too unwell all last winter and spring to take so much trouble, and Charles therefore excused himself.

"When, at length, Charles and I went together to Madame de Reden's, and were received and attended to in such a manner throughout the evening, that any stranger who had taken notice, must have supposed we could be nothing less than the Prince and Princess of Denmark, of all persons now in Rome. We have since renewed our visits as often as we could, and always receive the most pressing solicitations to continue to do so· With Madame de Reden herself, with her eldest daughter,* and her niece, Mademoiselle Wurmb, I have great pleasure in conversing, particularly with the eldest daughter, who I believe has both heart and head, and whom I wish I had opportunities of seeing otherwise than in a mixed society: we meet Baron Stein there sometimes, and many other people, and there is always music of one sort or other. That there is *something in Charles worth knowing*, all people know in time, and some people find out at once (like Baron Stein)—but to the Redens in the first instance the attraction in us both, was the circumstance of our living to ourselves, and yet not living without society.

"Charles has lately been much occupied with Baron Stein. All who know him, or could imagine his sort of character, would feel that he is one of that class of

---

* Henrietta de Reden, afterwards godmother to Emilia Henrietta de Bunsen, continued to the end of her life—as a chanoinesse of one of the *Stifte* of North Germany. an intimate friend of the Bunsen family.

persons from whom a request is equally felt to be a
command and an obligation, and would not wonder
that when Charles each day was asked to make an appointment for the following day, to spend from three to
four hours in walking or driving about, for the double
purpose of seeing sights and conversing, to comply was a
thing of course : and to this sacrifice of time there was
no difficulty in being reconciled, as besides the gratification of becoming acquainted with such an individual as
Baron Stein, the opportunity was invaluable for obtaining information as to political events in late years, such
as few persons can be equally qualified to give. Baron
Stein has from the very first spoken to Charles with
a degree of openness that could only result from the
conviction that the person with whom he was conversing
was worthy of the best he had to bestow, and was not to
be won with less than the best. At this conviction he
would naturally arrive the sooner, from what Mr. Niebuhr
must have said of Charles,—for although I cannot know
what that was, I am aware that Mr. Niebuhr knows how to
to praise—knows how to measure his words, so that much
may be left to be discovered, at the same time that he
discloses enough to prove that the discovery is worth
making.

"At Mr. Niebuhr's fête, when almost everybody removed
into the long gallery to take places to hear the music, I
remained in the outer room, thinking that the sound in
the gallery would be too powerful, and Baron Stein seated
himself by me. After speaking very graciously about
various things, he said. 'I think there is a draught of
wind here, shall *we* move to the opposite side of the

room ? ' I assented, and we went across, but that I might not seem to force myself upon him, I moved towards a chair at a little distance from that of which he was going to take possession, but he showed the chair next to his own, and asked if I would not sit there, as I should hear well in that place. Just after, the greater part of the assembly found it better to make their retreat to the outer room,—when Baron Stein said to me ' *We* judged right in remaining here.' These are petty details which would seem very empty to anybody else—but I think they will help my Mother to form an idea of Baron Stein's power of conferring an obligation by means of half a word or motion.

" William (Waddington) has been in Rome for some time, and I have that to tell of him, which will greatly shock you. He is ill of a fever with little hope of re_covery. . . . . Charles intends to watch for a lucid interval, to warn him of his danger."

" 10 *March*, 1821.—I did not think my own dearest Mother when I left off writing yesterday that I should see poor William expire to-day at five o'clock ! far less did I anticipate the satisfactory feelings with which I have watched his last moments. He received the Sacrament with perfect collectedness, joined in every response, spoke often to Charles of his sins and offences, but reiterated the assurance of his faith in God's mercy through the merits of our Saviour. . . . . My Mother will not wish me to write more. I am much worn, but she must not be afraid that I shall be ill."

" 14 *March*, 1821.—I have ventured to take off my darling Mary's long sleeves, and have now the constant treat of seeing her arms. If I could describe anything so round or beautiful as they are!—or anything so beaming as her eyes, or so pretty as her mouth, her chin, her throat, the nape of her neck, her shoulders!—and she is the merriest thing in the world and engaging beyond all conception, and, my Mother, she is eight months old!

" Mr. and Mrs. Niebuhr's two concerts, one in honour of Baron Stein, the other in honour of Prince Hardenberg,* have excited a prodigious sensation (in all people of surprise, in many of pleasure), and an opening was made for proposing a continuance of the same performances, the expenses to be defrayed by a subscription. All the princes in Rome, and all the ambassadors, immediately subscribed, and, of course, such names as theirs secured at once a more than sufficient number of other names. The tickets were signed and the business managed entirely by Charles and Kestner, the Hanoverian Secretary of Legation (who is, bye the bye, the son of Werther's Lotte—a very excellent person, and very good friend of ours). Two concerts have taken place, and have been a most exquisite indulgence. At the third it has been settled that the society of Sirleti shall together with the singers of the Papal Chapel perform the Miserere of Marcello. I have only yet heard the rehearsal—but alas! my Mother, I am spoilt by Palestrina. I am at a loss to conceive how I ever could listen with pleasure to Marcello—it seems to me now so empty, so unconnected, so unmeaning, so unmelodious! But it is nevertheless a great happiness to have heard the *best of the best*. even though I may never hear it more after I have left Rome, for the recollection of it is better than the sen-

* The Prussian Prime-Minister.

sation produced by what is inferior. Oh, if my Mother did but know Palestrina, having only heard the Miserere of the Papal Chapel, I fear she can scarcely imagine, however she may believe, of what infinite variety of effect and conception that style of composition is susceptible.

"The Miss Berry's were at the concerts, and each time happened to sit close to me, therefore I had a full opportunity of observing their behaviour, and hearing their conversation. In the fine and fashionable dress—the toques, and the caps, the satin, the gauze, and the blonde in which they are always attired, it is out of my power to recognise the little woman whom we saw one morning at Mrs. W. Lock's; but I observe that the Miss Berry who appears by far the youngest, and is the tallest, with a very good and youthful figure, is the person who has the harsh voice, the dictatorial tone, and the keen black eyes. The other Miss Berry looks much milder, is quieter in her manner, and speaks neither so much nor so loud. The first-mentioned attacked Charles at one of the concerts (for her speaking to anybody has the appearance of an attack) to ask the very learned question, whether Palestrina had not lived *just before* Marcello.* Baron Stein mentioned the Miss Berry's to Charles in this manner — 'There is an old woman who goes about Rome with a younger sister of sixty or seventy years of age. She is always talking about Horace Walpole: I have given her to understand that I despise the man, but nothing can keep her quiet on the subject.'"

"2 *May*, 1821.—This day se'nnight I went to Madame de Reden's. We did not arrive till ten, because Charles

* Palestrina, 1529—94. Marcello, 1686—1739.

had much to write, and we came away at one o'clock, but the greater part of the intermediate time I was waltzing, and was at the last so far from tired, that I could willingly have waltzed longer. Two days after I had a violent cramp, which made me quite lame, so that I hopped and hobbled about the house all Saturday morning, but on Saturday evening, Ringseis* came for his leave-taking visit, and we had some other people to meet him, who by degrees were so wound up by *singing*, that all set about waltzing—and soon I waltzed too—and the end of the story is, had no future cramp or fatigue."

"*Albano*, 22 *May*, 1821.—We came to Albano last Thursday, Mr. and Mrs. Niebuhr having removed here a few days before, to the villa of Cardinal Consalvi. Immediately after their arrival, Mr. Niebuhr wrote to say that they had wished to invite us to come to them, but had found that although the villa was spacious enough for two families, the number of beds was only sufficient for one. However they hoped that we would take a lodging at Albano, and live with them as much as if we were in the same house; adding that they would send the carriage to fetch us, in case we consented to the plan. We came accordingly, and have taken rooms in a house with a beautiful view, and a garden, at the end of the town nearest the tomb of the Horatii and Curiatii. Were not the present so bright, the multitude of recollections in Albano connected with images of pain,† would be enough to cast a gloom over the place, which, as a place, I never

---

* A German physician at Rome.

† The greater part of Mrs. Manley's married life had been passed at Albano—in a state of suffering not understood at the time.

liked as well as Frascati or Genzano.   Still, if we can find
a house to suit us, we shall probably settle here for the
summer.   Frascati, alas! can hardly be considered as
secure, on account of the bands of robbers; that is to say
the *town* is no doubt secure, but it would be too tantalising
to inhabit it without feeling at liberty to visit my favourite
haunts, and the road to Mondragone, and the wood towards Grotta Ferrata, are too little frequented to be safe,
since the robbers only the week before last carried off from
Camaldoli seven poor monks, in hopes of extorting a
ransom from the government.

"In the letter my Mother wrote, on first hearing of
William's death, it struck me very much that she should
have commented on Charles's *fetching* me, without my
having said anything to suggest to her the keener sense,
or rather the increased experience, I had had of his value
—of his more peculiar value to a person constituted as I
am—from all the circumstances attending William's last
illness.   From the first moment I knew he was seriously ill
my Mother will well believe that the wish to be personally
of use was perpetually recurring, but as often checked by
the consideration that the fever was believed to be infectious, and that with my three children born, and another
to be born it was not my duty, to expose myself to any
risk.   Those feelings were the same, but I was of course
more disturbed by the conflict, on the morning of the last
day, during the hours that I sat at home,—very glad that
I had a frock to make for Ernest, with which my hands
could proceed mechanically, and very glad that my children
were pleased to run from one room to another, so that I
could see and hear them, without being called upon to

attend to them. But I never said to Charles that I wished to go to William, satisfied that he knew my feelings, and that if it was right he would propose to me to go;—though when he came to fetch me, it was a relief which I as it were expected, without having done anything to procure it for myself. In the hurry of spirits in which I left the house with him, I forgot to put in my pocket my little prayer-book, which I afterwards on the way regretted, as I thought it might have assisted me in finding words of consolation; but on consideration of the whole of the dying scene, I am convinced the book would have been of no use. When I made one or two attempts to repeat texts of Scripture, William evidently received no benefit—there was not the look and movement of eager assent, which invariably followed when Charles or I expressed in our own words our own convictions. A remarkable instance was this—I had repeated the words of our Saviour to the penitent upon the cross, and William did not seem to attend. A few minutes after, Charles said to him, 'Mind that, William,—our Saviour said *To-day*:—immediately, without any interval of time, when this agony is over, you will be transported to His blessed presence, if you do but believe in His atonement, if you do but trust alone in His intercession:' and then William turned his head and eyes with the greatest animation, as if he was imbibing a cordial from every word. I mention this because everything that marks a state of mind is interesting to my Mother."

"*Albano*, 16 *July*, 1821.—My precious Mary has been very ill—but is mending daily."

"28 *July*.—My Mother, I wish I knew how to persuade

you that I am a stock or a stone, and that I do not feel!—
It has pleased God to take my Mary from me:—could I
but spare you the pain these words will occasion!

"On Sunday, the 22nd of July, her birthday, at noon—
she ceased to breathe, and seemed not to suffer:—and from
that hour, my Mother, my agony has been abating—God
has supported me, O how has He supported me! in body
and mind. For the last four days of her life, besides the
anguish of perceiving that I was to lose her, I feared to
become distracted at the thought that I had brought her
to this state, by venturing to wean her: but it is the signal
mercy of God which has removed from me the sting of
that reflection,—of myself I had no power to quiet my own
mind, as it is quieted. The meditations of every hour, on
what she was, and on the circumstances that preceded her
dissolution, strengthen me in the conviction that she was
not made for this world, and that no adequate cause can
be found for the sudden decay of all her vital powers,
except that it was the good pleasure of God to remove her
from sin, and sorrow, and suffering, to early blessedness, after a life of undisturbed enjoyment during eleven
months, and during the twelfth month of gradual decline,
with but little pain, for she never cried, and rarely uttered
a sound of complaint. She gently made her wants to be
understood, which were to drink, and to be carried about;
—and gently, without fretfulness, rejected what she would
not have, waving her sweet hand, and turning away her
lovely head. A rapid loss of flesh, and an indescribable
melancholy from the very beginning, were signs of a
degree of illness to which no other signs adequately cor-
responded, and these indications of danger weighed upon

my heart, and prevented from the very first my entertaining a real hope or anticipation of seeing her again as she was before. . . . . I have written without a tear, my Mother; I will now give some details, as many as I can, which will cost me more:—to my Mother it will be a solace to know all:—O did I but know how to prevent at least the bodily suffering which her sorrow for me will cause!

"I have been helped and supported in every way. What my Charles is to me, my Mother now knows, as well as anybody besides myself can know:—and the servants have done all they could, with all their hearts. My Mother will guess, from the manner in which I have ever been served by Angelina, what she has done and felt for me now: and Maddalena, a widow-woman, who has for nine months faithfully tended Ernest, has if possible felt more, as being a mother, and having lost five children, for none of which I am convinced could she have grieved more than she has grieved for mine; the manservant Francesco has children of his own, and has therefore known how to help me, as well as wished to help me. . . . . It was very good for me, my Mother, to have a great deal to do for my boys, in the course of their blessed sister's illness, especially for Henry in his threatenings of fever; had I not been compelled at intervals to attend to other things, to behold other objects than her angel countenance, how could I have prevented sinking under the continuance of bodily emotion.

"For two hours at least before she breathed her last—perhaps more, for I knew not how to reckon the time—I perceived what before I could not acknowledge to myself,

that the moment was near at hand; before that time, I
had the bed on which she lay carried into another room.
where the air was fresher. She looked up, and around,
with full intelligence, and was evidently aware of the
change of scene. Before this, I had kissed her cheek, it
was the last time; I had seldom kissed her before in the
last days, I could not do so without a burst of sobbing,
which it was my duty to avoid. I put my Ernest to sleep,
and laid him at the foot of her bed. I then gave my
Henry his bark, and as a reward for taking it well, was
bound to take him in my lap. I sate by her bed : I
glanced my eye from time to time, and at length perceived
a change of tinge which warned me not to look again.
Maddalena continued to moisten her lips. The physician
entered and asked me how she did. I answered according
to my conviction. After a moment Maddalena supplicated
me to leave the room,—I understood her and knelt down by
the bed : in another moment all was over, without sound,
without struggle. I knelt there sometime longer, all the
servants knelt with me—then, I went into the next room,
and left her whom I had never left, to Maddalena and
Angelina—I dared not remain, dared not look upon her

"It was my Charles's severer trial not to be present. The
two preceding days he had been bound to labour incessantly at Rome with Mr. Niebuhr. All would nevertheless
have been left, however at another time necessary, had he
known the real state of his child,—but it was a cruel
circumstance, that I had written him word of material
amendment on Saturday morning, for so it seemed—some
animation had returned, she had taken food, her thirst
had abated, she was not restless, she had slept so sound

for many hours! But from four o'clock, when the letter was sent, it became plain, even to me, that the remainder of life would only be measured by hours—although how many hours, my inexperience disenabled me from calculating. By the peculiar mercy of God, I never felt like many mothers in affliction, that I could not bear the sight of my remaining children,—on the contrary, it comforted me. Not long after their blessed sister was at peace, it was time for them to have their dinners, and they dined at the table near which I sat, and watched them. When the heat of the day had abated, I put on their tippets to walk out with Francesco and Annunziata: I myself went with Angelina on the road towards Rome, to meet my poor Charles: Maddalena remained watching by her who no longer needed any of our care.

"That night, my Mother, I did not sleep, but I lay in peace, thinking of her, who was perhaps near me, though unseen. The next day, I was seized with a craving to look at her, which however I would not gratify unknown to my Charles, and he dissuaded me: he was right. That afternoon I drove out with him and the children to Ariccia; —when I returned, I wanted again to see her—and heard that she was enclosed. O in this climate, it gives an additional pang, that all *must* so soon be over—that all, that little, that can be done!

"The next day, Tuesday the 24th, I left my Henry and Ernest for the first time, and went with Charles to Rome— our angel was before us, but we could not see her. After the first pang was over, I passed the drive in great peace. We approached Rome by the gate of St. Sebastian, then drove without the walls to the gate of St. Paul, close to the pyramid of Caius Cestius: it was within an hour of sunset, rather before the time fixed, which was good for me. I walked up and down on the grass, and afterwards sat under a tree; then advanced with Charles towards the spot. Schmieder (my mother knows the name of the chaplain to the Embassy) advanced to meet us. He said, turning to me—'The Lord support you.' I said, 'He has supported me.' He said again, 'Let not your faith fail and His grace will never fail.' I repeated—'He has been all-gracious to me.' We came to the spot: to see the bier, the grave, was very bad. Schmieder began to speak, and as he proceeded, I breathed easier; he said only what I knew before, but it struck me with new force, and all pangs abated as he uttered the prayers. His wife strewed flowers, and then the earth was cast—I thought I could not have borne that, but before it was finished the words of the angel to the apostles struck me—'Why seek ye the living among the dead? He is not here!'—and I looked no longer down, but looked up into the clear sky, and again I was at peace. Then, I turned to depart, and was again overcome by the sight of Mr. Niebuhr; with emotion that I shall never forget—he, who is so often complained of for not showing emotion, after taking our hands, threw himself down, to touch the earth that covered her—then came with us to the carriage, inquired after Henry and Ernest, and supplicated Charles not to leave me, saying if there was business, what he could not despatch alone, should wait. I had not expected to see him; he had already written to us, expressing from himself and his wife such grief, that I thought, considering their weak state of health, each would work upon the other to stay away from a scene too agitating. I went with Charles to our empty house. Schmieder came, and we both felt we could let him in : then I went to bed, and slept—I was much exhausted : before daybreak I waked, and thought of my angel, in peace. Next day, between six and seven o'clock, Schmieder was again waiting to see us : then we drove away, and returned to our darling boys.

"My Mother, the paper is almost at an end, and I have yet much to tell you—but I must leave some room, that you may have a line from my dearest, my best. O there is no word to convey what my Charles is !—I will write again soon, and in the meantime, fear not for me. I am in a state of bodily health and strength such as you could scarcely imagine possible—and my mind is in peace; the sting of her death is removed from me; nothing remains, but that which will ever remain ;—she is ever before me— every circumstance relating to her passes in unceasing succession before my mind; her loveliness in health !—her heavenliness in sickness ! I desired Angelina to cut off her hair, and keep it for me—some time I will send you a bit. I do not yet trust myself to look at it, nor at her clothes —Angelina has concealed all from me. Adieu, my dearest, dearest Mother ! Pray for me that the grace of God fail not to support me in the resolutions formed in the hour of sorrow ! "

BUNSEN *to* MRS. WADDINGTON.

" O my dear Mother, that you could be a moment present to see yourself how wonderfully F. is supported by God : nobody can believe it, who has not seen it—nobody, I mean, who knows how to appreciate her loss, who has

seen her sufferings, her grief, her despair, and her moments
of agony. . . . . O this angel was beautiful, lovely, in
death as she was in life, only with that expression of quiet
suffering which never left her face in the last six weeks.
It was harder than anything that I could not be with her,
kneel by her bed and gaze on her, only a few stolen
moments! O dearest loveliest face, O mild angelic countenance! now I have felt what it means that a pure
spirit returns to God to be a ministering angel to Him.
There is no pain, no grief in my heart, but a longing,
an irresistibly alluring attraction to think of her, to look
up to her, to pray to be with her! It has been only
after her death that I have told F. how often, particularly in the last six months of her health, I have
pressed her to my heart, and given her suddenly away
because I felt we *could* not keep her, because I felt I loved
her too much, far beyond any other love, and because she
was too like an angel, in beauty and loveliness and still
more in every glance of her soul. You could not give her
any particular character—lively, serious, sanguine, melancholy, she was nothing but love and loveliness."

MADAME BUNSEN *to her* MOTHER.

"*Albano*, 4 *August*, 1821.—My mind is tranquil now,
and I seldom or ever shed a tear. I employ myself in
everything as usual, without effort, and the only thing I
cannot do, is to speak of *her*—the thought is ever present,
but will not bear utterance. We have here a very delightful sitting-room, where my precious boys play about,
and run on the balcony to look at the carts and asses and
mules, that pass along the street, while I sit working or

setting work on a small bed that is arranged as a couch. At twelve o'clock the boys have their dinner and afterwards sleep. I then dine, and lie down for an hour, either to read or to sleep. When the heat of the day is past, we walk out; my favourite walk is the Villa Barberini, which I think my Mother never saw. We return home at sunset, my boys sup, and before I go to bed, I write out something for my Charles, when he is not here,—when he is, he reads to me.

"From the time my child expired, it has become more and more clear to me that she was never intended for me, or for this world : she was, in soul and body, too perfect to dwell here. I may believe myself competent to judge of the comparative merits of children, because I have two others, who always were very dear, and very engaging: but from the first they gave signs of human passions, human imperfections, which she never did,—always contented, always happy, though with more animation, more intelligence, than I ever saw in any other child. No words can convey an idea of her sweetness, her affection to her parents, more especially to me. I can for ever feel her arms clinging round my neck, her face pressed against me—O! blessed be God for having granted her to me, though for so short a time!—nobody that has not had such a child can conceive the joy she was—and there is no joy in this world to be purchased without pain, the one exquisite in proportion to the other. . . . . I have wished, my Mother, since I lost my angel, more keenly than ever, that you had seen her, but then I have felt that it is better as it is :— you grieve for me, O I know how you grieve for me! but had you seen her, you would so have loved her, so have fed upon the sight of her, that you would have had a weight of affliction more in her death, and you have already afflictions enough."

On the 4th of November, the feast of S. Carlo Borromeo, described by Bunsen as "the most venerable of all modern saints, and one of the most respectable of them altogether," the birth of Charles Bunsen brought back something of sunshine to the sorrow-stricken household. The extreme sympathy and interest shown by the Niebuhrs at this time, as well as after the death of Mary, made Madame Bunsen most anxious to efface any unfavourable impression she might have imprinted on her mother's mind at an earlier period of her intercourse with them.

MADAME BUNSEN *to her* MOTHER.

"12 *Dec.*, 1821.—Till I have accomplished the point I am *quite sure* of accomplishing—getting my Mother thoroughly to understand, and value, and admire Mr. Niebuhr, which she cannot do till she is possessed of facts, and details, and explanations, that can never be thoroughly given by letter,—she cannot conceive the pleasure I experienced from the indescribable kindness with which he greeted and congratulated me after the birth of my child."

"*New Year's Day*, 1822.—The first year of severe trial that I ever passed, is closed,—and I begin the new year in comfort of body and mind, such as I never before experienced;—confidence, that if tried, I shall be supported, as I have been. I might have known before, and indeed I ever have known, that it is impossible with God to inflict that which it is impossible to bear; but to have had experience of those supplies of strength from above which I know to be promised to all those who crave them, is of more avail to tranquillize the spirit than any degree of belief. My own dearest Mother, Heaven only knows whether I shall be with you, or still at Rome, at the close of this year! and I am satisfied that circumstances, that is to say, Providence, alone can decide our plans—beforehand, it is impossible to resolve, or even to form a wish, where the dangers and difficulties are so evident on either side.

"Most truly do I thank my Mother for the gifts she has sent to Mrs. Niebuhr. She is indeed very kind to me, and I am sure of her regard. I do not think I have ever mentioned how much I was affected by her manner of greeting me on our first meeting after my return to Rome at the time of Charles's great danger. There was a warmth, an animation of kindness and sympathy that I did not expect from her, however greatly and continually her character has gained upon me, in proportion as I became more acquainted with it;—and it was not a sudden feeling, an emotion of compassion, that was roused in her, for I have experienced in degree the same manner, and observed the same expression of countenance, every time that we have met since."

"21 *Jan.*, 1822.—To show my Mother how well I am, I must tell of the beautiful walk we took yesterday, with *all* the dear children, and she will be able to judge by looking at the map of Rome of my strength, and that of Henry, who walked every step of the way—but of the strength of Ernest, who walked three-quarters of the distance, she could not judge, without *feeling* the weight he has to carry—O if she could but feel it! I know she would delight in his size, however little able to lift him; it is as much as I can do to raise him from the ground, although when he is once up, I can carry him very well on my back.

"We went to the church of S. Pietro Montorio on the Janiculan, passing over the bridge Quattro Capi,—the nurse carried little Charles, who sat up and looked about him all that distance. Henry and Ernest walked like men, the former with his mother, the latter between his father and Angelina, having need of two hands to pull him on. After looking at the prospect, which was indescribably magnificent, in the finest possible weather, and going into the church, we proceeded to the Fontana Paolina, which extremely delighted the children, and the nurse not less, and then to the top of the hill, where we went out at the gate of S. Pancrazio, and returned down the hill on the outside of the walls, re-entered Rome at the Porta Portese, and came by Ripa Grande, and Ponte Quattro Capi, home.

"Mr. Brandis was married on the 2nd of September."

"*Feb.* 13, 1822.—On Monday morning I went with Charles to Thorwaldsen's studio. I had not been for an age, and I saw, with wonder and admiration, his statue of our Saviour—the most difficult object, without doubt, that he ever attempted, and one of the most remarkable proofs of his inexhaustible genius. It was not till two years ago that he ever executed a religious subject, and then, in compliance with the wishes of the Crown Prince of Bavaria, he made a design for a bas-relief of the three Marys at the

Sepulchre which was a complete failure, and he himself felt it to be such, and spoke in a tone of despair of the whole undertaking. Since that time he has been travelling, and doing nothing—but has meditated till he has comprehended the characteristics of that religion : the spirit of which he alas ! has never imbibed ; and the result has been the execution of colossal statues of Christ, of St. Paul and St. Peter, in a style that his best friends amongst judges of the art never expected him to be able to acquire. The church in Copenhagen in which these statues are to be placed is to be built in the form of a basilica—that is to say, like S. Paolo fuori le Mura—only not so large by many degrees. In front is to be a portico like that at the Pantheon, and on the pediment is to be a bas-relief of the Baptist preaching in the Wilderness, of which Thorwaldsen is to make the design, and which he wishes to have executed in terra-cotta, a material more endurable than marble when exposed to the weather. In the inside of the church, in the centre of the tribune, or semicircular apse at the opposite extremity to the entrance, is to be placed the colossal statue of our Saviour, and in niches in the side-walls of the church, statues of the twelve apostles, also of colossal dimensions. Thorwaldsen explains his own intention to have been to represent our Saviour as recalling to the minds of his disciples in all ages what He had done and suffered for them, and inviting them to come to Him : and dreading the appearance of the smallest degree of theatrical effect, he aimed at the utmost simplicity of attitude ; the head is bent forwards, the arms are gently raised and extended on each side, one hand neither higher nor lower, neither more nor less stretched out than the other ;

so that if the consummation of ease, grace, and majesty had not been attained, the figure must be stiff and unmeaning. The countenance is very, very fine—to call it quite satisfactory would be saying too much, but what representation of our Saviour could be so?—to my feelings, this head of Thorwaldsen's is the finest with which I am acquainted, except that by Raphael in the 'Disputa.'* Of other new things I was best pleased with a bas-relief representing Nemesis reading to Jove from a scroll the record of human actions—he listens till his wrath kindles, and he is preparing to cast the thunderbolt. I saw executed in marble the Mercury, and the Hope, which I had seen long ago in clay; I am sure that the Mercury is the finest of Thorwaldsen's works.

"After Thorwaldsen's sculpture in the morning, and an historical-philosophical-poetical discussion with Kestner in the afternoon, how do you think we spent the evening? In seeing the Puppet-show, at the theatre under Palazzo Fiano—and indeed, nothing could be better of its kind. Mr. Pertz† accompanied us, a friend of Baron Stein, whom we very much like.

* Thorwaldsen believed himself to have reached the climax of his powers in his statue of Christ. "I never was satisfied," he said, "with any work of my own till I executed the Christ —and with that, I am alarmed to find that I *am* satisfied; therefore, on the way towards decay."

† George Henry Pertz was agent to the association established by Baron Stein for discovering and collecting unpublished materials of German history. In this cause, to the end of his life, he edited "Monumenta Historiæ Germanicæ." He also wrote the Life of Stein. He was director of the archives at Hanover, and afterwards principal librarian at Berlin. His second wife was Leonora, daughter of Leonard Horner the historian. He died in 1876.

"On Tuesday morning I went to see a large cartoon by one of the three friends who lodge over us, Julius Schnorr von Carolsfeld. The design of the cartoon in question is from Ariosto, and is to make part of a series of paintings in fresco in a room of the Villa Giustiniani, opposite the Lateran Palace, belonging to the Marchese Massimo—the same villa in which Overbeck is painting from Tasso, and Veit (the son of Madame Schlegel) from Dante. Schnorr's cartoon is admirable, and I have indescribable satisfaction in anticipating his complete success in this great undertaking; for I have lately been sorry to see him entirely employed in executing subjects to which his powers are not suited. It is the fashion at present to give orders for nothing but paintings à la Raphael—Madonnas, Magdalens, &c.,—and that in a style in which it is not granted to all those who know how to paint, to succeed. Correctness in drawing the human figure, infinite variety of conception in the representation of the human countenance, great skill in grouping figures and still life, the liveliest fancy in the disposition of ornaments, such as draperies, trees, flowers, fountains and buildings—and more especially, the power of colouring with force, brilliancy, and delicacy—to this rare combination of merits Schnorr lays undoubted claim, but where sublimity of expression is required, he degrades the subject by theatrical sentimentality—and the only consolation for his friends is that he has sufficient understanding and taste to be aware of his failure."

"17 *April*, 1822.—The Pope (Pius VII.) did not give the Benediction on Easter Sunday, nor is he ever likely to give it again; his strength does not return, and it is believed his vital powers are worn out. It was on Easter Sunday that

I first related to my darling Henry the story of our Saviour's life, and sufferings, and resurrection :—and I shall never forget the manner in which he listened, clinging to me closer and closer, and looking up in my face as if he feared to lose a word. It was a natural transition to tell him of his sister, and of the state of the blessed ; and he promised that he would be good, that he might go to ' Gesù Cristo.' "

" 17 *June*.—I hope that the Princess of Denmark (I mean the wife of the Hereditary Prince) is admired in England, and I should be much surprised if she was not, for her person and demeanour appeared to me peculiarly admirable. I thought her very English, but remind-ing one of pictures rather than of life, of those times when the character of the face seemed to be communicated to the dress, not when individuality was lost in fashion. She used at Rome to dress her beautiful chestnut-coloured hair like Sacharissa, but had not features as regular : the tone of her voice is indescribably melodious, and her manner of speaking as agreeable as possible. She is not happy in her marriage, her husband being good for little or nothing, and appearing quite indifferent to her, attractive as she is, now that she is no longer a novelty : though he married her for what is called love ; and she has hitherto longed in vain for the charm a child would give to her existence, submitting with a good grace to what she feels to be so empty and joyless as a life of representation. When Mrs. Niebuhr at her command brought her children to show her, she watched them at play with the most animated delight, but at length burst into tears, saying that she envied everyone that had a child.

" At a ball at Madame Appony's the winter before last,

I was mortified to compare the Princess of Denmark, Therèse de Stein, and a Milanese Donna Camilla Falconieri, with the Englishwomen who were there, although many of them were very pretty, in particular two Miss Howards, but with such a want of individuality, that I should be at a loss to recognise their faces again. I have often attentively contemplated the profile of Therèse de Stein,* in the hope of recalling it, to be able to send it to my mother, but it is no easy undertaking, and it would at last give no idea of her brilliant dark eyes, or of the fine muscles, or, more properly speaking, as yet dimples, of her mouth. I shall wish, but almost fear, to see ten years hence what expression these muscles have assumed. As yet her countenance has only a general cast of seriousness, although a capability of any expression. I should say that she has already been able to form a sufficient notion of trial, to prevent the most disfiguring of all appearances, that of disappointment: and although with youth, health, beauty, riches, the consciousness of being the delight of her father's life, and the only person who has any influence over him, it might be said she must be too happy, she has a source of trial near to her who must successfully 'dash her cup of brilliant joy.' . . . . It might seem strange to write such a number of details of a person my Mother never saw, but it seldom happens to me to see anything that I feel sure would meet with my Mother's unqualified approbation."

"12 *Sept.*, 1822.—Charles is not able to write to you, as he must dine with Prince Henry of Prussia.† That personage I have never before named, yet he has lived in

* Afterwards Countess Kielmannsegge.
† Younger brother of King Frederick William III.

Rome ever since the Neapolitan revolution, and certainly merits mention from singularity. His manner of life is absolute retirement, shutting himself up with his books, and not seeing any of his attendants except at dinner, when it may be his pleasure to dine, but that is not his pleasure oftener than three times a week, when he dines very heartily; the intermediate days he takes nothing but a dish of strong coffee and a mouthful of bread, though wherefore he follows this plan, it has never pleased him to explain. Sometimes he never stirs out of the house for three months, and afterwards takes a fit of walking. He had the latter fit all this summer, and chose the hours between twelve and three for his exercise, probably because at that time of day he was certain not to meet so much as a cat stirring abroad, that could possibly find shelter within doors. He often gives dinners, and listens to conversation with fixed attention, showing approbation and disapprobation, but rarely uttering more than a monosyllable; he once called on Mr. Niebuhr, on his arrival in Rome, but has never called on anybody else, except Cardinal Consalvi, and has never summoned resolution to visit the Pope. He is a man of great learning, and understands a great many languages. He has a universal interest in political affairs, and takes in newspapers from England, France, and Spain, as well as Germany: he has served with distinction in the army, and is said never to have recovered his spirits since he was refused a particular command he had wished to have in the last war. He is advantageously distinguished among German princes by liberality in money-matters, pensioning persons that had been in his service at any part of life, or in any place; always giving, when a claim is made upon him, more than could have been expected of him, and being very careful at the same time to pay his debts. His dinners, as may easily be supposed, are a great penance, but Charles, although he would wish to avoid his presence, says it is impossible to help feeling a degree of attachment to his person.

"Ernest has just asked me—'Chi ti ha dato questo pane tanto buono mama—Iddio o Nonna?'"

Bunsen was first brought into personal contact with his sovereign during a visit which the King of Prussia paid to Rome with his two younger sons, in the autumn of 1822. General Witzleben, the confidential aide-de-camp who accompanied the King on this occasion, had been especially employed and consulted in the construction of the liturgy which, by the King's desire, was then in use at Berlin. To him Niebuhr spoke of Bunsen's studies and interest in the matter, and his communications to his royal master led to intimate conversations at the time on the subject which both had so deeply at heart; and thus laid the foundation of a mutually affectionate regard which seldom has the opportunity of arising between king and subject. It was at this time the intention of Bunsen, without regard to his worldly prospects, to throw up his diplomatic employments entirely, and devote himself altogether to the theological studies, by which he imagined that he could better serve not only his own but future generations. But this plan was fortunately rendered impossible by his duty to his sovereign after his appointment as Counsellor of Legation on the occasion of the King's second visit to Rome as he was returning from Naples, and by his further appointment as Chargé d'Affaires on the departure of Niebuhr from Rome in the following March.

MADAME BUNSEN *to her* MOTHER.

"14 *Nov.*, 1822.—Charles is running every day and all day long after Kings and Princes. I am sure I have reason to long for the King of Prussia's departure, for he is in such a state of good-humour and activity, and is so well entertained with everything, that it is his pleasure to run about from eight o'clock in the morning till dark, with only a short interval for dinner. He leads the way, attended by Mr. Niebuhr and Alexander von Humboldt, and the two Princes follow, attended by Charles, who is often called by Mr. Niebuhr to explain things to the King, in particular the churches, which Mr. Niebuhr says he understands better than himself. Charles has every reason to be satisfied that these royal personages like his company, which is some consolation under the bodily fatigue, waste of time and spirits they occasion. I must complain a little of my misfortunes : I am obliged to get up regularly in the dark, and hurry on some clothes to give Charles his breakfast in time for him to be in attendance at half-past seven ; then I never know what hour to expect him to dinner, for though the King fixes his dinner-time at two o'clock, he is very apt when busily engaged to make his dinner wait. Yesterday however was the worst day; in the course of the morning the King signified to Charles his wish that he should dine with him; they continued so late seeing sights that Charles could not even escape to change his dress, and he had nobody to send to let me know, therefore after waiting and wondering till four o'clock, I dined alone. Charles after his dinner drove about again with the Princes, and then attended them to see the illumination of St. Peter's, and the Girandola. After that was over, he was dismissed, but his labours were not at an end, for the King intending to go next day to Tivoli, and requiring *sixty-four* horses (thirty-two to set off with, and thirty-two to change half way, he and his attendants occupying eight carriages), Charles had to drive about in all directions to rummage out this number of horses, some in one place, some in another; then he went to report to Mr. Niebuhr that all was in order, and lastly, at half-past eleven o'clock, did he get home. At five o'clock this morning he went off to attend his Majesty to Tivoli, whence it is the royal pleasure to gallop back this evening at five o'clock. Charles is very much pleased with the behaviour of the King, who is throughout dignified, intelligent, and rational; and he likes both the Princes, but in particular Prince William, the elder of the two that are here; the Crown Prince is not of the party, but is expected in the course of the winter, and probably likes to travel independent of the King, who keeps his sons in prodigious awe: of the Crown Prince all parties and persons unite to speak in the highest terms."

" 11 *Dec.*, 1822.—The day after I sent my last letter, we had a visit from the King of Prussia, the two Princes, and their suite, to see the view from our windows, but before I give further particulars of the event of that day, I have to tell that the King, two days before his departure north-

wards, appointed Charles Counsellor of Legation, of his
own free grace and favour, without solicitation. This is a
considerable advancement in point of rank, and entitles
Charles to an increase of salary, and the most agreeable
circumstance attending the transaction is, that the King
has never been known to grant a similar favour so suddenly to any person, and the whole of his behaviour has
shown from first to last the very strong impression that
Charles's personal qualities made upon him. He staid at
first ten days in Rome, and three more on his return from
Naples, and each day took more notice of Charles than the
preceding, and the two last days, during dinner, and on
every other occasion, might be said to have conversed with
him alone, although he occasionally spoke to other people ;
this I was told by Colonel von Schack."

"16 *Feb.*, 1823.—As I have already told of my boys
sitting to hear stories in the evening, I must tell of their
present delight ; Ernest begs for the Argonauts, and
Harpies, and the brazen Bulls, and Henry begs for the
Hercules, and the Serpents, and the Lion, and the Hydra ;
these and many other mythological tales Mr. Niebuhr had
written down, in the most charming manner possible, for
his own boy, and we borrowed the manuscript, and I have
been very busy this last month in copying it, whenever I
can find an odd half-hour.

"I had the other evening a long conversation with Prince
Frederic of Hesse Homburg, about his sister-in-law Princess Elizabeth. He is a General in the Prussian service,
and is longer in proportion to breadth and thickness than
anything that ever was seen except a knitting needle, therefore I suppose he must be the very counterpart of his

brother, who is said to be as large as the Princess. He told me that he perceived by my observations on H. R. H.'s pursuits and manner of life in England, that I was acquainted with the interior of the late Queen's house, for they tallied with the Princess's own account of things; and desired to know by what name he should mention me to his sister-in-law. I told him it was better I should name the name of my mother, whom H. R. H. had known in her childhood, and to whom she had ever been very gracious; and he pronounced and *spelt* the name of Port after me, which I thought there was more chance of his recollecting than Waddington. From the wife of Colonel Schack he heard that Princess Elizabeth was universally popular, which is not surprising, and I also heard many of the jokes that have been made about her size; a fat Countess Goltz at Berlin asserted that when one had once made a journey round the Princess, one had had walking enough for the day; also, it was said that the Princess had great difficulty in finding a shawl that reached as far as her shoulders; that it should cover any part of her chest was not to be expected from a shawl."

"4 *April*, 1823.—Mr. and Mrs. Niebuhr left Rome this day se'nnight—and although poor Mrs. Niebuhr worked herself almost to death before her departure in settling and arranging about sale of furniture, as well as packing and preparing for travelling, for four children and her very invalid self, to say nothing of a husband who needs as well as deserves to be taken care of—a vast quantity of business was left for me to complete."

On the 28th of April, 1823, Madame Bunsen gave

birth to her fourth son, Frederick Wilhelm—who lived
only till the following June, when he was laid by his
little sister in the Protestant Burial-ground.

MADAME BUNSEN *to her* MOTHER.

"20 *May*, 1823.—Mr. and Mrs. Niebuhr passed through
Rome ten days ago, on their way from Naples northwards,
never to return; it was a very solemn parting, on many
accounts; Heaven only knows when, where, or under
what circumstances, we shall meet again, or whether we
shall ever again inhabit the same place, as we have done
for above five years, with the possibility of daily intercourse, in which time every successive given period has
slowly but surely drawn the bond closer between us. Mrs.
Niebuhr is going to a country in which she is nearly as
absolute a stranger as I should be (having been born and
bred in Holstein, and having spent only the three first
months after her marriage at Berlin), with many anxious
apprehensions lest a northern climate should prove more
injurious to her husband and children than beneficial to
herself, for Mr. Niebuhr has in Italy in a great measure
recovered his health, and the children have thriven asto-
nishingly in the country of their birth. I must however
rejoice on account of their removal, for this last year at
Rome she appeared dying by inches. She had suffered much
for years without its appearing, but latterly she showed
her sufferings to such a degree, that I hardly think you
would have recognised her, with hollow eyes and cheeks,
her colour gone, and her hair grey. At Naples she experienced some relief from the inexplicable pains she suffers,
and therefore recovered a degree of strength, but the air

of Rome had again an injurious effect, though she was only three days here.

"That most attaching child, Marcus, parted from me in a manner I shall never forget, shedding no tear, uttering no word, but clinging round my neck as if he could not let me go. It is in general more especially melancholy to part from children, because you feel that something in your life is utterly at an end, utterly cut off, for even if you can anticipate a time for becoming again acquainted with the child, that acquaintance will be something new, it cannot be considered on the part of the child as a continuation of the former, for he will nearly have forgotten you in the mean time. That is however a feeling that I have not in the same degree experienced with respect to Marcus; that child has a heart and understanding so extraordinary, that it is impossible not to reckon upon him as upon a person of formed character. He entered with his whole soul into the pleasure of seeing the sea, the ships, Mount Vesuvius, &c., at Naples, but though he anticipated great delight from imbibing new ideas on his northward journey, he was nevertheless very sorry to take leave of Rome. His father took him the last day to the Vatican, and observed that he was continually humming tunes, which he for a time disregarded, but at last said, 'Why are you so inattentive, Marcus? don't you like to see these things?' Marcus did not answer, for his eyes were full of tears, which he would not allow to come down." *

* Marcus Niebuhr was afterwards private secretary to the King, and wrote a book on Babylonian History. He married a Fräulein von Wolzogen of the family of Schiller's wife, and died in 1860. His sister Cornelia still lives (1878) at Weimar, as the wife of Herr Rathgen, President of the Tribunal.

"14 *June*, 1823.—I drove yesterday evening, my own Mother, to the Villa Albani, with all the children. It had rained in the morning, and therefore the smell of the earth and the trees was delicious. I enjoyed that, and the indescribable beauty of the view in the glow of the setting sun, while Henry and Ernest were happy beyond all happiness in riding upon all the sphinxes and lions they could possibly climb upon. Little Charles's happiness was trotting after and admiring his brothers, and trying to get into all the fountains that came in his way. I always recollect when I go to the Villa Albani having run my last race there with Augusta; I hope she recollects that I beat her."

"26 *June*, 1823.—I wish I knew what words to use, to spare my Mother a part of the shock she will feel, on learning that I have been summoned to resign the treasure so lately granted; and that my precious Frederic rests by the side of his angel sister. Be satisfied, my Mother, that I am not only composed, but thankful; thankful that it pleased God to take so soon the being that in so short a time was become so dear, for every week of added life would have added to the pang of parting; thankful, that I was not thus deprived of my little Charles, that infant preserved almost by miracle from the dangers to which he was exposed by my distress and exertions before his birth; thankful, that it was not my first child who was so speedily reclaimed ! . . . . It is certain that this infant had a peculiar look, a look of death, which I now find struck everybody that saw him, and which caused Charles and myself continually to feel (though we did not express the feeling) that we should not be allowed to preserve him: still, it is fortunately so difficult to distinguish a decided anticipation of death from the natural anxiety occasioned by infant life, that I had begun to gather hopes from observing how rapidly he throve, how fat. and active, and animated he became.

"On Tuesday, the 18th June, he completed the fiftieth day of his life, and was perfectly well. I drove to the Villa Poniatowski, and took him with me on the nurse's lap. On the following day he was not well, but not perceiving any reason to apprehend serious illness, I left my little angel, and took my other three treasures to the Corsini gardens, from whence we brought flowers, that I little thought to employ in decking the corpse of my little Frederic! When I returned he was better, and slept till four in the morning, after which came twenty-four hours, of which, my Mother, I could wish not to think and yet I cannot help it. When longing for his release, it was hard to help asking why such an infant must suffer so much, why the combat must last so long, but that involves the question why evil must come—that most needless, most impious question, for it implies a doubt of the perfection of God, and I hope I checked the movement as often as it occurred. When the last breath had been drawn, my Charles and I left the precious remains to the care of Maddalena and Angelina, and lay down for two hours. Afterwards we were even more refreshed by Dr. Schmieder: it is true he could tell us nothing that we did not already know, but he reanimated shrinking convictions. Then Charles proposed that we should go into the fresh air in some garden; and we drove to the Monte Cavallo, and walked in the shady walks of the Pope's garden, and enjoyed the summer breeze.

" When we returned, I went to look at my angel at rest. The look of pain was gone now, all was peace and loveliness. I scarcely left him for the remainder of the day, and there is no describing the sensation (scarcely to be called painful) with which I contemplated that form in the beauty of which I had so delighted in life, from whose earthly development I had promised myself so much : it was a fitly framed vessel for an immortal, early-glorified spirit ! But at night I took leave of it—that was a second separation. I could have wished ever to have kept it there before me. My sweet Henry had been very sympathising during the illness of his little brother, and Ernest also, in proportion to his age. Henry would hardly leave him during the first day of death, and begged that he might go to see him buried, and having heard that he was to be conveyed away early in the morning, woke of his own accord at half-past four, was very devout during the service, and has been particularly good, docile, and affectionate ever since.*

" My Mother, I entreat you not to be distressed about me. I assure you that I am very well, and except when I parted with the poor nurse, whose grief was extreme, and to whom I shall ever feel bound, for having performed her duty with her whole heart, I have not shed tears ; and I have too much to do, and too much left to enjoy, for it to be possible to feel depressed.

* The touching epitaph of the infant children in the Cemetery of Caius Cestius was written by their mother and rendered in Latin by Bunsen. It concludes with the words—"Hi parentibus non dati, at monstrati fuerunt; ut angelorum imaginem, innocentiae ore expressam, grato animo recordantes, beatae eternaeque visionis venturum diem laetiore fide expectarent."

" It is so completely a thing of course, to find in
my Charles everything—comfort, support, sympathy, the
power of re-animating—that it had scarcely occurred to me
to tell my Mother what she has long known. I shall now
conclude, that I may drive out with my boys; we shall try
to get into the vineyard where the ruins of the temple of
Minerva Medica stand; the day is delightful, a fresh north-
west breeze, and the distant prospect as clear as possible
To-night we shall take Henry and Ernest to see the
Girandola: it is Saturday, the 28th of June, the vigil of
St. Peter."

" 18 *July*, 1823.—The destruction of S. Paolo fuori le
Mura, which took place three days ago, has been so unceasingly matter of thought and conversation ever since,
that I can scarcely write of any other subject. My Mother
saw that church only once, and had nobody with her, as I
have had since, to show every part, and enable her to
become attached to the building as I have become; but yet
I am quite sure she will be shocked to know that it has
been seen for the last time, that the fire has spared but
little, and that little left in a state in which it is impossible
to restore, or even preserve it. In proportion as the walls
and columns cool, they crumble and fall in large masses;
and Charles, who made his way in this morning, says that
it is really inexcusable in the guards who are stationed
there to give anybody leave to do so, for it is not possible
to answer for the life of any person that ventures under
the porch. On Tuesday, the 15th, some masons and
plumbers were at work on the roof of the church, which
had long wanted a thorough repair. They were observed
to be drunk when they went up after their dinners, and a

quarrel took place amongst them, in the course of which one
of the plumbers threw his pan of burning charcoal at one
of the masons, and so utterly were they deprived of reason,
that so far from collecting the coals, or in any way guard-
ing against mischief, they did not even bring away the
pan, which has since been found among the ruins : these
facts the culprits have confessed. It was not till two o'clock
in the morning that the monks of the monastery adjoining the church received the alarm from some country-
folk travelling along the road, and as they had to run
to Rome, and rouse the watch to open the city-gate, to
awaken the Governor, and to collect the firemen, two hours
were unavoidably lost before the latter arrived from Rome
with their one engine and their water-carts—so little is the
danger of fire provided against in Rome. It is needless to
say that they came too late to be of any use; till the fire
had accomplished its work in consuming the whole of the
roof, it raged unabated. The greater part, and the finest
of the columns, fell in masses of lime, and more that remain
standing are so calcinated, that they will probably at the
longest only wait for the storms of autumn to be laid pros-
trate. The mosaics of the ninth century are yet standing,
but one of the prodigious columns of white granite that
support the arch on which they are fixed, is split from the
summit to the base. The mosaics produce a wonderful effect,
being now laid open to the glaring sun, whereas they were
formerly dimly discovered in the twilight of the church.
The beautiful tabernacle that covered the high altar, a
work of the thirteenth century, is also yet standing, although
damaged. It was an extraordinary circumstance, that on
the night of the burning of St. Paul's we went to bed at

ten o'clock, having for a fortnight before daily complained
that one cause or other had regularly kept us up till midnight. Had we that night staid up, from our high situation in the Capitol we could not have failed to have seen
the fire, and Charles would have taken care to have routed
guards and firemen. That old dunce Laura, who lives in
the apartments over us, did see the fire at midnight, and
had not sufficient wisdom or activity to give the alarm,
although she knew that two years ago Charles had not
thought it too much trouble to give assistance in saving
some hay-barns at that hour, which were perceived to be
blazing. But it is perhaps in a double sense useless to
regret that assistance was not more speedily sent, for when
in this climate at the driest season of the year, a roof
entirely composed of wood, and at the lowest computation
a thousand years old, had begun to burn, I cannot conceive
how even London fire-engines and firemen could have
stopped the progress of the flames.

"I am sure my Mother will be grieved at the extraordinary accident by which the few remaining days or months
which the venerable Pope could have had to live will probably be abridged. Happily he does not suffer pain. The
accounts given of the delirium which followed his accident*
are quite affecting; he continually recited psalms and
prayers, and the only difficulty his attendants had was in
preventing his attempting to get up and say mass; he
always knew Cardinal Consalvi and never failed to answer

---

* On the 6th July the aged Pius VII., who was far advanced in
the twenty-third year of his pontificate, had received a fatal injury
from a fall in his own room in the Quirinal Palace—the same room
which, on the same day, fourteen years before, had witnessed his
seizure by General Radet.

him rationally, but when not spoken to by him, he returned
to his psalms."

"29 *August*, 1823.—The death of Pius the Seventh has
made a great impression on the children, when they are
at play they often begin to talk about him; 'quanto io
volevo bene al Papa! e adesso è morto, non vede più,
l'hanno messo sotto terra; ma è andato in cielo, da
Iddio, e da Gesù Christo, è vero Mama?—e c'è pure lì zia
Emilia, e la sorellina, e il fratellino.' I took them to see
the remains of the Pope conveyed by night from Monte
Cavallo to St. Peter's, and they were perhaps the only
persons not disappointed by the spectacle. I had supposed
that the procession, consisting as I anticipated of priests,
and monks, and friars, and cardinals, chaunting and carrying torches, could not fail to produce an impressive effect :
but there were neither monks, nor friars, nor cardinals, and
only half-a-dozen priests; the remainder of the train was
made out of detachments of troops, and four cannon and ammunition waggons; and the torches were so thinly strewed,
that in narrow streets where the light of the moon could not
penetrate, the procession seemed to be groping its way in
the dark. The most plausible explanation of this most
unpontifical manner of constituting a funeral procession, is
that in times past, when there were so many popes of an
utterly different character to that of Pius the Seventh, pre-
cautionary measures for defending the corpse against the
apprehended marks of just abhorrence on the part of the
populace were absolutely necessary; it being well known
that a large band, after having been disappointed in their
intentions against the remains of Paul the Fourth, of the
Caraffa family, proceeded to knock off the head of one of

his statues, and after parading it about the streets, threw it into the Tiber.

"The remains of Pius the Seventh lay in state one day at the Quirinal, and three days at St. Peter's, but only for a few hours of that period was the face really visible, having been afterwards covered with a mask. I had wished to have seen his countenance in the serenity of death, but was prevented going when it could be seen. Although so advanced in age, and reduced in strength, Pius the Seventh had a hard struggle to enter into his rest; his death, after life's longest date, was similar to that of my blessed infant on the threshold of existence; his chest continued to pant with convulsive strength, after every other vital function had ceased! On Sunday the 17th (it was on Wednesday the 20th that he was released), he said to his physicians, ' Perchè fate tutte queste cose? io vorrei morire, sento bene che Iddio mi vuol ricchiamare ': and till speech failed him, he was heard to utter supplications for release. He was often delirious, and his ravings were those of devotional exercises, from which no voice but that of Consalvi could rouse him. Consalvi watched by him for the last three nights, as well as days, though his own state was obviously so precarious, that it is inconceivable how he can have survived his fatigue and agitation : he twice fainted in the course of the last night, and could hardly be brought away from the corpse. It might seem to many people absurd to sympathise in the grief of a prime-minister for the death of his sovereign ; but I know not why one should be denied the satisfaction of supposing the grief of Consalvi to spring from a legitimate cause ; to have lived more than three and twenty years in the confidence of such an individual as Pius the Seventh without becoming attached to him, would have required the insensibility of vice or folly; and Consalvi is neither a hard nor a weak man; he labours under the misfortune of habitually mistrusting his fellow-creatures, but there are many instances to prove that where sufficient evidence has been given of moral excellence, he is as capable of doing justice to it as any other intelligent being.

"The obsequies are to continue till the ninth day from the transportation of the body to St. Peter's, and the day after their termination, the 2nd September, the cardinals will be enclosed in conclave—literally, for all the entrances to the Quirinal are walled up, and provisions for the cardinals and their servants are put in through holes in the wall, which holes are sentinelled by prelates, to prevent communication; and yet, with all these precautions, there never yet was a conclave in which the state of parties did not become public before it closed. There are persons who assert that there are as many candidates as cardinals, but certain it is that on the most moderate computation there are not less than eight '*che passeggiano*,' as the Romans call it, that is, who seek after the Papacy, wherefore a tedious conclave is to be apprehended. I wish they might elect the Pope in time to allow us a breath of fresh air at Frascati before the winter; Charles will hardly think himself at liberty to move as long as the conclave lasts, and to us it would be no pleasure to go without him."

"20 *Sept.*, 1823.—On Monday, the 1st September, I attended in St. Peter's the last and most solemn requiem-service for the deceased Pope, and was much gratified; the greater part of it took place in that chapel into which I went twice with my Mother to hear vespers after our arrival in Rome. I sat in the gallery appointed for the chiefs of the mission and their wives; all other persons, strangers or not (the good days of Cardinal Consalvi being past) might take their chance as they could in the body of the church, which was on this occasion literally full, and filled with all that variety of costume which gives such a peculiar effect to a Roman crowd. Into the chapel nobody was allowed to enter, except the cardinals and prelates; the service was therefore undisturbed, the buzz of the multitude seeming more distant than it was. After the conclusion of the mass, in which the exquisite requiem of Pittoni was sung in even greater perfection than usual, the ceremony of absolution was performed five times, by five several cardinals; for Pius the Seventh as Pope, as Cardinal, as Archbishop, as Priest, and as Deacon; the five cardinals went in procession into the body of the church, followed by the papal singers, who performed a passage of a psalm or an anthem, after each absolution. These exquisite pieces of music were heard in perfection where we sate, but were nearly lost to persons who, though nearer, stood in the confusion of the crowd. The next day, we went to the apartments of Cardinal Consalvi at the Palace of the Consulta, opposite the palace of Monte Cavallo, to see the cardinals walk in procession into conclave, and it was one of the really fine sights to be seen. The piazza was as full as it could hold of people, and two lines of soldiers formed a passage for the cardinals. In the centre the two majestic statues, with the obelisk between them, appeared more colossal than ever, from the opportunity given of measuring them with human dimensions. Just

before them there is now a noble fountain, formed of the
enormous granite crater which my Mother may remember
lay broken in two pieces under the Temple of Peace the
winter she was in Rome: the water, springing into the air,
and falling into a lake rather than bason, glowed and
sparkled in the sun's rays, while the statues stood aloft
with their shady side towards us, and casting a long shadow
over the crowd; behind, the fine cypresses rising above
the walls of the Colonna garden, and the cupola of St.
Peter's in the distance, completed a picture, which as to
forms, lights, shades, and colours, was exclusively peculiar
to Rome.   The cardinals walked two and two, from a little
church at the other extremity of the summit of the Quirinal,
with one of the Guardia Nobile on each side, and preceded
by all the attendants who were to be shut up with them
during the conclave, also by the singers of the papal chapel,
who performed the *Veni Creator Spiritus;* the effect of this
might have been as fine as possible, but a noisy and disso-
nant military band at the close of the procession disturbed
all.   Within the first three hours of the entrance of the
cardinals, the diplomatic body, and the ecclesiastics and
nobiltà, are allowed to visit them, and Charles was much
amused to hear the various ways of expressing the compli-
ments of etiquette on the occasion; each several person
wishes each several cardinal a happy conclave, concluding
with some expression to signify the hope of seeing the
cardinal next time in a different dress, that is, as Pope.
The votes of the cardinals are collected twice every day,
and within a few days after their entrance they were disturbed in this operation by the discovery of a profane
spectator, namely, of an owl, which had entered through

the chapel window. With much trouble and exertion the cardinals contrived to drive the bird of wisdom from their assembly, but not without damage to the panes of the chapel window, to repair which damage became matter of much consultation. Should it be done in broad daylight, it was feared many strange suppositions as to the cause might ensue, and that it would appear as if the cardinals had quarrelled, and thrown their inkstands at each other's heads; wherefore it was judged prudent to issue orders to their Eminences' plumber and glazier to proceed with ladder and lantern at dead of night to replace the broken panes. One piece of policy however was forgotten, that of giving notice to the sentinels, who, as it happened, were not asleep when the work was commenced, and suspecting that incendiaries were coming to destroy the whole conclave, were upon the point (as it is said, but that is certainly a calumny, the Papal muskets never being arranged for murderous purposes) of firing upon the workmen, when the matter was explained to them. I give the story as one of those current in Rome, but cannot vouch for its accuracy, any farther than the circumstances of the operation by midnight. One of the jokes to which the story has given rise is truly Italian—that the owl must have been 'lo Spirito Santo mascherato.'

"From what transpired in the first week, it was feared that Cardinal Cavalchini would have the majority of votes, and the Romans were in a great fright, for it used to be his custom to declare during Lent that if ever he was Pope, he would erect a gallows before every public-house, and hang first those who ate and secondly those who cooked anything but meagre diet on a fast-day : and to persons who came to him on business, he used to give notice that he was not in a good humour, or disposed to attend to them, by threatening that if they did not instantly retire, he would throw them down the staircase, or out of the window. He was for a short time governor of Rome, when by acts of tyranny corresponding to these 'façons de parler,' he made himself deservedly hated; and yet, such is the bigotry of a certain set of cardinals, that he has obtained votes merely because it is certain that he will rather burn than conciliate heretics: however, there is no danger that he should be Pope, for even if it were possible that he should obtain a sufficient number of votes, he would without doubt be excluded by the veto which by long custom is allowed to the three courts of Austria, France, and Spain. Cardinal della Somaglia is reckoned likely to succeed, and he would be a very respectable choice: but according to the example of latter conclaves, the fortunate candidate is never found among those who at the beginning or towards the middle of the period of conclave collect the greatest number of votes : two or three parties in general mutually defeat each other's views, till the patience of all is exhausted, and then they all agree to choose an individual, obnoxious to none, but who has not been the peculiar choice of any.

"It is an indescribable gain to me to have now the daily use of a carriage, for if I had to drag my three boys out walking, as I did two of them last summer (Charles then gave me little trouble, being carried by his nurse) I should not very often get out of the house, having eighty-two steps to descend, and then the hill of the Capitol, both of which must be re-ascended when we return tired from the walk and the heat. . . . . My letter is interrupted by my having to interfere with Ernest's resolute determination to help the archangel Michael with his fist to chastise the devil, for my two big boys have got a great picture-book, reared up against my couch, containing engravings of the noble compositions of Luca Signorelli at Orvieto, with which the children are always greatly struck."

" 8 *Oct.*, 1823.—On the day of the election of Pope Leo the Twelfth,* Sunday, 28th September, we went to St. Peter's, and had the pleasure of standing two hours and a half to see him carried in, and placed to sit upon the high-altar, to be *adored* (that is the literal expression) by the cardinals, during the Te Deum. M. d'Italinsky† remarked on this most extraordinary ceremony, 'Il est vrai que je suis schismatique, et n'ai pas le droit de juger des choses catholiques : mais ce qui me parait extraordinaire, c'est que le Pape a mis le séant lá ou l'on met Jésus Christ.' We afterwards had a still closer view of the Pope as he drove away from St. Peter's, and were struck with the contrast between his emaciated features and death-like colour, and the brilliancy of his eyes, and almost too youthful animation of his countenance : but his is a face which can only by contrast recall the venerable visage of Pius VII. : in looking at him I felt that the sight as it were slid down his face as from the sharp extremities of a mass of ice, not finding a resting-place : not that the Pope is plain—on the contrary it is easy to believe what is asserted, that he was twenty years ago a very handsome man.

" It is impossible to deny that the first measures of the

* Cardinal Annibale della Genga.
† Russian Minister at Rome.

new Pope's government have been wise and salutary, if the execution only proves suitable to the design; they have consisted in the remission of taxes, and diminution of expenses. The new Secretary of State is a very respectable man, both as to understanding and character, but it is feared he will not at the age of eighty long endure the weight of business. The Pope was crowned last Sunday, the 5th, and the spectacle was really magnificent; we had full opportunity of enjoying it, being amongst the few entitled to posts of honour: there were no places reserved except for the Corps Diplomatique, the present Pope being resolved to do away with the long prevalent abuse of giving as it were exclusive attention to strangers: it is said *veils* are to be enforced with great strictness, and even that hats are to be prohibited in churches."

" 31 *Oct.*, 1823.—For the latter half of this month the weather has been beyond description vivifying, and we have reason to be thankful for having been able to make the most of it: we have daily spent several hours in one beautiful spot or another, and the revival of spring-verdure in inanimate nature, and of carnival-merriment in animate, has completed the effect of weather and prospect. Every tolerable afternoon at this season of the year, every villa, vineyard, and garden to which it is possible to obtain access, and the roadside to a certain distance out of every gate of the city, is full of people of the lower and middle classes, and most certain it is that general merriment has a most inspiriting effect, when one has no weight on the heart to counterbalance its influence. The marked character given to the different periods of the year is one of the things that I shall most miss when I am no longer in

Rome ; and only those who have experienced the effect of
the annually recurring mandate, by all understood, by none
pronounced, to be serious at one time, and gay at another,
can be aware how far this apparently arbitrary custom is
from being frivolous in itself. Among the places that
my Mother knows, we have been in Villa Pamfili, Villa
Albani, the garden of the Vatican, and Villa Borghese :
nothing out of Paradise was ever more exquisite than
the Villa Albani, in the sun and air of last Sunday.
Among places that my Mother does not know, we have
enjoyed none more than the vineyards on the side of the
hill behind the garden of the Vatican, and another situated
within the ruins of the once magnificent Villa Barberini,
on a little hill between St. Peter's and the Aventine, from
whence one of the finest panoramas might be made. We
have also been on Monte Mario, where my Mother knows
the cypress-avenue. What I regret continually when I go
to spots in Rome which my Mother has visited, is that she
should have seen so few, if any of them, in the degree of
beauty in which I have known them ; the splendour of the
summer-light and colouring is needed even by the scenes
of Italy. I recollected the other day by the lake in the
Villa Borghese how chilling the wind was when I was
there with my Mother, and wished she had experienced the
charm of the scene, in sunshine and stillness.

"We have usually been a numerous party, for as Dr.
Schmieder is on the point of departure, we have made a
point of enabling him and his wife to see as much as possible of places scarcely accessible to them without a carriage; and as they have two children, whom they as little
like to leave as I like to leave mine, you will easily

imagine that it was both convenient and agreeable that Charles should on such occasions go on horseback, there being five children in the carriage, one merrier than the other. My little Charles is always the best behaved, for however lively by nature, he always in a carriage sits quite still, watching the monkey-tricks of the others; in a garden he helps to play, but is very good, except that he expects his own Mother to carry him, and will not allow anybody else to perform that office."

CHAPTER VII.

THE CAPITOLINE COLONY.

"Good, the more
Communicated, more abundant grows."
MILTON, *Par. Lost.*

IN the preceding letters, allusion has often been made
to different members of the colony of German
artists in Rome, of which Cornelius and Overbeck were
long the guiding spirits. Dissatisfied with the state of
art in Germany, and participating strongly in the
religious reaction which took place at the beginning of
this century against the unbelief and revolution of the
last, they had come to settle in the Eternal City, in the
hope of initiating there an art-future for the Germans.
Being essentially *outline-men*, in opposition to the mere
colourists, the artists at this time went hand in hand
with the sculptors, whose leader and king was Thorwaldsen.

During Bunsen's residence in Rome, the German
painters and sculptors included Cornelius, Overbeck,
Koch, Führich, Veit, Schnorr, Wilhelm and Rudolph
Schadow, Wolff, Schwanthaler, and Kaulbach.

Niebuhr and Bunsen considered that amongst the living occupants of Rome in their time, the German artists alone had any worth; and that in their society, as far as their sphere reached, they could sometimes transport themselves into a better world.* The catholicism of Overbeck and the two Schadows excluded many subjects of conversation; and, besides Schnorr, Theodore Rhebenitz, a young student from Lübeck, the Tyrolese Koch—"an eccentric, petulant man, full of just thoughts and bitter sarcasms"—and Platner—"made a painter by an unlucky accident,—whereas nature intended him for a scholar and historian"—were perhaps most intimate in the circle of Niebuhr and Bunsen. "That the modern German school alone had struck out the right path, and was pursuing the proper aim, could not but be recognised by Niebuhr, who had already so early perceived and admired in the great historical artists, from Giotto to Raphael, the compeers of the ancient Hellenic schools of art,—brethren in spirit of Dante and Goethe. In spite of the individual defects and incompleteness of the early works of this modern school, Niebuhr perceived in its founders and their productions the vital principle which animated them in their opposition to the spirit of the age, and had confidence in that creative power which had united itself with a clear insight and a determined will." †

* See Bunsen's Essay on Niebuhr as a diplomatist at Rome, in the *Lebensnachrichten*.

† See Niebuhr's Letters. 1816.

The great works of the modern German school are now to be found in Munich and Berlin. Two important examples, however, remain in Rome. The house of the Zuccheri (64 Via Sistina) has a room decorated with frescoes by Cornelius, Overbeck, Veit, and Schadow, the order having been given by the Prussian consul Bartholdi, uncle by marriage of Mendelssohn. A room in the Casino Massimo, near St. John Lateran, is a more important work ; Cornelius and Overbeck were employed upon it, but the former was obliged to throw up his engagement for the sake of making designs for the Glyptothek, the latter by ill-health. The casino, however, contains a beautiful ceiling painted by Veit with visions from the Paradiso,* and an entrance hall by Schnorr: the whole was finished by the inferior hands of Führich and Koch.

The first settlement of the German artists in Rome was at the Convent of Sant' Isidoro, where they lived for their art, generally without any system of worldly prudence or reflection. "Cornelius is very poor," writes Niebuhr on Christmas Eve, 1816, "because he works for his conscience and his own satisfaction, and purchasers who would or could measure their remuneration by the same standard are not to be found."

But after the Bunsens settled at the Palazzo Caffarelli, the attraction of their society and kindness, the beauty of the situation, and its comparative economy,

* There is a noble fresco by Veit in the side chapel of the Church of the Trinità de' Monti.

drew into their immediate neighbourhood many of the artists who would now rather be sought in the Via Margutta and the streets near the strangers' quarter. The little German colony upon the Capitoline Hill then occupied almost an insular position in the centre of Rome. It was a world within a world. A bond of mutual kindness and sympathy seemed to draw the dwellers on the Capitol into a great family, which regarded Bunsen as its head.

One of the most valued residents on the Capitol for five years had been the excellent chaplain Schmieder, who left Rome in the autumn of 1823, to undertake a master-ship in the great public-school of Pforta near Naumburg in Prussian Saxony. His departure was greatly felt by the Bunsens as a present loss, though his future post seemed to promise an amelioration of the trial of parting with his boys, when it should be necessary to send them to a distant school for educa-tion. The successor of Schmieder in the chaplaincy at Rome was Richard Rothe, who was afterwards Pro-fessor of Theology at the University of Heidelberg, and who there continued a friendship with the Bunsen family, which had its strong foundation in the inti-macy of Roman life.*

Amongst the friends whose lives at this time became enwoven with those of the Bunsens, were the Baron Heinrich von Arnim and his charming wife, who were twice at Rome in 1823 on their passage to and from

* Dr. Richard Rothe died at Heidelberg, August 13, 1867.

Naples, where he was attached to the Prussian Legation, meetings which resulted in the almost parental
kindness, afterwards shown by these valued friends in
the north, to the sons of Bunsen, when sent away from
home for their school-education. In 1824, another
intimacy was founded with General von Radowitz, a
devout Roman Catholic, who in that year accompanied
Prince Augustus of Prussia to Rome, and who then
became, as it were, domesticated in the home-circle of
the Bunsen family. "On later occasions, when Bunsen was summoned by his royal master for consultation
from England, he may be said to have crossed the
track of Radowitz, as he was called upon in more than
one instance to consider a subject, and give an opinion,
in matters previously submitted to Radowitz by the
King; but, however various may have been the im-
pulses given by the two favourites, naturally so different, and however varying the lines that each may have
drawn over the chart of the royal lucubrations, it
would not appear that jealousy or mistrust had ever
arisen between them; so strong was the conviction in
each of the integrity and absence of all party-views or
of any crooked line of policy in the other."*

In the month of December, 1823, the thoughts of
Madame Bunsen were more than usually carried back
to Llanover by the marriage of her younger sister
Augusta—in infancy and early childhood an object of
her tenderest affection—to Mr. Hall of Abercarne and

* "Memoirs of Baron Bunsen," i. 233.

Hensol Castle, afterwards Sir Benjamin Hall and
Lord Llanover. The attachment which preceded this
marriage had commenced as boy and girl, years before
Mr. Hall attained his majority. After his marriage
he purchased a portion of the old Llanover estate,
which his father-in-law had never been previously able
to obtain, on which were the picturesque remains of an
ancient mansion called "the Court." On this newly-
purchased property, Madame Bunsen heard with constant interest during the next few years, that a third
Llanover mansion was rising within sight of her old
home, her brother-in-law having decided to make the
place to which his wife was so deeply attached his permanent residence, and Mr. Waddington having made
arrangements by which his eldest daughter, whose fate
seemed indissolubly connected with Germany, would
receive the value of the moiety of his landed property
after his death and that of her mother.

MADAME BUNSEN *to her* MOTHER.

"8 *Jan.*, 1824.—My own dearest Mother, I have begun
the new year with a degree of cheerfulness of spirit which
I would not by any considerations contrive to lessen, wherefore I have allowed myself to enjoy unrestrained a feeling
which I am thankful to say grows upon me every year, of
confidence, not in the prosperity of life, but in the power
of going through, with God's assistance, whatever life may
bring: going through, not as a beast of burden, groaning
under the weight imposed, but as a joyful bearer of the
ark of the sanctuary: human strength alone is as insuffi-

cient to support the weight of a feather as of a mountain, but with that aid which is ever granted to them that ask, the mountain will not be more oppressive than the feather.

"I have some new acquaintance this winter, my own Mother, who are people I know you would like : General Dörnberg, his wife (who is a niece of Count Münster's), their son, and two daughters.* The general has in several instances in the war shown himself quite a hero, and belonged to the Duke of Wellington's staff at the battle of Waterloo. It may truly be said that in person, manners, and conversation, he most completely answers his reputation ; so fine a figure, or so commanding a countenance, with such handsome features and mild expression, I am sure I never saw : his manner has the dignified seriousness of a thorough English gentleman, but at the same time a degree of warmth and cordiality which is in England more to be found in the lower classes than in those of polished exterior ; but which I cannot but believe must also have existed among English gentlemen and gentlewomen in better times, when the gregarious mixture of all conditions in society had not compelled the higher classes to be habitually armed at all points in defence of their dignity. Madame de Dörnberg has the remains of much beauty, or (to quote an expression of M. de Lageard) she was probably "plutôt excessivement jolie que belle ; " she is a thoroughly pleasing and well-bred woman, and the whole family have shown me from the first a kindness of manner that has truly gratified me.

"Of General Dörnberg I must tell you an anecdote.

* General Dörnberg was at Rome for the health of his only son, who died there July 17, 1824.

After the battle of Leipzig, when Davoust was retreating towards Hamburg, General Morand was commanded by him to collect contributions in Hanover: he occupied with a force of four thousand troops the fortified town of Lune-burg, and kept as prisoners there the richest citizens of the town and country-gentlemen of the neighbourhood, from whom he had extorted by threats all they had to give, but whom he afterwards sentenced to be shot on a given day, provided they did not procure him in addition a sum of which it was not possible they could furnish a single farthing. General Dörnberg received intelligence of the sentence only four and twenty hours before it was to have been put into execution: he was forty-five English miles distant, in a country in which the roads were seldom good, and at that season, the end of October, after heavy rains, nearly impassable. His force consisted of fifteen hundred troops of the Landwehr, which answers to militia; nevertheless he formed his resolution, and proposed to his small band to make a desperate effort to march to Lune-burg to liberate the prisoners. His troops assented with acclamations, the forced march was commenced, and com-pleted just as the night fell which was to be the last of the prisoners' lives. There was no time for a moment's repose after so violent an exertion, General Dörnberg in-stantly stormed the fortifications; the French supposing by the desperate courage with which they were assailed that their antagonists must have been supported by a powerful army, and dispirited by the fall of their commander Morand, gave way with precipitation, and left the town: when General Dörnberg and his gallant band took possession of it, and found the graves already dug in which seventy individuals, most of them fathers of families, were to have been interred after having been shot, at five o'clock in the morning!"

"28 *Jan.*, 1824.—Of the many things of which I have to write, the principal is the death of Consalvi, who was taken off by fever very suddenly, just six months and four days after his venerable master, but whose life for the last year had been matter of wonder, such was his complication of sufferings, while his incessant exertion of body, and unavoidable agitation of mind, would have been sufficient to have exhausted a man in health. His conduct since the sovereign power fell from his hands has been perfect; there has not been an instance of meanness, not a symptom of querulousness or discontent, he has been throughout dignified, courageous, and consistent, although the party that throughout his reign was adverse to him has taken care to put the strength of his mind to the test; not that the Pope has suffered himself to be made their instrument to that effect, on the contrary, although circumstances had occurred to render him and Consalvi decidedly adverse to each other when they were equals, on his elevation he gave a strong proof of his just estimation of the character and principles of Consalvi, by bestowing upon him the situation of Chief of the College of Propaganda Fede, a post of honour and of influence, to the boundless astonishment of most of his own most zealous supporters. After Consalvi had received extreme unction, about two hours before his death, he gathered sufficient strength to desire that the Pope might be informed that he lay at the point of death, and entreated his benediction; the Pope was himself ill in bed, but received the message with emotion.

and despatched Cardinal Castiglione to confer the requested benediction in his name, and Consalvi was still in a state of consciousness when the Cardinal came. I went with Charles to look at him ' ere the first day of death was past ; ' and his aspect was indescribably affecting ; his features were always too fine to be fit for the company-expression which they were most generally made to assume, as if to conceal the conflict of emotions within ; but now that all pain and passion had ceased, it seemed as if the soul shed more of its influence when its presence was removed. Yesterday, Charles and I, with Dr. Nott, made our way into the crowded Church of San Marcello, to attend the obsequies, which were performed impressively by Cardinal Bertazzoli, the personal friend of Consalvi ; and I was more than ever affected by the Dies Iræ of Pittoni."

" 19 *Feb.*, 1824.—Besides several balls, I have been lately at a very pretty fête, given on Madame d'Appony's birthday, at which a French comedy and a vaudeville were acted by her friends. A niece of Madame Récamier * played the part of a soubrette with such extreme grace and animation, and spoke French with that inimitable charm, possessed only by some French women, so that the rest of the performers would have been wise not to have admitted her amongst them, to set off their defects, for they acted and spoke French *very well*, when she was not on the stage. Between the two pieces were represented tableaux, and I had thus an opportunity of seeing for the first time what everybody has so long heard of. The charade which was to be represented was *Délire*. To

* Afterwards Madame Lenormand.

signify the first syllable, *Dé*, a set of players at dice, from a picture of Paul Veronese, were represented in very picturesque dresses, the wife and children of the principal player, forming a side group, being the beautiful Princess Razumoffsky and the two little Apponys. The second tableau was *Lyre*, Sappho playing on the lyre, surrounded by Grecian nymphs, a collection of magnificent beauties. Sappho was Lady Frances Leveson Gower—a statue of Parian marble, with limbs and features of the finest workmanship : the nymphs were Mrs. Dodwell; a resplendent Miss Bathurst; Miss Walker, a daughter of General Walker's, with a fine, intelligent, true English face of the right sort—the Mrs. Hutchinson sort; a perfectly lovely Italian, of the name of Bischi; and others. Then, to represent *Délire* all together, King Saul played pantomime, with Jonathan and Michal, and David sang to him—what do you think—a scene of Rossini's, from the Lady of the Lake! The Princess Razumoffsky looked very handsome as Michal, but the whole of this pantomime was to my perceptions very absurd. At this fête I saw Madame Récamier, who has long been in Rome, but who keeps very much to herself ; she is still handsome, large—but not out of shape ; and she has a good and mild expression of countenance. She is a person of whom everybody speaks well, although she has for years had no riches wherewith to buy ' golden opinions.' "

" 1 *April*, 1824.—The week before last, I may fairly say all Rome, all nations, classes, and conditions, were occupied by the loss of Miss Bathurst, the beautiful girl whom I mentioned in one of my letters as contributing to form a tableau at Madame d'Appony's. She was riding

out with an uncle and aunt, and the Duc de Laval-Mont-
morency. The latter offered to guide the party, and
accordingly conducted them along a road, or rather narrow
foot-path, beyond the Ponte Molle, having on one side the
Tiber, and on the other a high steep bank. He got off
his horse, and advised the others to do the same, but Miss
Bathurst preferred remaining on her horse, saying she
could trust to his quietness. The way every step becoming
narrower, her uncle became alarmed for her safety, and
in order to secure her, attempted to lead her horse; the
horse threw up his head, as many horses do when seized
by the bridle from beneath, and at the same moment his
hind feet slipped down the shelving and undermined
bank.—He struggled in vain to recover himself, the bridle
naturally broke with his weight, Miss Bathurst fell back-
wards into the water, and the horse over her; her uncle
sprang into the water, but while he swam about in vain,
she was seen by the bystanders to rise, and then she
disappeared for ever:—and though the most active search
was at once commenced by boatmen high and low in the
river, the corpse has not been found. Her mother is at
Turin; her father in the year 1809 was travelling with
despatches through a part of the Prussian dominions
occupied by the French, when he suddenly disappeared,
and no particulars ever have been obtained of his end,
nor has a trace been found of his corpse, the probable
conjecture being that he was murdered by the French for
the sake of the despatches:—singular that both father
and daughter should thus suddenly be summoned from
life, and their remains be consigned to the elements, without the rites of Christian burial. I could not help relating

the story, because the fate of Miss Bathurst has dwelt on
my mind, she having been a thing I delighted to watch,
as much as I could without ill-breeding, whenever I had
an opportunity of seeing her. She was not only more
complete in respect to beauty than anybody I ever met
before, but she had an expression of animated delight in
everything she saw, a freshness and fullness of youth and
health, with an utter absence of self-consciousness, that
made a most engaging contrast to the majority of fashionable beauties. I have mentioned her before as deficient
in expression,—that certainly was the case, but in her it
was scarcely to be called a want, everything about her
bespoke the freshness of existence, untouched as yet by
care, sorrow, or passion. The most dazzling complexion
and colour were relieved by dark hair, and animated by
dark eyes; and fine, full-grown proportions of figure were
rounded off by just the right degree of flesh, and harmo-
nised by natural ease and unstudied grace.

"The Duchess of Devonshire* died three days ago, and
though I cared little about her when living, I am thankful
to know that she expired in faith and peace. She sent for
Dr. Nott † three days before her death, and assured him
that she was 'perfectly composed,' that she had offended
greatly, but that she had repented, and that it had been
her habit of mind for years to seek pardon through Christ,
through whose merits and intercession she could alone
hope to obtain it. She has had cause to bless the memory

* Elizabeth, widow of the fifth Duke of Devonshire and daughter of
the fourth Earl of Bristol. Her first husband was John Thomas
Foster, Esq.

† Dr. Nott, Canon of Winchester, remarkable for his devotion to
the Fine Arts, was an intimate friend of the Bunsen family.

of her mother ; * had not notions of religion been instilled in childhood, after the life she has led, she would hardly have been able to imbibe them."

"24 *April*.—I three days ago saw a bas-relief of Thorwaldsen's, only just designed, about which all the world is mad. It is the Sale of Love, quite original—but that it is needless to particularise. First of all, beginning on the right hand, is a market-basket full of Cupids, packed one over another like chickens in the Roman market; and next the extremity of the marble, stand a girl of about twelve years old, and a boy about seven, touching and feeling and peeping, with vacant, indifferent curiosity, in utter innocence and ignorance as to the nature of that sort of fowl: on the other side of the basket stands a girl, who has taken possession of a Cupid, and holds him up on high, but the fellow has no fancy to stay with her, and is stretching his arms and legs, and fluttering his wings to go to a sitting girl, who with extended hands is inviting him to come. Next stands another female figure, hugging her Cupid, who is giving her the softest kisses in the world ; then comes a great sulky girl, walking away from the basket, looking vacantly before her, and swinging her purchase by his wings at her side, like a hen bought at market. Next is a man, sitting on the ground, with his elbow resting on his knees, and his head bent down, in listless endurance, while just on the nape of his neck sits a saucy fellow, looking triumphantly round, as if to bid defiance to all efforts that may be made to shake him off. Finally, over the head of the last, a Cupid is flying away, after

* Elizabeth, daughter of Sir Jermyn Davers, Bt.

whom a decrepid old man is hobbling on a stick, with his hand stretched out after the fugitive. Another recent work of Thorwaldsen is the bust of Consalvi, which is inconceivably fine ; there is no perfection in the bust, either as to form or expression, which was not in the living countenance, and yet the countenance in life seldom appeared so full of everything that is good, great, intelligent and energetic : but the marble cannot give the brilliant and penetrating eye, which in Consalvi was such a distinguishing feature."

" 12 *May*, 1824.—We have spent four delightful days at Tivoli, which place was more magnificent in verdure and vegetation than I had ever seen it. We left Rome early in the morning and arriving at twelve, went immediately to the Grotto of Neptune, and after dinner to the Villa d'Este, where the magnificent cypresses have diminished in number since my last visit. The next morning we set off after breakfast to accomplish the Giro. My Mother will remember the beautiful walk that is thus designated, going out of Tivoli by the gate nearest the Sibylla, and returning by the other gate, and the Villa of Mæcenas. I went the greatest part of the way upon an ass, from which I dismounted to scramble down a path only made for goats, lately discovered by Charles in his expedition with the Prince of Orange, leading to a spot on the bank of the river just opposite the Cascatelle. Henry and Ernest each had an ass, and were very happy. My little darling Charles I left with Angelina, to take a less laborious walk nearer the inn. After dinner we went to the Villa of Hadrian, in which there were not any girls gathering mulberry-leaves, but which in everything else appeared as it did seven years ago in June. The next day, before six o'clock, we were on our way to Vicovaro, ten miles from Tivoli on the road to Subiaco. The drive is beautiful, leading along the banks of the Anio in a narrow and constantly ascending valley, the mountains having the character of those about the lakes in West-moreland. At Vicovaro we saw the remains of the ancient walls, built of enormous fragments of stone with-out cement; and a beautiful old chapel,* a most perfect specimen of Italian-Gothic, a style of architecture dif-fering, but not radically, in conception and execution from the Gothic of England, France, and Germany, at the same period. The chapel was erected at the expense of one of the Orsini family, and that name, being inscribed within and without, has been retained in the knowledge of the inhabitants, every other circumstance relative to the foundation being related in the most absurdly fabulous manner. One account is, that it was a heathen temple, which once stood in another place, and was *transported piecemeal* and put up there. The clergyman of the parish did not insist upon the accuracy of the latter supposition, but was nevertheless convinced that the long, slender, Gothic cluster-columns were remains of an ancient Roman edifice, and observing us admiring the statues of saints and prophets in the niches of the portal, said, ' E queste figure erano fabbricate dagli *schiavi* della famiglia Orsini ' —imagining that the Orsini had been ancient Roman patricians in heathen times. We drove a mile and a half beyond Vicovaro to the monastery of S. Cosimato, situated

* Built by Simone, a pupil of Brunelleschi, who, says Vasari, died when he was employed upon it.

on a rock, rising to a great height perpendicularly from the Anio, which rock is perforated into cells, made by the original monks of St. Benedict in the sixth century. The prior of the monastery received us very goodnaturedly, he could not of course let *me* in, but showed us everywhere about, and took us a most broiling, but beautiful walk; and afterwards in a room next the sacristy (which was not forbidden to women, the entrance being from the church) gave us a most excellent luncheon, of ham, salad, omelet, eggs, and cheese. In the same manner these monks receive all strangers that come, and single men they allow to lodge in the convent as long as they please, expecting of course a trifling present, under the name of alms for the use of the church: but travellers have reason to be very glad to be so received, there being nothing like an inn for many miles round.

"The fourth day we again visited the Grotto of Neptune, and sat a long time in the Villa d'Este, and after dinner returned to Rome, driving half a mile out of the way to see the lake from whence the sulphur-stream flows, in which every year large incrustations form, which gradually collect together, swim a given time about in considerable masses, then attach themselves to the bank in a sufficient state of solidity to bear the weight of a man, although still in a floating state, and at last diminish the circumference of the lake, which in the memory of man was twice as large as it is now. It is on record that the ancients found the water to possess healing virtues, and the Emperor Hadrian built baths close to the lake, which have long been nearly levelled to the ground."

"21 *July*, 1824.—Two days ago the post brought the

long-wished for, but I had almost said no longer expected, official intelligence from Count Bernstorff,* that
Mr. Niebuhr not returning to his post, and the King not
intending to make another appointment, Charles was desired and authorised to continue as hitherto in the manage-
ment of business, with an increase of salary which will
make up our income in all to a thousand pounds sterling a year. For this we are both indescribably thankful,
and I am sure my Mother will join in our satisfaction,
when she knows that as we *start clear* upon the new salary,
we shall be very well off, not having to incur any extra
expense in our manner of living. . . . . Mr. Niebuhr will
probably remain settled for the present in Bonn, or some
other place on the Rhine. It is to be regretted for the
sake of public business that he should not continue concerned in it, as he has an astonishing talent for dispatching affairs, as well as judgment in directing them; otherwise we could only rejoice in his being left undisturbed to
continue his Roman history, in which he has made great
progress in this winter of leisure.

"About our being thus fixed here, probably for two or
three years longer, my own Mother, I have said nothing,
not because I have felt nothing; during the summer and
spring I was anxious to hear that another appointment
was made in Mr. Niebuhr's room, so that we could be left
at liberty to quit Rome at a time when our journey could
have been commenced and accomplished; but now, circumstances over which we had no control, have altogether
changed the case, I am no longer physically able to undertake the labour of breaking up housekeeping, and under-

* Prussian Minister of Foreign Affairs.

taking even the half of the journey to England, leaving out of the case the present season, in which the risk of removing the children would be too great to be incurred, if possibly to be avoided; and should I here await the birth of another child, if it please God to grant me its life, I am equally bound to this spot till it could with safety be weaned, probably not till this spring twelvemonth: when that time is arrived we shall see what it brings with it. The period I have mentioned, of two or three years, is stated at random, for Count Bernstorff specifies nothing, and we have no other data to judge from, as to what future resolutions he is likely to form. . . . . My own satisfaction rests upon the fact that our remaining here is not our own act and deed, it has been determined by circumstances independent of us, and therefore we may gather that it is the will of God thus to dispose of us; could I think we had brought about the decision, I should be full of fear and dread as to the result, and should feel the bitterness unallayed of hope deferred: as it is I will believe, that what has been so long delayed, will not finally be denied."

"13 *August*, 1824.—I enjoy indescribably the summer-stillness, the freedom from interruption, and the glorious weather. I continue to drive out at six o'clock in the morning to the Villa Borghese, where I find a place to sit down, under the pines, while the children play about. At that hour, the air is invigorating, and although fatigued, I am never exhausted by going out then; in the evening, the atmosphere is never sufficiently refreshed to be enjoyable till about a quarter after dark, when I enjoy it upon our own loggia. My darling Ernest completed his

fifth year in most perfect health and had a very merry
birthday. We went down to breakfast in the garden at
half-past six, and there it was very delightful till eight,
when we brought the children in, and produced some playthings for the amusement of all, which Ernest was to
divide as he pleased. . . . . After I had helped them to put
in order a fortress in iron-work, and a Turkish caravan (all
Tyrolese toys), I left them to arrange or disarrange at
their pleasure, and went to lie down in Charles's sitting-
room, to enjoy rest, and quiet, and an Italian translation
of Thucydides."

In September, 1824, Mrs. Waddington was first informed by her daughter of an approaching change in
their family arrangements. In his unmarried life, the
ideal of Bunsen's future had been to make a home for
his unmarried half-sister Christiana, and one of the
charms of his Indian project had been that she would
have accompanied him to the East, and that her health
would have benefited by a tropical climate. His real
intercourse with Christiana had however been confined
to a few weeks in 1814, when he saw in her the long-
suffering victim of oppression, and when his chivalrous
spirit was roused by the desire of putting an end to her
sorrows. Since then she had been maintained by his
remittances, and cheered by constant letters, in which
his whole life, with its occupations, cares, projects,
and aspirations, was ceaselessly poured out before her,
as before a superior being capable of guiding and
advising. Now that his residence seemed likely to be

fixed with certainty in Rome for some time to come, his earnest desire was that his sister should leave her home in Holland, and come to Rome, where he thought that she would be the maternal-friend of his wife, the presiding genius of his home-circle. He believed also that his boys would not only find in her, who had been the object of chief reverence during his own boyhood, the wisest monitress of their youth, but that her presence would have the desirable effect of naturally leading them to talk German, as she could speak no other language, except Dutch.

The mistake made in the invitation to Christiana, was bitterly repented of. Her presence, joyfully hailed at first, soon proved a burden almost unendurable. Nothing pleased her. She had come to Italy expecting to find everything perfect, and she found everything imperfect. She immediately wished to return, but she had given up her own house, and the expense of the journey back, in those days of vetturino travelling, was not easy to meet. Thus, for seven years and a half, she continued an element of the household, "a ceaseless trial, putting feelings and principles to the severest test, and acting as a 'refiner's fire' upon all sterling realities."* And, though the chief struggle of endurance under the strange vagaries and even violence of an imperious temper, rendered more way-ward and irritable by constant ill-health, fell upon her sister-in-law, daily contact with his sister dispelled

* "Memoirs of Baron Bunsen."

from Bunsen the darling illusion of his life, which had represented her as the model of female excellence.

With the arrival of Christiana was anticipated that of M. Simon, as a tutor for the boys, whose connection with the family for seven years—during which he was "an instrument of moral flagellation to parents and children"—proved almost equally unfortunate.

The next winter, however, was a happy one. Familiarity had not then rendered the Bunsens conscious of the thorns which were in store for them, and the presence of Mr. and Lady Emily Pusey* at the beautiful Villa Mills on the Palatine, gave a charm to the English society which it had never possessed before. In the spring, also, the Bunsens formed their first acquaintance with Neukomm, the composer, who continued till his death one of the most valuable and valued of their friends. A great personal sorrow to Madame Bunsen was the death of her mother's unmarried sister, her beloved aunt Harriet Port, of whom she frequently spoke as one "in whom the energy of a loving nature, the enthusiasm of self-sacrifice, and the ardour of devotedness, existed in ceaseless outpouring of its heart's-blood upon fellow-creatures, without the due response in kind, without receiving from others that which it gave so freely of its own." The death of

---

* Daughter of the second Earl of Carnarvon.

another dear aunt, Mrs. Granville of Calwich, in the following year, loosened for Madame Bunsen all immediate ties to England which were not connected with Llanover.

MADAME BUNSEN *to* MISS PORT (the last of a series of letters to this beloved aunt, written before the news of her death, which had already occurred, reached Rome).

"2 *Oct.*, 1824.—My own dearest Aunt Harriet. The Sunday before last, I longed to begin a letter to you, as I came out of church, to give some idea of a sermon I had just heard. It is the general practice of our clergyman, Mr. Rothe, to preach on the gospel of the day, and the gospel of that day contained the account of the *ten lepers* who were cleansed, of whom only one returned to give thanks. Mr. Rothe observed, that it being the universal custom of our Saviour to require of individuals for whose benefit He intended to exert His healing powers, a certain degree of faith in those powers (for reasons not expressly stated, but easily to be gathered by attentive consideration of His modes of dealing with mankind) it is certain that even the nine ungrateful lepers were not destitute of faith. This may also be proved by collateral circumstances, first, their having supplicated for relief; secondly, their having instantly obeyed when bidden to '*go and shew themselves to the priests*,' instead of waiting to see whether their journey would be of any use, or whether the command was a mere mockery—for it is said, not that their cure was performed the moment the words issued from our Saviour's lips, but that 'as they went, they were healed.' Therefore the question is, how should they have been capable of faith in any degree, and yet so stupefied, so hardened, as to be incapable of thankfulness for the mercy received ? And it may be supposed, in explanation, that they argued as follows : ' We have suffered severely, have suffered long, have suffered patiently, although we have never done anything in our lives to merit punishment so severe; we have not been worse, perhaps better, than our neighbours, whom we see in the enjoyment of health and of society, but God saw fit to afflict us, we know not why; it is easy to understand why He now withdraws the affliction; we may be glad to be relieved, but in receiving relief, we have received no more than our due.' But the Samaritan joined to his faith in Divine power and Divine mercy an utter self-renunciation; his mind had been so penetrated with the consciousness of sin, that he had not an idea of possessing a right, or making a claim, to the mercy for which he entreated; and therefore on receiving it, instead of being bent like the others on hastening to obtain from the priests the temporal advantage resulting from his cure—of re-admission into society—he was irresistibly urged to return and proclaim aloud the glory of God and his own thankfulness. Of the eloquence with which this was stated, the consequence drawn, and the application made to the soul of every Christian, it is not in my power to give any idea; and having in my own mind the impression made by the whole together, I cannot in the least judge whether, in the bald account I have given of the substance, it will appear to you as original and as edifying as it did to me.

"This view of the subject has led me to reflect on the apparent inequality of God's dispensations to His creatures on

earth, a matter even more difficult to those who do not suffer
by the inequality than to those who do, that is to say, when
the latter have the spirit of the Samaritan leper; but which
need not stagger or disturb, any more than any other difficulty of the sort, when we consider that it is probably
intended, amongst other good ends, to serve the purpose of
reminding us of that spiritual world, in which the hardly
tried (that is, the highly favoured) in this life, are to meet
with full and overflowing compensation; from which, even
here, they receive their hidden supplies of strength; and of
which, even here, they have probably a clearer sight and
perception than can enter into the conceptions of those
who, even without forgetfulness of God, are in full enjoyment of the best share of earthly comfort."

To her MOTHER.

"23 *Oct.*, 1824.—I need not tell you how incessantly my
thoughts beat round and round like a bird against the
wires of a cage till I heard from you.   But do not suppose
that I have been depressed, or have spent the days in tears
since the arrival of your letter.   I shed a few tears, and very
few, when I went to tell Charles in his room that my Aunt
Harriet was dead—and I shed a tear, but not more, on
telling of my poor Augusta's delight at the birth of her
child. . . . . My box has arrived in perfect safety, and
well might I complain of my Mother's too great magnificence in loading me with such a provision of things. . . . .
I shall not allow myself to say anything of the feelings
with which I looked upon my dearest Aunt Harriet's gifts,
although I did not know when I received them that her
warfare was accomplished!   Perhaps she now knows my

feelings towards her, better than she would have done had she remained on her bed of martyrdom long enough to receive my written expressions."

On the 7th of November, 1824, Madame Bunsen gave birth to her fifth son—George Frederick.

MADAME BUNSEN *to her* MOTHER.

" 24 *Nov.*, 1824.—I may now allow myself to write to my Mother of my little angel. I am sure that in loving children, as in other things, one improves by practice. I loved the others from the moment of their birth as well as I was capable of, but I never had as much delight in any-one as this. . . . . We intend to christen our new treasure George, after one of my own dearest Mother's names."

" 30 *Dec.*—I long to describe the appearance of my little angel, but of that I can give no idea: so lovely an infant I never saw, except my Mary, and though his features are not like hers, his sweet smiles, his early intel-ligence, his perfection of temper, his rapid growth, and undisturbed enjoyment of existence, remind me of her continually, and that being the case, it is no wonder that I rejoice over him with trembling."

" 1 *Jan.*, 1825.—The new year is begun. Last night Charles and I sat up together till the clock of the Capitol had sounded the close of a year, so marked with blessings to us both that it is impossible not to look forward to another with more than usual mistrust—mistrust in the changeable course of human things, not in the mercy that has ever hitherto in joy or sorrow accompanied us. Those who possess so much, have much to lose !—and the side may be pierced by the very staff that supports. But, blessed be God for his inestimable gifts, even though it should be, in the secret dispensations of His providence, that they should to-morrow be withdrawn!"

"27 *Jan.*—I have been seeing much lately of Lady Frances Sandon.* I think her quite charming. She is in the first place very pretty, and would be beautiful, if it were not for her mouth: otherwise her features, the shape of her head, and her throat, are perfect, and she has a good figure and fine complexion. But if she had been less pretty and pleasing, she would have bribed me to like her by her evident delight in my children, whom from the first she desired to see, and from whom she could hardly take off her eyes."

"15 *Feb.*, 1825.—Our two new inmates arrived on the 1st of February. It would be too sudden to attempt to give you a full description of my sister-in-law after a fortnight's acquaintance; suffice it to say, that I have nothing to tell now that is not in the highest degree satisfactory, she seems to answer in every respect the idea I had formed of her, from her letters, and Charles's description: everything that I have seen denotes the clear head, sound understanding, and high principles, which he always attributed to her. She has many of Charles's peculiarities, without being in person like him. Her exterior and manners are perfectly gentlewomanlike. She has a very good figure, and a mild and intelligent countenance; her features,

* Lady Frances Sandon, afterwards Countess of Harrowby (fourth daughter of John, first Marquess of Bute) continued an intimate and valued friend of the Bunsen family till the end of her saintly life in March, 1859.

which must always have been too strongly marked, appear
much too large for her face, owing to its thinness, the
result of long and severe suffering, but the expression is
not harsh, although the lines have all a tendency to be so.
She has a sensible manner towards children, but Henry
is the only one to whom she can make herself thoroughly
intelligible, though the other two are already fond of her,
and get on in speaking German. She has been tried in
life more hardly than anybody whose well-attested history
I ever yet heard. I trust and believe that it will be
possible for us to make her happy and comfortable here,
although with a terribly suffering body, a house in Rome,
even arranged as well as it can be, is a bad thing at last;
and a person used to Dutch neatness must I fear be in
hourly penance when waited upon by Italians."

"17 *August*, 1825.—The death of my Aunt Granville
and the desolation of Calwich, dwell upon my mind with
a degree of pain for which I can scarcely account, considering how long I had been accustomed, and I had
supposed reconciled, to the idea that I should never see
her again in this world ; and considering how much the
pleasure which the face of nature, and her kindness,
occasioned me in Calwich, was counterbalanced by other
circumstances :—but on opening Göthe's ' Torquato Tasso '
the other day, a well-known passage met my eye, which
suggested an explanation to my feelings. I must surely
have translated at the time of reading it that passage to
my Mother—' The spot trodden by the virtuous is sacred ;
and their words and deeds re-echo there to the ears of
posterity.' Now I believe it is the very reverse of this
being the case, which makes those feelings bitter, that

ought only to be sad and solemn, not even mournful—for, to her, death was rest and reward, the prize obtained after the fight well fought, the race well run, the burden nobly sustained!—But that those who inhabit the place of her abode, who possess what once was hers, what her care embellished, in which her eye delighted, that they all should forget her 'as a guest that tarrieth but a day,'* is the intolerable sensation: foolish to be sure, for to the blessed immortal spirit not even the folly and wickedness of men, any more than their pains and sorrows, can be a disturbance: her will, so resigned even in life, is now wholly merged in the will of God, and she knows what we can only believe, that all evil shall work together for good at the last; she beholds in the spirit, the destruction of the last enemy:—'The last enemy that shall be destroyed is death.'——O my Mother, I cannot suppose that the death mentioned in that awful passage can mean anything so comparatively insignificant as the mere separation of soul and body:—I must look upon those words as a ray of light disclosing depths of mercy even for the most perverted: devoutly as I believe at the same time that the tremendous threatenings of God in the Scriptures are to be taken as literally as His glorious promises, and that a soul without relish for God and goodness, incapable of faith and humility, and thus self-banished in the time of mortal life from the presence of God, will be equally self-banished in another state of existence, and that in that banishment consists the condition of torment, described under so many poetical images, and generally

* Calwich was afterwards sold, and became the property of the Hon A. Duncombe, Dean of York.

received as a place of imprisonment and arbitrary punishment. Every individual figures to himself his proper heaven; and those who have in their time of trial formed no taste for the Heaven of God, such as it exists, would remain dark and frozen even in the midst of its glories, if they could be transported there: on the other hand (to borrow the daring image used in a most extraordinary book, published by Luther, but written a century earlier), could Satan himself be capable of a longing, an aspiration after the joys of Heaven, he would at once be there! his pardon would be sealed, because his nature would be changed!"

"18 *August*.—Last night, an unusual hour of quiet after putting the children to bed enabled me to dilate on a subject on which I little thought to touch when I began to write; and now at last it is most unconnectedly and inadequately stated. Without attempting to explain it better, I will only tell my Mother the course of my reflections upon it. I never doubted that the literal meaning of the Divine threatenings was to be received undoubtingly, as matter of faith, however difficult for human powers to reconcile with the equally certain matter of faith that the mercy of God is infinite; and I well remember in our first summer at Frascati expressing that conviction in a conversation with Charles. About a year after that conversation, I read the extraordinary work to which I have alluded, which consists in a small number of very short, very concise, most comprehensive essays or chapters, of which every sentence is an ingot. It was written, of course, in what are called Catholic times, but the author was a Christian, and no Romanist. All that is known of him is that he was a Teutonic knight of Frankfort on the Oder, his history and earthly distinctions are 'lost in the abyss of things that were.'* The work was published by Luther, since the age of the Reformation has been out of print, and was republished a few years ago: a Latin translation was made of it at an early period, through the means of which it was known to many English divines in the seventeenth century. This book, my own Mother, contains much which made to me as clear as daylight the great point, that what is called hell is, no more than heaven, confined to place or time, but is a condition of the soul, into which the soul degrades itself, which may well begin even in this life, although here its torments will be lessened by that same veil of flesh, which the joys of heaven cannot pervade: it is a natural consequence of the order of things by God established, a natural consequence of the rejection of offered salvation; and if the expression may be used, it is impossible even for Omnipotence itself to grant that which his creatures have become incapable of receiving. With Mr. Erskine† I had much conversation on this subject; and as well as I remember, it was he who suggested the possible interpretation of the passage— 'The last enemy that shall be destroyed is death'—as the other member of that mighty paradox, the solution of which is not for us in this world—into which even the angels desire to look! A similar view of the world of spirits I found implied, strange to say, in a Spanish poem

* This book "Theologia Germanicè" (this is the correct title) was translated into English by Miss Catherine Winkworth.

† The admirable Thomas Erskine of Linlathan, now well known from his Letters.

of the fifteenth century:—perhaps the author might be
one of the many thousand Spaniards who had to expiate
in the flames their aspirations after purified Christianity."

"*Rome*, 30 *August*, 1825.—On Charles's birthday, the
25th, we had delightful weather, the sky being clear, the
sun bright, and the air delicious. We began at seven
o'clock by breakfasting in the garden. At dinner we were
fourteen in number, besides children. Before dinner,
some favourite hymns of Charles's were sung, arranged
for four voices, which had been composed (by Reisiger)
and practised by the singers without Charles's knowledge,
and were therefore an agreeable surprise to him; after
dinner we went to Villa Lante, and took our dessert with
us, and enjoyed the view and the garden most exceedingly.

"The presence of Reisiger* in Rome has been and is a
great source of pleasure to us. I wish I could pack his
music, composition and execution, in my letter, how my
Mother would enjoy it! He is a young man, but has
already celebrity as a composer."

In the middle of September the family removed for
the refreshment of country air to the Villa Piccolomini
at Frascati.

"*Villa Piccolomini*, 13 *Oct.*, 1825.—I did not think I
should again have dated from Frascati, yet I am well
reconciled to remain by the unequalled beauty of the
weather and country, although out of virtue I should have
returned, to put an end to the confusion of the divided

---

* The popular composer—Kapellmeister at Dresden.

household, and get something done of the much that is
wanted to cover the children's nakedness this winter.
They have in the villeggiatura so torn and worn the remains
of their summer clothes, that I shall not be able to show
them in Rome till I have bought and cut out and had
made something new.   However that is a trifling distress,
a much greater, resulting from our absence, is the death
of my canary-bird, which was announced to me yesterday.
My Mother will wonder at my having such a favourite, but
I must surely have mentioned, now four years ago, the
bird's having flown in at the window. It sang most
sweetly, and was quite tame and happy, and therefore it
was no distress to see it in a cage.

"I have only to tell in Frascati of uninterrupted enjoyment. The quantity of exercise I habitually take is to
myself inconceivable. I will give an account of what I
have done this morning, as the most recent occurrence.
We got up an hour before day, and went up to the tip-top
of the hill of Villa Aldobrandini, where we walked up and
down till the sun was pleased to rise; then we saw it gradually illuminate the Lateran and the Vatican, and other
buildings in Rome, the mountain casting a long shadow
over the campagna. We had ordered the servants to
bring our breakfast after us to the top of the hill, but I
proposed going down again to meet it, and placing ourselves in the beautiful hall of the Palazzo Aldobrandini;
and it was well we did so, for it was eight o'clock before
fresh milk was to be had, and the gentlemen set themselves to playing at bowls, the children led the ass (which
had carried their aunt) about to graze, and I betook myself
in the corner of a delightful old-fashioned leather couch,

and slept most comfortably till the coffee came. After we had made an enormous breakfast, the bowls were again put in motion, and I, and the children, and the ass, and the servants, and the baskets with empty cups and plates, went home, and I set myself to write,—and after dinner I shall be quite fresh and ready to take another walk or ride.

"Yesterday we were equally in movement the whole day : in the morning I was sketching, and after dinner we rode on asses to Grotta Ferrata, and saw the chapel of Domeni-chino. We came home after dark, and then received an in-vitation to hear an Improvisatore at the Casino Piccolomini. The name of our host is Angiolotti, a rich *possidente*, or farmer, from whom and his wife we have received great civilities. We were the day before yesterday at their farm, or *tenuta*, where the vintage is going on. They gave us ham, and cheese, and *frittata* and *pizza*, and wine, and grapes as much as we could eat. We had our friend Reisiger of the party, and he played, and sang German, and the vigneroli sang Italian. We had the nurse with us, who rode like a man on an ass, with my darling before her, who enjoyed the party as much as anybody : my little Charles rode before his papa or Simon : his two brothers ride independently.

"Some days ago we made an expedition to Monte Cavo, the highest point of Monte Albano, where there is a monas-tery. The monks gave us bread and wine, and we had cold meat and grapes with us. We rode down on the other side of the hill towards Albano, where the carriage met us in the *Galleria di sopra* by the Capuchin convent : we then drove to Castel-Gandolfo, whence we went down to the brink of the lake to see the emissary, and returned home to dinner

at five o'clock. Another day we drove to Genzano, Charles
and his sister and Simon and myself and the three boys
packed in the carrettella: my darling was left at home
with his nurse and Angelina, and Kestner rode on horseback. My Mother will remember the name of Kestner,
whom we now value more than ever, since he has been our
constant companion on parties of pleasure for many days
successively, without ever giving opportunity for an observation as to his character that was not to his credit. We
had provisions for dinner with us, and our servant Antonio
to cook, therefore all we wanted in Genzano was a kitchen
and dining-room; but on our arrival we found the rooms
of our old acquaintance all occupied, and were glad to be
conducted by Kestner to the house of a *possidente* whom he
had formerly known, whose wife in the most obliging
manner granted us all we wanted; she was a very handsome woman, and in deportment, I had almost said, a
princess. While our dinner was preparing, we made the
tour of the lake of Nemi on ass-back: that *mirror of Diana*
as it was called (the woods and a temple on its banks
having been in ancient times consecrated to her) never
appeared to greater advantage, for there were light fleecy
clouds in the clear October sky, which produced those
occasional false shadows which I must always long for in
mountain scenery, from recollection of the lakes of West-
moreland.

"I shall be glad at last to return to our own dear home,
and yet our pleasure in Frascati has been so altogether
without drawback, that I could almost find in my heart
to be afraid of what may follow a change of abode. I
have had time to read here too, and enjoy most extremely

a German translation of Herodotus. I have also enjoyed reading in the Bible more than I have time to do at home —I mean, time uninterrupted, and to read with interruptions is of little avail. I have been greatly struck with many historical parts of the Old Testament, which in connection I have not read for years; and must ask my Mother whether she does not think the narrative of Nehemiah most particularly touching."

"*Rome*, 19 *Oct*.—We returned home on Sunday morning, the 16th, and find our own dear house very delightful. My boys are all as well as possible, and, at present, very good."

"14 *Feb*., 1826.—I have to communicate the intelligence of the King's having bestowed upon Charles the order of the Red Eagle, a distinction which is a matter of much satisfaction, as indicating the favourable dispositions of the King and his ministers, for there are few if any examples of a person not belonging to a privileged class receiving it after so short a period of service. The first intelligence was communicated by the good Baron von Reden, now Hanoverian Minister at Berlin; the nomination took place on the 18th January, and last week the cross and ribbon were delivered to Charles by General de Lepel, the Aide-de-Camp of Prince Henry of Prussia, who had travelled from Berlin with great speed to return to his post. Only the day after the arrival of this decoration, arrived the intelligence of the failure of the banking-house of Benecke in Berlin. They were Charles's agents for the reception of his salary, and had only eleven days before received for him his quarter's allowance, for which they had transmitted a bill of exchange, which bill of course there had not been

time to negociate, before it became of no avail. . . . I wish
that I may prevail upon my Mother to be as little disturbed by this piece of ill-luck as I am myself; I cannot
possibly deny, when I state the case to myself, that it is a
very serious thing, and that as we have never yet had *more*
than *enough* with our whole year's income, I cannot explain
how we are to have enough when the quarter's salary is
wanting; yet I cannot get rid of the feeling that we shall
not *need the lost sum*, whether it shall be made good, in
some unforeseen way, or whether we shall be able to do
without it. All accounts, from the Baron von Reden and
others, tend to prove that Count Bernstorff, as well as
Prince Wittgenstein, uniformly speak of Charles with
strong expressions of esteem for his character and conduct,
and something approaching to admiration for, not mere
commendation of, his talents for business; and also that
the great liking which the King showed towards him in
Rome, has been kept up more than could have been
expected, by what I may call *correspondence* since, for the
King reads everything he writes to Berlin, and you may
readily believe that what he writes is worth reading. So,
my own Mother, pray hope the best with me, and do not
be more distressed than I am.

"Lord Sandon left Rome on Thursday, taking for my
Mother a sketch-book, and for my father a Latin document,
which was a *petite attention* of Monsignor Marini to me.
He found the original in the Papal archives, and thought
I should be overjoyed with a proof that a person bearing
the name of Waddington held a situation of credit in the
Church in the early part of the reign of Henry III., for
that is the date of the document."

"*Easter Sunday*, 26 *March*, 1826.—M. d'Olfers is here, with his amiable wife, on his way to the Brazils as Chargé d'Affaires. He has been for two years attached to the Prussian Legation at Naples, his connections at Berlin having reckoned upon getting him into Charles's post at Rome, an arrangement which the circumstance of his being a Catholic would at any time have rendered impossible, for the business of the Prussian Legation here could not in many respects be well got through by a person in any way hampered by private ties to the Church of Rome, without considering the important point of the Protestant Chapel, which could not be kept up under a Catholic *chef de légation*. On his way through Rome to Naples with Count Fleming two years ago, he and Charles formed a personal acquaintance as cordial as if they had not stood in the relation of a sort of rivals to each other, and they have kept up from time to time a degree of correspondence, which I hope will continue, for Olfers's letters are always indescribably entertaining. He is one of the sort of men that I know my Mother would like, of sound and sterling attainments, and polished but inartificial manner, with a great deal of quiet fun, and a stillness of deportment not the least resulting from phlegm or insensibility.

"We have lately to our great pleasure formed a new musical acquaintance of the name of Neukomm, who is come to Rome for, I am sorry to say, a very short time, after a singular course of travels. He was born at Saltzburg, and became a pupil of Haydn at Vienna; his first removal from Germany was to become *Maestro di Cappella* to a Russian prince, and he spent some years between

Petersburg and Moscow; after which he became *Maestro di Cappella* to the King of Portugal when in Brazil, but the Court having a decided passion for *waltz-masses*, Neukomm was not satisfied to remain where his style of composition was not approved, nor satisfied to adopt a style such as could have secured approbation, wherefore he returned to Europe, and has ever since been attached to the *Court* of —— Talleyrand ! !—who is said to rank music amongst the luxuries which he considers worth possessing in the highest perfection. With Talleyrand Neukomm set out towards Rome, but the former having found the weather not to his taste, remained by the way at Nice, allowing Neukomm leave of absence to proceed to Rome and Naples.

" On Wednesday in Passion Week Neukomm returned home with us from the Sixtine Chapel, and played to us in a manner that could give delight even after the Miserere. To give an idea of his playing, I must describe the course of my own feelings,—I was at first sorry for the arrangement to bring him home with us, not wishing to be disturbed, and only reconciled to it on the ground of giving pleasure to M. d'Olfers, who had known and valued Neukomm for years as a man as well as a musician ; but from the moment he began to play, I was thankful to have the state of feeling protracted, which had originated in the Miserere. He played airs with variations of his own composition (amongst others 'See the Conquering Hero comes'), and afterwards gave an idea, as far as one pair of hands and a very feeble voice could give an idea, of passages in an oratorio which he has this winter composed, but which has never yet been executed.

The words are selected from Klopstock's *Messiah*, and the chorus he played to us is grounded on the passage in Isaiah, ' Who is He . . . . that is glorious in His apparel, travelling in the greatness of His strength ?—I that speak in righteousness, mighty to save ! '—the whole to be performed by a choir in two divisions, answering each other in the manner of Handel's ' Who is the King of Glory ?—The Lord of Hosts, He is the King of Glory ! '

" O my Mother, how I wish you could see Lady Frances Sandon, and still more, know her : I am sure you would think her ' a thing of other times.' She seems to me to realise things I have known in description—a class of women to which the finest ladies I see are not fit to be chambermaids. She goes away for good the end of next month, and Heaven knows where, or when, or how, we shall meet again, but I shall always rejoice in the indelible image she leaves, of a species of creature from which every-day women are as different as negroes from whites.

" The more I see of Lady Bute, the more I am convinced that she is a thoroughly kind-hearted and well-principled woman, but in the scale of human beings I am sure she takes an inferior rank to her daughter, who is almost an angel."

" 25 *April*, 1826.—The presence of M. Neukomm in Rome is a very great pleasure to us, and we make the most of it by seeing him daily. Independent of his most extraordinary, and to me unequalled, musical talent, he is of a most attaching character, and has those sort of placid manners, combined with rationality and intelligence on all subjects, which make a person a welcome inmate at any time and at all times. Charles takes advantage of this delicious weather to go about Rome with him, and I join the party whenever I can. This winter Charles has formed several very agreeable English acquaintances, all through the Sandon channel; first and foremost Lord Binning, with whom he has had much intercourse, and for whom he has a great liking and value. Further, Mr. Egerton Vernon, a son of the Archbishop of York's; two Mr. Smith's, one John Abel, the other Augustus, both related to Lord Carrington; and a Mr. Bramston, are all persons we like in different ways."

On the 1st of June, Bunsen joyfully announced to Mrs. Waddington the birth of a daughter, who received the name of Frances from her god-mother, Lady Frances Sandon, and that of Helen from her father's half-sister, Madame Müller. At the same time he had the gratification of telling the ever-kind mother-in-law, who, as usual, was wishing to make up the loss he had suffered, that the sum swallowed up by the Benecke bankruptcy, had been graciously made good by the King.

MADAME BUNSEN *to her* MOTHER.

"12 *July*, 1826.—I have a mind to write down some of the interruptions of the morning, to give my Mother an idea of the day; a thing I should often attempt, were it not for the long notes of explanation, which ought to be appended to each name that will occur. I was up at six o'clock: while I was dressing, Charles slept on, and I would not rouse him, because for the last few days he had rested too little and run about, or in some way or other been too busy in the heat and sirócco; as soon as I was dressed however, he got up, and went out on horseback. Of all the children, Charles alone was awake and up: I therefore proceeded to open my writing-desk and begin my letter, in the *camera gialla*, with the windows open and green blinds closed, to keep out the sun and let in the air: but soon Henry and Ernest made their appearance, and I broke off from my letter to hear them say their prayers. Then Charles returned, and we went to breakfast, with Neukomm (my Mother will remember the name of the musical composer, whose company, as well as his music, delighted us so much at Easter—he has since been at Naples, and is now with us again, day after day, as before, and every part of the family looks upon him as belonging to us). The place where we breakfast I must draw some-time for my Mother, I can now only describe it as near the loggia where the water is drawn up,—a partition has been made in the mangle-room which reserves to us a delight-ful little gallery, with a magnificent prospect and fine air without the morning sun. After breakfast I went to dress my little angel, but by the way met a messenger who announced that a certain Klitsche was seized with a fever. This person is established in the house of the late Bartholdy, to mount guard upon the valuable collection of antiquities, until the heirs shall otherwise have disposed of them. Klitsche came to Rome a year and a half ago with the false notion by which many people at a distance from Rome are possessed, that here institutions accessible to strangers for the study of theology were to be found: that not being the case, his condition here was pretty nearly destitute, and Charles has in one way or another

helped him forward (sometimes procuring him employment in transcribing deeds) awaiting a favourable opportunity of finding a better provision for him. These few
particulars may account for his so far, after a fashion,
belonging to us, that it was necessary I should leave
every other business to perform the most needful, of
procuring him attendance; wherefore I left my little
angel to wait in her night things, and after ordering the
carriage, went downstairs to Madame Eggers (whom the
children call Signora Elisa *—and who is always willing
and able to give counsel and assistance, to ask whether she
supposed I could obtain the help of a woman, of whom she
knew more than I did, and settled that we should go together
to fetch her; then I came up again to make a hundred
arrangements to keep the wheels of government in motion
during the interregnum, and hold seven hundred and one
conferences with Antonio about dinner, with an interlude
of rummaging amongst the dust of the bookshelves for a
pamphlet for Charles, 'Sur l'Orgue expressif de M.
Grénier.' Then I packed Charles the less with Madame
Eggers and myself into the carrettella, in order to lessen the
number of jarring elements left at home, and proceeded
to bespeak the physician, fetch the woman as nurse, and
establish her by the sick person. Then I proceeded to
one or two shops, being on the way, and returned home
at twelve, found a new cap which my sister-in-law had
ordered, and went up to her bedside to explain and
interpret, and hear whether it was right, after listening to
the narrative of the manner in which she had passed the

* M. Eggers, the landscape painter, afterwards settled in Berlin.
His sons were the authors of a Life of Rauch the Sculptor.

night—the heats, and the chills, and the ups and downs. Then I dressed my sweet girl, settled her three eldest brothers to sleep (George was put to bed by Angelina), and was thankful to lie down on my own bed. At two o'clock with some difficulty I waked, and before three collected the whole family from all corners of the house at dinner; after dinner, consultations with Antonio about things to be sent to Klitsche, directions to Agnese about work, part the first of a discourse with my sister-in-law about a ruff and a hat, luckily broken off by Neukomm's offering to hear me practise, an offer I am always rejoiced to accept. I excused myself from driving out, having been out already, sent Charles the less and George with my sister-in-law and her friend Augusta Klein, and Henry and Ernest into Madame Eggers's garden. At eight o'clock everybody returned, I gave the children their supper, heard their prayers, and took them to bed: and at last came to my corner of the couch, the rest of the party being my sister-in-law, Charles, Neukomm, and Kestner. I sat lazy, instead of working as usual, with my Mother's candle-screen, with impressions of leaves, before me, to save my eyes, which were quite tired with puzzling at the score of *Judas Maccabeus*, which Neukomm had insisted on my making out. After looking at the moon, the two glorious planets, and the Mont' Albano in the summer night, at a quarter past ten I went to bed."

"16 *August*, 1826.—I have a long story to relate to my Mother, which I have as yet delayed, from not liking to tell her that Charles had committed an act which I considered imprudent and extravagant, but I will now state his sin in all its magnitude, and leave her to find an excuse for him. He has thought proper to order from Paris what is called an *orgue expressif*, the new invention of M. Grénier, having fallen in love with the description made by Neukomm of this extraordinary instrument. I stated my opinion that the measure was imprudent, because it was highly improbable that after Neukomm had left us we should ever hear the organ again, for it would be difficult to find a dilettante who understood the art of managing it, and as for me, in my old age, with five children, it was too much to expect that I should accomplish learning to play upon a new instrument, never having yet been a proficient in playing on the old one. Further, I insisted that it was extravagant, to incur a great expense, calculating upon being able to save it up in the course of the year. To all my wisdom Charles replied by a number of sophisms, but maintained the point 'that once for all, we *must have* an *orgue expressif*, and that if we must have one, it was the best economy to have it at once, for then we had more time to enjoy it in our lives.' Wherefore I withdrew my opposition, the organ was ordered in April last, but having first a packing to undergo, and then a long journey to make, did not arrive till Tuesday the 8th of August. Neukomm delayed his journey for the sake of enabling us to hear the organ once in perfection, although thereby greatly diminishing the time he had allotted for the north of Italy and Switzerland, having fixed to be in France at latest the end of September. The effect of this instrument is beyond description, it is capable of unlimited expression, the sound being produced by the gradual pressure of the feet alternately upon two pedals, and the tones are soft and swelling like those of the human voice when in great perfection, or like the most exquisite wind instruments. When hearing Neukomm play, I continually caught myself holding my breath, as when listening to the *Miserere* in the Sixtine Chapel. As to my own prospect of learning to play upon it, I am happy to say that in these ten days I have already surmounted some part of the difficulty, which consists in the movement of the feet, and have good hopes of proceeding further; and the delight of touching it is so great, that I shall only be in danger of giving up more time to it than I really have to spare. It has made *furore* in Rome, the Cardinal Secretary of State was enchanted, and began to *sing* himself from excess of delight: the Maestro di Cappella Baini said it brought him into a cold sweat and that he could not stand it if he was to hear it every day; Monsignor Capaccini (who was private secretary to Consalvi and wrote all his dispatches) ordered such another organ full speed for himself: and the Corps Diplomatique was out of its wits for admiration. I must not forget to state that the expense did not turn out as great as I expected, for, including the carriage from Paris, it amounted to ninety pounds sterling: yet the instrument is as perfect as to make and materials, as a piece of furniture, as in sound."

" 6 *Sept.*, 1826.—I wish I could here give a shadow of the darling figure, in a great brown pinafore (sent by grandmamma for Ernest), that is now trotting near me, enjoying in stillness the condescension of his brother Charles in playing without plaguing him, as is too often the case; to me it is a great gain when Charles is so gracious, for then I can keep both my little boys with me (tho

elder brothers are with Simon), otherwise I am compelled
to interpose and part them, and at length banish my
George to the maids, who *can* sometimes keep him good
and happy, whereas Charles is nothing less than 'the
Deil himsel' with people whom he does not acknowledge
to have a right to direct him : I maintain my sovereignty
after a fashion, but it costs me many a hard battle. My
George, and his little sister, are the matter of unmixed
delight; there never was any creature more alive to all
impressions than that dear boy, he shows me the clouds
when the sun is setting, points to the river and gazes at
it, watches the course of a flight of birds overhead, and
his great enchantment is a herd of oxen grazing: he
strokes and caresses his little sister, laughs loud at her
motions, and shows her to everybody. He cannot bear to
hear one of his brothers cry, and the only thing he takes
very ill of me is punishing Charles. I begin to expect
that in process of time he will speak, for he now utters all
sorts of sounds, and seems to have attained the idea that
by means of sounds as well as signs he may make himself
understood.

"I had not time in my last letter to make a statement
in qualification of the impression I produced by mentioning playing in score: my Mother must not form too magnificent notions on the subject, it is like a child's spelling
out words in a language it does not understand ; to be
able to give to the words their proper tone and accent,
and to the sentences their meaning, it would require to
be much further ad-anced than I am; still, although it is
a great matter of doubt whether I shall ever find time
fully to turn to account the instructions of Neukomm, the

trouble he took with me has been of essential use. As of late years we have many times made attempts to get people to sing, I have often practised writing out parts in the different keys, and therefore could read them : but when Neukomm insisted upon it that if I would, I could play a piece of music in which the notes were to be sought out of four different sets of lines, and written in four different keys, I never believed it would be possible in any degree; however, a few days' practice convinced me of the contrary, and I hope in time to learn at least to play what I have picked out with him : even should I never do that, the practice of the score has had the advantage of making other things appear comparatively easy. My obligations to Neukomm are very great in enabling me to enjoy, and making Charles enjoy, the delicious organ : I get to it at odd half-hours often in the day, the pleasure of touching it is greater and greater, and I obtain great praise for my progress : I must tell my Mother that M. Neukomm always insisted upon it that I should play well upon the organ, although in the three days which elapsed between its arrival and his departure, I was far from producing a tolerable tone : as he is a great *Gall-ist*, perhaps he was led to the conviction by having detected (as he asserted) the organ of music plainly in my forehead. I wish my Mother might ever know Neukomm, as well as hear him play; his gift of producing music I know would be a feast to her beyond everything, but I cannot doubt her liking himself. He has stood the test of being our daily inmate for two months at a stretch, without reckoning the time of his being in Rome at Easter; and at last all of us were as melancholy at his departure, and missed him as much at breakfast and dinner, in walks and drives, and in quiet evening conversations, as if he had belonged to us for years, so perfectly did he suit every individual of such a set of creatures as we are : all our acquaintance, however dissimilar, delighted in him, and Thorwaldsen in particular quite worshipped him.

"I have this year made the acquaintance of Sir William Gell: Charles had known him longer. He is a cripple from gout, and was obliged to be carried up our staircase : he however causes himself to be lifted upon a horse, and then takes enormous rides of discovery in this most undiscovered country. He has found many interesting ruins of ancient cities, hitherto unknown to antiquarians, is actively engaged in making a map of Latium, and interests himself greatly in the study of hieroglyphics, according to Champollion."

"16 *Nov.*, 1826.—From the quantity of things I have had to do since we returned home on the 1st of November, accounts to be put in order, a few visits made, an immense number received, and an expedition to the Papal Chapel to hear the *Dies Iræ* of Pittoni,—have so filled up the short mornings, that I scarcely know when I have been more hurried to less purpose, for so much remains to be done, that I feel as if nothing was done. And in the evenings we have so seldom been free from casual visitors, that it is not often I have accomplished playing on the delicious organ.—but it goes on well, my Mother, and I can play some things upon it with satisfaction to myself. How I thank my Mother for enjoying the accounts of it, it is indeed a great delight in life."

" 14 *March*, 1827.—I had last week an impediment in writing to my own dearest Mother, of which she will be surprised and pleased to hear,—a journey to Orvieto, resolved upon in a moment, executed at once, and which turned out admirably. We had spoken of going there pretty nearly every year for the last five, but the difficulty of moving all together, or of separating, always prevented our doing so, and the distance being seventy miles, we should probably never have accomplished going there, had we not made up our minds to leave the children in the care of Simon, and set off as a trio with post-horses. On Wednesday, 7 March, we left Rome at half-past six, Henry and Ernest accompanying us as far as the door, Charles in his shirt and muffled up in a shawl causing himself to be carried to the staircase window, my darling George asleep, and my angel of a girl sitting upright in bed, with two eyes wide open, waiting for the nurse to dress her. As far as Montefiascone, our road was the same as that by which my own dearest Mother travelled away from Rome, and I think however little in a state her mind then was for enjoyment, she must with her eyes have observed the beautiful situation of Ronciglione, where the road begins to ascend the mountain on the other side of which Viterbo is situated, and have taken in the exquisite expanse of the Lake of Vico, which is for a long time visible during the passage of the mountain; and then she will the better guess the sensations of pleasure with which I viewed them; pleasure resulting from many causes, the sensation of breaking the ice as to a journey, such as in ten years and a half I have not made, not to be forgotten amongst them. We arrived so early at Viterbo that we might have pro-

ceeded further, but preferred walking about to see the
churches and prospects, while our dinner was getting
ready, and remaining in the very excellent inn that night.
The weather was delightful, but like that of a fine early
spring day in England, the sky not being in a state of
Italian clearness; and the sort of air, the outline of the
hills about the Lake of Vico, the effect of the unclothed
woods, casting a shadowy brown tinge, altogether brought
me back not less than twenty years!—to the journey from
Tenby just at the same time of year, and the effect of the
hills of Dynevor, Dreslin Castle, and the Towy in the vale
of Caermarthen.

"At Viterbo we found two friends, one of them Maytell,
whose name I may perhaps have mentioned as a person
whom we greatly valued. He is a Russian subject, but of
German extraction and education, and had the day before
taken leave of us to return to his native country, the province of Liefland (also the country of Baron Stackelberg);
and his intention of going to Orvieto in the first place, was
the reason that pinned us down to this precise day for our
expedition. On Thursday morning at sunrise we proceeded
from Viterbo to Montefiascone, where we walked about to
see the churches, and the exquisite prospect from one of
the gates towards the Lake of Bolsena, and then went on
to Orvieto, which is eighteen miles distant, magnificently
situated on an insulated hill in the midst of a valley, which
appears like a park surrounding a castle, and is enclosed
by most picturesque hills, surmounted in the distance by
snow-capped mountains: the town is mounted on a per-
pendicular rock, and has no need of other walls of
enclosure. We spent the whole remainder of the day in

and about the magnificent cathedral, which even surpassed
the expectations we had formed ; the next morning we
were there again by seven o'clock, returned to the inn at
nine to breakfast, and spent the remainder of the time till
we left Orvieto at two o'clock, in re-examining the paintings of Luca Signorelli, Fiesole, and Pietro Perugino, in
one of the chapels of the cathedral. The weather, which
had hitherto favoured us, now changed for the worse, and
we returned to Viterbo through an absolute hurricane.
After resting there that night, we reached Rome in safety
and prosperity at three o'clock on Saturday the 11th,
although the prospect of the Lake of Vico, so peaceful and
sunshiny three days before, was obscured by a storm
of rain and wind accompanied by thunder, lightning, and
hail, through which we traversed the mountain of Viterbo.
I came first up the staircase, in the midst of which Henry
met me, a little further stood Charles, waiting till I came
to him, then came Angelina with George, and the nurse
with my darling. Ernest had not been allowed to move
out of his room, for he is suffering from his eyes, which
has been a great means of preventing my writing since my
return home. I am accustomed to scramble on with
various employments with *only* Charles and George to
interrupt, but the addition of a third, between whom and
each several brother I must keep the peace, and for whom
I must find occupation without exertion of the eyes, is a
great addition to the *distraction* of attempting any occupation requiring the *thoughts*. Independent of children I
have had a succession of things which have scarcely left
me breathing-time. Some of these interruptions I shall
try to note down, because I know my Mother likes to have

that sort of peep into my daily existence. The first thing after breakfast, when I was about to take out my letter to write, I found I had three or four notes or packets, books or newspapers, to write or fold, seal up and dispatch; each was nothing, but all together made something as to time; that ended, kitchen discourse; then, interview the first with the Banderaro, or upholsterer, about a leather cover for the organ, about which the Banderaro ought to have come before, but it is a rule, that everybody is sure to come on the morning when I have to write. I had dispatched the Banderaro, when Charles called me to a consultation, about a letter to be written, a plan to be formed and an appointment made for going out, and an invitation to be sent for next day: the consultation ended, I was in full retreat towards my writing-box, when it was announced that the milliner was waiting, having brought two caps for me, one for my sister-in-law, and a wadded quilted white silk bonnet for my sweet girl; I might to be sure have bid her leave the things, and said I would send the money, but knowing her to be a widow, and poor, I felt bound to examine, speak, hear, and pay; had just finished when my sister-in-law came down—a narrative of health, or I should say sickness, but *short*. In the midst of this, a poor Swiss with three children announced—and thereby hangs an explanation. This individual, of whom I knew nothing before, belongs to a class of the necessitous that particularly excite my compassion, and have for the last two years been extremely numerous. In some of the Swiss cantons, and many of the southern parts of Germany, the philosophers who speak so wisely about checking the increase of population, have brought about a law prohibiting marriage unless the parties can prove themselves possessed of a certain capital; the consequence of this law has been in the countries themselves, as I have heard, that couples come together as before, but in most cases, hold themselves exonerated from the marriage ceremony: in those cases when a scruple of conscience occurs after the connection has been formed, they have nothing to do but to expose themselves to the complicated distress of a distant journey for the purpose of being married, and just because they have no means of subsistence but their daily labour, with other details, it may be guessed what cases of misery occur—the risk of sickness and absolute destitution in every instance, not to mention the degrading necessity of begging, for persons whose appearance and deportment denotes their having been accustomed to honest independence. I was glad the other day to have expatiated on this philosophical iniquity to Mr. Empson, the successor of Sir J. Mackintosh in the East India College, who seemed struck by the details I gave. To return from this digression, the Swiss was to be spoken to, and some odds and ends rummaged out for her and her children; then came the Banderaro again, in superfluity of zeal to show patterns of leather for the organ-cover: then the children's dinner was ready, then I ran to help Charles to seal for the post, then in all haste ate my bason of gruel with the yolk of an egg and sugar beat into it—my usual luncheon: then put on my hat and pelisse, at the same time keeping the peace during the toilet of Charles and George, who went with me to form their taste (or more properly to be kept out of mischief) at the Vatican; heard that Charles was engaged with a Mr. Middleton, who had brought him a letter from

Sir W. Gell, and went in to show, not myself, but my hat and veil, and to give Mr. Middleton a hint to go : the hint after a quarter of an hour took effect, and then we set off, Charles on horseback with Kestner, the rest in the carrettella, Henry on foot with Simon, Ernest provided with company in Albert and George Eggers : my sweet girl dispatched to walk with Angelina. The day was glorious, and the Vatican beamed and glowed in sunshine. I could not however get far in the gallery, so was I fagged with the morning's scramble, at which you will not wonder."

"31 *March*, 1827.—I wish beginning to write so many days before the post-day might secure my dispatching a letter with somewhat fewer omissions of things I wish and intend to say, than usual.—The sentence, thus begun, is finished to-day the 3rd April — a plain proof how far I can reckon upon my days ; since the first words, I have driven through the time that has elapsed, or more properly been driven, with the sensation of passing from one necessary division of the day to another with such rapidity as to become dizzy and scarcely recollect what is the most necessary thing to be done next, so rarely is my occupation a matter of choice and selection ; this I do not state as matter of complaint, but matter of fact and of self-justification, not towards my Mother, who does not require it, but towards myself, who often unjustly complain of myself for leaving undone so much that I wish to do. My present vexation is, that I do not expect to be able to manage to give any sign of actual existence, in the shape of scratch or smear on paper, to be conveyed to England by one who could have taken it safely. What I wanted to have done, and considered most feasible, would have been a coloured sketch of the inside of our sitting-rooms, which I think would enable my Mother more than anything else to figure it all to herself. On two different mornings, when I felt as if I could ' catch a minute by the tail and hold it fast,' I began to cut a sheet of drawing-paper, and look after pencil and crow-quills,—but as if the said minute had been resolved to laugh me to scorn for pretending to dispose of it at my pleasure, not till late the same evening, on the way to bed, did I secure the needful number of seconds to settle the litter I had then made—far enough from executing the intention with which I had made it.

"Mr. Erskine has been some time in Rome, and I was greatly gratified to find that he met us both just at the point where we parted, though we have had no communication with him in the interval; he is a very remarkable and most interesting person, of whose individuality it is difficult to give an idea by description; there is a sort of high-wrought spirituality about him, without a shadow of affectation of singularity; he never dwells for a moment on mere decencies or commonplaces, but proceeds naturally and at once to matters of thought and feeling. But he is at present quite *forestico*, and not to be caught."

On the 29th of May, 1827, Madame Bunsen gave birth to her second daughter, christened Emilia, after her lost sister, Mrs. Manley. It was at the same time that Dr. Arnold, of Rugby, paying a short and hasty visit to Rome with some pupils, laid the foundation of his great friendship with Bunsen. Later in the summer the family moved to Castel Gandolfo.

MADAME BUNSEN *to her* MOTHER.

"15 *August*, 1827, *Castel Gandolfo*.—The idea of the bare possibility of my seeing here all those beings, who have so occupied and do so occupy my thoughts, but who for so many years have existed to me but in the visions of recollection and imagination—has scarcely been out of my thoughts : I have not looked at one of the children, without considering how they are likely severally to strike my Mother: I have not looked at Charles, without endeavouring to measure the alteration (even to myself a very sensible one) which ten years have brought about ; I have counted the lines in my own face, as far as I could with such a looking-glass as our present residence affords ; I have not looked within at the rooms, nor out of the windows, of our present delightful place of abode, without speculating on my father and mother inhabiting it with us, with Augusta Charlotte and Hanbury.*

" An accident befell Ernest on the 4th of August, which I will begin with saying, passed off most happily, and then my Mother will feel a less shock on hearing that he broke his arm. We set out very late (from Castel Gandolfo), that is to say a short time before sunset, on account of the heat, to walk in the *Galleria di Sopra*, the shady avenue which leads to Albano along the ridge of the basin of the lake. Our party consisted of Charles and myself, Mr. Erskine, Mr. Simon, and the four boys, followed by the servant Nicola. We had just passed the gate of the Villa Barberini, when the three eldest boys

* The infant children of her sister, Mrs. Hall, afterwards Lady Llanover. It was November, 1829, before the meeting really took place.

ran with Nicola a few steps down a narrow path going
from, or rather lower than the main road, having called
upon him to make them whips; we then perceived some
loose horses coming after us, and the man who was with
them answered to a question of Nicola, that they were to
go along the narrow path which the children had entered,
wherefore we all at the same moment summoned the
children to come out of their way. My attention was
occupied by George, who stood just at the entrance of the
narrow path, and just before the horses' feet, but Mr.
Erskine was quicker than myself in springing to seize
him. In the meantime the other three boys were making
their escape up the bank to get into the main road, Nicola
helping Charles as the youngest, and supposed more help-
less, when Ernest's foot slipped, and he fell, upwards.
The whole was the occurrence of a moment, and when I
turned my head from witnessing the safety of George, I
heard him scream, and while seeing him lifted on his feet
by Nicola, *saw* what had happened, so that I answered
Charles's exclamation of ' What's the matter ? ' by saying,
' He has broken his arm, I see it.' Nicola took him up
in his arms, and I made a sling of the silk handkerchief I
had in the bag which contained my sketch-book: he continued to scream and I said to him, ' My boy, God has
suffered this to happen, and God will help you, don't you
know that ? ' upon which he became quiet, and from
that moment never cried or complained : a circumstance
which I can never recall without the tears starting to my
eyes, from thankfulness that he should already be capable
of being quieted under suffering by confidence in divine
support. As we passed through the street of Castello,

people without end wanted to help to carry Ernest, but Nicola would not give him up. The operation of setting must of course have been very painful, but it was over in a moment, and he only uttered a sound at that moment. . . . The surgeon said at the end of a week, which was on his birthday, that he might be allowed to leave his bed. and walk about with his arm in a sling."

CHAPTER VIII.

ABSENCE.

"They are never alone that are accompanied with noble thoughts."

SIR PHILIP SIDNEY.

IN September, 1827, Bunsen left Rome on his first official journey to Berlin, suddenly summoned on the ostensible reason of conveying thither a noble work of Raphael—"La Madonna della famiglia Lante"—which he had been enabled by a happy accident to procure for his country; but really, that his knowledge of the intricacies of the Papal government, acquired during a long residence at Rome, might be made useful in difficulties which had arisen with dignitaries of the Roman Catholic Church in Silesia and other parts of the Prussian dominions.

The distinction with which Bunsen was received at the Prussian court, the favour of the King, and the friendship of the Crown Prince, drew forth such universal courtship of the man, who appeared for the time to be in the very brightest sunshine of royalty, as was excessively trying to one who was still only entering

upon his thirty-seventh year, and who since his marriage had always been satisfied with a quiet life of
laborious duty and usefulness in the animated solitude
of the Eternal City. It was observed on his return to
Rome that his appearance was changed and that the
period of youth was passed. The chief subject of the
royal conversations with Bunsen was that which the
King had most at heart, his anxiety to heal the religious wounds of his own dissevered dominions, and to
promote peace between the Reformed or Calvinistic, and
the Lutheran Churches. For this purpose, with the
assistance of General Witzleben, he had long since put
together a form of prayer for his private chapel, which
had gradually become the authorized form of worship
for the " United Evangelic Church of Prussia."

Repeatedly commanded to prolong his stay, Bunsen
lingered at Berlin till the beginning of March, when,
before taking leave, he considered it his duty to submit
to the King the form of Liturgy which he had drawn
up, with the assistance of Rothe, and to reveal that this,
rather than the form enjoined by his sovereign, was
already in use in the Protestant chapel at Rome. Many
of Bunsen's friends considered that by this act he would
utterly forfeit the King's favour. At first it was evident that Frederic William III. was displeased, but he
received Bunsen's explanations with the kindness which
he had always evinced towards him, and eventually not
only permitted the use of the Liturgy, but made a
public acknowledgment of its merits, by causing it to

be printed, with a preface by his own hand. Bunsen
was himself enjoined to correct the press, so that his
return to Rome was delayed till May, 1828.

MADAME BUNSEN *to her* MOTHER.

"*Palazzo Albani, Castel Gandolfo*, 1 *Oct.*, 1827.—I have
to communicate that on the 8th Sept., the day I dispatched
my last letter, the post brought Charles royal orders to
travel to Berlin as soon as the vacation in the Roman
tribunals should leave him at liberty to quit Rome without
occasioning interruption in the dispatch of business ; (you
will remember that the greater part of Charles's occupation here consists in transacting the business of the
Catholic dioceses in the King of Prussia's dominions with
the Pope, they not being allowed direct intercourse with
the court of Rome). On the 24th September he accomplished getting ready to set out, and at five o'clock in
the afternoon of that day we saw him drive away from his
own door, with post-horses, in a well-closed travelling
carriage, with an excellent and agreeable travelling companion, and an active and clever servant; the carriage so
constructed that he could lie down at length in it, which
was very necessary, as the plan of the journey will make
it often indispensable to travel through the night as well
as the day. His travelling companion is an architect of
the name of Stier, whom we have known for years, and
have every year seen more reason to value, and that he is
useful and agreeable in travelling, we all know by experience, from having had him with us at Orvieto last March.
You will remember that some time ago Charles hinted at
the possibility of this journey, which we afterwards had

reason to believe would not take place, and therefore
wrote to Berlin for leave of absence to go to Naples. In
answer, he was told that the ministry had need of personal
conference with him, with respect to some difficult points
which yet remained to be arranged with the Pope; and on
which (I believe) the ministry do not know what to demand,
until they have heard from Charles what, according to the
system of the present Papal government, can be expected
to be obtained. This opportunity for Charles of seeing
Berlin, not as a mass of building or a mass of population,
but as a centre of intellectual movement,—of again seeing
the King—of being made personally known to the Crown
Prince, who is highly prejudiced in his favour—of forming
the acquaintance of Count Bernstorff, who has already
shown him all the personal interest that can be shown to a
person unknown—of feeling how he stands with his old
and constant protector Prince Wittgenstein, and measuring
the degree of toleration felt for him by the King's private
minister, General Witzleben; cannot but be felt to be
highly important: and may God direct him and direct
them, so that this crisis may tend to establish, not to shake
his position in life. I hope and believe I do not deceive
myself in saying that I have no feelings of ambition on
this occasion : most certainly do I fear and dread that which
many people expect, that the predilection which the King
showed for Charles when in Rome will so far strengthen,
as to induce him to desire his presence at Berlin, in some
post of trust and honour. If such a distinction was to be
inflicted, I trust in Providence that the requisite strength
to endure it would be granted; but humanly speaking,
there is nothing I could so earnestly wish to avert as any

circumstance that should lead Charles, with his acute feelings and irritable fibre, into the midst of court-cabals and
city-intrigues; the happiness of life would be the least to
be sacrificed : only thick-skinned and phlegmatic people
can get through such an ordeal without a material change
for the worse in character. But I trust I shall see him
again, at the end of November or beginning of December,
with much increase of knowledge of the state of things
from the near view he will have been enabled to take, and
with no other alteration, either in plans, wishes, or situation in life. At Berlin he hoped to arrive on the 12th or
13th October, and if not detained by express commands,
would not stay longer than to the end of the month; but
his journey back would take more time than the journey
there, because he would of course profit by the opportunity of being in Germany after eleven years' absence, to
take a glimpse of several friends whom he might never
have the opportunity of seeing again, in particular his
remaining sister, Helen, Madame Müller, who lives at
Corbach, where he will also visit the graves of his parents.
If it is possible, he will go to Bonn, to see Mr. Niebuhr
and Brandis. The latter is as happy as possible in his
marriage, but his wife is almost always ailing : God grant
her life may be preserved, for the calamity of his losing
her would be too terrible. Mr. Niebuhr wrote Charles a
very long letter lately, very happy in the gradual and
complete development of his Marcus. Mrs. Niebuhr drags
on a suffering existence, never well, and never in danger."

" 10 *Oct.*, 1827.—I have had a long and delightful letter
from Berlin, where Charles has met with the most gracious
of receptions from King, Princes, and Ministers. The birth-

day of the Crown Prince, three days after his arrival, was celebrated by the King at a little country-house, which he inhabited when he was Crown Prince, twenty miles from Berlin ; and Charles was invited, although no other person was there except the Royal Family and their attendants."

Madame Bunsen *to her* Husband.

"*Palazzo Albani, Castel Gandolfo*, 26 *Sept.*, 1827.—Having been busy all morning looking over papers, and putting accounts in order, I may now allow myself the refreshment of beginning a letter. My own Dearest and Best! it is a strange sensation that my thoughts have such a long space to travel over before they can reach you : but most thankful do I feel that this separation should take place now, instead of at any other time,—this year, instead of last. On the past summer my thoughts will repose as long as I live with thankfulness, at no time did I ever feel you so near to me, at no time did I ever feel so fully how much you loved me, at no time did I ever feel so much satisfaction and delight in you : so it was just that a period of privation should follow one of fulness. I assure you I am not depressed : I am serious, but not melancholy, at your absence, and in the consideration of the very important crisis that this journey must form in your life.

" The morning after you left, I unceasingly despatched business till half-past twelve, when I set out for Albano, with your sister, the four boys, Augusta Klein and Albrecht, and Giovanni's brother as lackey. Not till four o'clock did we arrive, for they had given us tired horses, however we had no distress, except the hunger of the children, and I enjoyed sitting in quiet in the delicious air.

After dinner the children enjoyed a game at Boccia with Augusta Klein. Before they went to bed, I examined Ernest as to his studies in the absence of Simon, and received from him a compendium of the history of Moses: with such exactness of detail, such accuracy of chronology, and such choice of language, as confirms me in the hope that whatever knowledge he may acquire, he will fairly *possess*, it will not be as it were lent for a time.

" 27 *Sept.*—Yesterday we made an expedition to the outward extremity of the Emissary, *alle mole*, which we found an easy distance, and a very beautiful road, and the spot itself is well worth seeing, though there is nothing of antiquity visible. The post brought letters from Niebuhr with commissions for Latin books, and for an antique brick for Marcus.

" 28 *Sept.*—To-day we have been at Marino, and Frances was with us, and enjoyed greatly riding upon an ass on the old woman's lap. My George rode also, and was the happiest of human beings at being held upon the ass, but he and I have had many a dispute."

" *Castel Gandolfo*, 4 *Oct.*, 1827.—On Monday we profited by the fine day to go to L'Ariccia with all the children, who rode alternately, Frances and Emilia of course with their accompaniments of nurse and waiting-maid, and George with one of his brothers behind him. We fell like a flight of locusts upon John Veit, who sent for his wife from her devotions to receive our visit.

" On Tuesday we drove to Genzano, and afterwards proceeded to Nemi, and there visited the garden of Palazzo Braschi, which is really enjoyable—being contrived upon the steep descent of the rocks under the palace.

" Your sister is on the whole surprisingly well, though she has daily fever, and often severe rheumatic pains. Judging by her feelings, she is of opinion that the bad weather is drawing to a close; if it should do so soon, it would be worth our while to remain here longer, and to go to Monte Cavo, Grotta Ferrata, and the Centroni. Yesterday I had a great battle with George, to whom I found it necessary to refuse *Butterbrod* at breakfast. After urging his right and privilege to it for some time, he resolutely exclaimed, 'Giorgio prende butiro, ammazza Mama me!' You may believe I kept my countenance till I had done whipping him and putting him in prison, but then allowed myself to laugh."

" 7 *Oct.*—I hope before I leave to have dry weather and leisure combining to make some sketch or another as a record of my dear Castel Gandolfo, a place that I shall ever remember with gratitude, and which can in recollection stir up no feeling but what is soothing."

" *Palazzo Caffarelli, Rome,* 14 *Oct.*, 1827.- I had the comfort of your letter, my own Best and Dearest, on the evening before my safe and happy, but somewhat wet return from Castello. There had only been an interval of rain for two days, in which your sister made her escape very wisely to Rome. I never felt so much alone as in the day and half I was at Palazzo Albano without her, and was quite happy to find her again in our own dear house, where everything renewed to me the idea of your absence. The day before I left Castello, besides packing up, I went in the morning to visit the Marchesa Coosa, and then to take leave of the Villa Barberini, where I greatly enjoyed a solitary walk, after establishing the children at play, along the long avenue as far as the pines: the Libeccio blew a tempest, but the sun shone, and the wind spent its fury on the summits of the trees, the walk itself being sheltered; all which circumstances assisted the solemn, but not melancholy state of mind, in which I bade adieu to Castel Gandolfo. Afterwards I took leave of the Pope's garden, and after dinner went down to the lake, and as far as the Emissary, where my George was much pleased with the sight of the swimming lights, which curiosity was not new to his brothers."

" *Rome*, 15 *Oct.*—I had on Saturday evening, and again to-day, a long visit from Mr. and Mrs. Shirley,* the former the same that we ever knew him, and looking the picture of happiness: the latter has produced on us the most agreeable impression, I am quite rejoiced to know her, and wish more than I can describe that she might still be here when you return."

" 20 *Oct.*—My thoughts are much occupied by your description of Cornelius's paintings, and a spirit of criticism will rise in spite of me against the manner in which he has treated the taking of Troy. I think there is much cleverness in the combination of means to produce strong emotion, but that real genius would have been more sparing in the representation of human brutality. The art of painting had better not exist, than that it should be exercised to display the degrading side of what is noble in the ancient world and in human nature; and in the honour

* The Rev. Walter Shirley, afterwards Bishop of Sodor and Man. He married a first cousin of Madame Bunsen, Maria only daughter of William Waddington, who was naturalized in France in consequence of his marriage with Miss Sykes, heiress of S. Remy, in the département de l'Eure.

that we pay, and that we owe, to the memory of Homer's heroes, we should as much as possible keep out of sight and out of recollection the fact that they were ignorant of those refined humanities which Christianity has taught; and the taking of Troy might be represented, and truly represented, without the introduction of those images of passion and atrocity which lower the Grecian heroes to a band of wild beasts, who, after wearying themselves with slaughter, are ready to contend among themselves about the division of the defenceless remainder of their prey, each thinking the other has the better portion. The idea of Cassandra prophesying the vengeance to come, is very magnificent, and the escape of Æneas must be a point of consolation for the eye to rest upon; but I could wish in the other Trojan princesses somewhat less of 'female noise, such as the majesty of grief destroys.' A calamity, for which a number of preceding sorrows had prepared the way, would, as it were, condense the feelings into composed endurance; and historical painting has no need of theatrical emphasis to be intelligible.

"I have been at the Villa Spada, the Villa Pamfili, and the Villa Borghese; at St. Peter's, and S. Maria del Popolo. Rome is very delightful as well as Castello, but one has less leisure here."

To her MOTHER.

"23 *Oct.*, 1827.—Mr. Shirley and Maria are here, and enjoying Rome most thoroughly. When they wrote me word they were arrived, I felt as odd at the idea of encountering them without Charles, as I used to do years ago at the thought of forming new acquaintance without my

Mother; it seemed as if I wanted him to make amends to people for the trouble they took in knowing me. . . . . I am disappointed in Mr. Shirley's not speaking German enough to converse with my sister-in-law, for I am sure it would be a pleasure to both; and I always wish to everybody capable of appreciating intercourse with the extraordinary mind of my sister-in-law, the refreshment and invigoration I have experienced myself from her consummate originality. I do not mean originality in the commonplace sense of the word as implying mere singularity; but to signify, that whether she communicates the plainest or the most refined result of intellectual or spiritual experience, it is always in such a manner as conveys an absolute conviction of its being self-derived and not received from without for the purpose of transmission. When I recollect the hints I have from time to time given you, my Mother, as to this very uncommon person, I am struck with the idea of their apparent discrepancy, and yet cannot by letters undertake to reconcile them: all are true, however paradoxical."

To BUNSEN.

" 24 *Oct.*, 1827.—The company of the Shirleys, whom I see here, or go to, most evenings, is a great gain to me; it is a refreshment to come in contact with people so right-headed and right-hearted, and with whom mind, principles, and feelings, are all sound and healthy."

" 7 *Nov.*—Every sentence in your last letter leads me to ejaculate, to you, my Dearest, to myself, to all of us, ' Watch and pray, that ye enter not into temptation,'— temptation to self-satisfaction, to self-gratulation ; temptation to worldly ambition; temptation to forgetfulness of God and his Providence! Surely, it is an awful trial to which you are exposed, but may the grace of God brace every sinew of your soul to resist unto the end, that you may neither fall into the error of contemning His favours, nor that of looking upon them as your due.—The full tide of gratification beyond wish or expectation, I am called upon in some degree to check, by communicating to you the intelligence of Mr. Cathcart's death. . . . .*

" This is the birthday of our darling George, as last Sunday was that of Charles. A whole set of treasures awaited them both, and the little Eggers' came both days to help to make a noise, and a fine noise was to be heard the whole day long."

" 17 *Nov.*—I have just been in the Campo Vaccino with your sister, my George, and the nurse with Emilia. We saw a number of men at work, excavating opposite the Coliseum, at the foot of the temple of Venus and Rome, but could discover nothing new, except that some archways appear since the removal of the mould, under the substruction of the steps that surrounded the portico of the temple. My George picked up pieces of stone, repeating with great satisfaction ' *questo é bello, 'tico,*' meaning *antico.*"

" 19 *Nov.*—May God guide and protect you! is my prayer now and continually :—if it is His will, your going to Berlin, and remaining in Berlin, will be good for yourself and others; and then I shall not regret your prolonged stay. Your purpose, to attain the point of being well understood by those persons who direct the spiritual existence of your

---

* Mr. Cathcart was the friend of Bunsen's early life, who had been the means of bringing him to Rome.

country, thus stated in general terms, I greatly approve: but I wish I knew who those persons were . . . . and, till you give me more data, I know not how to assent to your assertion 'die Reise war der Mühe werth!' I wish you may not awaken mistrust and suspicion by all your liturgical conferences. O the gossip of Berlin!"

To her MOTHER.

"26 *Nov.*, 1827.—My own dearest Mother's letter was written on the 7th November, my darling George's birthday. O! could but the spirit of joy and satisfaction which was diffused thro' this house on that day, have spread to my Mother, how it would have cheered her gloom, how it would have renovated her weariness, how it would have soothed her spirit! The child is and was the same child on that day as on other days, but that day all were happy in the privilege of doing something or another to make him particularly happy from morning till night, and he was so happy, and did so enjoy himself! I do not love him better than my other children, my own Mother, but he is altogether the one in whose promise I have the fullest satisfaction: there is such a vigour in him, moral and physical,—such proportion, such fullness, such intelligence, such tenderness of nature. Oh! how you would delight in him, and be refreshed by the sight of him! My Mother, it is indeed more and more necessary, as you say, that we should meet, but how?—When I think of the risk about my Father, I dare not allow myself to *wish* that you should come to Rome, so entirely do I feel what you express, that any degree of illness would cause the bitterest self-reproach. But, blessed be God, it is God alone that can bring us together, it is God alone that keeps us apart,—therefore the prolongation of trial must be best for both and we must by no forced measure attempt to put an end to it, lest the trial should take a still worse shape, and turn to punishment. . . . . With regard to my troubles, one cannot be thirty-six years in the world without having anxieties of some sort or other, and I always think, with respect to them, of my Mother's expression when sending me of an errand—' Gallop up stairs again, and give such a message—it's all in your day's work.' That idea of a *day's work*, as much as one's strength can perform, and not more, but also not less, but limited to a term, the day—was always fully satisfactory to me, at those times ; and it is equally so now. I am well content with my present portion of the day's work, my own Mother, and you would be so too, if you knew it, that is, if you knew the whole of my situation, in all its bearings, of which it is so difficult to give an idea in letters written at scraps of time, and amidst interruptions. And as to the future part of the day's work, I do not fear getting through with it.—How should I sink under discouragement, who have the everlasting arms under me, the wisdom of Heaven to direct and guide me, and the infinite treasures of goodness to supply all my necessities ?

" I have constantly the same accounts from my dearest husband, of his receiving unceasing and universal marks of grace and favour at Berlin : may the Providence that brought him to this situation of honour and danger, defend him from the envy, hatred, malice and all uncharitableness by which he must be surrounded ! From the spiritual dangers of his situation, I have the fullest trust that the mercy of God will protect him : He who 'granted the early will grant the latter rain,' and bring His own work to perfection."

" 29 *Nov.*—I have seen the Allens often, morning and evening, and the company of Mr. Allen* is a real pleasure to me. I am more than ever aware of all that is good and excellent and respectable about him, but his foibles have grown old with him as well as his good qualities, and he is as fond as ever of repeating anecdotes of Brooke's : he has however changed the chit-chat of Holland House for that of Woburn, and the names of Scarlett, Brougham, &c., for those of the Russells and the Seymours."

To BUNSEN.

" 14 *Dec.*, 1827.—On Wednesday, our new carpets being down, I invited several people whom I thought myself bound to ask in some form or other. Therefore I got together some musicians. Sardi was pleased to come, and to sing admirably something from the Creation of Haydn : besides him there was Röstell's little Corinaldesi, whose singing was much admired, and a harp-player named Fraziani : the Vannitelli played admirably on the piano-forte, and altogether it was an abundant feast of music, so that the evening passed off extremely well. I took care to have *un rinfresco sufficiente.*

" My George last night jumped up in his sleep and said ' Papa, papa via, papa torna.' On coming down-stairs this morning, Charles related that he had dreamt of his Papa : and Henry, on hearing it, said that he had often dreamt of his Papa's return. Last Sunday I had a long

* Allen of Cresselly, brother of Mrs. Drewe.

walk with the four boys, Giovanni holding my George's hand, and carrying him part of the way home. It was one of those delightful Roman winter days, in which every object seems illuminated and ennobled by the atmosphere, and every breath of air inhaled seems to invigorate soul and body. We went by the Coliseum to S. Clemente, where we examined paintings, monuments, marble-enclosures, and mosaics, to the gratification of all the children. From thence we proceeded to the Baptistery of the Lateran, where the words *Indulgentia Plenaria* gave Henry an opportunity of asking particulars as to the belief of the Catholics, which he received much to his satisfaction, wisely shaking his head. We then went through the Lateran, looking at everything, and issued forth by the main entrance, where Santa Croce and the Porta Asinaria, and the range of mountains behind, with the green meadow before, burst upon us in full splendour of sunshine and colouring.

"At Lady Compton's I have made acquaintance with Mr. Hallam and his wife. Mr. Hallam is not exactly agreeable, but he looks like a person made of sterling stuff.

" My Best-Beloved! the year will be at an end when this letter reaches its destination : probably you will not open it till the new year has begun. May it be to you a year of new blessings, a year of sobriety of spirit, a year of self-resolution, a year of advance in spiritual life! As to all that is temporal, it is impossible for me to form a special wish, lest it should be either granted or rejected in wrath! I can only pray for myself, for you, for our children, for all those we love best, that the power of God may be granted, to enable us to support the will of God! The past year is one I look upon with peculiar thankfulness, for the renewed and strengthened assurance of your love that I have received in it: for the peace and enjoyment of our summer residence: for the progressive improvement in mind and body of our precious children. Again and again, God bless you, my Dearest! It is nine o'clock, and Kestner, Hensel,* and Grahl† are sitting in expectation of me."

"17 *Dec.*, 1827.—My Best-Beloved, what ticklish ground you are standing upon! So useful to each and all, so indispensable where advice on given points is wanting— where all are in a scrape, and all would be glad of a suggestion how to get out of it, but trust you rather than any one else, as being believed to understand the subject better! Oh what shall save you from splitting on rocks, or running aground on shoals! And yet, there are no rocks, no shoals, for him whose steerage is ever regulated according to the true compass of the soul:—who with singleness of eye and heart marks alone the noiseless vibrations of that needle of conscience, which ever points to the pole, the one fixed point round which all that is earthly revolves. My Dearest, shall I admit that I did not like your exultation in *la difficulté vaincue:* were you not too full of self-confidence in your own powers ?—If you have, as I trust and believe, laboured not only faithfully but efficiently for the peace and welfare of the church of Christ, I shall indeed be the last person to grudge you the praise you deserve, but I wish you had not taken so much to yourself. That Providence which brought about your journey to Berlin, may make use of you to produce public

* An eminent Prussian artist.
† The well-known miniature painter to the King of Prussia.

benefit: but to be the instrument of good will not make you better, unless your inward abasement before the cross of Christ is proportioned to your external exaltation. My best-beloved, most precious, will you forgive my preaching? If you have not needed it, you will not take it ill! You are placed on a pinnacle, and you will not wonder that I call to you from a distance, supplicating you to keep your eye still fixed aloft, lest, should you cast it below or around, you should grow giddy and fall."

"26 *Dec.*, 1827.—On Christmas Eve I took care to ask all the stationaries, Kestner, Platner, Rothe and his wife, Hensel, Grahl, the three Eggers and their children, which with the standing-dishes of Simon, Röstell, and Rhebenitz, and the new acquisition of Herr Georg, made up a tolerably large party, and we put up Rhebenitz's transparency between two beautiful trees. . . . . My darling George had a hammer and a pair of pincers, and was the happiest of God's creatures, lugging about the two treasures, one in each dear fat hand ; after looking at everything, and enjoying everything, he took them with him to bed, and slept with them under his pillow. For everybody else present I got some suitable Christmas-box."

"5 *Jan.*, 1828.—My Best-Beloved, your view of the state of people and things in Berlin is made in *your* temper of mind, and I must consider it with *my* temper of mind, which was always one of fear and trembling from my childhood. When anything looks very bright, I always expect a reverse, and so it is in the present case. However, be that as it may, let the will of God be done! I fear not to look forward to a change of fortune, knowing by experience how little outward things have to do with

the satisfaction one may feel in existence. When we were
in the narrowest circumstances, I had less of care and more
of enjoyment, than I have had since what are called our
days of fortune. . . . . You, as the acknowledged favourite
of everybody, are now flattered by everybody (I mean the
world of distinguished beings in the first place, and the
world of little beings in the second) and therefore *all* people
can scarcely show themselves to you in their true colours.

" On the last evening of the year I sang 'Gottlob,
ein Schritt zur Ewigkeit' alone : I wonder where you were,
and who sang a hymn to you !"

"*Jan.* 17, 1828.—My Dearest, I cannot express the pleasure your account of your Christmas gave me, nor what
affection I feel towards the Gröbens * for making you such
amends for not being at home. I also feel real affection
towards the King for the regard he showed you. That
invitation on Christmas Day, and the yet more flattering
arrangement for your hearing the Russians sing, I take to
have resulted from the pleasure which your letter accompanying the Raphael on Christmas Eve gave him. I
doubt not that letter was written with all your heart, and
so it reached the King's."

In the beginning of February, Madame Bunsen
received the news of her father's death. He retained

---

* Count Carl Gröben, of Neudörfohen in East Prussia, had been
Blücher's aide-de-camp during the late campaigns, and held the same
position at this time towards the Crown Prince, afterwards King
Frederick William IV. He lived to an old age, a splendid specimen
of the last generation. His wife was a daughter of that General
Dörnberg described in a former letter from Madame Bunsen to her
mother.

his active habits and his systematic application to reading, to the last, and walked in snow and frost the day
before he died. He retired to bed as usual, while on a
visit to his daughter Augusta at Abercarne, and the next
morning was found by his servant speechless, having
been struck with apoplexy. Mrs. Waddington was
immediately summoned from Llanover, 13 miles distant, but he was never apparently conscious of her
presence. He expired the 19th January, 1828, in his
80th year, and was buried at Llanover.

MADAME BUNSEN *to her* MOTHER.

" 6 *Feb.*, 1828.—My own Mother, I experience that for
a shock of this sort there is no preparation : I had thought
myself prepared for it, with such certainty that I anticipated it;—but that does not alter the fact, or the impression made. My sensation in reference to myself is that
produced by the idea of a ship let loose from its cable,
and drifting before the wind :—the longer I was separated
from the only *home* I ever knew, the more I have ever
clung to the idea of having one fixed point in the world,
the abode of my parents ; and shall that perpetually recurring vision now be incomplete ? must I figure to myself
the empty place, the deserted room ? must I give up the
waking dream of showing my children, of hearing the
comments made upon them—must I give up, worst of all,
the hope cherished of being myself, of being through the
means of my children, some gratification, some occupation, some amusement, to him whom I must look upon as
a benefactor for whom I have never done anything—

towards whom I might have appeared as a mere thankless receiver? Perhaps these dreams might never have been realized, but to have had them cut short by death is the same pain as if every probability had attended them, and we that are earthly must cling to what is earthly, must suffer from what is earthly. But if all this touches me, my own dearest Mother, and touches deeply, what have you not to feel, to be bowed to the ground by? and am I never to be with you at such times?—a foolish thought, for what could I do for you? You are strong to endure, strong in the aid which has never failed you. ' 'Tis dread Omnipotence alone can heal the wound he gave;' your trial and your comfort must come from the same source. O my Mother! how my soul is penetrated by your self-accusation!* and what can I say, how shall I contradict you? I can but remind you of what you know, that you were, and had been, the sole pleasure of his life, the sole occupation, the sole subject-matter that mixed with his thoughts and plans; the thing that he looked for at every period of the day: that you made all his happiness: can you not rest upon this fact? O no,—at first I know you cannot ward off that self-reproach which pours poison into the wound, and converts sorrow to anguish. But you will in time, I trust and pray, feel the practical influence of what your understanding admits. From the blackest stain of sin of which human nature is capable, down to

---

* This alludes to the distress of Mrs. Waddington because she had remained at Llanover when Mr. Waddington, by his own wish, went for a few days' visit to Abercarne. His death was quite sudden, but he had the affectionate attentions of his youngest daughter and her husband, who were with him.

the faintest shade of wrong which a tender conscience can perceive, all must be brought to the 'one fountain opened for all sin and uncleanness:' there the one is obliterated as well as the other; and He who rebuked the winds, and bade the waves be still, can also quiet the human spirit, and bid it cease from troubling the defenceless heart. I am thankful for the circumstance of a precious note being written to you! the very fact of *writing*, of performing that act of all then the most irksome, tells worlds as to the feelings of tenderness towards you that occupied him. And that you were away from him at that moment, was for his satisfaction; he did not anticipate his end was so near, and therefore it was his wish that you should arrange his affairs, in order to forming a plan for the future. You made a sacrifice to his wishes in that short separation. My own dearest Mother, I have no conception how you should ever keep your promise of giving me an account of what took place from the time the chaise came to fetch you, till the note was put into your hands; but if you ever could tell me anything of that time, the comfort would be great indeed: my thoughts wander to it in unceasing conjecture.—That solitary return to Llanover! I had almost said, I cannot bear to think of it: but that is a manner of speaking, my Mother has to bear the reality.

"All Charles's letters contain accounts of the King's unceasing kindness to him: even to *favouritism:* I mistrust all these flowers growing on the soil of a court; they will all have their thorn, although that may later be discovered. . . . . My own dearest Mother, I know not how to bid you adieu!"

To BUNSEN.

"14 *Feb.*, 1828.—I feel my father's death most for my mother, but also as a great personal shock. . . . . My mother attended the funeral. It must have been a most affecting scene: more than four hundred farmers and country people present, and yet all as still as death, though many children were amongst the crowd. Ever since I received on the 20th of December a drawing of my father by Augusta—the most incomparable of all like-nesses—I have felt as if that gift was sent to prepare me for his death: yet, when it was sent, he was in perfect health."

"19 *Feb.*, 1828.—I have had an interruption which gave me much concern, the necessity of breaking to our excellent friend Kestner the news of the death of his mother, who was Werther's 'Lotte.' She was from all accounts a very estimable person, and never deserved in any other respect than being attractive to be raised to the 'bad eminence' of a heroine in a novel."

"20 *Feb.*, 1828.—Of your long-delayed return I can say nothing more than what I daily pray, God grant a good issue! God bless your going out and coming in! Heaven knows of your *coming in* we feel a great need, but I see we shall have much longer to wait. As to other matters, the principal ones in your letter, I pray in the words of the hymn,—

Lava quod est sordidum,	Flecte quod est rigidum.
Riga quod est aridum,	Fove quod est frigidum.
Sana quod est saucium.	Rege quod est devium."

"7 *March*, 1828.—We spent my birthday with as much satisfaction as we could, under the consciousness of your absence, though that was indeed a great weight upon me. That morning I was in some danger of breakfasting alone, for I could get nobody in the house to come, for all the children, with Rhebenitz, Hensel and Grahl, were collected in your sister's room, where she made them wait for Kestner, who was late, in order to come to me in grand procession, the least first. My two sweet girls carried flowers and *roba dolce*, my George a pair of gloves, my Charles a ribbon, my Henry and Ernest each a flower-pot with a flowering-plant in it; your sister brought me a canary-bird in a cage, Grahl a picture of my Frances, Hensel a copy of verses, Rhebenitz a very beautiful drawing from a painting of Pietro Perugino, and Kestner a copy of verses, with a drawing of your sister, which is very like. Afterwards came the Rothe's, she having embroidered a ruff for me: then came the Eggers' procession, Albert with a flower-pot, Georg and Otto with a basket lined with green silk, the gift of Augusta Klein. As soon as the children had dined, we went to see the wild beasts, now outside the Porta del Popolo, and then to the Villa Borghese."

To her MOTHER.

" 1 *March*, 1828.—My dearest husband is still at Berlin, and God grant it may be to good purpose. During this long stay at Court plentiful seed of future trial will have been sown—that is certain: but be it so; 'it is all in the day's work,' and there is but one thing good or evil in life. What I cannot understand is the possibility of people's *seriously* congratulating me (as they do) upon the advantages to be derived to the children from Charles's present favour. One should suppose nobody had ever heard, or read, what a Court is.   I have more hope of the children's doing well in life, from good instructions begun, continued, and ended in faith and prayer.

"The boys are now very busy *cutting out* at one table, while I am writing at the other.   They were at first all about my table like bees, for they always suppose where I sit must be the most convenient place.   After we have dined about five o'clock, and the children at the conclusion of our dinner, have had mashed potatoes, or stewed fruit, or bread and butter, for their supper, they play about a little, and then go up to Simon, who, as I understand, speaks to them about their conduct during the day, then reads a hymn, and prays with them, and then they return to me.   Rather more than a month ago I began the practice of cutting out for them (without moving from my great chair) something from a card, that they might trace it round, and cut it out for themselves—there being no end to my drawing things for each of the three to cut ; and this has proved a delightful occupation, to which they return with fresh zeal every evening from seven to eight o'clock, when they go to bed. The things most usually cut out are from my Mother's book of horses, and birds from Bewick, and beasts from Goldsmith's *Animated Nature*.

"Henry and Ernest have their regular drawing lesson every day, and singing twice a week—the drawing makes progress, but not so striking as the singing.   Rhebenitz keeps them to making out outlines for themselves, from real objects, and Henry has begun to draw from the window ; but this method, which is laying a solid groundwork, cannot at first make a show.   With their progress in singing I am quite astonished—that those two little things should keep firm at their posts, and perform their part of the Psalms of Marcello, while the tenor and bass, and the accompaniment are going on at the same time, is what I witness with surprise, for the quantity of teaching they have had has been really very small, and subject to many interruptions. Their master has accustomed them to writing out their own parts, and it is most amusing to see the important faces they make, when copying out music like great grown-up people, and I am never obliged to remind them of doing it, they always find time, altho' the business is not allowed to encroach on lessons of any sort."

" 19 *March*, 1828.—Maria (Shirley) has left me a legacy of 'pious acquaintances' in Rome, amongst whom I have had an opportunity of learning more of the way of the world than I knew before, and really I am not edified with what I have learnt. . . . . Do you remember a little book which my dear aunt Harriet sent me, the *Memoirs of Mrs. Mary Cooper?* There was much in it to me a subject of melancholy contemplation, as to the seducing spirit now going about the world, of 'Pride dress'd like Humility.' The heroine of the book, I doubt not, will be received among the pardoned and accepted; but I maintain that nevertheless it implies doctrines, and suggests sentiments, more mischievous than anything in Delphine. Mrs. Cooper quotes from a favourite preacher, and often repeats with high satisfaction, 'Do not be satisfied with your religion till it makes you happy.' This implies, first, that it is lawful for you to be satisfied with your religion, that you are allowed to consider it possible to be so religious as to be enabled to say 'It is enough.' Secondly it implies, that we may expect and require to be

happy, in this world, thro' religion. O my own dearest
Mother, what do people mean by such suppositions? Have
they ever thought or reflected? Is not the first step towards religion to acknowledge yourself less than the least
of God's mercies, and not only dust but sin—and when
any step is made in religion, does it not lead you more and
more to wonder at the desperate wickedness, the deep
deceit of the human heart,—to feel 'the iniquities of your
holy things,' and renounce with abhorrence even what the
world may call your good deeds, as knowing them to come
from the same source, to be formed of the same stuff, as
your sins, and therefore unfit for the sight of a God of
purity, however they may take forms useful and convenient
and fair-seeming to men? the result of which is and must
be, the reception, as a matter, not of dogma, but of deep
and heart-felt conviction, of the truth that thro' all-sufficient merits, not our own, if claimed by humble faith, we
are assured of acceptance. Maria once talked of feeling
great happiness since she was convinced of the vanity
of everything earthly, a sentiment I do not understand,
but which I found no opportunity of expressing my dissent
from. I do not comprehend what is meant by the *comfort
of a good conscience*, although I well understand what Jeremy
Taylor calls ' a false peace, and a silent conscience.' My
own Mother, it is risking a good deal to begin on such
topics with my Frances sitting on the table *mending my
glove*, and my George building a house and chattering
opposite: but I believe you will understand what I mean,
however incoherently put together; and not suppose that I
have learnt of Dr. Nott to cast a sweeping sentence of
excommunication against sectaries; on the contrary, I

believe my tendency *was* the reverse, that of over-rating
their merits, nor will you suspect me of requiring everybody to 'bow their heads like a bulrush' and expect to
rise to Heaven only from the depths of despair."

To BUNSEN.

" 20 *March*, 1828.—This day I receive my Best-Beloved's
letter announcing a yet longer absence.—But, God grant
his blessing to the cause, and then, whatever the result, it
will be satisfactory : the result to yourself must probably
be trial, of some sort or other, but if all consequences are
encountered with singleness of heart, strength will be given
to endure them. My Dearest, it is hard work to be patient ;
could I but believe the delay would only be for ten or
twelve days, or only for any given time, I could then make
up my mind to the necessity. But the mischief is, that
after having been so often disappointed, one has no confidence left. . . . . I thank God for the gracious treatment
you receive, and for the fine mind, the candid spirit, and
exalted views of the principal person you have to deal with.
And I thank God, my very Dearest, for all the love and
affection you express towards me : it is my trust in your
love that alone makes it possible to endure this piecemeal
penitence of your lengthened absence."

" 9 *April*, 1828.—It continues to seem odd as well as
disagreeable to me to have to see all sorts of things,
and take part in various *passatempi*, according to the
different seasons of the year, and that you should still be
absent ; and you too go on, through business and pleasure,
through labour and refreshment, between friends and
enemies, through the disturbances of men and the festivals

of the Church—and all without me! I was with your sister on Good Friday in the Sixtine Chapel, as well as on Thursday, and thought much of my dearest Charles on both days, in our own chapel and in that of the Pope; but what day is there on which I do not think much of him! The sun is shining in at the open window, and the breezes bear all the freshness of new vegetation to every organ, and I feel health and strength and spirit to enjoy, but it is tantalising to feel that the principal means of enjoyment is far away."

To her MOTHER.

" 18 *April*, 1828.—I must answer my dearest Mother's question, whether I ought not on account of my health to come with my children to England, very decidedly in the negative. My health is really very good, the illness of this winter was an accident . . . . indeed I consider that I have many grounds for apprehending that my health will not be as good as it is, when I shall be exposed to the intense cold of a German winter, or the continued raw damp of an English one: however, let that be as it may; sufficient unto the day is the evil thereof, and if a burden is sent, strength to bear it will be granted. When I consider the wear and tear I have gone through in the birth of so many children, and the cares and anxiety, the exertion of body and mind, inseparable from the happiest earthly condition, I am only astonished that in these last almost eleven years I should not have experienced a more sensible decay of powers. I know that I am older, and that I look older, but I believe not more so than I should have done from the simple effect of years, wherever or in whatever circumstances passed. Further, my own Mother, even if I did not decide the question so positively against a removal on account of health, I should in no case be satisfied to leave Charles. He has been called upon to leave me, and the journey and protracted absence having been brought about by circumstances quite independent of us both, we were both bound to acquiesce: but we ought never to bring such a separation upon ourselves; I certainly never shall, and I am convinced he will not; whatever might have been his feelings before, as to the practicability of living without me, I have every reason to imagine he has found the reality of absence worse than the anticipation. As to the reasons of his detention, I must explain a long story as briefly as I can. He was in the first place called upon to discuss a matter of great importance in the relations of the King of Prussia with his Catholic subjects, namely the terms on which mixed marriages (between Catholics and Protestants) may lawfully be contracted; the Court of Rome, as things now stand, giving no dispensation without an engagement that the Catholic party will enforce the education of *all the children in Catholic tenets*. This is of course a state of things which cannot go on, but it is not easy to guess how the parties are to be conciliated: however Charles went away from home with a contrivance in his head, by which the matter was to be accomplished, and the result time will show. Then he has had much to do, in speaking and writing, with respect to a difference between the Catholic Bishop of Breslau and his own Diocesans. But the third thing was the principal. The King of Prussia when he was in Rome established in the Chapel of the Legation the liturgical form which he had been endeavouring to induce his subjects generally to adopt, and which in many congregations of the Prussian dominions has been adopted. To this liturgy serious objections have with reason been made : it was put together by persons little suited to such a business, in compliance with the King's desire for something like the mode of worship of the Church of England; and consists of fragments strung together, each good, but wanting a principle of connexion for the furtherance of devotion. This liturgy may be said to require a regular choir, and such was actually got together in Rome, amongst the Painters and Sculptors, to very good effect. But in the course of the second summer after the King was here, many of the principal members of the choir travelled away, and their places were not to be supplied, and therefore Charles, with Rothe the chaplain, availed themselves of the pretext to *re-model the whole :* and they introduced a form, in everything material the same as that of the Church of England, though varying in arrangement. I was amused, and so will you be, to think of the liberties which the subjects of a despotic monarch sometimes take! Of course no report was made to Berlin, for that would not have done :—and Charles now being at Berlin, had every possible reason to hope for an opportunity of communicating the matter, in such a manner as to ensure its not being quashed at once by Royal displeasure. This opportunity was at last found, and on the 28th January the form of divine service here in use, with accompanying treatises and elucidations, was laid before the King. An awful pause ensued, in the course of which Charles learnt that the King had shewn himself much displeased, but had said 'that he would leave the congregation at Rome at liberty to do as they pleased:' he laid aside the papers, and there seemed no hope of his entering into the subject. However he bethought himself, had the papers brought before him, read and explained by his private secretary, General Witzleben, and at last, had Charles summoned to a private audience, in which the business of reconciling him to what had taken place was completed. So far all was well. Charles was invited to a farewell dinner on Thursday, 28 Feb., after which he was graciously dismissed. On Friday morning he was in the act of taking leave of the Crown Prince, his horses having been ordered for the next morning, when he received the King's command to come to dinner at 2 o'clock. On entering the King said to him, that he wished him to delay his journey a little longer, and that General Witzleben would explain the reason. The reason was accordingly explained, that the King was resolved to have the whole printed: and that Charles must superintend the printing: for that it was to appear in the world with the Royal approbation and recommendation. Upon this business he has been detained the whole of March, but his last letters lead me *really* to believe that he will have begun his journey on Easter Monday the 7th April. In that case, he may be here the middle of May."

To BUNSEN.

"23 *April*, 1828.—My own Best-Beloved! the idea of your certain and near return now blends itself with every thought, and gives importance to every action: for almost everything is done or let alone with a reference to it. . . . . You will tell us the dear bright day of your arrival, and then we will drive in a great troop to meet you, at least as far as La Storta, and bring you home in triumph, and feed you, and let you rest, and I shall place a sentinel at the door to say that nobody shall dare to come in. And then the next morning, before the enemy has time to make his approaches, we will put ourselves into the carrettella, and run away to Tivoli, with the object of freely and confidentially speaking, hearing, discussing, and being mutually understood by each other, at this recommencement of our conjugal existence. For you must admit, that if you stay in Rome in your own house only one day, a regular plan of siege will be formed, and all the outlets barricaded, so that you can no longer escape, and even if you escape as easily at the end of four days as at the end of four hours, the best and freshest hours would be past, and your head so full of Roman cares that you would not be able to belong to yourself and to me, as exclusively as I want and expect and desire and require. The eight months of your absence have been marked by joy and grief, pleasure and plague, which we have each had to go through alone : those circumstances will have left their results, and produced their modifications in both of us. And after we have spent our days of enjoyment at Tivoli, where we shall sit out of doors, and saunter, and dawdle, and talk all day, we will send out a grand invitation to everybody we know, to come some evening, and then announce and give out that you are every evening to be found between seven and nine o'clock, but never in the morning."

Bunsen returned to Rome on the 21st of May, and in June the whole family moved to Frascati where the first floor of the Villa Piccolomini was now engaged for their occupation, and continued to be their happy summer home during all the rest of their stay at Rome. In a glorious situation, close to the magnificent Villa Aldobrandini, the Villa Piccolomini, embowered in groves of bay and ilex, looks out on the changing glories of the view which is unlike any other in the world, over the vast expanse of the historic Campagna, in which the world's capital alternately gleams white in the sunlight, or is lost in the luminous immensity of the pink haze. Happy were the long succession of bright summers spent here; " happy was Bunsen in the undisturbed exercise of his faculties in productive labour, in teaching his elder sons and superintending their studies; happy in the relaxation and recreation furnished by that beautiful neighbourhood; happy in the society of chosen friends."*

A welcome addition to the daily society of the Bunsens at this time was given in Herr von Tippelskirch and his wife, *née* Countess Kanitz. Tippelskirch was appointed to succeed Rothe in the chaplaincy at Rome, and both there and at Frascati lent his cordial assistance to Bunsen in the education of his sons.†

MADAME BUNSEN *to her* MOTHER.

" *Villa Piccolomini, Frascati,* 6 *July,* 1828.—Our spare room here is at present occupied by Tholuck, a clergyman who is here as temporary successor to Rothe, till now chap-

* See *Memoirs of Baron Bunsen,* i. 357.
† Herr von Tippelskirch afterwards had a living near Halle, and in the latter part of his life was chaplain of the great government hospital at Berlin, called " La Charité."

lain to the Legation, but who has had an appointment at Wittenberg, and was therefore relieved at his post till his definitive successor can arrive, which will not be till Easter. Tholuck's presence is a great pleasure, and 1 trust will be a great benefit to us, at least he has greatly the gift of instructing, as well as of interesting and entertaining. He has distinguished himself by one or two works, and is a great orientalist: he has been in England, I believe chiefly amongst the *liberal* Evangelicals (I would not use that name, if I knew by what other to call them). Lord Bexley and Sir George Rose are the only names I know amongst the people he was much with. The summer is delicious, and the children, more particularly the three little ones, enjoy the exercise in the villas, which they have such constant opportunities of taking. . . . . My own Mother, I hope to draw and do all sorts of things while I am at Frascati, so much am I impressed with the delightful sensation of the possibility of *employment*, not *hurry*. Since we have been here Charles has at least once a day wished you were here with us to enjoy it: that he always does when he is very happy."

BUNSEN *to* MRS. WADDINGTON.

" *Villa Piccolomini*, 6 *Aug.*, 1828.—My dear Mother. It would have been my duty, and it has been continually my most earnest wish, to communicate to you immediately after my return from Berlin the result of this in many respects most important period of my life. God knows that I have not found time to do it as early as I intended, but at Rome I was from the first moment to the last overwhelmed by accumulated business and never-ceasing visits of old and new friends, and here in the country almost three weeks have been required to secure to me that external and internal repose, without which I strongly dislike to write letters, destined, as this is, to convey a lasting image of one's own life, and to serve as a fixed point and a sea-mark, as it were, to look upon till the long period of separation is at an end, and more satisfactory explanations can take place.

"I will now begin the account I owe you; not of the detail of my Berlin life, because that is impossible, but of the results of the journey as to my situation in life, our prospects and our plans for the education of our children.

"You are aware that hitherto I was, as it were, a stranger in the interior of the State, whose service I had embraced. Risen to a high station in the diplomatic line, I had no *root* in the country where my children were to be established. Firmly resolved not to die a diplomatist and exile, if I could help it, I was unable to form a positive plan, as to my further career in the King's service. God be thanked, that both these inconveniences have disappeared, and given room to prospects, and, humanly speaking, certainties, far beyond all my wishes and expectations. A stay, three times protracted to the extent of six months, not only without my instrumentality, but on the contrary against my decided wish and intention, was at last found to have been necessary to call forth those proofs of confidence of the King, the Prince Royal, and the ministry, which enabled me to establish my *character*, in the moral and intellectual sense, and to mark out to myself the point, upon which, under the present circumstances, I was to bring to bear those powers and acquirements I may possess to serve my King and benefit my country. These results have been as decisive as favourable.

"Having thus, to a certain degree, the free option of preparing for myself either a speedy return to Berlin, or an establishment at Rome more fixed than before, my decision was and remained, to keep and to fortify that station, where more than ever I thank God to be placed. It is its retirement, leisure and independence, which has enabled me to pursue those studies which at once have placed me so high in the Royal confidence, although I never contemplated in their pursuit anything but my own information and the discovery of truth for myself and my fellow-creatures. Moreover, as its independence has given weight to all I had to say on the momentous subjects under discussion, thus it enables me now quietly to wait for the right moment of acting. When therefore towards the end of my stay all eyes were fixed on me, and some considered it likely that I would remain at Berlin, as one of the King's Ministers, questions were put to me from many sides. My open declaration was that I claimed no favour of the King's, besides that of keeping the place, where my services had given satisfaction to His Majesty: and I did not conceal from those, who had a right to more, that should ever the King claim my services in the administration of the church and public instruction, I would be unable to withhold from His Majesty that I concurred entirely in the object which his government wishes to attain, but that I did not think the means employed, in any way proper to this great object in view.

"All my friends, and amongst them my present chief, Count Bernstorff, approved the view I had taken so decidedly of my situation. The Count therefore directed his kind care to the amelioration of the post entrusted to me. I was given to understand that after having executed some commissions of importance, I was to be made Minister Plenipotentiary with an increase of my appointments.

"When you now look back to the precarious nature of our establishment hitherto, and when you consider the impossibility resulting from it, to pursue a regular system of studies and researches, and to form a steady plan of education for our children : when on the other hand you present to your mind the unparalleled enjoyment of a situation like mine, on the Capitol, or the delightful hills of Tusculum, having six months the choice of the most interesting society from all parts of Europe without the turmoil and noise of other great towns, and the remainder of the year leisure to live as a philosopher and a good father of my family—when you take all this into due consideration, I am sure you will be fully impressed with thankfulness for the immediate result of my journey. You will be still more so, when you see our mode of life, our domestic customs, our place in society, and our quiet enjoyment of the united beauties of Nature and fine arts, in short all which I know and feel to coincide so entirely with your natural taste and the wishes of your heart and mind."

MADAME BUNSEN *to her* MOTHER.

"*Rome*, 12 *Nov.*, 1828. . . . Most assuredly religious party spirit is the worst of all bad things ! The spirit of the most bigoted Catholics towards those they called Heretics, is completely reproduced in the sentiments of Evangelicals towards such of their Protestant brethren as do not tie themselves down to a certain ceremonial law, or think themselves better than others for not going to balls! It is however a comfort to hear that there are still such people in the world as Lady Louisa Stuart! how I rejoice in the idea of your having had the refreshment of her presence.* Mrs. —— will have observed very soon that my Mother and Lady Louisa were above using the despicable Shibboleth of a certain party, and having at once concluded them not to be of the Evangelicals, and *therefore* of the reprobate, will have been frightened to death at the thought of the contamination, and felt herself bound in conscience to hurry away.

" The state of my sister-in-law is now most extraordinary and melancholy. She continues seriously and alarmingly ill, and will not see either myself or Charles. I have the comfort of knowing that she wants for no care or attention at the hands of Louise; but last week when Louise was confined to bed with an inflammatory fever, I went to see her uninvited, to know whether the Italian girl who waited upon her in place of Louise did her duty; and persisted in returning again and again: till at last, not satisfied with merely repulsing me, she drove me from her with a degree of fury that I do not consider myself justified in again exciting, and Heaven knows when I shall see her again, for not having done anything to occasion

---

* There was a very close tie of friendship between Lady Louisa Stuart and Mrs. Waddington, which originated in the almost motherly protection and kindness shown by the Countess of Bute (mother of Lady Louisa) to the heart-broken and desolate niece of Mrs. Delany after the death of her aunt and adopted mother.

this fit of humour, I can do nothing to undo it. The advantage of this misfortune is, that I have my time at my own disposal, for the first time for three years and a half, with the exception of the first six weeks at Frascati this summer : and that is an indescribable relief, from which both body and mind gain.

"I have lately had curiosity gratified, but nothing else, in the sight of Chateaubriand, who is a vain creature : thinks himself handsome, and really speaks French so that it is a treat to hear him. The sentiments he utters are as yet a sort of mask, perhaps the time will come when he will utter opinions, supposing he has any."

CHAPTER IX.

ROMAN SUNSHINE.

"Beholding the bright countenance of Truth in the quiet and still air of delightful studies."—MILTON.—*The Reason of Church Government.*

IN the autumn of 1828 Bunsen went to Florence to meet the Crown Prince, afterwards Frederic William IV. of Prussia, and to conduct him to Rome. He arranged that he should enter the city by that descent from Monte Mario, dear to all Roman pilgrims, by which the whole glories of the Eternal City are gradually unfolded to the traveller who follows the windings of the long descent; while, instead of gloomy walls and a poverty-stricken suburb, the first buildings he reaches are the Vatican, and St. Peter's, and the pillared piazza which two gigantic fountains illuminate with their silver spray. The fortnight of the Crown Prince's stay was delightful to all who came in contact with him. Whatever he visited, he saw with indescribable enthusiasm. "His soul is filled with the highest and most splendid designs," wrote Bunsen to Schnorr von Carolsfeld, "and with an amount of knowledge and of capacity for entering into details, of contemplating an object on all sides, of weighing and balancing, and then holding fast the best—such as in a sovereign, present or future, will hardly ever be found." When the Crown Prince left Rome, he was accompanied by Bunsen as far as Venice and Verona.

The next few years—in which the chief outer events were the death of Leo XII., the short reign of Pius VIII., and the accession of Gregory XVI.—were passed happily by the Bunsens, between their Capitoline home and the Villa Piccolomini at Frascati. The duties of the Legation were however so onerous as not to leave much time at the disposal of Bunsen for his literary pursuits, the interest of which was so fully shared by his wife. One object which he had at heart, urged thereto by his friend Edward Gerhard,* was the establishment of an Archæological Institute,† for the assistance of representatives of all nations, who might be interested in the study of ancient Italy. This was accomplished amid many difficulties, and the Institute, liberally endowed by Frederick William IV., not only still exists upon the Tarpeian Rock, but is now very influential. At the same time, by the unremitting exertions of Bunsen, amid endless opposition, the Protestant Hospital (Casa Tarpeia) arose by the side of the Institute, and the *Collegium Preuckianum,* an old Roman

---

* Then "an early pioneer, and long an honoured centre of antiquarian studies in Germany." Dr. Gerhard died at Berlin, May, 1867.

† Instituto di Correspondenza Archeologica.

Catholic establishment, founded by a Baron von Preuck, for the assistance of young Roman Catholic students in Rome, was unearthed and brought again into working order, two cherished inmates of Bunsen's intimate circle being the first to profit by its restoration—Ambrosch, who died many years later as Professor at Breslau, and the young student of history, Papencordt, early snatched away from a life of unusual promise.

The time of study which Bunsen could retrieve from the "Description of Rome"—which he always felt burdensome, but to which he considered himself bound by an arrangement (detailed in an after letter) with the publisher Cotta, for the assistance of his friend Platner—was now devoted with hearty enthusiasm to Egyptian research and the study of hieroglyphics. He was the first to urge the importance of such investigations upon Richard Lepsius, afterwards one of his most valued friends, whose expedition to Egypt, undertaken at the expense of the Prussian Government, was crowned with important success.

Madame Bunsen's own days were increasingly occupied by the care and education of her children. She had a peculiar talent for making her lessons interesting by illustration, and for fixing the facts of the world's history in the minds of her sons, by connecting them with the scenes they visited with her. Their Scripture lessons were often alike recalled with pleasure by mother and sons. "All my children knew and loved their Bible early," wrote Madame Bunsen long afterwards—"my Ernest, when driving out with me in the carriage, would sing to himself the history of Abraham, or some other part, language and tune being alike an improvisation."

MADAME BUNSEN *to her* MOTHER.

"8 *Jan.*, 1829.—Charles and I have had much pleasure in seeing Mr. Gally Knight. We were brought together by Mr. Wilmot Horton, who consulted Charles on the subject of his plan for a bill in favour of the Catholics. Charles, at his request, wrote a memoir on the subject of the negociations of Protestant Powers with the Court of Rome, which, as Mr. Horton left Rome three days after Christmas, was sent after him by courier to Florence. The courier was to be sent off on New Year's Day, and Charles had not been able to begin his memoir till three days before. In the afternoon of one day, and the morning of the next, he finished it, to my amazement, considering the bulk and the importance of the matter; then he gave it to me to read, and, as far as I could, correct, in what leisure intervals I could make in the afternoon of the second day : then came the grand business of transcribing, which I alone could undertake for him, as neither of the two Secretaries possess more than a very slender portion of English, of accuracy, or of speed : and this business I began upon at eleven on the last day of the year and finished writing sixteen folio pages by two o'clock on the morning of the New Year,—not having of course written without intervals. First I wrote from eleven till half-past three, then Charles took me a walk in a bracing north wind, which was very refreshing : we came back to dinner at five, after dinner rested, let the children sing a hymn suited to the close of the year, sent them to bed, and at eight o'clock set to work again : at eleven we left off, rested, and, together with his sister, read, spoke, or meditated on the *tide of time*, and *time of tide*, till the bell of the Capitol announced the end of the old and beginning of the new year; soon after which we set again to work, and the writing and dictating were at an end before two o'clock. I had great satisfaction in this undertaking from the idea that thus a quantity of very necessary information, such as English Statesmen do not possess relative to the Court of Rome, and are not in the way of acquiring, and such as on the whole nobody is so qualified to give them as Charles, should thus be conveyed into a channel, in which, please God, it may serve to ward off much evil."

" 6 *March*, 1829.—Since I sent off my last letter we have had for the first half of February such intense cold as I never felt in Rome; in one part of our own house, the water froze indoors, and when, on the 15th, we went to the Villa Pamfili, after the weather had been milder for forty-eight hours, we nevertheless found every fountain, and the surface of the pool, still incrusted with massive ice, to the great delight of the children. This degree of frost having been accompanied by the keenest north wind, was more penetrating to the human system than a far greater degree would have been in a northern climate, and the sicknesses and deaths that have taken place in consequence have been innumerable, to begin with the Pope and Torlonia, whose deaths have produced the most singular contrast in public feeling, the latter death having been as generally lamented (on account of the extensive alms by which he endeavoured to buy off his offences) as the former was indecently rejoiced over, nothing but the season at which it took place having been contrary to the wishes of the Romans. In their sentiments it is impossible rationally to participate, as their hatred is grounded on those parts of the character and conduct of the Pope for which posterity will applaud him, and not his defects; but his merits were displeasing and inconvenient to them. Charles sincerely regrets Leo the XII., from his experience of him in the transaction of business, and it is a great question whether his successor (whoever that may be) will possess that knowledge of the state of public spirit in foreign countries which rendered it so easy to argue with him, and get him to understand reason. Humanly speaking, it was most unfortunate for Charles that the Pope did not live a few months longer, as he was upon the point of completing an important negociation relative to the mixed marriages of Catholics and Protestants in the Prussian dominions, the decision of which is now of course rendered not only distant but uncertain.

"On my birthday we went to the Villa Pamfili. The day was delightful, and we enjoyed ourselves most thoroughly; and the quantity of flowers was so great, that I broke my back with stooping after them, for although I had assistants enough, there was no prevailing with myself to pass by a red or purple anemone. But the greatest enjoyment of the day was seeing my sweet Emilia insist upon walking, and scolding Angelina for holding her hand. When Frances saw her walk, she also set off leisurely, having before seated herself on the grass, spreading out her pocket-handkerchief to put the flowers in, as she had once seen me do when I had forgotten to bring a basket.

"While Charles was laid up with a cold, a friend brought him 'Tom Jones' for his amusement, and I was induced by observing how he laughed over it, to make a trial myself; and I confess the spirit of the narrative led me on for some chapters, but then I remained sticking in the mire, and I much doubt whether I shall ever read further, and most cordially do I apply my dear Father's favourite epithet, ' 'Tis a blackguard book.' "

On the 11th of June a fourth daughter was born in the Palazzo Caffarelli and christened Mary Charlotte Elizabeth.

BUNSEN *to* MRS. WADDINGTON.

"26 *June*, 1829.—I did not mention in my last letter a most entertaining journey I have taken to the sea-shore, with Dr. Nott, a German professor, a German painter, and M. Kestner—the Hanoverian Chargé d'Affaires, as my companions. We proceeded first by Civita Vecchia to Corneto, where the site of the most ancient city Tarquinii, the seat of Tarquinius' ancestors, of Etruscan origin, and the common cemetery of that town, have lately been discovered. This cemetery has an extension of six miles, and presents a natural plain covered with innumerable smaller and bigger hills, that mark the site of the tombs. These tombs are all hewn in the rock that lies under the surface, and formed in two or more chambers, some of which are still found to contain the bones and the finest vases, arms, &c., that the deceased possessed : some of the paintings which abound on the walls are likewise preserved. Imagine that many of these tombs are of an antiquity of 2,500 years and more, and show a high civilisation, although the fine arts were also here an importation from Greece. From thence we proceeded to Musignano, near Canino, the present residence of Lucien Bonaparte, who has established here his head-quarters in order to survey the most interesting excavations which are going on in his territory. Imagine a wide plain of three or four miles in circumference, entirely filled with tombs, hewn into the rock. In the midst of this plain there rises a hill, 60 feet high, and 200 feet in circumference, which has been found to be wholly artificial. It was originally surrounded with a fine circular wall, of huge square stones, with an entrance paved with slabs of *gilded bronze*. The inside presents chapels, towers, rooms, &c., all destroyed and stripped of their costly ornaments, and the whole was undoubtedly the sepulchral monument of the royal dynasty. The tombs are for the greatest part still filled with the most beautiful vases, of which Lucien already possesses 2,000 at Musignano, among which there are 200 of the first rank, whereas in the whole of Europe there are not twenty others of that merit. Now imagine the odd way in which he lives there and in which we found him. About two miles from his castle he has erected two tents, in the one he sits himself, with his old Franciscan friar, who always accompanies him, surrounded with inscriptions, papers, and books: the other gives shelter to the horses who are always ready to carry him or his aides-de-camp to any point of the field. Now and then one of them comes in to say: 'Eccellenza, a new vase has been found,' or 'a golden ring is here,' or 'an inscription,' &c.

If the object is small, it is brought to him to be registered, and if gold sent to the Princess, who has a rich collection of gold *parure* of God knows how many and how old Etruscan queens and ladies, some of which she wears herself, as bracelets, chains, &c., of most beautiful workmanship. If it is a vase, he goes himself to the spot, and gives his directions how it may be removed, washed, and sent to Musignano. We were ourselves present at such a discovery. It was a great and beautiful vase, all covered with mud. When brought to the light, it was washed, and one figure after the other, witnesses of the once active genius, came out of darkness and mud. Then we went with him to his castle. Before it there are two winged lions, of natural size, sculpture work of the Etruscans : twelve such stood as guards at the entrance of the royal tomb before described. The family life of Musignano is very good, simple, and worthy. Lord and Lady Dudley were present. Ladies and gentlemen speak of nothing but vases, Etruscan arts and kings ; no politics, no regrets. The Franciscan friar is the master of the house. The young princes seem modest and good-natured. We dined there and then went to Canino : in the morning we returned to see the collection a second time. What a curious spectacle to see Napoleon's brother, as busily employed among the tombs of Etruscan kings and lords, and roaming about the monuments of past ages in a deserted country, as once among kings and princes of the day."

MADAME BUNSEN *to her* MOTHER.

" 22 *July*, 1829.—This the anniversary of the birth, and of the death, of my first precious Mary, who has now been seven years ' set free from sin, and sorrow, and mortality:'

—and I am now blessed with a fourth girl, and a second Mary, as perfect and as full of promise as an infant can be : and if the remembrance of what has been experienced checks the flow of sanguine expectation, the conviction, which all experience hourly strengthens, that mercy alone dealt out the pain, as well as the joy, leads to the tranquillising result, that to rejoice in hope is not only permitted, but commanded : and that, on the ground, that even should the gratification of hope be denied in things human, the denial will be the more abundantly compensated in things divine. My own Mother, the feeling that arose in writing the date, I wished to communicate, but I know not how much of it is expressed, or how much you will have to guess, for George is by me, writing on the slate in great capital printing-letters, a Latin declension, at every stroke of which I have to hear and answer some question or observation : you will be amused at this branch of study, which is a most delightful occupation : Mother and son go solemnly together to *fetch* a word from Papa, because if I was to send George alone, he might forget some *case* or other, and then I should not know how to put him in : and then he writes his slate full, which, what with getting the word right, and the spelling right, and the letters as right as he can make them, lasts a long time, during which period I have, many days, cut out several frocks and such like things, but writing does not go on quite as well in his company, and I should choose another time, were not choice of times and seasons a matter that with respect to me is a manner of speaking. Besides George on one side. I have my poor sick Frances on my lap, sometimes with her head on a little pillow, and sometimes on my left arm, which will account for scrawling ; but an interruption I cannot call her, for she is still too unwell to be capable of being amused. Emilia is very engaging and attaching in her behaviour since her sister's illness, so full of concern to see Frances lie down and be carried about; rejoicing to see her eat again with a *spoon ;* caressing her and stroking her on all occasions, and what most of all delights me, showing no jealousy of her sister, altho' a great anxiety not to be forgotten by me: for when I am busied about Frances she never teases to come to me, but whenever I try the experiment of sending Frances to Angelina, she sets off, and comes to me, and stands modestly by me, fixing her large eyes on my face, and silently begging to be taken in lap; and when I take her, there is nothing she does not do to show her quiet happiness.

"My own dearest Mother, my precious Mary was baptized on the 12th July, and received the names of Mary Charlotte Elizabeth, Mary being the name of my own Mother, and of my sister-in-law (also godmother) who held the precious darling's heavy weight. I stood to represent my Mother, and two acquaintances of ours represented the Countess Bernstorff and her mother the Countess Dornath, who were the two other godmothers : Charles represented his friend M. Strauss (a celebrated preacher and theologian in Berlin), and our friend Major Scharnhorst arrived in Rome in time to represent Count Gröben, the other godfather, the excellent and gallant son-in-law of General Dörnberg, whom Charles saw more, and delighted in more, than anybody else, when he was in Berlin, and with whom I became acquainted when he was in Rome — aide-de-camp to the Crown Prince."

"15 *August*, 1829.—My Mother expresses surprise at hearing of Charles's being engaged in a work on Rome, and I am still more surprised that I should never have written her word of it; but still, on reflection, I can account for not having done so, from Charles's only having become entangled in the business, so that it was an old story as relating to other people, before it became a new story as relating to him; and it has now for many years been such an old story altogether, that I must have supposed I had related it to you long ago. The commencement of it dates from the first winter after our marriage, when Mr. Niebuhr and Mr. Brandis, in conjunction with Charles, were puzzling their heads to find out an occupation for Platner, by which his talents and knowledge might be made to turn to account for his family, Platner having till that time been by profession a painter, in consequence of his Father choosing to make him one, whether nature chose it or not.* At last Mr.

---

* The father had been forced against his will to become Professor of Latin and Greek at Leipsic, when his own longing was for the life of an artist. His son Ernest was consequently forced to an art life, though he was naturally a bookworm, and could not paint. He executed a cartoon of Hagar and Ishmael represented at the two opposite ends of a vast canvas, the space between being intended for the "stone's throw!" The German artists in Rome had agreed that when any of their society finished a work, the rest should see it and give a candid opinion of it. Cornelius expressed his opinion of the cartoon of Platner by leaping straight through the canvas and saying, "Now, if you will join the two ends there may be some composition." The obligatory system of education in the Platner family was carried on into the third generation, in which a young man whose natural tendencies were all towards the life of an artist, was compelled to classical studies.

Brandis suggested his undertaking a new edition of Volk-
mann's and Lalande's Description of Rome, for which he
believed him well qualified, from his very complete knowledge of the arts, and of the antiquities of the Middle
Ages, and of the history of Italy altogether; but as from
not possessing the Latin language, Platner was dis-
qualified from going farther back than Italian would carry
him, Mr. Niebuhr and Mr. Brandis promised to manage
between them the classical part of the work, and Charles
promised to help Platner whenever he should have need of
reference to Latin works in the execution of his portion
of the undertaking. Cotta the celebrated bookseller was
that winter at Rome, and entered with the greatest alacrity
into the plan; the work was to be executed on his account,
he was to pay two louis d'or for every printed sheet, and
gave carte blanche for the purchase of the necessary books
of reference. This was very liberal, but at the same time
a good speculation, for Cotta judged, and judged rightly,
that a work for which Niebuhr and Brandis were the
vouchers, would be worth his money. The contract was
made just a month before Henry was born, and Platner
set to work in the first place, to make a historical account
of the Basilicas, or principal churches, of Rome. But here
he was every moment at a stand without Charles, from the
quantity of Latin necessary to wade through; and came
about three evenings in every week for advice and correc-
tion of style—the latter being with Platner the most tedious
of all matters, as he considers it his duty to fight tooth and
nail for his own arrangement of materials, and his own
use of German words. Nearly three years passed before
anything was considered so far finished as to be shown to

Mr. Niebuhr, but when he saw at last a description of the Lateran, which had cost Charles *time* and *breath* not to be calculated, and patience more than I should ever have thought that he possessed—his exclamation to Charles was, 'But can you, my good friend, for a moment imagine that what Platner has here written can be sent to press?' This was a comforting decision! but one against which Charles could not protest: he answered Mr. Niebuhr, 'Then I must write the thing myself! for I cannot do more than I have already done to help Platner to write it.' Wherefore Charles began at the beginning—and soon brought Mr. Niebuhr a history, description, and a detailed criticism of the Lateran, and of S. Paolo fuori le Mura, which obtained not only approbation, but high commendation: and now it was settled (as it ought to have been at first) that Mr. Niebuhr was to keep to ancient Rome and its vestiges, Charles to the Middle Ages and their remains, and Platner to the Museums and Galleries—to which he has proved himself fully competent. Mr. Brandis had been long since 'over the hills and far away!' and the time soon came when Mr. Niebuhr was also to depart, without having contributed anything to the work except a short dissertation, small in bulk tho' great in importance, on the history of the building, improving, increasing, diminishing, and destroying of ancient Rome: he was very sorry not to have done more, but his having been prevented from fulfilling his promise originated in one of the weaknesses of his character. He had promised Gau the architect to be Editor of some inscriptions found by Gau in Nubia, which the latter wished to publish together with engravings from his drawing taken in that journey, but which could only be published after the revision of a critical scholar. But Mr. Niebuhr never intended to do this till after he had finished his portion of the work on Rome. Gau, however, being at Paris, published an advertisement of his work, mentioning Mr. Niebuhr's editorship, and promising all *within the year*, and thus entrapped Mr. Niebuhr, who felt himself bound to enable Gau to keep his word, which I do not think he was:—and as soon as he had laboured thro' his Nubian inscriptions, the time of departure was come, and he left Charles alone with the weight of the Roman work on his shoulders, and the whole business of the Prussian Legation, for which Mr. Niebuhr and Charles together had not been too much! Since that time, he got rid of a part of the antiquities to Professor Gerhard, an excellent as well as learned person, and our very good friend : and a part of the Middle Ages to our good Röstell, now for the last year attached to the Legation. These two persons will derive from Cotta the payment for the sheets they write, which Charles does not, as he works for Platner : in addition Röstell, has undertaken to *correct* Platner, and *dispute* with him."

" *Frascati*, 19 *Oct.*, 1829.—My own dearest Mother! and are you indeed on the road to me! and will this letter find you within a few days' journey of me! I write the words, think the thought, and feel—but cannot yet believe the fact!

" And now, my own Mother, a new set of anxieties arise, which I try to keep as quiet as I can. What will you think of the *new-old* thing that you will find in me? Judging by myself (for I have not the power of fancying either you or Augusta a day older than when I last saw you) I doubt not that you will be struck, and shocked, at my aged appearance,—not considering that 12 years are 12 years, which besides *tell* more after six and twenty than before: and if their 'times, their seasons, and their change,' operate on the *physique*, not less does their weal and woe, their rough and smooth, their sweet and bitter, affect the *morale* whether by relaxation or tension, whether parching or chilling, whether furrowing or obliterating. And then, my own Mother, what will be your feelings towards my heart's treasure, my delight, my comfort,—I had almost said my idol—perhaps the expression is more just than justifiable—my Charles! If defects should strike and displease you, will you make allowance for the severest of trials thro' a long course of years,—the gratification of every wish—the flattery of the great—the love, adoration of the good—the admiration, applause of the intelligent—in a word, the favour of fortune in its most seducing form? and will you then instead of counting up human inperfections, only wonder at the sterling worth that has remained so unspoiled? and if at last something remains to be covered, will you take my love, my admiration, my approbation, as one grand mass of conclusive, comprehensive evidence, and consider that as I am the nearest and know the most, I must be able to judge the best?

" And then, my own Mother, will you take my children for such as they are, and not wonder and be displeased at finding, generally speaking, but common-place sort of things?

" My sister-in-law bids me say for the thousandth time

how tantalising it is to her to think of seeing you and not being able to converse with you. That vexes me as much, or more even than it can vex her—could you quite form the acquaintance of that astonishing, unique person, it would be a key to many an enigma, with respect to me, and to her resistless influence over everybody with whom she has to do.* My own Mother! is this the *last* letter? when I think of that, I am half blind, and my hand trembles, and why need I write on? To be sure I have a world to communicate; but soon I shall not need ink or paper."

In the beginning of November the meeting so often deferred, but looked forward to with such ecstasy, really took place, and Mother and daughter were united after twelve years' separation, finding that absence had rather strengthened than weakened the bond between

---

* Christiana Bunsen was believed to possess the powers of second sight to an extraordinary degree. On the occasion of the visit of the Crown Prince (afterwards Frederick William IV.) to the Palazzo Caffarelli, when all were filled with admiration of his natural charms and predicted for him the most brilliant future, no one paid any special attention to the weird and unprepossessing woman who sate in a corner, grim and silent, but all-observant. Afterwards her brother asked her what had been the— apparently engrossing—subject of her thoughts. "I was thinking," she said, "of the words in the 12th verse of the 8th chapter of the 2nd Book of Kings, 'I know the evil that thou wilt do unto the children of Israel.'" In later life Madame Bunsen frequently described Christiana's strange insight into character:—"She used to give me descriptions of all the different persons who came to the house, not gathered from their conversation, for she never understood a word they said, but yet, whenever I knew the facts, her descriptions were quite correct, and where I did not know them—why, it was very amusing and interesting for me to hear what she had to say."

them. Mrs. Waddington remained at Rome till the following July, and thus enjoyed the happiness of obtaining something more than a mere nominal relationship to the many young lives which had sprung up unseen by her; while her ever calm judgment and bright intelligence rendered her a most welcome addition to the circle of friends who formed the society of Palazzo Caffarelli. Madame Bunsen, on her side, rejoiced to make the acquaintance of her brother-in-law Mr. Hall, of Abercarne, and to renew her relationship towards her sister Augusta, whom she had last seen as a child, and who was already the mother of two children, to whom a third was added at Rome in the summer of 1830.

MADAME BUNSEN *to her* MOTHER.

"*Villa Piccolomini*, 14 *July*, 1830.—My own dearest Mother! in the unceasing bustle and fatigue of the last two days, it is not yet clear to me as matter of feeling that you are literally gone, and that I have it not in my power to go and see you! Oh I am thankful indeed for having had you so long near, for having seen you so much! But I will say nothing of feelings, for I would not for the world cause a tear. I wish I could think my own Mother had shed as few as I have done since we parted! I have had so much to do, and have been obliged to think of so many fiddle-faddles, that I have in general succeeded in avoiding thinking over what will not bear thinking of.

"At half-past four in the afternoon Charles and I, with nurse and baby, Frances and Emilia, and Angelina in the

carrettella, set out from Rome, having before sent off three
cart-loads of belongings, to follow up the three cart-loads
sent on Monday.   The drive was intensely hot ; we arrived
however safe, and it was with a peculiar feeling that I
commented to Charles on our doing so, having had on my
mind all day an apprehension that we should not get to
Frascati without an accident.   We began arranging beds
and couches with great activity, and were agreeably surprised at the appearance of our carts at nine o'clock, which
we had feared would have kept us up longer, as without
some of their contents, there were not mattresses enough
for all the family—eighteen souls and bodies.   About an
hour after ourselves, the second carrettella arrived, which
contained my sister-in-law, Simon, and the four boys.   As
I was in incessant movement from one end of the house to
the other, and only still when I was feeding others and
myself, it is to be accounted for that I never uttered the
usual question 'Are you come safe?'   Wherefore guess my
sensations to-day, on hearing from my sister-in-law, whom
I asked the reason of a terrible bruise, that they had
been overturned by the way, and all pitched out of the
carriage like so many balls ! but how can we be thankful
enough, that nobody was hurt but her unfortunate self,
though she fell with her head against a stone, and was for
a long time senseless.   The coachman's supplications to my
sister-in-law were the cause of their not telling of the misfortune till he was clear off in the morning, and had received his *mancia*.   It was rather hard work to George to
be silent, and he asked Mr. Simon if he might not at least
tell the nurse."

   " 15 *July*, 1830.—Charles has had a number of the *Edin-*

burgh Review lent him by Dr. Wiseman, in which I have read, to my information and amusement, a long article on Dr. Hahnemann and the Homœopathic system ; it is evidently written by a person more taken by the new theory than he thinks proper to admit, for fear of being ridiculed, and I wish what is there stated, for and against, by the head of the party and his antagonists, may make upon my Mother the impression it has made upon me, confirming what I had been inclined to think before, that altho' the abuse of this and of all modes of practice is and must be most mischievous, yet *there is something in it* of more than plausibility.

" I wish my Mother could have seen this house, that I might make her comprehend how comfortable we are now in it. We have contrived lying-down places for everybody, the luxury of which we fully feel, now that the heat is so intense. On Thursday evening we drove down to Grotta Ferrata, and enjoyed an approach towards coolness in the air: afterwards, in the short interval between feeding the children, letting Henry and Ernest sing their hymns, dispatching all to bed, and going to bed myself, I read the newspaper accounts of royal exits and entrances, and was surprised at the *Times* article on the history and character of George IV. I was so afraid of being disgusted by the common practice of canonizing the dead, merely because they are dead, that I was gratified by the unsparing reprobation, without bitterness, of the private character and habits of the King, altho' I thought his political conduct rated too high, and could not but be offended by the continuance of the tone of unqualified approbation applied to Queen Caroline. Yesterday morning Charles went with his boys between six and seven to the Villa Conti. After breakfast, George read one of Watts's Hymns out of his Grandmamma's book, and was greatly delighted to ascertain that it was given to himself; and then wrote a little, but the heat was such, that I would not let him do more, in the intervals of being with Simon. As to myself, except cutting out a frock for George, I did nothing all morning but what could be done lying down, so utterly inert had the heat made me. I am reading the Life of Columbus, by Washington Irving, a book in the style of a book-maker, full of words, and with a great pretension to the communication of new information drawn from manu-script documents, which, however, as far as I have pro-ceeded, I do not detect. My Mother, at every turn I find some little thing or another that you or Augusta have left me, which is always a new pleasure."

BUNSEN *to* MRS. WADDINGTON.

"*Frascati*, 17 *July*, 1830.—My dearest Mother. I was very sorry that a first sheet went without a line from my hand, because I really *wanted* to write to you, as I have always wanted to *speak* to you, to open to you my heart, to gaze upon you and catch every glimpse of that countenance full of benevolence and kindness. The more I feel this, the more I feel thankful for the great blessing conferred upon us by your kindness in coming over to see us: the heart has so much to feed upon, and the mind has enjoyed so much *reality*, that all farther wishes, ardent as they may be, are in comparison thrown into the background and vanish. I never loved you enough, nor do I so now, when I contemplate all I admire, respect, and love in you;

and I feel more than ever that so noble a soul, so generous a heart, a mind so entirely occupied with the happiness of others is never known nor loved as it ought: but that feeling again is happiness."

MADAME BUNSEN *to her* MOTHER.

"*Frascati*, 17 *August*, 1830.—My children are all well. Mary in particular is the wildest of the wild, and is the most amusing, droll, saucy thing that ever was, insisting upon having her own way in everything, and sometimes most exceedingly *naughty*, scolding, demanding, insisting, and triumphing when she gets the better. You will be surprised perhaps that not one of the children has oftener spoken of you since your departure, than Emilia, who often alludes to 'quella Nonna di noi.' Charles had a letter the other day from Sir William Gell, in which he says, 'I charge you and Mrs. Bunsen to beware of eating pears, for his Britannic Majesty's Chargé d'Affaires for Hanover has made the observation, that *one very fine young lady eat one pear, and immediately had strong dollars in her boddles* ' : dolori nelli budelli.

"I hope and believe that you have had newspapers, and that you may not have been without particulars of the revolutionary state of France, and to enable you to admire the conduct of the people of Paris : God grant that the bloodshed may have had an end, not to be renewed, and that the spirit of moderation may continue. I wish the Duke of Orleans was of a character suited to his high destiny, but his conduct appears to me wholly without dignity; he is no William of Orange! I have stupidly forgotten who said of the late era of the world, beginning

with the fall of Napoleon, 'Les évènemens de nos jours ont été grands—mais ils ont trouvé les hommes petits.' Charles was told, two years ago, by a person well informed, that the Duke of Orleans had been thus addressed, by a member of the *côté gauche*—'Monseigneur, soyez tranquille, nous ferons la révolution pour vous, et malgré vous.' *
We have been and are in such a state of excitement in anticipation of political news, that I hardly know how the time passes, and forget the days of the week and month. Charles works like a horse, at his collection of hymns, and the introductory essay on that description of sacred poetry in Germany. I read with pleasure in Coleridge's book, which I think is of the class that are a gain in one's existence. I have been one evening at Cardinal Weld's; they all seem to me very good, kind people."

"*Frascati*, 30 *July*, 1830.—O my own Mother! how enjoyable is our existence here! and O if you could but have been with us! I will not say that again, but could not help saying it this once, under the fresh impression of your journey. We have established a porter at our gate, as usual when we are settled here, and thereby keep the ragged population of Frascati out of our garden, having enforced the stopping up gaps in the hedges. As a characteristic trait of this nation, I must mention that when we were deliberating about the choice of a porter, great interest was made by people resident close by, who got our own servants on their side, to induce us to choose a

* Mrs. Waddington and her youngest daughter were in considerable danger at this crisis—being surrounded by a mob in a French town they were passing through, in consequence of the fleur-de-lis on the arms of their carriage leading to the suspicion that some of the family of Charles X. were in it.

man, represented as possessing every desirable quality and qualification, who is in the awkward predicament of not being able to be with his family at Frascati except by night and by stealth, from having some time ago stabbed a man in a quarrel, which man died of the wound! and the murderer of course has reason to fear that the vengeance of the relatives of the murdered man would stimulate the reluctant police to seize him, if he should reappear in his native town without sufficient protection, which sufficient protection the Italians think Charles would be doing a most benevolent action in affording him! As a pendant to this story, our present porter (who really as yet has never murdered anybody) the day after he was installed, asked Charles in a supplicating manner for permission to wear 'questa piccola arma.' Charles was about to examine the thing he produced from under his coat, when he cried out, 'Bada, bada, c'é la palla dentro.' It was only a loaded pistol, which had he entrapped Charles into authorising him to wear, he would most probably not have borne in vain, had any object of his spite come near him."

"16 *Sept.*, 1830.—Your box is arrived, and its greatest delight is the books, many of which have come into immediate use for the children. The most perfect of all things is 'the Boy's own Book': I enjoy the clear-headed description of the games, the execution of the vignettes, and everything: I wonder who wrote it. Dame Dumpling, Dame Trot, and the rest, have all furnished amusement of all sorts to all sizes and descriptions of persons.

"To-day Charles is gone to Rome, to return to-morrow. After he drove off, we set out on a walk, my sister-in-law on an ass, Simon and myself, with all the children, nurse, and Angelina on foot. As we meant to make a good circuit, I intended to have sent back the little girls after they had accompanied us a little way, but they walked with such spirit, and were so delighted at making a part of the company, that I resolved to try to take them on, and with a very little help, each of them being carried alternately by the servant, they accomplished the whole way, Emilia singing for joy, and Frances running and chattering, and my Mary doing everything that was sweet and delightful; choosing to walk, to hold her sister's hands, then to be carried by Henry, then calling after each of the party, then wondering at seeing her aunt upon the ass. Heaven grant a continuance of health to these precious little things, that I may not bitterly repent leaving them to go to Naples! I have taken myself to task often and often as to the motives of this journey—for mere pleasure, I doubt whether it would be justifiable: but I look upon the complete change of scene, of thought and occupations, as quite necessary for Charles after the un-remitting labour he has had here, and previous to entering upon the life of interruptions, labour, and various excite-ments which awaits him in Rome. Then—our four boys we can take, they are all old enough to enjoy, and profit by the journey."

"*Rome*, 5 *Oct.*, 1830.—We have been enjoying our-selves very much to-day, going in the delicious October afternoon to the Villa Borghese, where the verdure is now more beautiful than in the spring, and which at this season is every day full of gay groups. Yesterday I went on foot with Simon and the four boys to the Monte

Testaceo, where we saw the sun set gloriously: I took my Frances and Emilia with me, having them carried by turns, and they walked nobly, and were delighted to belong to such a grown-up party. We left our dear Villa Piccolomini on Michaelmas-Day, and I have to look back upon the time spent at Frascati with great thankfulness: we had the enjoyment of much leisure, and yet of much social pleasure; and altho' Charles laboured so much for himself, seldom, if ever, has he been able at the same time to busy himself about the children so much as he did this summer, by means of the morning walks regularly taken before breakfast with them and with me. The beauty of nature, of the walks and views about Frascati, strikes me each time of being there with such added force, that I could almost suppose I had been before insensible."

" *Ischia*, 15 *Oct.*, 1830.—If it was only for the sake of the date, I must make the beginning of a letter to my dearest Mother, in the midst of a state of enjoyment which seems at the time a dream, and will probably appear so when past. O that I could by words give an idea of all that I have *drunk in* during the last seven days! It is a line I think of Sir W. Jones's—' He was all eye, and saw thro' every pore!' This is a new world—much too luxurious, too intoxicating, to wish or even to consent to *live* in;—but to gloat over, to expatiate in for a time,— and 'then back to busy life again,'—is *rapturous*, no common word will do."

" *Naples*, 24 *Oct.*—Being now established in a lodging, and calling myself *at home*, I feel almost as if I could write a regular letter, and yet it will perhaps at last be nothing but a bundle of unconnected scraps. Before I begin at

the beginning, I will state the blessed fact, that all of us
are well, and have passed through the manifold risks of
so much journeying by land and water unhurt, and that
the three sweet angels left at home are also well. I had
a letter from Simon the fourth day after I left home,
which would have delighted my Mother—so detailed that
it was a picture of the existence of those darlings—the
behaviour, the looks, the occupations, the *words* of each,
all characteristic,—even the words of my Mary, when
seeking the whole house for her Mamma, her Papa, and
Giorgio. Then I had to fast for twelve days, employed on
our coast and island tour, and on returning to Naples on
the evening of the 22nd I was cheered by a laconic
assurance in a letter from Rhebenitz that all were in the
most thriving state.

"The day after my last letter from Rome, we breakfasted at Velletri, having beforehand run to the Palazzo
Lancellotti, where we saw the sun rise from behind the
splendid mass of the Volscian mountains on the left, while
the sea became visible in the distance on the right, with
the beautiful outline of the Monte Circello, formerly island
of Circe. The staircase and gallery landing-places of the
Palazzo Lancellotti I think the finest I ever saw. From
Velletri we flew rather than drove over the finest road
possible thro' the Pontine Marshes, delighting in every
mile of the way, and wondering what can cause people to
call them tiresome. They are enclosed on the right by a
range of mountains (ornamented with picturesque ancient
towns) such as the eye might feed on for ever without
fatigue: and whatever luxuriant vegetation, expanses of
water peopled with wild birds, and the effect of an inter-

minable avenue of trees within which the road passes,
can do to obliterate the recollection of an unwholesome
flat, is done. Terracina struck me rather less than I
expected, and yet it is most picturesque : on the other
hand, I had never heard enough of the mountain-pass
between Fondi and Itri, where the hills to the very edge
of the road are full of myrtle, *lentisca, cefalia,* intermingled
with heath, the first I had seen since England. I wish
you may happen to know the two shrubby plants of which
I have given the Italian names—the former, between
glossy evergreen leaves, has small coral berries growing
thick round the stem like holly ; the latter, a tough
slender stem with sea-green spear-like leaves, has at the
extremity berries of cornelian, heavy enough to curve it
towards the ground. How many vignettes did I make in
idea for my intended letter to my Mother in driving along !
But people who draw, and who keep a journal in travelling, cannot be such as have to pack and unpack, take
care of and provide for, a husband and four children.
But my own Mother, I do not know what travellers are
made of, who do not talk of Mola di Gaeta. I doubt
whether anything in the world can exceed the view from
the inn called Villa di Cicerone. We arrived there when
the sun was setting, and saw it rise next morning over
the Gulf of Gaeta, reddening the smoky column of the
far-distant Vesuvius. From thence every bit of the way
is beautiful, except from Capua to Naples, where the
uninterrupted succession of tall abeles, connected by
garlands of vines, concealing the soil and the distant
prospect, is as tiresome as in Lombardy. Professor
Gerhard drove to meet us the first stage, and we entered

Naples by the splendid new road made by Murat, on Saturday the 9th. On Sunday, after church, we went in a boat, the thing I entreated to do first of all, along the shore to Posilipo. Monday we resolved to set off on the island tour with Count Platen,* and drove off to Pozzuoli : here the inn was full, but on inquiry we found a private house, which pleased us much better, though there was no pretension to refinement of accommodation. While our dinner was getting ready (which consisted, besides soup and fresh fish, of two such haycocks of maccaroni that we could have played at hide and seek under them) we drove past the Lake Avernus, within sight of the ancient Cumæ. Next morning our eyes opened on the Gulf of Baiæ !

> ' Bear me, some god, to Baiæ's gentle seats,
> Or bury me in Umbria's green retreats ! '

are two sufficiently prosaic lines of Addison's, which have chimed in my ears some twenty or five and twenty years ago, and now I know what moved the mild-spirited Addison to that vehement ejaculation. We embarked in a large boat, and coasted along, landing at all the spots where antiquities were to be seen : in the first place we went on asses by the side of the Lucrine lake to the Avernus, and there saw the Cave of the Sybil, as it is

---

* Count Platen Hallermünd, the fertile lyric and dramatic writer, remarkable for his warm efforts in behalf of the liberation of the Poles. He was a celebrated but not a popular poet, and he died, forlorn and poor, at Syracuse, in 1835. Many instances are remembered of his wonderful insight into national character. Of these perhaps none were more remarkable than his remark to Bunsen—" In Germany we say, ' he is a priest, he is a judge,' in Italy they say, ' *fa* il prete, *fa* il giudice.' "

called—a subterranean passage probably for communication the nearest way between the ancient Cumæ and Misenæ.
Having crossed at last the promontory of Misenæ at Bacoli
while we sent the boat round, we embarked on the other
side, and pushed off from the main land to Procida, walked
across the island, and again embarked for Ischia, where
we arrived at sunset, and found most comfortable quarters
in the Sentinella, an inn formerly a villa, delightfully situated. At Ischia we remained three days, one day longer
than we had intended, on account of the sea being too
rough for our more considerable voyage to Capri. But we
enjoyed every hour spent in Ischia, and could with pleasure
have stayed longer; we made the entire circuit of the
island, and ascended the Epomeo. We were seven hours
on the sea from Ischia to Capri, however all was enjoyable, and half seas over, I obliged Charles to hear, and be
delighted with ' He who has bent him o'er the dead : ' in
the sight of such shores and such a sea, one has need of
the words of inspiration, one's own words will no longer
do for one's feelings. That passage is a description, and
the only description, of Magna Græcia, as well as of real
Greece—it is not Italian. I do not despise nor reject, for
I love what is Italian, but what is Grecian is another
thing : and no enumeration of objects, no geometrical elevation of rocks and hills, can communicate even a shadow
of the reality, they give ideas of other things. Capri I
think yet more beautiful than Ischia, and in Capri I felt
at home, whereas the volcanic mass of Ischia conveyed in
every part the impression of a soil and nature foreign and
heterogene. From Capri the second day we rowed to
Sorrento, floating over the smooth sea, close in sight of a

coast diversified with every species of beauty. At Sorrento we slept and got away next morning as soon as we could, for it was the only place on our tour that we did not like. Mr. W. described it to me literally—'the most beautiful prison in the world, but I don't like to be imprisoned.' We rowed to Castellamare and drove thence to Salerno through the valley of La Cava—indescribably beautiful; and were utterly astonished, after all that we had latterly seen, with the view that opened upon us on descending from Vietri towards Salerno. There we inhabited an inn which had been a bastion of a fortification, and we issued from each of our rooms upon a broad terrace, looking on the sea, over which, three mornings running, I saw the morning star, the break of day behind the coast of Pæstum, the first rays of the sun gleaming on the cliffs on the right hand, stretching from Vietri towards Amalfi, by the clearest and most tranquil atmosphere. The situation of Amalfi, my own Mother, and the valley behind it, is striking beyond description. At Pæstum also all expectation was exceeded by the temple of Neptune: the desolation is frightful, and the asphodel, ever found 'within the place of thousand tombs,' grows all over Pæstum. We saw Pompeii on the way to Naples. The impression which it makes must always be peculiar to itself, and I was not insensible to the effect of places of abode as fresh as if inhabited yesterday, the inhabitants of which have yet been for 1700 years mouldered into dust: but Pompeii is the thing I least of all enjoy, or rather do not enjoy it at all: it is so *little* in every sense of the word, so completely *dans le style de coudoir*.

"The rooms which Count Pourtales has taken for us

in Naples are beautiful, with a range of windows looking on the sea. At the Palace of Portici, I was delighted with a whole grove of *Georginas*.* I hope my
Mother knows the flower, brought by Humboldt originally from the Brazils; it grows very tall in a bush,
and the flowers are every variety of the colour of the
ranunculus, with more outline and light and shade. The
bronze statues in the Museum are inconceivable ! With all
marble remains of antiquity, one puzzles to make out what
is ancient and what has been injured by restoration : but
the bronzes are perfect throughout, fresh and uninjure l.
There would be no end to enumerating objects of delight,
but a bust of Julius Cæsar, of consummate workmanship
and undoubted authenticity, is an object to feast upon in
recollection, as communicating a fund of new ideas. Even
the marble cannot quite deaden 'that eye whose bend
doth awe the world;' while the fine chiselling about the
mouth marks it irresistible in words and expression. The
people of Naples are most hideous and uncivilised, so that
the Romans appear princes on recollection : but I delight
in what I have seen of the country-people and the island-
ers. At Procida and Ischia I have again seen *feminine*
creatures in petticoats, with soft voices, speaking Italian
with a melodious cadence, and looking upon you with a
melting gaze, instead of the brazen stare of Rome."

"*Naples*, 6 *Nov.*, 1830.—Although Count Pourtales was
a new acquaintance, his sudden illness and imminent
death touch us very nearly, and turn to serious sadness
the dream of enjoyment and idleness in which we have
passed the last five weeks. We found him here in the

* Dahlias.

prime of life and possessed of everything that youth and
health and friends and fortune can give to make life
desirable. On the 25th he was with us in the palace and
gardens of Portici, and we little thought that the hand of
death was so soon to touch one of the party, and still less
that the lot was to fall upon him. He is the fourth
person amongst those whom we may call our associates
who have been carried off by sudden illness within the
last three months, as if we were to be allowed every
possible warning, without being afflicted by actual distress ! ''

'' *Rome*, 16 *Nov*.—Count Pourtales breathed his last on
Wednesday the 10th, and on Thursday, 11th, Charles saw
him buried. On Friday at four o'clock in the morning we
left Naples. We saw Caserta and the amphitheatre at
Capua, and before seven on Saturday evening had mounted
our own Capitol, and found our darlings grown, and
fattened, and well, and merry ! How is it possible to
be thankful enough ! Mary came to me at once, but
looked at me with fixed eyes, as if trying to recall an
image of the past, and did not for the first five minutes
smile or rejoice—at the end of that time however all was
clear to her, and she embraced me, and clung round me,
and then sate on my arm gazing at me with a look of
sweetness never to be forgotten. Her father in his travelling cap frightened her, but her *mustering* her brothers is
not to be described :—George, ever her great delight, was
the first that she took hold of by the neck, and kissed,
and called by his name, which, as the easiest of pronun-
ciation, she then applied to each of the other brothers,
stroking and kissing each at the same time, but when

corrected she took all possible pains to repeat the right names : then gazed at each brother, saying ' Bello ! '—and when she lost sight of any one of the four, she would hunt about, and call for whichever was missing, as if she was afraid of losing them again. My Frances was most affectionate, and in different ways she and Emilia have not known what to do to show their delight, ever since I came back.

" I must not forget to tell my Mother that our expedition up Vesuvius turned out very well; we had the finest weather, and the volcano in great activity : it is an inconceivably magnificent spectacle, but which could not so far absorb me as to prevent my often turning my back upon it, to gaze upon the exquisite outline of coast to be traced far below—the three successive bays, from the promontory of Gaeta to the extremity of the promontory of Sorrento, called Capo Minerva; and the unequalled islands of Ischia and Capri, so distinct tho' so diminished. The day at Pompeii was very enjoyable. After witnessing an excavation, we dined with Professor Zahn, who has been for a time resident there to make drawings for the museum at Berlin : he caused the custode-population of Pompeii to assemble and dance the Tarantella for our amusement after dinner, on a terrace with a view of Vesuvius and the sea, and one of the sub-directors of the excavations sang buffo songs to our great delight. At the excavation before dinner, Sir William Gell was present. Pompeii itself will not please me, I cannot help my vulgarity, but I must think of calf-sheds and cow-houses and hen-roosts, and everything that is not refined, when I see such narrow spaces, let their elegance of decoration be what it will !

What is really striking is the street of tombs. We contrived to spend another day between Pozzuoli, Cumæ, Baiæ, and Misenæ, to renew the most delightful images of the whole journey. Now, my own Mother, I wish I may have forgotten nothing essential to be told—thousands of things I have got to say, but between children, visitors, household affairs, and settlings, have not a moment left for recollection, and as the children's dinner is coming, I will close my letter. O my Mother! how dreadful is the state of the world. We all cry 'Peace! peace!' and there is no peace to be hoped for.

"Pray tell Neukomm that we have Felix Mendelssohn here, and that I have already heard him play a Fantasia of Beethoven, and the Preludi of Sebastian Bach, and he will then tell you what enjoyment that is. Felix Mendelssohn's adagio-touch is the only thing I ever heard like Neukomm's."

In December the Bunsens again witnessed a papal funeral, for Pope Pius VIII. expired on the first of that month, after a reign of little more than a year and a half.

MADAME BUNSEN *to her* MOTHER.

"*Rome*, 26 *Dec.*, 1830.—I have not for many years felt so well and strong as since the thorough refreshment of our delightful journey to Naples; but last Christmas my Mother was with us, and so many others were also wanting, that Christmas Eve would have been melancholy from recollection, had not the three eldest boys imagined, contrived, and arranged something for the pleasure of their sisters, which amused everybody, and pleased me I believe most of all, from the thought and its execution. I believe the separation occasioned by the journey to Naples had its beneficial effects, in proving to the boys that they really had pleasure to gain by the presence of their sisters, for I had observed ever since I came home that they were caressed and played with, instead of being teased, as was too often the case formerly : and for the last three weeks I had seen the boys at work at all sorts of things at all odd times, wanting paste every two or three days, and scattering snippings of old visiting cards about all my tables, to say nothing of using all my scissors, &c. ; and when I asked what it was all about, I was told it was for their sisters at Christmas, but a great mystery was made, and George was not let into the room behind the nursery for some days. At last, after my arrangements had been seen and admired, and they had received their gifts, we all went in procession to see their devices, and were really surprised at the good effect they produced. They had converted my dearest Mother's fire-screen into a tree, by dint of green twigs and garlands, and connected it with a real tree on each side, formed of a branch of bay planted in a garden-pot, by festoons of green tied together ; the whole stuck full of wax tapers, a picture in the midst of the screen, and in front of the screen a little table with gifts for their sisters and for the maids, made or bought by themselves, out of their own pittance. They afterwards sang their hymn, had their tea and cake, and went to bed, but as Henry well observed, 'Last year we were so many and noisy !—this time we could make no noise.'

"One of our new acquaintance this winter is Madame de Staël,* the widow of Auguste, *your* Madame de Staël's only son. She is a very charming person, mild and intelligent, but deeply afflicted, having lost her only child the year after she lost her husband. She is, according to the laws of Geneva, the heir of that child; and possesses Coppet, but her riches can give her little comfort. Her delight is my Mary, and when she comes here, she can scarcely take her eyes from her: she fancies her like her own child."

"*Rome*, 24 *Jan.*, 1831.—My own Mother, the newspaper will have told you of the death of Mr. Niebuhr! and you will in part have imagined the shock it has been to both Charles and myself; but quite the degree of shock you cannot have imagined. Charles's feelings have been of the same kind, but even keener than when he lost his father, for the relation of the heart was the same, and with respect to Mr. Niebuhr existed in full force and vigour, whereas from the decays of age, his father had long been dead to him before he expired. And then, the loss of Niebuhr was so unforeseen! he was in the best years of a man's life, not more than fifty-five, his health had strengthened of late years, and tho' he was often ailing, he had no complaint to threaten life. His illness lasted only eight days: from the third day, he asserted that he should die, but till after the fifth, no other person saw cause to apprehend danger. A violent inflammation of the throat was the last death-stroke, but it was without a struggle, or apparent pain, that he expired in the night between the

* Madame de Staël, often mentioned in these volumes, died at Geneva in 1876.

1st and 2nd of January. His mind was clear to the last. Oh! what I would give to know that the highest grace had been granted to him which I think can be granted to a parent on the verge of the grave—that of yielding up a set of unprovided children into the hands of the common Parent, satisfied that God is not bound to any given means for securing their temporal and eternal interests, and that whether he himself had lived or died, their welfare must equally have been the gift of Providence! Mr. Brandis in his kindness wrote many and full particulars, but did not mention anything *said* by him in the prospect of death. But I will comfort myself with the belief that the power of composure and resignation—the most at variance with his anxious and agitated nature—may have been communicated in his last moments by that Voice which rebuked the winds and bid the sea be still. Oh! my own Mother! think of Mrs. Niebuhr! I cannot even think of her yet without tears: and yet I will answer for her bearing her affliction as she ought, that is to say, without complaint or murmur. I answered for the manner in which she would bear the burning of her house,* and every account of her corroborated my supposition; she has ever by principle and habit accepted what came from the hand of God, without pitying herself. But how is she now tried! her *all* is taken away—the object of every thought and action, of every feeling, of every exertion! for even her children

---

* Niebuhr's new house at Bonn, in the arrangement of which he had taken great pleasure, had been completely destroyed by fire on the night of the 6th of February, 1830: but his books were for the most part saved by being thrown out into the snow from the windows of the second story, and the MS. of the 2nd volume of his " History of Rome" was found amongst them.

were so united with him in her affections and occupations, that their existence will be at first but aggravation of misery to her. She was ill when he was taken ill, and not having left him day or night for six days, was then compelled to take to her bed, and when he expired, her fever was so high that she was considered in great danger! However, when Mr. Brandis's letter was sent, on the 4th January, she was recovering.

" I know not how to be thankful enough to Mr. Brandis for having written so immediately, for the death of Mr. Niebuhr was in the newspaper of the same post by which his letter came, and had Charles seen that, without having a letter of particulars and certainty, I think he would have been half distracted. Charles had a long letter from Mr Niebuhr not three weeks ago, very remarkable in many respects : he was quite wretched at the state of the world, and the prospect of the breaking up of governments and of society, without the chance of a better order of things coming out of the anticipated chaos. Time must prove whether his anticipations, or those of more sanguine politicians are just; but in the meantime we are not authorised to condemn as absurd the apprehensions of a person, the study of whose life had been history and politics, and who therefore could see events in their causes more than ordinary mortals. The third volume of Mr. Niebuhr's Roman History he had shortly before prepared for the press, whither he had sent it with a short introduction relative to passing events, written with a freedom that had startled the few people whose comments have as yet reached us. One of the expressions was quoted in a letter to Charles from the publisher of his hymns—' The foolhardiness of the French

Court has broken the talisman which held in thrall the demon of the Revolution.'

" Mr. Brandis's letter contained besides details of his own afflictions. Last summer, a fire broke out in the house of his only and most beloved sister, and consumed in a few hours the whole abode, and a manufactory, which was her husband's sole property and dependence, and that husband, and her eldest son of seventeen, perished in the flames! She has six other children, and the eldest daughter sickly! My Mother, what afflictions fall upon other people! Poor Mr. Brandis received the intelligence when about to go and recruit his debilitated body at Carlsbad, after having endured not only fatigue from long exertion, but affliction from the loss of his second boy. He gave up the water-drinking at once to go to his sister, and found that, before he arrived, a subscription had already been made by the inhabitants of Kiel in Holstein, where she resided, to form a fund for her and her children's support. He however nobly declined this generous proof of the regard in which she was held, saying that he, with his father's assistance, engaged to provide for her. He then went on to Copenhagen to arrange with his father. What proportion the father gives he does not tell, but he mentions that his wife having in his absence made a contrivance to do without half of their house, and let the other half to a friend, they would be enabled by the rest to make good the obligations he had entered towards his sister.

" 25 *Jan.*—And yesterday's post brought the news that Mrs. Niebuhr was released from her sufferings just one week after the death of her husband! The letter did not come to us, and my sister-in-law concealed the intelligence till this morning, that we might not have to think of it thro' the night. Nothing could be less a surprise. I have never felt it possible that she could long survive. But think of those children! the eldest fourteen, the youngest nine years old, all of an age to know what they have lost, bred up with such extreme tenderness, with only too much indulgence, shut up from the rest of the world, and now at once to be cut off from the whole of their past life; to come into the hands of persons to them unknown, even tho' kind friends of their parents! The report conveyed by the letter from Bonn was that they were to go immediately to Kiel, to the sister-in-law of their father, and guardian-aunt of their mother, Madame Hensler, a very superior and excellent woman; and I hope the plan would soon be executed, for to remain in the house of death and desolation might produce a terrible effect upon them. It was the house of which greater part had been burnt in February, and which had been built up in the summer, and in which they had settled themselves again since September! Charles and I wrote to Mrs. Niebuhr last week: I had a feeling that she would not be able to read the letters.*

"Last week we passed several fine afternoons in seeing sights, Charles feeling the need of something to divert his thoughts from the subject to which they ever revert. We went with the four boys to the top of St. Peter's, and even into the ball, one day, and another to the Galleria Borghese. My own Mother, I will conclude. Do not

---

* Niebuhr and his wife rest together in the same cemetery at Bonn, in which the Bunsens also now repose.

think me melancholy, but I cannot help being sad. O what things are passing in families and nations, and we are spared!"

"10 *March*, 1831.—We are all recovering, my own Mother! (after an attack of scarlet-fever) and I have driven out to-day in the most delicious weather, and it is not to be described how beautiful everything was—the abundance of spring blossoms, the brilliancy of sun and sky.

"I am delighted, but not surprised, at the manner in which Neukomm has *attracted* you (though people would laugh if I was to speak of *attraction* as belonging to Neukomm). He is a most extraordinary person, possessing a few more senses and powers of perception than anybody else, and employing them with consummate skill to give pleasure, and avoid giving pain, to those persons whom he likes ; and even those whom he dislikes (and he *can* take in utter aversion) he never offends. No cat walking and winding between wine-glasses without touching or causing to vibrate ever exceeded him in the talent of going *his own way* amongst all sorts of clashing characters, without dislodging anyone, or discomposing the frame of society. He is a person whom when once you know, it is impossible *only to like*, you are compelled to have an *affection* towards him, to feel, not a common-place wish to see him again, but a *want* of his society, a consciousness that what he was to you, nobody else can *exactly* be, that his place is only to be filled by himself. I should not have used these expressions to my Mother before she *knew* Neukomm, as I perceive she does now know him, otherwise they would seem too paradoxical, *now* I am sure she will enter into them.

His affectionate disposition, his power of strong attachment, stand in contrast with a power of calculation that
never was exceeded : never, I suppose, did he do anything but what he intended, and never was he taken by
surprise. To enumerate the apparent contradictions in
him would be endless : all that is most exquisite in art or
nature is matter of his chief enjoyment; and the female
character, and the character of children—the flower and
quintessence of creation—are his especial delight and
study, while for the Creator he can find no place in creation ! This is a fearful fact, my own Mother, only ascertained after multiplied opportunities of nice observation ;
for Neukomm scrupulously avoids *speaking out* as a general
rule, but more particularly uttering anything to shock his
friend's opinions. He is a deeply unhappy person ; the
keen susceptibility of his feelings is misery to him, for no
wound that his heart receives can ever heal—the arrows
of death, the deaths of his friends, are ever rankling
there, and reminding him of that termination of his
own existence, of which he *will not* think. I should be
interested inexpressibly to know his history—I never met
with anybody that did : and he never tells anything himself
but *dotted* facts here and there without connection. It is
my belief that a fund of religious conviction in the hearts
of his friends, forms to him, unknown to himself, an
additional attraction. One evening, when he was going
away late, having worked himself into deep melancholy
with music, he said (I forget in answer to what) in the
words of Hamlet—' When we have shaken off this mortal
coil, what dreams may come ? ' &c. in the manner of a
question.—Charles answered, ' Then, I think, we shall

awake from all dreams.' But he did not assent. I could fill pages in commenting on this most singular of all human compositions, but I must make haste from this subject.

"I hope and trust, my own Mother, that you never believe a word of newspaper or private accounts of disturbances in Rome. Here we have *none*, but the stories that are every day fabricated, and written from Rome, are beyond all belief. A sentinel in the Campo Vaccino went to sleep over his musket, which went off and shot him dead; and a poor dog was shot in the dark for not having answered to the cry of 'Chi viva'—but this is the only blood that has been shed. To be sure the Romans have almost died of fright to hear that some insurgents were advancing on Civita Castellana, but then the Grand Army of the Pope, consisting of one thousand men in uniform and five hundred ragamuffins (who being nearly *in buff*, should be denominated *the Buffs*), have frightened them off.

"I am enjoying Major Napier's 'War in the Peninsula,' it is indescribably interesting; but what a fearful picture of a demoralised nation do the Spaniards present! What self-deception, faithlessness to themselves, and treachery to others! Wherever *exclusive* and *ultra*-Catholicism has robbed a nation of the right use of its moral faculties in the most material point, the moral and intellectual sense becomes blighted and inefficient."

In September, 1831, as will be seen from the letters which follow, Bunsen, on the urgent advice of his friend Herr von Tippelskirch, suddenly determined to relieve his wife, who had latterly spoken of her pecuniary trials as "only a feather in her burden," from the twofold domestic incubus which had weighed upon her for so many years. "I had once or twice said to Charles," she wrote to her Mother afterwards, "my thoughts start back from the subject of our life this winter : all I know is that help always comes, when help is indispensable. He never could make any answer, his distress was equal to mine."

Yet the parting with Christiana was affectionate on both sides, and many friendly meetings afterwards took place. "I could not write before on the subject of my sister-in-law," wrote Madame Bunsen when she was gone. "She had not chosen for months to speak to me, drove me from her room when I attempted to visit her, and abused me and her brother to every one she saw. Yet we parted on the most affectionate terms, and about me she has cast her spell."

BUNSEN *to his* WIFE (*at Frascati*).

"*Rome, Sept.*, 1831.—I have taken a great resolution, because we live in a moment of crisis.

"The enclosed to Christiana will explain to you everything. I have received an invitation to come and see her in her room. I shall be firm and inexorable as to the execution of the plan.

"I am meditating to propose to Simon this afternoon whether it would not be better for himself to give up his situation and return to Germany.

"God give us the right resolution, and bless what we do. I expect to hear your unbiassed feeling and opinion."

"26 *Sept.*, 1831.—Christiana has become an angel: she has cried—accused herself—complained of herself—but *still* she goes, for you might consider from this that she does not intend to go.

"She goes next Thursday week. Simon goes with her.

"Everything is settled."

Madame Bunsen *to* Bunsen.

"*Frascati*, 27 *Sept.*—Your letter has comforted me indescribably, in every way—most of all with the intelligence of that softened state of spirit, which I anticipated would take place at the last, but I had supposed not *till the last*. O I wish that softening might extend further than your person! but although it should go no further, it is still a balm to one's heart that the parting so far should be without bitterness of feeling.

"I have passed a happy day, happy in seeing and feeling that a *real education* of our poor boys is taking its commencement. Henry is to-day as if he could leap out of his skin for joy! and knows not what to do, to show his affection to me, and to Ambrosch. With Ambrosch, after the boys were in bed, I have had the most satisfactory conversation; and I must form the most cheering hopes, from his evident insight into the manner in which not only our boys are severally to be *taught*, but in which their characters are severally to be worked upon and formed. The boys, all four, little guessing what journeys are projected, use for ever at intervals a *certain name*, as of a phantom the return of which is expected.

"Adieu my own very dearest! I feel such a superabundance of happiness that I must fear a reverse of some sort."

BUNSEN *to his* WIFE.

"27 *Sept.*, 1831.—This is the week of surprises and changes. You will not have dreamt probably of what I am to write to you, viz. that next Saturday Christiana and Simon and I shall come out to Frascati, and that you will be begged, as you are now, to return together with the boys the same day here, that we may have four quiet and happy days together.

"So it is. Last night she began to speak on the subject. We planned to invite the whole family here: then, we bethought ourselves of the impossibility of placing them for want of beds, and she resolved to go to Frascati to take leave of the dear girls, and to propose that the four boys might come here with you, sleeping on their paillasses.

"All is arranged to mutual satisfaction, and it becomes clear to each of us that the only remedy was the plan proposed by me—God be thanked for it now and ever.

"You may, I think, announce to the boys Simon's departure."

MADAME BUNSEN *to* BUNSEN.

"*Frascati*, 28 *Sept.*—The blessed intelligence in your letter had not been out of my *hopes* since I received the account last night of the happy change in your favour— but again, I did not think it would have taken place so rapidly. Thank God for it! Pray give to your sister my kind love, and tell her how I shall rejoice to see her, and spend the last few days with her. I cannot write to her to-night, being quite knocked up, for the measure of emotion being full, I fancy the body is rather giving way, having participated beyond its present powers in the elasticity of mind within the last two days."

On October 6, a letter from Bunsen to Mrs. Waddington announced that his sister and Simon had that morning set off—"an awful moment, after seven eventful years!"

MADAME BUNSEN *to her* MOTHER.

"*Rome*, 30 *Nov.*, 1831.—Before we left Frascati, we spent a day at Marino, where I stayed and went about with the boys, while Charles went to wait on the Pope * at Castel Gandolfo, who desired him to stay to dinner with a Cardinal, Maggior Domo, and others who were with him. The Pope himself came in at the desert, for altho' he may *in the country* dine with ordinary mortals, he nevertheless takes his meals alone, not to make ostentation of keeping to his monk's fare. He was very cheerful, and the whole party so full of October merriment, that it was quite an original spectacle for M. de Sydow,† just arrived in the country.

---

* Gregory XVI. (Mauro Capellari), who had been elected in the preceding February.

† Herr Rudolph von Sydow, a man of intense religious fervour, to the end of his life a faithful and devoted friend of Madame de Bunsen. He was Secretary of Legation in Rome, and after filling several diplomatic posts, became Under-Secretary of State for Foreign Affairs in Berlin. After his retirement from office, he was President of the Association of the Red Cross under the Queen of Prussia.

" On the 20th I made a visit, the first of the kind I ever made ; odd as it may seem, after having been fifteen years in Rome, and Charles accredited to four successive Popes, that I should never have been presented to any Pope. The Prussian Minister at Florence, Baron de Martens, and his wife, being for a short time in Rome, Charles had made an application to the Pope to receive them, and thought it right that I should not stay away on the occasion ; and we were appointed to come on Sunday afternoon, 20th November, to the Pope's pavilion in the garden of the Vatican, the place appointed for receiving ladies. When we had accomplished the long walk along the terraces of the garden, and were thinking (I at least for my part) of taking breath before the ascent of the staircase of the casino, we found, issuing from the hall-door of the said casino, actually on the steps before it, nothing less than the Pope himself, only *devancé* by his monsignor in waiting, and two or three other *gentiluomini* to the right and left ; —he had chosen this manner of reception in order to cut off the ceremony of curtsies and obeisances ; and saying ' Siamo in campagna,' he led the way up the stairs, and himself showed us into his saloon, where he caused us to sit down with him on chairs placed round a table at one end, and there being one chair too few, he was about to reach one himself, but that Charles got it instead. He kept us with him more than half an hour, and was very agreeable, with real *esprit de conversation*, showing neither the embarrassment of a monk, the obsequiousness of a secular ecclesiastic, or the assumed dignity and extravagant condescension of a Cardinal—one or other of which extremes I should have thought scarcely avoidable in a person called upon to play the part of a temporal and spiritual sovereign. He began by speaking of the improvements he had made and should make, in the garden and casino of the Vatican, giving his reasons for fixing upon the Vatican as his principal residence, founded upon the far greater importance of the presence of the court in that forsaken quarter of the city, in giving employment to the lower class of inhabitants."

The 3rd of January, 1832, greeted the birth of the twins, Theodore and Theodora, who, in their joint life, were to shed joy over the lives of their parents, and who, from the first, were equally welcomed with the large circle of their predecessors—"the two blessings of God are thriving wonderfully; we almost see them grow," wrote Bunsen on the 14th.

BUNSEN *to* MRS. WADDINGTON.

"24 *Jan.*, 1832.—The twins were of course to receive one and the same name. After having balanced between Cornelius and Cornelia—Constans and Constantia—Theodor and Theodora—we decided on the last as expressing best our feeling in being so richly blest, for the meaning of both names is *God's gift*. Nothing can be more touching than to see the two dear little angels lying by each other's side in the cradle, and they are the object of interest and admiration to all the Roman *principesse* and English ladies who come to visit Fanny. Among these ladies there is one whom we feel particularly attached to, the French Ambassadress, Comtesse de Ste. Aulaire. She is one of the most distinguished, and at the same time most unassuming ladies I ever saw. I knew her already in 1825, during her first stay in Rome. Since then she has made great progress in the knowledge of Christianity, I mean of that real, inward religion which is founded on an internal evidence of the grace of God in the salvation through Christ. She had already in 1825 a decided tendency towards the religion *of the Gospel* (she is, as well as her husband, of one of the most ancient Catholic families): and her intimacy with the Duchesse de Broglie, to whose brother, the Baron de Staël, she had an early attachment, sanctified by religion, has developed and directed her religious feelings and principles. She has written a really Christian Preface to the *Extraits de Lettres Chrétiennes,* which she published last year anonymously at Paris. These are letters of Madame de Guyon, in extracts, divested of all that was extravagant and enthusiastic in that distinguished and really Christian woman. It is very extraordinary that such a person should be French Ambassadress to the Holy See! She and two other Catholic ladies are members of a society of about sixteen persons, who meet every Thursday in the afternoon to read the Bible together. Nothing can be more touching and edifying than her domestic life. The whole family read every morning a chapter of the New Testament, and when she is alone with her three daughters, models of simplicity in their manners, she makes them write down their explanations and meditations upon the same. Of course all this is concealed from the world, and done as in time of persecution. Strange compound of human things in which we live! The other day she was distressed by the news that the eldest daughter of the Duchesse de Broglie, of fifteen years, was dangerously ill and near her death. Madame de Staël (the widow) and the Duchess wrote to her in the most edifying manner. Then came letters that gave some hope, but a fortnight ago a courier arrived with the news of her death. I have since read the letters of the Duchess and Madame de Staël. They would be more worth printing than any histories of saints. Madame de Staël describes the agony of the last night. Then, when death was approaching, and the child began to comfort her father and mother, saying: 'Je meurs en paix, ne pleurez pas?' the Duchess, overcoming her feelings as a mother, rose and pronounced these words—'Mon enfant, va en paix : ta foi t'a sauvée ; laisse nous ta paix que Dieu t'a donnée.' After this benediction the girl expired, smiling."

MADAME BUNSEN *to her* MOTHER.

" 24 *Jan.*, 1832.—My own Mother, to-morrow it will be three weeks since I was blessed with two more dear treasures—more prized and delighted in, I think, than any before, not because the preceding ones were less valuable, but because by practice one learns to enjoy, and learns to be more thankful. . . . . Their father has high satisfaction with the progress the boys are making. Oh my Mother ! what a blessing it is to see these boys, indeed all these children, as happy as the day is long, and going with spirits and gaiety from one thing to another."

BUNSEN *to* MRS. WADDINGTON.

" 9 *March*.—Last Sunday our dear babes were baptized, in our chapel, where a very considerable congregation had united to see the twins with their two nurses, and their

seven brothers and sisters, whom I made to stand in a line
on one side of the baptismal font: * a sight which touched
me so much when I saw it that I was quite overcome
during the ceremony. The afternoon we spent all together,
with the friends of the house, in the Villa Pamfili: it was
the first perfect spring day, the clearest sky, the sweetest
air, and the meadow of the Villa quite covered with thousands of anemones and violets."

MADAME BUNSEN *to her* MOTHER.

" *Rome,* 10 *May,* 1832.—My own Mother, I have lately
written a few lines to you, and if they should ever reach
you, I hope you will kindly receive for my sake—who do
you think—a Frenchman ! and no common Frenchman.
It is M. Rio, of Vannes in Bretagne, whom we have seen
much of this winter : he glories in being a *Breton,* in
having spoken all the years of his childhood exclusively
the Breton language, but as this is preserved in Bretagne
in much less perfection than the Welsh in Wales, he
makes it the principal object of a journey to Great
Britain to study his native language at its source. He
was overjoyed and astonished at my promising him a
letter of introduction on the Welsh frontier. I hope his
being a man of distinguished talents, and heroic courage,
and sincere devotion to his opinions, will gild over to you
all the circumstances of his being an *Ultra-Royalist,* an
Ultra-Catholic, and ready at any moment to shed the last
drop of his blood in defence of the Drapeau Blanc and the

---

* This font was first used on this occasion. Its pedestal, with
designs by Thorwaldsen, was the gift of Mr. Pusey ; the vase of gilt
bronze, executed by Hopfgarten, was the gift of Bunsen.

sovereignty of the Pope! I do not most assuredly approve of his creed either religious or political, but his sincerity, and commanding character, enforces respect. He speaks English very well, and also Italian and German, is possessed of a quantity of information on all subjects, and has so much interest in the fine arts, that conversation may be held with him on a variety of matters, without touching the dangerous point of politics: but yet I hope when you see him you will set him to relate the remarkable history of his own campaign at the age of sixteen, during the *cent jours*, when he helped to organize an insurrection against the authorities constituted by Napoleon.

"We saw a great deal of Sir Walter Scott the first week of his being here, and he once dined with us: the first time of seeing him was quite a shock to me, for though I had been told how infirm he was become, I was not prepared for his difficulty in speaking. But tho' his articulation is gone, his conversation is much of the same sort as formerly, and his expression of goodness and benevolence really venerable, in the midst of physical decay. He is very weak in body, and I am afraid not well managed by his daughter, who is nervously anxious about him, but does not influence him. He is going away next Friday, provided he is not knocked up by an excursion to Bracciano, on which Sir William Gell is taking him to-day, intending to set off at ten o'clock, and drive in the burning sun twenty-five miles. I am sure they ought not to have kept him so long in the south, for heat cannot be good for him: I fear he will not live long." *

* Madame de Bunsen ever remembered Sir Walter Scott's touching last words to her on leaving Rome—" I hope and believe *your own*

"*Frascati*, 29 *June*, 1833.—I must tell my own Mother something of our delightful and throughout fortunate expedition to the mountains. We drove on Tuesday morning to Cavi, four miles beyond Palestrina. At Cavi we stopped to bait the horses, and got out of the carriage without knowing where in the little town we should seek a resting-place for ourselves better than the stable into which the horses were conveyed: we sent Franz to examine the room that was offered us in the Osteria, but he came back and reported that 'it was used as a henroost, and the people were just driving out the hens'; so we asked a man on the piazza whether there was not a private house where we might be let in to rest for an hour or two, and he answered—*perchè non entrate là ?* pointing to a palace, to which we had not dreamt of aspiring. But we took the hint, and sent up Franz to make our request, which was no sooner uttered than granted, the *Guardaroba* and others came to receive us like expected guests, we found clean rooms with excellent new furniture, beds, and couches, placed at our disposal, a well-provided kitchen, and such a cordial welcome, that we might have been tempted to consider the whole as a dream, having been five minutes before in an unknown place, not knowing where to enter. Upon inquiry, it came out that the possessor was a neighbour of ours in Rome, and his *Guardaroba* and *Ministro* well acquainted with Mary's nurse and her husband, and other families of our nurses, in the neighbouring town of Zagarolo, so that we were not so unknown as we had supposed. We brought some provi-

feelings prove your reward for the kindness and hospitality you have shown me."

sions with us, and the people of the house furnished us
with so much besides, that we made a great dinner, and
having enjoyed the view from the terrace into a beautiful
rich valley, bounded by steep and wooded hills, and opening to give a prospect of the clear blue Volscian mountains, we set off again, refreshed and pleased, at four
o'clock, and drove six miles further along a good road,
which then came to an end, so we left the carriage to
return to Cavi, and went the remaining two miles of steep
ascent on foot to Olevano, where we were cordially received by Signora Costanza Baldi,* an old acquaintance of
many years' standing, who possesses a casino in a delightful situation out of the town ; in short, every situation in
that country is beautiful, where the view is not shut out
by walls. I had heard much of the neighbourhood of
Olevano, but had not fancied anything so fine as it is—
such an assemblage of the finest materials of landscape, so
consummately grouped, and so continually varied—mountain and plain, bare hills and woody knolls, green patches
and wild thickets, rugged rocks and rich vegetation, chestnut groves, vineyards and cornfields : and the numerous
towns either perched like eagles' nests on the summit of
mountains, or fastened like pigeon-houses to a precipitous
declivity, or rising in the shape of ant-hills on a rock of
their own, in short situated as if the eye of the painter had
been more considered than the convenience of the inhabitants, which is to be explained by the circumstance of their
having been all originally fortresses, the position of which

* The delightful though primitive casino-inn of Olevano—one of
the most gloriously situated in Italy, is still in the hands of the Baldi
family.

was selected *on account* of the difficulty of approach. The next day we remained at Olevano, going out in the morning early, in one direction, sitting in the shade to draw when it grew hotter, and after dinner being conducted by Signora Costanza and Signor Giacomo the organist of Olevano on the other side, first up to the ruined castle, then thro' the town to the Vigna dell' Arciprete, a beautiful spot which we had often seen in the sketch-books of painters. We had observed by the way that we were followed by the Signora Costanza's maid with a covered basket on her head, and on our arrival at the Vigna the materials of a *merenda* were produced, Signora Costanza having been quite distressed at not having prevailed upon us at dinner to eat as much as she thought necessary. On our way back, she sent Signor Giacomo up a high cherry-tree, from which he broke off whole twigs loaded with cherries, to the exceeding delight and enjoyment of the boys. The Signora Baldi is a *possidente* of Olevano, who lets her spare rooms every summer to painters, who come to study the scenery and the features of the inhabitants, who are a very handsome race—the women with a Vittoria * cast of features, but taller and with better figures. It was a treat to see some of the saltarello-dancers: and all or most belong to a class of which much is heard in novels and poetry, and something in books of travels, but which are rarely seen in reality—country-people not rich enough for luxury, but sufficiently well off to afford themselves leisure for amusement. In the Casa Baldi we lived as if on a visit, but the Signora had a present for the food and lodg-

* Vittoria was a beautiful peasant-girl of Albano, discovered by Kestner, and often painted by him and other artists.

ing she had afforded us, reckoned according to what would have been fair at an inn, if there had been such a thing.

"We set off before six on mules and asses to go across the mountains to Subiaco, a distance of twelve miles, along the most rugged roads, but presenting the finest variety of prospects. Subiaco is situated in the valley of the Anio, 27 miles above Tivoli; therefore here we had river-scenery, and abrupt mountains, the character of which reminded me of those which rise above the Rydal Lake in Westmoreland—indeed this tract of country being lime-stone and not volcanic, may by nature bear a similarity to home-scenes; and our great enjoyment was the observation of the wild flowers, among which, at a certain elevation, for the first time in Italy I found my Mother's favourite veronica, and also *leaves* of primroses, it was of course too late for flowers. The beauty and variety of flowers in these regions is not to be described, numbers growing wild that we cultivate in gardens,—Venus's looking-glass, devil in a bush, adonis, lupins, and a quantity more of which I do not know or have forgotten the names. The unusually long continuance of cool and rainy weather had preserved everywhere the freshness of the verdure, and the ripening corn completed the effect, so that it was more like an English June, but with the high colouring of Italy. The early part of this day was overcast, and we had a storm or two while passing chestnut woods, and a more serious shower which obliged us to shelter in the village of Rocca di S. Stefano—but as we did not get wet, the clouds did us good service in protecting us from the sun. At Subiaco the day cleared up and we went after dinner to see the celebrated convents of San Benedetto and

Santa Scolastica. . . . . In returning we slept again at Olevano, and intended to have seen much more of its walks, but were detained at the Casa Baldi by a merry party of the inhabitants, who sang national airs, accompanying themselves on the guitar and mandoline, and afterwards danced the saltarello in every variety. We staid another night at Cavi with the same hospitable people who had received us on our entrance into the town, and on the following evening before dark we were safe at home at Frascati, and found the dear girls and sweet babies well and brisk : and having enjoyed our five days' idleness and exercise, we now set in good earnest to our regular, quiet, and busy summer course of life.

" Oh my Mother ! I wish I could describe how delightful the twins are ! the boy in particular—the manner in which he opens those big sensible eyes, and fixes them upon somebody he knows, and then bursts into a smile and trembles with delight ! The dear little girl is also full of smiles and intelligence, but in a quieter way, and does not *crow* as much as he does."

" *Frascati*, 24 *July*, 1832.—This year our summer existence is unmixed enjoyment, without having anybody to plague, or thwart, or disturb us. Having allowed the boys and ourselves the refreshment of the journey to Subiaco, on resettling at Frascati they were settled in a regular plan of lessons, so contrived as to economise time and strength as much as possible, in order to make the most of this invaluable season of relief from interruption, in which their Father can urge, aid, and enforce, as well as instruct. They get up at five o'clock, and we breakfast at eight, and between those hours they prepare themselves for lessons, and walk out with us for half an hour. At nine o'clock they set to work again, and are kept to it in good earnest till twelve, when we *drive* them all to lie down on their beds, where they have no difficulty in sleeping till dinner-time at one o'clock, except indeed that Henry often gets up before that to practise on the pianoforte, for which he has little or no time except on Sundays. After dinner they play at ball till three, when they set to again, and work till six, and then walk out till dark, sup, and go to bed. What the lessons consist of Charles will best explain: that of which I take cognizance is their English, in which the younger ones spend two hours every day, and Henry one hour; besides which, two days in the week, Charles and George read with me in the English Bible chapters relating to the portions of ancient history which they have gone through with their father. My dear Henry's state of constant activity and strenuous exertion is an indescribable blessing. Ernest and Charles too make evident progress, altho' with them it is against inclination: George in the act of acquiring is in his element, and he has a natural instinct for going to the bottom of a thing. I have the comfort of seeing my own dear Frances and Emilia steadily advancing in good habits. My little sweet Mary gives me more trouble and anxiety than her sisters, she is so *very* often so *very* naughty—so resolved to establish her own absolute dominion, and to be herself exonerated from all observances and obligations."

" *Frascati*, 16 *August*, 1832.—You suffer more, my own Mother, in the anticipation of my dear Henry's departure to school than I do—that is a fact upon which I entreat you to rest for your comfort. The explanation of so strange a fact is my over-filled life—filled to overflowing; which leaves so many *present* matters of attention to occupy my thoughts in the narrow intervals of engrossing occupa-tions, that the idea of the parting—the first separation— the *chasm* on which we stand, only casually recurs to make my heart swell; and I have hitherto succeeded well in driving it away, for it will not bear dwelling upon. What-ever *is* to be gone through, *may* be gone through: and therefore all will be well when the time is come and gone: but there is no *imagining* the possibility. Well do I remem-ber how I was struck long ago, when little C. and F. drove away from Llanover, at your saying, ' There! that is at *an end!'* It is an idea quite foreign to a young person that anything can *end,* but which the experience of years renders familiar. When my dear Henry shall have been launched on the ocean of a great school, afterwards to go to a university, after that to enter upon a profession, I may have, I have the greatest hope that I shall have, the satis-faction of knowing him to be advancing in every respect as I can wish; but the period, in which he belonged to myself, will belong to the past and exist but in grateful recollection. But this is as it ought to be: he was not given to me for myself, but I was allowed to have the care and enjoyment of a child of God, to help him on his way to the best of my power: and now my power will—not end altogether—but give way to one more efficient, the bracing influence of a social system. But although this last year of being at home is in many respects a most important and useful year to him, I have hourly opportunities of observing that it should be the last: if he remained longer he would be par-tially matured before the time, he would be brought too far into life, he would imbibe too much of other people's experience : it will be good for him, or rather essential for him to be kept back among boys for a given time, in which the body may be strengthening, and the mind acquiring the materials of knowledge. In his present scrupulous and indefatigable attention to a succession of duties, he is already too little like a boy. . . . . It is already a subject under consideration whether when we send Henry to Schulpforte, we ought not also to send Ernest—probably to the military school at Berlin !

" My own Mother, think as little as you can help of the parting of next spring; but think rather that there is no knowing what a year may bring forth, and that if it is best for parents and children, we too may soon have a summons to follow them northwards. If I was to say what I don't know how to bear in the business, it is our not being near enough to have them in the holidays, and the risk attending those holidays if they are allowed to leave school to go elsewhere.

" I have less leisure than ever this summer, altho' now always well and brisk; but the *reason* is what I rejoice in, that I have this year *much* to do with my children, and I trust to some purpose. . . . My dear George is in his best state, well in health, mild in temper, and taking in knowledge at every pore. Of my sweet twins there is so little to be said, and so much to be felt ! they are always well, always growing, and increasing in intelligence. And how little in every day can I manage to nurse them ! but I enjoy the sight of their enjoyment of existence."

" *Rome*, 5 *Nov.*, 1832.—My own dearest, dearest Mother ! I received five days ago your letter of the 15th Oct., and hard it is to know how to begin an answer,—hard to check and choke down all that multitude of insufficient expressions of love and thankfulness, which as being insufficient, I will not write . . . .

" I have never yet told you. my own Mother, that I shall *not*, as I believed, have to part from Henry next spring, though Ambrosch cannot remain with us after next February. We were at Frascati in habits of daily intercourse with Abeken, the nephew of one of Charles's earliest and dearest friends, who had been in Rome ever since last winter, and became convinced that he was not only in character, principle, and acquirements, fitted for becoming the successor of Ambrosch for a year, but that he was well inclined to take the office. This being the case, Charles made up his mind, after much consideration, and consultation with Tippelskirch and Sydow (who both have the kindness to give very material assistance in the instruction of the boys), that he would be doing right by both Henry and Ernest to detain them another year, and then send them both away together. There was always an objection to sending Henry without Ernest, as the spur of emulation would then be removed from the latter. And as to both of the boys, it was an awful circumstance to put them, so soon, out of reach of all paternal influence— for it must be considered that being obliged to settle them in public schools at such a distance, is throwing them off like a ball that cannot be caught again. We may perhaps not see them again till they are fixed in character as men ; wherefore, if it could be made clear that in their learning they would not be kept back by a year's longer detention at home, in other respects it was evidently right to detain them :—and, *with* this conviction, you may conceive how

our feelings are relieved by this change of plan. . . . .
Charles has begun again to give lessons to the boys, who
in the remaining days of October after our return, went
over their summer lessons by themselves, and yesterday
stood an examination in form by their father, Ambrosch,
and Abeken, which on the whole was very satisfactory."

"*Rome*, 12 *Nov.*, 1832.—I will at last begin to tell my
dearest Mother of our late journey in the Abruzzi. . . . .
The threatened arrival of Prince Augustus of Prussia in
Rome, made it necessary for us to conclude our *villeggiatura*
by the middle of October, that we might be settled before
he was likely to come upon us: and it had long been our
intention to spend our last days in the country in a little
tour, that the boys might have a thorough refreshment
after the very good earnest studies of the summer, before the
studies of the winter should begin. Many were the directions in which we might have found objects of interest, fine
tracts of country, and mountain air, but we decided upon
the province of Abruzzo Citra, and the Lake of Fucino, or
Lago di Celano as it is called in the maps. Kestner, who in
all his travels in Italy had never been there (for near as it
is to Rome, it is out of the common beat), resolved to be of
the party with his nephew—Kestnerino.* So, after having
on the 30th of September, taken leave of Monte Cavo and
Nemi, by riding on asses, *en masse*, including the little
girls and Miss Thompson (the governess), over the mountain, dining at Nemi, and then driving home by the direct
road—we spent Monday and Tuesday the 1st and 2d of
October in packing and arranging the awful breaking-up

* The nephew of M. Kestner, Hermann, went by the name of
" Kestnerino."

of our *villeggiatura*—awful in joke, as comprising such a quantity of trouble, such cart-loads of luggage: and awful in serious feeling, as closing a period of four months spent in peace, in the enjoyment of all the splendour of nature and climate: of all the comfort of leisure for important duties, and without any drawback from sickness on our part, or that of the children.

"Being at Rome, on Friday, the 5th, at half-past four in the morning, we packed our party into our own open-carriage, three boys sitting opposite their parents, and the fourth—the very substantial George—being crammed in between: the servant Franz on the box. Travelling dress whether to wear or carry was a difficult question, but as many things as were indispensable for the boys were crammed into bags hung generally on the outside of the carriage, it is hard to be explained where; the small carriage box under the front seat having enough to do to carry the indispensable for the chiefs of the party. We were very proud of being at the Porta Salara before Kestner; day broke as we reached the Allia, where the Fabii perished; and by ten o'clock we arrived at the Passo di Correse, where an osteria is situated, at which our horses were to bait. Near this spot a river joins the Tiber, formerly called the Cures, and held sacred by the ancient Sabines, and though every trace of their city of that name had disappeared even under the Roman Emperors, the *name* of Correse still remains: it is a beautiful stream, alternately glassy and broken by pebbles. Here we left the Campagna di Roma, and entered the defiles of the Sabina, where the country is beautiful—narrow vallies and steep declivities, and a number of little towns or rather fastnesses, a great deal of wood, and the road good, tho' hilly: we slept at Poggio S. Lorenzo, where there is no inn, but we obtained clean beds in a private house, and the use of the kitchen, where Franz and Kestner's servant (called Vincenzo di Annovera) cooked our dinner. The next day we arrived before noon at Rieti, situated on the same river Velino which afterwards falls over the rocks above Terni, in a valley as luxuriant as the country about Naples, and in the same manner disfigured (to my perceptions) by a continual vegetation of tall trees with festoons of vines, which in a small number are beautiful, but when spread over a whole expanse of country destroy all beauty— the undulation of ground and variety of cultivation being concealed, and nothing but the summits of the hills seen over them. However we climbed up the tower of the Cathedral, and the hill of the Capuchins, and thus discovered all the fine forms of mountains from which we had come, and to which we were going. Charles called upon the Bishop whom he had known in Rome, and the Cardinal Delegate: and before he could return from the latter, the former came to return his visit, and to bring him a packet of letters of recommendation for the journey, which gave me an opportunity of seeing Monsignor Ferretti,* who distinguished himself last year in the time of insurrection, by being the *one* faithful of a thousand, and not merely passively but actively; for by his resolute manner of dismissing the messengers of the insurgents, and by putting his own hands to the preparations for defence, he made the people of Rieti understand that it was out of the question to show their ill-will or faintheartedness, and that resistance *must* be made, even tho' they had but *one* piece of

* Cousin of Pope Pius IX.

ordnance, no ammunition, and on one side of the town no ramparts. He related to me himself how he fabricated musket-balls, and parcelled out his few materials of resistance, altogether putting so good a face upon the matter, that with the assistance of a tremendous storm of hail which pattered in the faces of the insurgents, the latter were so disconcerted, that Rieti was enabled to hold out until the arrival of Colonel Manley, who made a forced march to come to the rescue with a body of Papalini. But he did not tell me himself what he had once told Charles, that when the messengers of the insurgents came to summon him to surrender; he first admonished them solemnly as to the great sin of rebellion, and assured them, *in termini da vescovo*, that he should not be guilty of it : but finding that he had not thereby succeeded in convincing them he was in earnest, he took off his Bishop's cap and gown and took out the cross of the Legion of Honour (which he had obtained in the time of the French), stuck it in his button-hole, and then poured forth against them, *alla Romana*, all the terms of vituperation which the Italian language affords : which made them comprehend he was not to be dealt with. He belongs in appearance as well as character to earlier times, and has the finely chiselled features and powerful colouring of an old Italian portrait. He was accompanied by the Principe di Francavilla, who was just returned from Aquila, and a relation of the Governor, who informed us of two things, one that permission had been sent from Naples for the entrance of our horses at the frontier, and the other, that the Governor expected us at his own house—which second piece of intelligence was as embarrassing as the first was satisfactory.

" Sunday morning, the 7th, we proceeded on our journey thro' the celebrated pass of Antrodoco, which the French forced with great loss of life in the time of the Revolution, tho' only defended by half-armed peasants, and which it was supposed would have entirely checked the Austrians in the year 1820, so great is its natural strength : but the latter met with no resistance. The scenery is magnificent every step of the way from Rieti, and in addition to the more usual ornaments of the Italian landscape, I saw ash-trees of the finest form and growth, in natural woods, such as I had never seen out of England. At Antrodoco a friend of the Bishop of Rieti asked us to partake of '*un brodo, e qual-cosa,*' and startled us by the immense dinner of which we were called to partake. Night closed in before we perceived the shadowy forms of the buildings of Aquila. We intended to have slipped into the town unperceived, and avoid the Governor's house, there being in Aquila an inn, which in no other place after Rieti was to be found ; but a servant of the Governor (Prince Capece Zurla) was stationed at the gate to show us the way, and therefore we saw no way of avoiding this *troppa gentilezza,* which we had been far from intending to bring upon ourselves : but it seems that instead of the simple notice to be given to the Custom house to let our horses pass freely, orders had been sent to all possible officers under government to assist and further our progress, which they interpreted into receiving, lodging, and feeding us. If we could have guessed beforehand that the Neapolitan government would have been to this degree obliging, we could never have made up our minds to give all the quantity of trouble we thus occasioned : but as we *had not* the fault upon our consciences, and as we *had* health and spirits to go through with the undertaking, we enjoyed the opportunity of taking a view of Italian manners and character, such as no other set of circumstances could have afforded. The Prince Capece Zurla was fortunately alone, his Principessa having gone to visit a married daughter: he gave us an apartment which he had fitted up for the King when he came last summer, and scarcely could he have treated the King himself with more attention or a more sumptuous ceremonial. When we came out of our rooms in the morning between 7 and 8 o'clock, he was already in the ante-room waiting for us, and after giving us breakfast, he went about with us to see sights the whole of the first day, which put us into utter despair, and we told him we must the day after proceed on our journey. But he made such a point of our staying a second day, that we gave way, on condition of his not interrupting his customary occupations. We should indeed have been sorry to leave Aquila after only one day's stay, for it is a most interesting town, full of fine architecture and fine pictures, and in a most striking situation, on an elevated plain of the finest forms,—not a dead flat, but full of undulation and highly cultivated, bounded by hills of exquisite outlines, not rugged, but covered with short fine grass for sheep, behind and above which tower the barren summits of the Gran Sasso d'Italia, the Majella, and other of the highest of the southern Apennines. We were guided on the second day by the Marchese Dragonetti and the Marchesi Torres, who had also been of the party the day before: the former was an old acquaintance, and is a very superior man, of talents and acquirements most astonishing, considering the absence of all advantages under which he has laboured—except indeed that greatest of all advantages, the desire of improvement, and the consciousness of surrounding ignorance. The two brothers des Torres are much more *des nobles de Province*, but intelligent and well informed as to everything that has come within the sphere of their observation, and obliging beyond description. Both they and Dragonetti are of Spanish origin, and Aquila altogether, the manner of our reception, and the high ceremonial in deportment and language, reminded me of descriptions of Spain in former times. The Prince Capece Zurla, for instance, proposed to return from a drive by saying,—'Adesso, se comanda, torneremo a *casa sua*,' meaning his own house,—and the des Torres in taking leave, and in urging our return to Aquila, to make a longer stay, said, ' Si ricorderà che avrà sempre in Aquila *una sua casa*, almeno una capanna!' meaning the Palazzo Torres. During those two days, we went from one fine church, from one fine painting, to another, and returning within doors when it was dark, had such French cookery and French wines, that it was a matter of alarm for both grown-up people and children, for all, as you may suppose, were famishing. In our second day's sight-seeing we were introduced to the house of the Marchese Dragonetti, and kindly received by his handsome pleasing wife, who in the desire to be hospitable, ordered ices for us, when, being extenuated with fatigue and hunger, a morsel of bread was the luxury intensely longed for; as Kestner observed afterwards, the offer of ices under such circumstances was like ' giving one's stomach a cruel box on the ear.'

" On Wednesday, the 10th, we got under weigh, and

thought that at last we should *levare l'incomodo* from our good Prince : but he having a journey of a few miles to make, to inspect some public works going on in his province, declared he should go with us part of the day in his own carriage, and there was no begging off. When we got to the end of the first post, where he was to change horses, he represented to us that the post-house, where our horses were to bait, was an uncomfortable place for us to wait in, and insisted upon cramming us all *into* and *upon* his large travelling carriage, and carrying us on eight miles further, to Popoli, where the Signor Sindaco (a sort of chief magistrate) fed us most amply. Popoli is in a luxuriant valley, where the river Aterno, which rises in the plain of Aquila, becomes a considerable stream. From thence we drove on to Rajano, taking leave of the Prince, whose last care of us left the most pleasing impression of all, for it seemed an act of freewill and kind-heartedness : at Aquila we might believe him to be only actuated by scrupulous notions of his *dovere*, but once on the journey, as he had made all possible arrangements for us, he might with a safe conscience have left us to our own inventions. At Rajano we were lodged and most hospitably received at the house of a *giudice*, a droll old bachelor, who was greatly distressed that we could not eat all the supper he had prepared for us. Rajano is beautifully situated on an elevated plain, the site of the ancient Corfinium, smaller than that of Aquila, surrounded by fine mountains, in which the Aterno flows in a deep bed ; but its waters are of no avail to the plain of Rajano, being on a so much lower level, and it would therefore be barren, were it not for an antique canal, which perforates the ridge of hills, and

brings water from a higher valley, so that the whole surface is carefully irrigated and wonderfully fertile. From
thence we crossed the lowest part of the ridge of mountains surrounding the Lake of Fucino, called *le Furche*,
which is an ancient name for a mountain-pass: and
descended to the town of Pescina, in prospect of the lake,
at two miles distance. Here a most comical scene took
place on our arrival. We were going to Don Giuseppe
Melchiorri, an antiquarian friend of some friends of ours,
who expected us, and came to meet us: but the Sindaco
and the Bishop also sent emissaries to insist upon our
coming to dine with Monsignor Vescovo; we however
made good our entrance into the house of Melchiorri, but
were then obliged to give way, and go and eat the
Bishop's dinner, and I was greatly entertained at sitting
by the side of a Roman Catholic country Bishop, who had
probably never seen such a number of heretics together in
his life before. He was a venerable-looking and well-bred
old gentleman. After we were released from the dinner,
we rode with Melchiorri by the side of the beautiful lake,
and saw some antiquities, less worth seeing than land,
water, and sky, and came back to endure the infliction of a
great supper. Next day was Friday, and we supplicated
Melchiorri not to make any alteration in the meagre diet of
the day on our account, but he replied—'Sono gli Speziali
che hanno gli *scrupoli*, io no '—and I fancy was glad of an
excuse for not eating meagre, for he had served in the
French army at Marengo, and had *seen the world*. After
visiting the site of the ancient Marubium, and riding about
near the lake, we returned to dinner at one o'clock, and while
we were in the middle of a course of dishes *alternately* fish,

fowl, and meat (the greatest abomination to strict Catholics),
a visit was announced from Monsignor Vescovo, who must
have been much edified by the spectacle : this misfortune
might have been supposed precluded, as Charles had taken
care to call upon him and take leave that morning, but
there was no help, and he came in, with his suite of
two or three priests. After dinner, we made our escape
with difficulty from Pescina, for our host declared he
required a *month* to show us the antiquities properly—
altho' to judge by the samples he did show, there is little
remarkable on that score at this end of the lake—and
drove on to Avezzano, where we were recommended to the
Casa Mattei, by Cardinal Cappelletti, the Delegate at
Rieti, Donna Chiara Mattei being his cousin, and we were
glad not to *incomodare* the Sotto-Intendente. From the house
of the antiquarian gentleman-farmer and former officer at
Pescina, our removal to Avezzano brought us into a new
world ; the family of Mattei were thorough gentlemen and
gentlewomen, of old-fashioned formality, but not awkward,
and their house was a palace, in every respect handsomely
arranged : and it was to be felt that Donna Chiara managed
her own house. This was the first time of our journey
that we had seen a *padrona* di casa, elsewhere either there
was no such thing, or she kept out of sight. We spent
Saturday in seeing the Emissarium of Claudius, which a
number of workpeople are employed in excavating; we
entered it from the side of the lake, and then rode over the
mountain which it perforates, to see its outlet in the deep
valley of the Liris, afterwards called Garigliano. From
this side the excavation has been effected to a considerable
distance, but the point of difficulty will be just under the

summit of Monte Salviano, and there some people doubt
whether further progress will be possible, and others do
not wish it should, fearing that too much water would be
drained from the lake, which now furnishes fish to an
immense extent of inland country, and thereby supplies
food, and the means of earning necessaries, to a great
multitude of the poor inhabitants of its banks. All that
it is to be wished the Emissary should effect, would be
the prevention of those overflowings of the lake, taking
place at intervals of centuries, which occasioned its original
construction in the time of Claudius, and latterly, in
1816, devastated a great quantity of cultivated land.
Nothing can be more beautiful than the valley of the
Liris above the outlet of the Emissary. I made a sketch
there of the Liris rushing at a great depth at the
bottom of the defile, the steep sides of which were chiefly
covered with chestnut wood, while a magnificent mountain
in front bore the name of *Serra di Sant' Antonio*, called
Serra, in the sense of closing up the valley. Much was
the Signora Mattei astonished at our admiration of the
country, and when I showed her the point of view that I
had delighted to draw, she observed—'A me! mi pare
tanto brutto!' The next morning produced a real embarrassment : it was clear from many circumstances
that the Mattei had no idea of looking upon us as
anything but Roman Catholics, for they regarded with
a sort of reverence those who lived in sight of the Pope
and could give accounts of him, so I was urgent with every
member of the family to be up early as well as myself
and to mount our various steeds before the hour of mass ;
but as everywhere in Italy the difficulty was great of get-

ting off, and while we were waiting for our animals. Don
Ladislao Mattei came up in all ceremony to ask, 'se
vollesse vostra Eccellenza esser servita di sentir la messa,'
the fact being that they had a private chapel and chaplain.
Nothing remained for it but to plead haste, and the
threatening condition of the weather, and thus hurriedly
to say farewell with an unpleasant sensation of having disappointed our kind host. After seeing the wonderful
Cyclopean fortifications of the ancient Alba, we proceeded
to Magliano, where we were most kindly received by Don
Giovanbattista Masciarello, of a long-established family of
patriarchal proprietors, having 6,000 sheep, and I know
not how many head of cattle : living in an immense palace
full of expensive furniture, but not so well arranged as
Palazzo Mattei, because Donna Pepa Masciarello was a
sort of Roman, a native of Rieti, whose notion of life
was taking her ease, and nothing was in order but what her
husband's good head could regulate ; otherwise she was a
goodnatured woman, and they had both less ceremonial
and more natural instinctive good-breeding than we had
anywhere found, and therefore we felt quite at our ease in
their house. The day we spent with them, snow fell on the
lofty Velino, which rises close to Magliano, and we visited
under umbrellas the ancient Alba Fucinense—a hill artificially levelled into three terraces with fortifications far
older than the Roman time. From Magliano we saw at a
distance the plain of Tagliacozzo, and, on the slope of the
hill, the church of Santa Maria della Vittoria, built by
Charles of Anjou to commemorate his victory. In that
battle, which crushed the descendants of the great Emperor
Frederick, seven members of the great Ghibelline family

of Capyx or Capece were present: these the Guelfs showed particular zeal in destroying, and six fell, but the seventh being only a boy, was concealed from the pursuers. From this boy seven families called Capece have descended: one was that of Capece Zurla our hospitable host at Aquila, another that of Capece Latro, Archbishop of Tarento, a fine old gentleman whom we saw at Naples. It was he who had the large Angora cat called Portaleone, who used to sit on a particular stool and cushion close to his master, and whose manner of receiving strangers was supposed to influence the estimation in which they would be held.

"The 16th and 17th October we spent in crossing the mountains where there never yet was a road, yet, in one of the many villages of the Cicolana we were received by an ancient feudal lord, not only with hospitality, but luxury. Our guide was a smuggler by profession, who on being asked whether he knew the road, said by day he had never passed it, but often enough by night. We were expected to stay at the house of a land-owner in a village called San Pietro, but it was resolved to ignore this invitation, and we rode straight on un-challenged, to Rieti. Our intended host has since been in Rome, and when I answered his eager questions as to our route and party, and described our numbers as consisting of three gentlemen and myself, with four boys of different ages, a manservant, and a guide of the country, mounted in part on horses, the boys on donkeys, myself on an English saddle and in an English riding-dress, he started up exclaiming that then indeed his messengers had seen us, for he had placed one at each end of the village, but they had brought him word that no signori whatever

had passed, but only a company of strolling players—
comediante di campagna! We came home from Rieti by
Terni, that I might see the waterfall, which we did in the
greatest perfection, with the finest weather, the finest tints,
and the heath in blossom. On Friday the 19th we were
in Rome again, after a journey without any disaster and
having found the Kestner's the best of travelling companions."

"12 *Jan.*, 1833.—The old year closed upon me, my own
Mother, and the new year began, only too well, in fullness
of blessings, and with a sensation of satisfaction, a consciousness of present comfort and enjoyment, of the degree
of which, if I could give an idea, I might (strange to say)
on one ground be afraid of doing so, lest you should suspect me of being indifferent to the *one* circumstance of
distress in our present situation. But as you will *not*
suspect me of such indifference, I trust this statement of
feelings will be a matter of unmixed comfort to you, and
perhaps even tend to communicate to your mind that hope
for the future with which mine is filled. Amongst the
wishes, for the gratification of which I felt most urgent,
and in which I could *allow* myself to be urgent, during
those three last hours of the old year, in which Charles
and I sate together and for the most part silent, was that
my Mother's mind might be relieved about our worldly
condition : and I feel as if that prayer would be granted.
The removal of all embarrassment in circumstances is one
of those things for which I dare not ask in prayer : I can
ask, and do, that I and mine may be provided for the
future, as we have been in the past, with all that is needful ; relief will come *when it is good for me.* For my dear

children's advance in the course of the last year I cannot be sufficiently thankful."

"*Rome, 5 March,* 1833.—This winter has granted us much social enjoyment. Lady Raffles is the widow of the Governor of Java, and is one of our new acquaintance of the winter who will not be blended in the mass of those seen for a moment and thought of no more : the combined impression produced by her manner, countenance, and conversation, prepares one to believe, or even guess beforehand, all that is great and good attributed to her. She brought us a letter from Madame de Staël, whom she had known long and well at Geneva. She has an only child, a girl of twelve years old, the wreck of a large family which fell a sacrifice to the climate of Java. Mr. Julius Hare, one of the translators of Mr. Niebuhr's Roman History, has been here, and is a most sterling person ; we have also seen much of Mr. Walter Kerr Hamilton, a nephew of the Mr. Hamilton whom we saw in Rome many years ago on his way back from being minister at Naples : and he with his cousin Mr. Farquhar, and Mr. Hare with his travelling companion Mr. Worsley, came to us many an evening, when there was no other person present but M. Turguéneff, who had been Minister of State under the Emperor Alexander, but is now a voluntary exile from his native country, owing to the implication of his brother in the conspiracy against Nicholas. He is a person whom it would take pages to describe, so little does he belong to any of the common denominations of society : a Tartar Prince, and looking like one, yet of the most polished manners, and most consummate talent for conversation ; knowing almost everything, having read almost every book, having been in almost every species of society, having worked his way through all sorts of opinions, and yet retaining an unspoiled taste for what is good, and an unwearied longing for what is best. How much I could tell you of him that would be interesting as a picture of human nature! We have also had great pleasure in the society of two Americans, one of the Episcopalian Church, and one a Baptist—Mr. Burgess of Providence, and Mr. Chase of Newton near Boston. One person of whom we see a good deal is the Grand Duchess of Baden— Stéphanie Beauharnais: she is a widow, and is here for the winter with her very pleasing daughter. She has remains of beauty, and is in manners and conversation very attractive; she has the tact of a Frenchwoman in softening off form, instead of liking it as a *parvenue* might be expected to do. She sings very sweetly, and is full of talent; and her conduct thro' life in a difficult position, having been forced by Napoleon on a family that did not wish to be degraded by an alliance with his *fille adoptive*, is said to have been thoroughly meritorious. Dear Mrs. Stuart and Lord and Lady Northland are on the point of departure: they have been a great pleasure to us."

"*Frascati*, 11 *June*, 1833.—To-day is my Mary's birth-day and she is four years old, and a most engaging creature; I look upon her with a singular and indescribable compassion, for she seems to possess the gift of attraction— every stranger takes notice of her, and she delights in being taken notice of : she can interest, please, and obtain caresses, without the slightest effort, and therefore, how doubly hard her task to attain to moral worth—to doing right for the sake of right!

" We continued to see a great deal of Mr. Hare till he left

Rome, and with continually increasing regard and esteem; he is now gone straight back to England to settle down for life in a country living in Sussex in the gift of his family. He is a great friend and admirer of Dr. Arnold. Our old friend and favourite, Mr. Christopher Wordsworth, passed through Rome on his way back from Greece, and we saw him with much pleasure. On our return from a most interesting little tour to Toscanella, Viterbo, and Orvieto, a new social gratification awaited us:—our friend Turguéneff had returned from Naples, accompanied by a very remarkable person, Joukovsky, celebrated in Russia as a poet and in every respect intellectually distinguished, who has been some years tutor to the young Hereditary Grand Duke,* and greatly favoured by the Emperor and Empress, without having become a courtier. His health being very precarious, he had been allowed leave of absence to travel, but being in haste to return to his important post, he had but very few days for Rome, and those few days Charles helped him to enjoy most thoroughly, in showing him objects of interest, which he had looked at before in part, but without the consciousness of all that was to be seen and felt in them. He has much of the manly, kind-hearted simplicity of manner of Walter Scott, with of course difference of national characteristics; in conversation perfectly unpretending, but yet never letting fall a commonplace word; and I have seldom met with a foreigner, to whom I felt myself from the first so much drawn, as if there was in him nothing foreign or strange. Turguéneff and Joukovsky and a very distinguished German officer in the service of Russia, de Reutern, were with us the other day, with Thor-

* Now the Emperor Alexander.

waldsen, Cornelius, and Overbeck—the three first artists
of the age: it was one of those remarkable combinations
which scarcely any place but Rome can offer. All were
very animated, and increased the social spirits of the others,
so that it was a day to remember. The Russians I have
mentioned have been with us most evenings, and often in
a morning, and besides a sculptor, Woltreck, who has
wanted to model some of the children, and as it is not an
order, but a thing done for his own pleasure and my profit
in the end, I could not send him away.

"I have lately read the 'Meditations de Fénélon' with
great satisfaction: few indeed are the passages exclusively
for Catholics, it is truly a Christian book."

"24 *August*, 1833.—It is little use beginning upon so
interminable a subject as Madame d'Arblay's nonsense *—
but surely such a quantity of unmixed nonsense never was
written before as her book. Still, I do not wonder that
people have found it entertaining, for so did I, if reading a
thing intently, eagerly, and greedily, being provoked and in
a rage at every page, can be called being entertained. The
book is gossip itself, though not clever gossip: and gossip
is the great thing needful for pleasing people. If anybody
—a valet or a lady's-maid—will in any way write down anything that they have heard and seen of such characters as
Madame d'Arblay treats of, it will always be sure to be
eagerly read, as long as there is a presumption that the
writer does not wilfully deceive, and gives the objects with

* Madame d'Arblay had been well known to Madame Bunsen in
early life, through her mother's intimate acquaintance with her as
Miss Burney, when residing in her girlhood at Windsor with Mrs.
Delany, by whom the authoress of "Evelina" was first introduced to
the notice of the Court.

all the truth of which the medium is capable. But will you explain to me, my Mother, how the Dean and Chapter of Westminster could admit that blasphemous unchristian epitaph, with which she in so self-satisfied a manner winds up her book ? Generally speaking, everything in the work may be tolerated and swallowed (although a good gulp it would often require) except her defacing the subject of religion : to be sure she meddles with it little enough, but when she does, it is in a manner that makes one shudder, to think that a person so near her grave should see even in that nothing but a matter to turn a sentence on, and make a sentimental face about. Worst and most painful of all, the letter to ' mon ami' about Dr. Burney's last moments— when she regrets not having been able to cheer the soul passing from time to eternity, by making him understand the cause of the bonfires and illuminations for the victory of the Allies—gives, unconsciously, a soul-harrowing picture of a human being, at the extremest verge of life, yet clinging to mortality, and agonised with the physical fear of dissolution, incapable himself of spiritual-ising his thoughts or feelings, and having no one to help him to a happier frame !—while the image with which she wishes and endeavours to harrow up the soul, is that of herself, called upon most inconveniently to grieve for the death of a father, just when she wanted him to rejoice with her in the destruction of Napoleon and return of her hus-band. In short, surely never was such self-idolatry as hers ! and we might be tempted to pity her for having been exposed, with so weak a head, to the intoxication of so much applause, were it not for the proof she gives of indis-criminating appetite : being as self-satisfied in the homage of Pamela, and taking it as much for sterling coin, as in the praise of Burke or Johnson. But she is herself *une comédienne*, nothing else : her mind was evidently formed by the impression Garrick made upon her : she had the gift in youth of entertaining people : and the equally useful gift (which she has lost in age) of not committing herself and discovering the poverty of the substratum ; and thus alone can I account for a character so insignificant having been so valued. But I wish I could talk instead of write : my Mother would help me to construe her, which I am very curious to do."

"*Frascati*, 14 *Oct.*, 1833.—To-morrow we intend setting off on a scrambling tour to the neighbouring mountains, of which I greatly enjoy the thoughts : we do not intend to be away more than eight days, but when we return we shall directly pack and return to Rome, as to which I feel as if I was about to plunge up to the neck in a torrent, where I should have to struggle hard to keep swimming for a given number of months, until I reached this quiet shore again. We returned on the 11th from a three days' expedition to Cora and Norba in the Volscian mountains, by way of Velletri, as far as which place we went on Wednesday in the carriage, that is, Charles and myself, and the four boys : M. de Sydow and M. Abeken accompanying us on horseback. At Velletri we procured horses to ride to Cora, which has no carriage road as yet.* I requested that mine might be at least a quiet horse, and was assured that it belonged to a convent of nuns, which was to be

---

* There is now a railway to Velletri and an omnibus to Cora !—so that this exquisitely beautiful place may be visited in one day as an excursion from Rome.

taken as a proof of good education : I must say from this example I should be inclined to trust the proof in future, for the horse was a pattern of good behaviour. The boys were happy beyond expression at riding 14 miles. We slept at Cora, after having seen a beautiful temple in great preservation, and other remains of antiquity, and the next day undertook a ride to the ruins of Norba, a Cyclopean city in a most picturesque situation, by a most dangerous mountain track, in which however the horses kept their feet admirably : but we returned by the town of Ninfa in the plain, by a longer but safer road, having had enough of the sensation of danger. Friday morning we rode back to Velletri, by the same rich and beautiful country by which we came.

"There is no describing how engaging my Theodore becomes : I certainly have valued the other children enough as babies, but I think nothing was ever so delightful as he is."

"*Rome*, 4 *Dec.*, 1833.—Not to have written before is one of the privations that I have, and must have, in the bustle of a Roman winter. But when I speak of bustle, you must not suppose the causes of the bustle to be disagreeable. As usual in the winter at Rome, the number of things to be done makes quiet impossible, and enjoyment difficult, but yet *much is enjoyed*. We have the most delicious season, and I have been often in the garden, having it put in order, and making a hedge, or rather reforming a hedge which I have replanted with roses, oleanders, volca-merias, and geraniums : it is not to be described how geraniums have flourished in the garden in the short time I have had it to myself—a set of short slips put in in March have become almost trees in the course of the summer.

"I have strength now for all I have to do, go from one thing to another throughout the day, and have no need to lie down : and in the evening, if we are at home and have not too many visitors, I finish up my sketches. For this I had a bit of praise from Mr. Clifford which greatly pleased me. The day after he had seen me thus employed, he said, ' How I like that making the most of odd times ! it is what everybody ought to do, and what *I* never do ! and thus I have done nothing, and learnt nothing, in my life.' Mr. Clifford's being here is a great pleasure to us : he is really a delightful person, entering into everything and enjoying everything like a child. Lady Northland and dear Mrs. Stuart * have also been here since the 2nd November, and Lady Northland † has been kind enough to desire me to be godmother to her baby, who is to be christened to-morrow."

"14 *Dec.*, 1833.—I have been writing to the Comte de la Ferronays‡ for a letter which may have influence on the fate of M. Rio.§ I wish —— may know in some measure who

* The Hon. Mrs. Stuart, a very early friend of Mrs. Waddington, daughter of Lady Juliana Penn (see Chapter III.) and widow of the Primate of Ireland.

† Afterwards Countess of Ranfurly, daughter of the Primate of Ireland and Mrs. Stuart.

‡ Described in the beautiful volumes of his daughter, Mrs. Augustus Craven, called the " Récit d'une Soeur."

§ A. F. Rio, the well-known author of " The Poetry of Christian Art." He had gone to Llanover with letters from the Bunsens requesting Mrs. Waddington to give him introductions which might facilitate his Welsh studies. In Wales he made the acquaintance of Apollonia (aunt of the present Mr. Herbert of Llanarth) to whom he was eventually married.

and what la Ferronays is—that they may be assured that *nobody's* approbation could have more decisive weight. He is the only Frenchman I ever saw who had consummate English dignity of appearance and manner, and this appearance in him is the shining forth of the inward character. How high he was in office under the former government is probably known, and how uniformly conscientious all his acts of public and private life. The last period of his public life was being French ambassador at Rome, and he gave up the post as a point of honour after the Revolution of the Three Days: though a devoted adherent of the old Bourbons, he is a yet better Frenchman: and though a man of very decided religious opinions, he never was an ultra in religion any more than in politics.

"Our last winter's friend, Turguéneff, the Russian of whom we saw so much with such pleasure, is just returned, but for a short time: as yet there has been no other person of the sort that greatly interests us, and whom we wish daily to see, except Mr. Clifford, who is the picture of enjoyment. We have nobody like Mr. Julius Hare, or Mr. Kerr Hamilton, or Mr. Christopher Wordsworth as yet. Yesterday however I had a great pleasure—seeing again Lady Boyle, formerly Mrs. Courtenay Boyle. She received me most affectionately and has always the same engaging manner. She had her youngest daughter with her, and her son Captain Boyle; her daughter the Maid of Honour will join her in the spring."

"*Rome*, 31 *Dec.*, 1833.—On this last day of the year I begin a letter, before sunrise, to my own dearest Mother, who will easily guess that the close of the present year is unusually solemn to me, but to detail all that fills my heart

at this time would take up pages. I look back upon a
year most particularly marked with blessings, in which I
have been allowed a quantity of enjoyment, and growing
satisfactions of many kinds—first and foremost that of
more and more loving and approving him whom I have so
long loved and approved, whose character ever rises upon
me, and continually 'works itself clear, and as it runs,
refines.' Then, the improvement of all my four boys,
which in different ways and degrees is equally certain; in
particular the increase of character in my dear Henry, who
is the only one at all *maturing*. Then the thriving and
promising state of the twins is a great joy—and if the three
little girls are not yet all that I wish them to be, yet must
I not be unmindful of the text—'Shall I receive good from
the hand of the Lord, and should I not also receive evil?'
and *receiving* from the hand of the Lord means *receiving
thankfully*, as what is a certain good, because coming from
Him, although it may seem 'no way joyous, but rather
grievous.'

"We have had a great pleasure in the arrival of Mr. and
Lady Emily Pusey, who are more like a brother and sister
than merely friends. This evening we are to part with
Abeken, who has been with us ever since the departure of
Ambrosch."

"*7th Jan.*, 1834.—And now I will let you know that
Neukomm is come back at last, and the pleasure is very great
of having him here. We have found him a quiet corner
and a writing-table in Charles's room, and he has composed
one of a series of Practices for the organ this morning, and
since dinner has been explaining to me the grounds of
thorough-bass : in short he is already in full activity in the

house, and every person in it seems to feel as if he either had been, or ought to have been, always there. He is come just at the right time, to animate us all after the departure of Abeken, who left us in the night between the old and new year. There are so many things inefficiently and superficially detailed in my letters, my own Mother, which yet occupy my time, thoughts, and feelings, that it is no wonder amongst others that you should have heard so little of Abeken: of whom perhaps I might have mentioned two years ago, that a nephew of Charles's most beloved college friend was come to Rome, with a brilliant reputation for classical attainments and abilities in every way, who had been from the first moment very much at home in our house, Charles having at once felt him to be of the right sort, and having even used jokingly the expression—' Kestner shall not be the only person that has a nephew—I too have found a nipotino for myself.' But I must admit that Charles was the only person who from the first justly estimated Abeken, for tho' I admired his powers, and was aware of his superior understanding, sterling principles, and warm affections, I could not for a time like his company, because he overwhelmed me with his superabundance: having in a high degree the want of tact of many fresh fish from the universities (even in well-mannered and regularly drilled England) and never knowing when to have done with a subject that interested him, and speaking too loud, and without modulation. This time twelvemonth, when Ambrosch was about to leave us, Charles determined to ask Abeken to fill his place in our house, and assist him in the care of the boys; the whole first year of our acquaintance, spent in close contact, having continually drawn him nearer to us. He accepted gladly, tho' utterly objecting to receiving any other remuneration than what he was pleased to consider as such in becoming a member of the family. During the year that he has thus been in the house, his instructions to the boys have been invaluable, and not less invaluable his assistance to Charles in every possible pursuit: in every respect the favourable impression he made at first has been confirmed, and the roughnesses that at first disturbed have been wearing off, so that nobody can prize him more than myself; and as he likes reading aloud in the evening, I have had a degree of pleasure in that way which was quite a new thing to me, and has procured me a good deal more leisure for drawing, than I should otherwise have had, for if he had not read aloud to me, I should probably have thought it right to read to myself. On the journey that we made in October, the people with whom we lodged used to take Abeken for my eldest son (which he might be in point of age) and it struck me they had well hit off our mutual relation, for he used to attend to me, and consider me as Henry does, and it has long seemed to me as natural to think of his pleasure and indulge him, as with respect to my dear Henry. He had long chosen the profession of a clergyman, and Charles obtained some time since of the King that he should be appointed the successor of Tippelskirch, who will leave his post in the spring: Abeken is now gone to Geneva, to study the state of religious feeling and opinion there, and will then proceed to visit his family at Osnabruck, but will meet Charles at Berlin, and return hither in May. As a substitute for Abeken, we are very fortunate in having Kellermann, a

Dane by birth, though his breeding has been German, a very distinguished scholar, and besides a man of principle and character. He is an acquaintance of two years' standing, so we can hardly be mistaken in our estimation of him, and it is a great comfort to me to think I shall have an efficient person to manage the two boys, in Charles's absence, at least as to learning; for they have long had a great respect as well as liking for him. But Kellermann is not as an associate what Abeken was, and therefore Neukomm appears the more a person to fill the void, and besides comes opportunely as an additional help to me to avoid thinking of the parting now so very near."

CHAPTER X.

LAST YEARS AT ROME.

*" Truth is as impossible to be soiled by any outward touch
as the sunbeam."*
MILTON, *Doctrine and Discipline of Divorce.*

IN March, 1834, Bunsen set out for Berlin, taking
with him his two elder sons; Henry, to the great
school at Schulpforte, of which one of the masters was
Dr. Schmieder, late chaplain to the German Protestant
Chapel at Rome; and Ernest, to the military college at
Berlin. At the Prussian capital Bunsen was as warmly
received as ever by the King and the Crown-prince—but
manifold troubles were in store for him, through the
question of great importance for Church and State,
which was then in full agitation—that of mixed marriages. While, according to the law of Prussia, a
father has the sole right over the education of his
children, so that all stipulations before marriage are
forbidden; according to the Roman Catholic Church, no
marriage can be celebrated unless a promise is given that
all children shall be brought up as Roman Catholics, and
in the newly annexed but almost entirely Romanist

provinces of the Rhine, the clergy absolutely refused to perform a marriage under other conditions. While Leo XII. and Pius VIII. lived, the court of Rome was pacifically disposed, and would have been willing to enjoin priests in Germany to grant their *passive assistance* in case of a mixed marriage, refusing only the usual nuptial benediction. But, in an evil hour, Prussia insisted on the full marriage ceremonial; delay ensued, and the chance of compromise was lost. Thus, on his return to Rome, the feeling shown against Bunsen as representative of its Protestant antagonist was so bitter, that he implored to be released from a position which he felt to be scarcely any longer tenable. To this he at that time received the flattering reply that his services at the court of Rome were indispensable to his country.

MADAME BUNSEN *to her* MOTHER.

"*Rome*, 1 *April*, 1834.—On the 13th March I parted from my dear boys and their father. My own Mother, I believe that you have suffered and will suffer more pain from this parting than I have. I say that to you, who will not suspect me of not caring for our boys, and who know that my husband is the thing *par excellence* that I live for. I have so much to do, so much more, literally speaking, than I *can* do, that I have no rest for thought, no interval for dwelling upon what is painful; and that is what stands me in stead, my strength would be worth nothing if it was to come to a combat with the pain. I cannot help going into Henry's empty room on some errand or other, but I generally get away without a tear. The worst thing is, not remembering, but catching myself at forgetting: the other day I called to Henry at dinner, and was only reminded by the sound of my own voice what name I was naming. He writes to me, dear boy, that he cannot yet believe that he is parted from me, that when he packs or unpacks he thinks 'it is a task I have given him to do.'

"This morning at six o'clock Neukomm left us. These three months' intercourse have been very delightful to us, we have enjoyed his company and valued his character more than ever. I say *we* in full plural, for all our friends and associates have been drawn towards Neukomm as we are ourselves. He has been in full activity, and has composed many fine things, and played to us a quantity of his compositions. I think his style of composition ennobled and improved since he was here before: the oratorio of Mount Sinai and that of David appear to me splendid works of genius. I wish I could hear them executed."

"2 *April.*—This is my dear, dear Henry's birthday. My Mother will remember it. O how thankful I am to have him at sixteen what he is! My dear Ernest too, my Mother would find greatly altered to his advantage. Charles the less has been very good since his brother's departure, exerting himself to fill Henry's place, taking care of the babies, liking to do anything for them, showing the greatest alacrity in helping me, and more than all, bearing reproof humbly and being very pains-taking with Kellermann. Doing lessons with George is as usual my most agreeable occupation: we read French and English, and he repeats the lessons of geography to me which he used to receive from the invaluable Abeken; whom we none of us know how to do without, I as little as anybody else: all long for his return, though when he returns we cannot have as much of his time and company as we had before, because he will have to take upon himself the business of the Chaplain to the Legation.

"I have gone through worlds of thought and feeling since I sent my last letter. By this I do not mean distress, but subjects which take up one's whole mind for the time being, and make the admeasurement of time very difficult. One of these subjects is Mrs. Augustus Hare; I have seen her much, and feel that it is no common connection. . . . . I have enjoyed the society of Mr. and Lady Emily Pusey: they are real friends. Good and sensible and well-principled people are often alike in the serious business of life, but in the choice of pleasures and recreations there is a grand difference between people—therefore with the Puseys and the Hares and some others, I can go on, and I shall always get on and come nearer, but with others I am at a stand-still at the first step."

To her SON HENRY.

"*Rome*, 5 *April*, 1834.—My dear, dear boy, how much I have thought of you on your birthday! That day will have marked the period of the greatest change in life that you perhaps ever can make, at least the most absolute change of all surrounding circumstances. I have prayed, and do pray, that God may be with you—that you may feel yourself ever in His sight! and then you will proceed securely, whatever trials may be in store for you in the course of life. My dear boy, this separation is bitter, and yet we must not forget that the probabilities are that we pass our lives in separation : it is highly unlikely that you and your Mother should ever again live much together. Therefore let us make the best of separation, and not put off communication to the uncertain time of meeting again. Tell me always as much as you can of what you think and feel, my own dear boy ; that is often matter of effort in absence and distance ; but it is difficult to begin again if once discontinued : and if long discontinued, estrangement is almost unavoidable. Yet you must not take time from exercise or sleep to write to me, and your day will be taken up in study. But I wish you would take a sheet of paper, and write a bit at a time, just when you have time, and send the sheet off without minding whether the letter has beginning, middle, or end."

" 6 *May*, 1834.—My heart has been with you most constantly during the late important period, and the many particulars which your dear Father has made time to write to me, have been matter for continued thought and thankfulness,—indeed for continued prayer : for what can be the issue of every reflection, the outlet of every feeling, but a supplication that God would render us all more fully sensible of the unbounded mercy of His dispensations towards us, and that He would give us a heart capable to accept from Him everything that He may send, with willingness and thankfulness, even though it may not always be, as now, that which we most desire ? It makes my heart full to overflowing when I think to what a degree all that I can most desire has been granted to me as to you, my dear boy : your situation in Dr. Schmieder's house, the whole arrangement of the school, above all the manner of your entrance, and your being yourself satisfied to have entered in that manner. I was thinking of you more especially on the 18th, which I supposed to have been your critical day : and most assuredly my wish floated between two points—the one, that you might do yourself credit, the other, that your entry might not be a brilliant one—in the fear that you might be tempted to feel yourself secure, and as if anything less than your best, most urgent and unremitting endeavours could be sufficient to enable you to attain to the point which you are called upon to reach, in the time that you will enjoy the advantages of Schulpforte. I have seen and known on many occasions that succeeding too completely is a bar to future success, and the greatest possible evil that can happen to any one, is to have his energies lamed, and his activity checked, from within. Therefore, my dear boy, though I think with pain of the terrible puzzle you were in, when called upon to put Schlegel's *Dramaturgische Vorlesungen* into Latin, I most cordially rejoice in the result, which had the effect of detaining you in that lower class in which it is so necessary for you to feel yourself at home, before you can with any freedom move in a higher sphere. I am very thankful to be informed that you judged rightly of yourself, and had no wish for the present possession of honours which you did not feel competent to wear. May you, by God's grace, be preserved through life from the misfortune of over-valuing your own powers or attainments ! or imagining the circumstances and qualities which make us accepted and valued amongst men, to be always a standard of intrinsic worth."

" 9 *June* . . .—It is most useful to be among a number

of youths of the same age, in order to become conscious
that man was not made to stand wholly alone, that he
must combine with one or other class of his fellow-creatures, and that if he will have nothing to do with the ordinary herd of the insignificant—who go to the business of
life like slaves to their daily task, and submit to laws and
regulations only in so far as they fear the rod of retribution—he must in his actions strive to belong to those whose
conduct is regulated by uncompromising principle, and
whose guiding-compass points ever to an immovable ideal
standard of excellence, higher than any real one that the
experience of life will show."

"25 *July* . . .—The beginning of your school-life, my
dear boy, has been so prosperous, you seem to have
enjoyed and profited by the good with so little mixture of
attendant evil, that I fear your worst trial may be yet to
come, at the important crisis of the ushering-in at Oxford.
But yet grown-up men must be less rough and uncivilised
than when in school-boy years : and whatever the conflict
of antagonistic elements of society such an university may
present, I must believe it is yet ever possible for one who
acts in singleness of heart, with no object but that of doing
right, to pass on unharmed by all the various powers of
evil which present themselves in forms of seduction or
intimidation. The worst of trials is the trial of faith : but
through that also, when it comes, the same singleness of
heart will lead you. The conviction, if a difficulty arises
within, or is suggested from without, that it is not the
fault of Christianity, but your own fault, that it appears
such,—that the mote is not in the glorious sun, but in the
glass of the dim telescope through which you are viewing

it,—will always give time for help to arrive: and such help will never fail those who encourage the action and long for the presence of the Holy Spirit of grace in their minds."

To BUNSEN.

"7 *April* 1834.—Yesterday I had a visit of an hour from Mrs. Augustus Hare, whose conversation transported me into another world—a world of soothing and edifying contemplation. It does one good to think that in the case of her married life, two people so calculated to love and benefit each other were brought together by Providence, even though it pleased the same Providence to allow them but five years of mutual enjoyment. They had been attached for five years before their marriage, and their acquaintance was of seventeen years' standing. Much has she told me that was deeply interesting, and she has promised to come again. Her plan is to take a cottage in the parish of Julius Hare, or as near to it as possible, that she may have the comfort of seeing as much as possible of him who was dearest to her late husband, and of endeavouring to assist him among his parishioners, which will be a continuation of the habits of her life in the parish of her husband. Is it not a blessing when the laws of a country hallow the relation of brother-in-law and sister-in-law, and make it as sacred as the tie of blood between brother and sister? Were it not for this both Julius Hare and his sister-in-law would be too young to venture upon this plan of near residence and future co-operation, for fear of the comments and suppositions of the world."

" 15 *April.*—Yesterday the Hares went away. I saw
them on Sunday, poor Mrs. Augustus Hare feeling more
than anything having to part from the room where she
had watched her husband to the last, and go far away
from the spot where his remains repose. I feel that next
to God's words she will find His works her best com-
forters. She begged me to visit her husband's tomb.
I cannot express how much I have been gratified by
her manner and expressions towards me : and those
of Marcus Hare. She showed me a letter of Dr.
Arnold's, in which he compares you and Augustus Hare,
and says no two could be more similar—concluding with,
' God grant to me to resemble them in the nobleness and
beauty of their goodness.' "

" 21 *April.*—I wish you could see how delightful the
darling twins are : they are now singing about me like
two little birds, waiting for their breakfast. You have no
idea of the enjoyment we have from the garden, and as
we have water in the fountain we keep it watered—but I
cannot yet get over looking at Henry and Ernest's deserted
gardens."

" *Villa Piccolomini,* 16 *June.*—What pleasure it is to be
again in this delicious place, where I arrived yesterday
evening, a few minutes before the most glorious sunset,
together with Kellermann, Charles, George, and Emilia;
Miss Thompson and the rest had arrived the evening
before. I had feared the entrance into this house, where
the want of so much that I was accustomed to enjoy here
appears new and fresh : and most certainly it was very sad
to see my Henry's desk and Ernest's, and to pass your
empty study."

To her MOTHER.

"*Frascati*, 19 *June*, 1834.—We have been enjoying our-selves here since last Sunday, the 15th. I had almost dreaded coming, or rather not almost, but had quite an absurd aversion to resolving on leaving Rome, apprehend-ing the first impression of the absence of so much that I love on coming to this place, where we have all lived so happily together. But that was a morbid vision, and has given way to the actual reality of so much good as I am allowed to possess and enjoy here. Miss Thompson and Kellermann and I, with the five children, breakfast and dine at a smaller table and in a smaller room, that we may not be reminded in the great hall and at the large table how many places are unfilled : but still we occupy the hall to our great comfort as a sitting-room. Frascati never was more beautiful ; after all the fears entertained from the drought, all is fresh and green, in the most delicious summer-weather, without any heat to complain of."

To BUNSEN.

"*Frascati*, 3 *July*.—We all go down after dinner into the shady alley and enjoy the *aura estiva :* the girls play and talk much with Adèle Vollard, Kellermann draws Theodore in the little cart—he whipping as hard as he can to make the horses go on, I sit with Theodora in my lap till Hannah has dined, Charles shoots with a bow and arrows of his own making, and George climbs trees at Kellermann's bidding, from which I turn away my eyes, though well aware it is right he should try."

"8 *July*, 1834.—When you are not here it seems to be

such a clear case that nothing can be more than a quarter enjoyed, that I am much too apt to make all days working days, all hours working hours: it occurred to me yesterday that I scarcely take the requisite time to stand and enjoy the view out of the window, as I used to do last year. The season is indescribably delicious! yet I could find it in my heart to wish that it would rain, that it might be fine when you return. I am just returned from a drive to Marino, with both the dear twins. Whenever I can take up a book (mostly when one of the twins is asleep on my lap) I read Evan's 'Church of God,' given to me by Mrs. Augustus Hare, and reckoned by Julius Hare to be worthy of Hooker."

"25 *July*.—Kestner went yesterday afternoon to Rome, and Miss Thompson and I drove with him in his *scappavia*, down the hill to the place where I had long wanted to draw that Casino with the pine that you remember: the boys were also there, playing at Piastrella, and we walked home."

"11 *August*.—The last letter of Abeken, our adopted son, touched me as usual from the extreme affection which it expresses. I sometimes take myself to task for not being angry at being canonized, or whatever I ought to call it, as I am by him: but it is so impossible to doubt the reality of the filial-regard which he proves to me at every opportunity, and I am so conscious of deserving it by the regard I feel for him, that I cannot but be gratified by the expression of it, however well aware of being enormously overrated. How I have been spoiled for the last three years, my Best-Beloved! To the iron rule of your sister and Simon has succeeded a period, in which I have been drawn closer and closer to you, my own dearest; in which you yourself, being relieved from an intolerable household burden, surrounded by associates and helpmates that answered to your needs and tastes, in full and suitable and not exhausting activity, could for the first time in the whole period of our married life thoroughly expand and develope on all sides, and be yourself entirely and uninterruptedly, to mine and everybody's enjoyment. Then as household-friends I have had Ambrosch, and Sydow, and Abeken, to spoil me, and indulge me, and praise me, and approve me—and, as dear Lady Raffles said, ' I do so love to be spoiled by those I value!' And now, whereas during your former absence at Berlin I was a ball thrown from one to the other of the two spikes of your sister and Simon, never finding a resting-place, and worn out of all independence of judgment and self-possession, in your late absence I have had no creature to control or thwart me. I have had Sydow's constant support and counsel and sympathy, Tippelskirch's kindness and friendship, Miss Thompson's * grateful attachment—and if I have had cares, which felt the heavier for your not being present, yet with the help of homœopathy to procure me the undisturbed possession of my own physical powers,† nothing has been overwhelming. And now I conclude with the delightful idea that I am writing to you for the last time, and that, please God, I shall pass but one more Monday

* The governess of her daughters, afterwards Madame Abeken.

† Madame Bunsen had been subject to violent headaches, which, occurring sometimes two or three times a month, deprived her in each case of at least a whole day's usefulness. By the advice of Neukomm, she tried homœopathy, with excellent effect, owing much to the advice of Romani, homœopathic physician to the Queen of Naples.

without having been reunited to you. Farewell, my Best-Beloved, may God please to grant his blessing to the end of your journey, and to the re-commencement of our home-life ! May you not have so idealised your wife in absence, as to be less satisfied with her in presence ! "

To her MOTHER.

" 27 *August*, 1834.—Charles returned safe and sound last Thursday. On Monday, the 18th, I went to Rome with a carriage-full, sent the carriage back on Tuesday morning to bring the rest on Tuesday evening, that we might all be ready to drive out on Wednesday evening on the Florence road, which we did, but in vain, as he did not come till Thursday morning. He arrived accompanied by Abeken, the general favourite, and Dressel, a person of much promise, whom he has brought as tutor to the boys. On Sunday afternoon, the 24th, we all moved to Frascati."

" 26 *Sept*.—Nothing was ever so strange, so unnatural, and apparently impossible, as that I should not till this day write a line to my own dearest Mother to express some part of the feelings which have occupied me so unceasingly since I received the letter, which told me she would come here, and that she would come into my house. My own Mother, there is no describing the happiness of every hour and every moment in the consciousness that I shall have you here, that I shall really be able to enjoy your presence !—to know that I am again to live with you ! to have you always at hand ! to have again my own place in the room you inhabit !—to have my husband, my children, known to you in their daily habits, not as visitors at set times !—to have the opportunity, the means, the time, as

well as the will, to make my whole heart and my whole
life known to you! All this comprises such a fullness of
happiness and comfort, such a realising of wishes and
desires, as I can scarcely believe or comprehend. My own
dearest Mother! how I ought to thank you for overcoming
all the many difficulties that stood in the way of my gratification, and yet, how strange, that the last thing that
occurred to me was to thank you! It is such a fact, such
a thing understood, that you always do, and always have
done, everything possible, almost what was impossible, for
my comfort and benefit, that to thank you is rather a part
of my love for you, than a separate act and sensation.

" Charles enjoys the idea of my Mother's coming, almost
as much as I do—he is for ever speaking of it, morning,
noon, and night. And good Kestner is so heartily pleased!
I told him of it one evening, and he came the next day,
saying, ' I cannot think of anything but that your Mother
is coming.' "

To her SON HENRY.

" 6 *Dec.*, 1834.—I hope you will receive this on Christmas Eve, that you may not on that day be without an
external mark of the feelings with which you will be
recalled, in the far-distant place of your birth. May God's
blessing be with you, my dearest boy, as on every day of
your life, so more especially on the first Christmas you will
have passed without your parents, and sanctify the feelings
with which your heart will be filled : make you serious,
but not mournful : reminding you that to those who strive
to be united in His faith and fear and love, *the past* and *the
distant* are not lost, and the future, in whatever external

form it may come, will abound in good, and ripen into glory and blessedness."

"19 *March*, 1835.—I hope this letter will reach you on your birthday, and convey the heartfelt prayer of your parents, that every blessing may attend you throughout the year upon which you will enter. You have hitherto been blessed indeed, with health and every advantage to further your progress, and enable you to qualify yourself for a situation of usefulness: and may it please God to continue them to you, and more particularly to give His grace to the religious instructions, or recapitulations, that you are now going through, and to the whole preparation you make for the most solemn act of your independent existence, by which you as it were confirm the Sacrament of Baptism received in a period of unconsciousness, and solemnly undertake to be a ' doer of the word,' and not merely a hearer; an actor, and not merely a recipient. My dear, dear boy, may God help you to become indeed independent! to feel that you are come to an age of self-responsibility, in which, from this time forth, the guiding advice and directions of others may be sought as an assistance, but not trusted to as a support: in which you are introduced to ' the glorious liberty of the children of God,' and called upon to act as ' free, but not using your liberty as a cloak of maliciousness, but as the servant of Christ.' In your intellectual acquirements, as well as in your moral consciousness, you are equally called upon to develop an individual existence, and I trust that your best endeavours will not be wanting, and then the blessing of God will not fail. I know, and have experienced, my dear Henry, that it is a difficult step to take in life, to resolve to look upon it as one's duty to judge for oneself, not in the sense of opposition, but in the sense of independence. In the law of Christ is given us ' an anchor of the soul, both sure and steadfast;' and that is what is to keep us firm, however the winds and waves of this troublesome world may buffet us."

Mrs. Waddington's projected journey was delayed for some time by her own alarming illness at Llanover. But she arrived at Rome in the late autumn of 1834, accompanied by Mr. and Mrs. Hall. When they returned to England with their infant Caradoc—being recalled by the sudden general election, and posting in eleven days from Rome to Boulogne, Mrs. Waddington, with her little granddaughter,* accompanied the Bunsens to Frascati, and spent the summer in the ground-floor of the Villa Piccolomini, of which the first-floor was occupied by the Bunsens, the whole family living in ever-increasing enjoyment of the view, as well as of the fine airy rooms of the old country palace. At this time the upper-floor of the villa was occupied by M. de Sydow, and M. Abeken, who had been recently married to Miss Thompson, the valued English governess of the Bunsens, after her recovery from an alarming illness, which had at one time seemed hopeless. Madame Bunsen was especially thankful for her mother's presence and advice during this summer, in which the increasing lameness of her second daughter, Emilia, now almost

* Now the Hon. Mrs. Herbert of Llanarth.

entirely confined to her couch, began to cause her great anxiety. In June the sad news of the death of Mrs. Hall's youngest child, Caradoc, nearly caused Mrs. Wadding-ton to set out suddenly homewards, but the risk of travelling with her young granddaughter was so strongly represented to her, that she was induced to put off her departure, and was eventually led, by the urgent solicitations of her daughter and son-in-law, to remain in Rome another winter, in the Palazzo Caf-farelli.

Mr. Pusey having promised a living to Henry Bunsen, and his own decision being quite formed for the life of an English clergyman, it was decided to remove him from Schulpforte, and send him to Rugby and Oxford. Meantime he was allowed to return for the winter of 1835—36 to the land of his birth, pro-ceeding in the following April with his grandmother to England, and to Llanover, before going to Rugby.

MADAME DE BUNSEN *to her* MOTHER.

"24 *April*, 1836.—Having drank tea, sung a hymn, accompanied by myself instead of Henry, seen Emilia and Mary into bed, and heard them say their prayers, I sit down to write to my dearest Mother, in a place in which she never knew me sit, in the first window of the yellow room, at the round table which used to stand before the corner-couch, and which has been removed to make room for the sofa-table, till now used by my Mother. After you left we set off to Fiumicino, having settled Emilia in the garden, dressing dolls with Angelina, and Mademoiselle cutting out a doll's frock, the dear twins *à la chasse des escargots*, picking them off the lilies. The road to Fiumicino is very prettily varied the first half of the way, hills and dells, brooks and meadows, cultivation and country-houses; the trees all out, even oaks and walnuts, a quantity of asphodel in blossom (surely Henry will see, and show that classical plant, the flower of death); several views to draw, particularly looking back from an ascent at S. Paolo and the broad reach of the Tiber and Mount Albano, which I hope to drive to some day, for it is not far. When we reached the sea-shore, the waves were dashing very tolerably for the Mediteranean, and surprised the children much. Sir Thomas Acland and Lord Clifford packed us into two boats to go to his yacht, where we staid till nearly dark.

" My own, own Mother, you blinded yourself by your (farewell) words of tenderness, and they must remain uncommented upon, lest I blind you again; but they are treasured up. Your expressions of approbation revive all those feelings of penitence, which I think were the ruling ones at, before, and after the parting with you, my own Mother. If sin and wilfulness did not mingle in everything, even the best of what is earthly, how much more might I have been to you, my own Mother! if you were to seek to blame, as you seek to be satisfied, how would your approbation have been qualified! But all I could say on this topic shall be unsaid, because it would upset us both. To be able to feel through all that deserves to be felt, to think through all that deserves to be thought, to live up to the level of the situation in which the soul is placed, must be the happiness of a better state: here it is only by

dint of avoiding what we cannot bear, that we prevent
being shaken to the foundation : and perhaps everybody's
experience tells, that the most intense feelings, of whatever description, never are and never can be communicated."

"7 *May*, 1836.—Mr. Meyer and Dr. Braun * dined
with us yesterday, having returned from their archæological tour of nine days. They brought a terrible story of
the Princess Canino's sons, Pietro and Antonio, who have
been roving about the country, performing all the atro-
cities of banditti, robbing, carrying off women, and at
last committing murder. This murder was on the person
of a man almost as bad as themselves, and Meyer, who
had been told that one of them had, *per disgrazia*, shot
a robber, took it into his head to compliment the Princess
upon her son's having rid the country of a public nuisance !
The unfortunate mother answered with embarrassment,
said she was greatly distressed by the accident, but probably took comfort from the idea that the deed could be
represented in the light of a public benefit. However,
scarcely had Meyer and Braun left the castle of Musignano, when they learnt that one of the Bonapartes, the
guilty one, had escaped, but that the other had been
arrested, after having killed on the spot one of the Pope's
officers and mortally wounded another, of those sent to
arrest him. He is now in the Castel S. Angelo, and the
opinions of the Romans are divided as to the manner of
the death, which it is supposed he cannot avoid : whether

* The well-known archeologist, who was nicknamed " Storto
Collo," from the way in which he held his head on one side to
examine coins, &c.

'to save public disgrace,' he will be privately executed, or poisoned!! It seems that 17 years ago such a means of *preserving appearances and satisfying justice* was had recourse to. But that poor unfortunate mother! Whether she has or has not done her utmost to teach her children religion and morality, in any case, how tremendous is the visitation!

"I have profited by one of your injunctions in letting Meyer get me the 'Heart of Midlothian.' Reading it has done good, first by taking off the edge of a curiosity to read the many *later* and unknown works of Sir Walter Scott, based on the merits of the few *earlier* ones known to me. I now know him as a book-maker, as which I never knew him before. It is a proof to me of the present idle taste of the multitude, that so many people have told me this was the very best of the novels! To my feelings it is the very worst I have ever read—without one merit to redeem it, except being founded on a fact in real life, more affecting and more admirable in its real circumstances than in his working out. It is *remplissage* from first to last, mostly or entirely unreadable, but from curiosity; and I am sure the public only like it because they want *goats' flesh and asafœtida sauce* to stimulate their palled appetite. There is advantage taken in this work of every circumstance of natural interest to harrow up the reader's feelings,—instead of sparing them, with the good taste of 'Waverley.' Then the improbabilities are not to be swallowed — the contrivances clumsy and commonplace beyond description.

"We have had much pleasure in seeing Mademoiselle Calandrini, who has had such an astonishing success, though a Protestant of Geneva, in establishing schools for children of various ages at Pisa, beginning with places for receiving and training infants of from a year and a half to two years old, and proceeding to regular schools for the same children when older. I have not seen for a long time a new acquaintance who so much gave the impression of the head and heart being both right; and she is perfectly natural and pleasing, not the least *apprêtée*, as the Genevans are apt to be.

"Dr. Arnold has sent a short specimen of the style of his Roman History. O were it but finished and published! It will be a treasure to children and to everybody."

"12 *May*.—Lepsius has been here since Monday. He makes a very satisfactory impression as to character as well as talents, in short he fulfils the expectations created by his letters, which were clear-headed, straightforward, intelligent, full without overflowing. He has a natural polish of manners, but no ceremonial, and is neither forward nor shy: it is inconceivable what materials he has collected for the study of Egyptian antiquities, and his drawings are admirably executed. You may suppose that Charles is very happy to be able to talk of Hieroglyphics, but it does not make him idle: he is very busy all day, and only gets to his treat at meal-times, and in the evenings."

In the month of June, Bunsen and his wife, with four of their children, enjoyed a carriage-tour to Gaeta, Benevento, Avellino, Salerno, and Naples—"a journey filled with enjoyment, bright with cheerfulness, unembittered by distress or inconvenience." The later summer was saddened by the lingering illness of Madame Abeken, who had removed to the rooms in the Villa Piccolomini recently inhabited by Mrs. Wadding-ton,—" her powers of resistance and endurance incon-ceivable, and her state of mind most edifying, full of faith and hope, and anxious to be gone." She died in the middle of August, commending her heart-broken husband to the Bunsens in her last moments, so that he became even more than before an object of solicitude and affection to them, and she was buried in the ceme-tery of Caius Cestius, near the graves of William Wad-dington, of Augustus Hare, and of Bunsen's infant children.

MADAME BUNSEN *to her* MOTHER.

" 27 *Oct.*, 1836.—An event in Frascati the week before last, I must now detail: it was nothing less uncommon than the passage of the Pope on the way to Camaldoli, but the circumstances were unusual. Charles had been told of the Pope's having let fall expressions to the effect of 'Bunsen keeps quite away—I have not seen him these two years' — which suggested his doing something to prove that his having refrained from seeking opportunities of personal interviews had not originated in any want of respect, but rather in delicacy, from the nature of the negotiations and correspondences going on all that time. He therefore sent an official letter, stating that he had been informed by the Governor of Frascati that his Holiness would come there one day, as usual in passing to Camal-doli to dine; and that he hoped he would take breakfast

by the way at the Villa Piccolomini. You may suppose
that he wrote this in his best manner, and also you will
imagine that although, all things considered, it was not
very likely we should have to go through the undertaking,
yet still I was somewhat in hot-water till the answer came
—gracious beyond expression, though *for this time* declining, as having promised to stop at Cardinal Pacca's and
the Villa Falconieri. At the same time Charles was informed that this *personal* attention had given great pleasure,
and when he went over to Castel Gandolfo the day after
the Pope arrived there, to wait upon him, he was overwhelmed with caresses. The Pope dwelt with emphasis on
his owing his cure* to a Prussian, and said further '*E
proprio un suo fratello il quale è venuto per guarirmi*'—
from a likeness, real or supposed, in person, between Dr.
Alertz and my husband. A day or two later, when the
intended visit of the Pope to Frascati took place, it had
been settled that Charles should take the opportunity of
presenting to him several Prussians, mostly Catholics,
when he was in the sacristy, as being far less troublesome
than such presentations in Rome, and accordingly he
appeared with his train, two ladies and four men, in the
small sacristy of the church of Frascati, and was made to
approach close to the Pope's chair, on one side, in order
the better to make his presentations. The Pope spoke to
each of the three Catholic young men (one of them Urlichs)
and expressed himself pleased with them—'*Buone faccie,
mi piaciono !*'—and after the whole set had retired, Charles
prepared to retire also from his post of honour, but the
Pope said, '*Restate, restate*,' and went on talking to him,

* From cancer.

so eagerly that he could not move, all the while the Pope
remained there, having his foot kissed by a crowd of friars,
ladies, and persons of all sorts, as fast as they could come
in and go out.

"Alertz has received princely rewards for his cure of
the Pope."

To her SON HENRY.

"19 *Nov.*, 1836.—At present there is no prospect of the
gratification of our wish for removal to the south of Germany: I must be satisfied that when God sees it good for
us, it will be contrived, for your Father has done all he
could to further it. The reasons for wishing it are very
decisive—not that an unknown country can in itself be an
object of desire to me, and probably neither he nor I will
ever have elsewhere the enjoyment of existence that we
have in Rome and Frascati; but to be established in a
really cheap country, where we could feel that our income
was *enough and to spare*, would be an enjoyment such as I
have never known yet : and to be within reach of Ernest,
and not to be compelled to cast away Charles and George
like balls to such a distance as not to be able to catch them
again, is the first and most pressing of all reasons for
desiring a removal to the north of the Alpine barrier :
which, if we had once crossed, there need be no impossibility of our visiting England, and seeing my dear Henry:
although, so great is the comfort I experience from having
been allowed such a renewal of intercourse and as it were
acquaintance, in the last winter, that separation is now
comparatively nothing to me, compared to what the separation from Ernest is becoming. When you both went with

your Father to Germany, I parted from you as children :
now I have seen you again, in comparative independence
and fixedness of character, you understand me, and I
understand you, and your letters I can take as really reflect-
ing the state of your mind and thoughts. But each year
seems to make Ernest more a stranger, and I confess, not
to be enabled to see him, is gradually becoming heavier
and heavier to me.

"We have seen much of Papencordt this summer—a
first-rate being and a real acquisition. Lepsius is also
much here, and helps your Father to refresh himself with
Hieroglyphics : indeed your Father is calculating Egyptian
chronology (which you know was an old passion) and is
making out delightful things. Lepsius is a person of
astonishing mental gifts, and of all sorts of talents,—
amongst others, musical : he sings and plays delightfully.
He is busily engaged, in short there never was such a
working colony as that of Frascati."

"19 *Nov.*—Dr. Arnold has written to us his decision for
your going to Oxford as soon as Easter. . . . . I have
only therefore to remind you that nothing is demanded of
you that is not within reach of straight-forward industry
and application, and that it is a certain fact, nothing of
lawful and laudable attainment can resist the human will,
if only strenuous and unremitting. I think it was a
maxim of Maupertuis, ' Qu'est ce que c'est que *bien vouloir ?*
—C'est ne vouloir qu' une chose, mais la vouloir toujours,
dans tous les instans de la vie.' "

On the 5th of January, 1837, a twelfth child was
born to the Bunsens, making a tenth in the large family

of living children. She was baptized by the names of Augusta Matilda, Dr. Arnold being her god-father.

MADAME BUNSEN *to her* MOTHER.

"14 *Feb.*, 1837.—I have nothing but causes of thankfulness to communicate. My darling baby thrives and grows fatter and heavier every day. . . . . One thing that I have long had to tell, and yet have not written, is the satisfaction I feel in the growing *practical* affection I experience from my children. I have felt, more than I could or would tell them, how eager all have been to help me, to be of use to me, to do anything with me or for me—in their various ways."

"22 *April.*—The Cliffords have had a great loss, and Rome too, in the death of Cardinal Weld, who has died probably in consequence of mistaken treatment. To-day the English College has celebrated a mass for him, in which the music was Mozart's *Requiem.* Monsignor Wiseman held a funeral sermon, in which he introduced a sketch of the Cardinal's life.

"We have parted with the Seymers with great regret, having found them continually improve on acquaintance. I have quite a regard for Miss Seymer,* and hope not to lose connexion with her altogether."

"*Frascati*, 3 *July*, 1837.—Fancy, my dearest Mother, if you can, anything so extraordinary as our having now a diplomatist-courtier by profession as our daily inmate! You will say how can that be, with the scrambling arrangement, the make-shift furniture of the Villa Piccolomini. Because the Baron de Buch is a good-natured person, with

* Afterwards Mrs. E. Denison, wife of the Bishop of Salisbury.

straight-forward understanding, and perfect good-breeding.
He has succeeded Usedom, to whom we had constantly
become more and more attached, for he is a most valuable
character, with first-rate abilities."

In the three years which had elapsed since the last
visit of Bunsen to Berlin, the differences between
Prussia and Rome had remained unsettled, and in the
meantime the gentle Pius VIII. had given place to
Gregory XVI., and the Archbishop of Cologne under
whom hopes of conciliation had been entertained had
passed away, leaving his place to be filled by the
strange appointment of Baron Droste von Vischering,
an uncompromising zealot, who, with the character of
Thomas à Becket, was resolved to yield no atom of his
spiritual power. Still, in June, 1837, hopes of concilia-
tory arrangements were again entertained at Berlin
from the expected arrival of Monsignor Capaccini, the
confidential secretary of Consalvi, who since his death
had been the one great statesman possessed by Rome,
equally " the faithful servant of his Government, and
the faithful friend of humanity, which he desired to
serve by promoting peace and a good understanding
among all sorts and conditions of men."

That Bunsen should again be summoned to Berlin
was natural, especially as he had long lived at Rome
with Capaccini in relations of personal friendship and
mutual esteem.   He was desired to come as quickly as
possible, so as to arrive before the Papal envoy, and to

use what pretext he chose for his journey. The pretext was found in his taking with him his third and fourth sons, Charles to be placed at Blochmann Institution at Dresden, and George to the school at Schulpforte. When he arrived at Berlin, Bunsen found the King already determined upon the arbitrary removal of the obnoxious Archbishop, who was accused of having entered into the Ultramontane combination of the Belgian bishops, and had given further offence by having proscribed the theological teachers in the University of Bonn, which had been endowed and was supported at the expense of the Prussian Government. Accordingly, on the 20th of November, 1837, the Archbishop was arrested, and conveyed away from his diocese, never more to return. It was a rash act of despotism, and as such aroused the indignation, not only of the Catholic, but of the Protestant population of Germany. Its imprudence was afterwards felt by the Government. Bunsen, who had been employed at Berlin to draw up a statement of the whole quarrel between Church and State, was unjustly pointed at as its instigator, although his liberal wishes might have been conclusively proved from his having recently by his personal influence with the King obtained that Catholic soldiers after parade should be held excused from attending the Protestant service, which had hitherto been compulsory.

During his stay at Berlin a way of escape from the difficulties of his position at Rome had seemed to open

for Bunsen in the vacant place of Director-General of
the Royal Museum, and in September he sent positive
directions to his wife to pack up and prepare for instant removal with the whole family to Germany. But
cholera was then raging both at Rome and Berlin, the
cordons and quarantines between the two places rendered an immediate journey impossible, and before it
could be carried out, Bunsen had discovered that the
museum directorship was to be united with other duties
which rendered his acceptance of it most undesirable,
so that his wife received directions to unpack again,
and await further directions. Her calm courage in
danger of pestilence, and imperturbable patience amid
so many wearisome changes of plans, will be apparent
in her own letters, where least of all she sought to exalt
herself. Amid the agonizing suspense of the cholera
period, surrounded by so many young children, and hearing daily that some valued friend had fallen a victim,
she had the support of her son-like friend Heinrich
Abeken, whose noble exertions during this trying period
were afterwards rewarded by the King of Prussia with
the Order of the Eagle, the royal munificence at the
same time paying off all debts on the German Hospital
at Rome.

In the beginning of December, a Commission was
established at Berlin for transacting the affairs of
Rome, and immediately after this grand mistake, with
enmity behind him, and hostility before him, Bunsen
left Berlin. He passed through Vienna, where, owing

to the friendship of the Comtesse Ste. Aulaire, he was kindly received by Prince Metternich, who urged him to delay his journey till the arrival of a fresh courier with some indication of the state of feeling at Rome ; but, being overruled by other advice, he proceeded to Trieste. Here letters from his wife awaited him announcing the declaration of the Pope that he would never receive him again. Still, instead of returning to Berlin to defend himself, or awaiting directions from head-quarters, he imprudently pushed on, and he arrived at Rome just before Christmas.

MADAME BUNSEN *to* BUNSEN.

" 17 *July*, 1837.—It costs a sort of effort to begin to write to you, because it presupposes the certainty of your total absence !—which as yet I can scarcely comprehend. Frances and I breakfasted in inconceivable solitude, and then went to church, which was an inexpressible comfort : in no other way than in taking part in public devotion as a means of edification, could the troubled waves have been equally brought to rest—even had it been possible, by any efforts, to procure two hours of equal quiet in one's own room, in which to meditate on all that could compose and strengthen the mind, yet just at the moment of need, the mind is not, with me at least, independent enough to find what it most needs, and would either prey upon itself, or at best fall into unprofitable stupour. Abeken chose the hymn ' In allen meinen Thaten,' which was just what I could have wished : and his sermon, saying that all fears and exaggerated anxiety as to the future is a sort of denial

of God and his providence, such as those who call themselves Christians should see that they correct and conquer,
if they will deserve that name, was peculiarly what I
wanted. After church, George's and Charles's poor nurse
came, ready to break her heart that she had not been able
to take leave of them. At half-past five we set out to
return to Frascati, and had a most delightful drive."

"*Frascati*, 13 *August*, 1837.—I have little to communicate except what is not new, that home and daily occupations, and home-objects, and walks, and drives, and what
not, are all very different without my Best-Beloved, to
what they were with the addition of his presence. This
worky-day world, as Shakspeare calls it, never puts on a
festal garb, when you are away; there is nothing, thank
God, to complain of, there is as yet no distress, but I have
not the sensation of enjoyment.

"There is no cholera in Rome, at least I believe not:
but there are *algide perniciose*, and *gastriche coleriche*, which
those who have a mind to be frightened suppose to be only
thin disguises for the dreaded monster."

"21 *August*, 1837.—Thank God, all is well with us,
although the storm which has so long been gathering has
burst over Rome, and the cholera is an admitted fact there.
What the mortality really is, it is difficult to know, but no
doubt greater than it need be, if help was granted, and
rational measures taken. Monsignor Marini and Monsignor Morichini are said to be very active in distributing
food and other assistance to the distressed in Trastevere,
but in other quarters of the city it does not seem that anything is done. In that part of the Quirinal occupied by
Monsignor Capaccini there have been four cases and two

deaths. The Pope does not leave his apartments. Prince
Henry is as yet well, that is, in his usual state. Vollard*
is firm at his post.

"As to myself, what should I tell you but that I want
you every hour of the four-and-twenty? God bless you
and keep you in health of body and mind, guide your
steps, and rule your actions."

To her MOTHER.

"*Frascati,* 22 *August,* 1837.—The cholera is at last in
Rome certainly. The Princess Massimo † had her usual
Saturday evening party and was dead on Sunday morning.
The dreadful idea of poison possessed the ignorant savages
of Rome, and in the Piazza Montanara (very near the
Capitol) they fell upon a poor Englishman, a master of the
language, who it is said had the imprudence to caress a
child, and give it a *ciambella;* he received eleven wounds,
was with difficulty dragged away by the soldiers, and
brought to the Hospital of the Consolazione, where it is
feared that he is by this time dead. This occurrence has
startled the Roman government, and a proclamation has
been issued announcing summary and severe punishment
to anyone who shall dare to speak of poison. It is said
the women were more savage than the men. A report
went about that the wounded man was a *Prussiano*, and he
was even improved into a *Maestro Prussiano—il Maestro del
Ministro di Prussia*, so that Bravo ran in a fright to the
Capitol to know if it was indeed Urlichs, Abeken, or

* An intimate friend of Bunsen, private-secretary to Prince Henry
of Prussia.

† From the terror which pervaded all classes, the body of the Princess Massimo had to be carried to the grave by galley-slaves, as no
other persons could be found to perform the office.

Kellermann. A priest has also been ill-treated by a *limonaro*, for giving sugar-plums to some girls of his acquaintance, but carabinieri were luckily near enough to save his life. In Trastevere there is considerable mortality, but then no physician dares practise there, the temper of the people is so savage, and the idea of poison so general. Tremendous was the uproar of devotion on the Madonna-festival; processions barefoot and howling out litanies crowded the Gesù-church, whither the wonder-working image has been brought from Sta. Maria Maggiore. Of these processions it was observed that the one from Monte Caprino out-screamed two or three others. In the evening there was a general illumination to propitiate the Madonna, and the whole population paraded the streets in their best clothes.

" Here in Frascati we have as yet no cholera, tho' much sickness, as usual when the heat bursts out all at once after a long period of unusual coolness. Frascati is apparently rational and enlightened, as being the only town around Rome that is not closed against all that would enter. Albano, Marino, little Grotta-Ferrata, &c., let no creature in, but Frascati trusts in —— S. Rocco·! He is the patron-general of *pestiférés—he* saved Frascati from the plague in the 16th century, when it was just at the gates, and caused a miraculous image of himself to be found, which is still in his church, *noi siamo divoti di S. Rocco*, and how should the cholera get here? So they let all fugitives in, and such carriages-full come from Rome, that I cannot guess where they sleep. I confess I cannot manage to get frightened, which I really think must be stupidity and want of imagination."

To BUNSEN.

"26 *August*, 1837.—So I have passed your birthday without yourself—for the first time for twenty years : I wish it may be the last. I asked Papencordt and young Abeken* to dinner, and treated all with some ice, which made the children exceedingly happy. In the evening we went to the Villa Muti, and returned late enough for Theodore to see to his satisfaction the *Milch Strasse*, which he has learnt to pronounce in German, and had asked to be shown many evenings when the moon had been bright. After dinner I allowed myself also an amusement—which you know to me is a great one, though rare—that of reading a novel of Walter Scott's—' Quentin Durward.'

"Abeken will give you the details of the awful scenes going on at Rome—the death and burial of poor Houseal, the murdered Englishman, and the death, alas ! by cholera, of the Norwegian from Drontheim, who was such a faithful member of our congregation, and of the choir. Such a scene of misery and confusion and terror and unreasonableness as Rome at this moment, can I suppose hardly be imagined :—nineteen galley-slaves, employed to form the new burial-ground near S. Paolo, have seized the arms of the soldiers when piled, and made off : some have escaped, and others were taken :—there have been two attempts at insurrection in Rome, to prevent the establishment of cholera-hospitals within the town, the fools not considering that the only chance for the life of those attacked is to have no long journey to make. But each several individual of this

* Wilhelm Abeken, first cousin to Madame Bunsen's " son-like " friend. His first writings on the " Remains of Etruscan Civilization " were much applauded. He died young.

enlightened population, as long as not attacked himself or herself, considers every cholera-patient as an excommunicated being, of whom it matters not what becomes. The Princesses Massimo and Chigi have been conveyed to the same public burial-ground with the rest near S. Paolo. All Rome is sighing after the Austrians, that is, that class which has property to protect, and believes the Pope has begged them to come: but I daresay that is not true. The convent of the Trinità de' Monti was among the first places attacked, although hermetically closed: several nuns have died, and the report goes that Lord Clifford's daughter is ill. But this proof that nunneries are not safe, is of no avail; every private house that possesses the means is closed against all comers."

"28 *Aug.*—As yet Frascati is not attacked, except by fear. Hitherto the *divozione a S. Rocco* keeps up such a degree of courage, that free passage is allowed to all such as do not confess to having had deaths from cholera in their house at Rome: only everybody is fumigated at the entrance of the town, to the great suffering of the daily-passing *vetturini*, some of whom are said to spit blood from the quantity of Chlor they have inhaled. At Monte Porzio they now let no one pass, as Urlichs and Papencordt experienced, who rode yesterday to make a visit to Monsignor Wiseman, and could not get the guard to receive their cards. The reason of this proceeding is said to be, that having formed no idea of fumigation but making a great fire before the gate, and then driving people round it or through it, they scorched a woman and burnt her ass, to a degree that made it clear the practice must be abandoned. Thus as the neighbouring *paesi* will let nobody in from Frascati, Frascati has established a system of reprisals, and has guards at every corner to keep out all that are from the neighbourhood. At Albano, where they were so savage in exclusion from the first, cholera has appeared.

" My Best-Beloved, I write on other things with a sort of shuddering aversion to communicating what is uppermost— that Tommaso * has been seized with the cholera! It was in the night of Saturday, but not till Sunday morning did he send for a physician: every care has been taken of him, by Abeken's kind superintendence, but as the second stadium had commenced before the medical assistance could be given, there is little hope. Before this letter is closed I shall be able to tell you whether this severe loss has befallen us or not. He at least has not wanted what most of the poor patients have been deprived of—care and kindness. Angelina and Pietro are most zealous and fearless, and also Rosa from the hospital. Pantaleone has attended him, and the advice of Tagliabò was asked. I have the less hope that he can get over it, because he had been long in a state of spiritless terror, which gave him no chance. . . . . All are yet well in this house, and I feel thankful for every day passed in health, which one ought always to feel, but it needs a nearer threatening of the horrors of pestilence to be reminded of mercies daily received.

" 28 *August* (Evening).—My Best-Beloved, our faithful Tommaso is indeed lost to us. He expired on Sunday evening, 27th, at sunset—before I had received the first tidings of his illness, which was of 24 hours' duration. I

* The Bunsens' house-steward, brother of the faithful Angelina.

can write no more now, for I am obliged to take to my bed, by an unusual degree of migraine: it was aggravated, no doubt, by the great shock I have received. But you know I always tell you the truth, so that you will not apprehend anything more or worse. . . . . I am indescribably thankful now that you are not here, you would feel bound to go to Rome, and what a misery that would be."

"*Frascati*, 30 *August*, 1837.—What shall I say of the turmoil of thoughts and feelings, caused by your letter of the 14th?* But all that I can think or feel is absorbed in one feeling, in the conviction, that whatever you decide upon, I shall be satisfied with. Causes of anxiety I have enough, as to the fulfilment of all you write of, because you know not the present awful state of the country: but all may yet be well. If it please God to save us from the pestilence, He can do so under any circumstances—here at Frascati, or through the bustle of packing and settling affairs in Rome."

"2 *Sept.* 1837.—Yesterday Kellermann breathed his last! O my Best-Beloved! it is indeed walking in 'the valley of the shadow of death:' and I feel so relieved that you are not here in the midst of the danger, that I know not how to wish for the speedy return that your last letter promised! But if things are wonderfully so arranged as to enable you to realise your plans, it will be a sign that it pleases God to take us away from hence, and then He will help us through. We are, thank God, all well as yet, and the pestilence has not reached Frascati: but if you come, you will find all looking less fresh than when you

---

* A letter desiring Madame Bunsen to pack up and come to Berlin, with full directions, soon afterwards contradicted.

left us. The season, independent of the pestilence, must have been a trying one. You will believe we take all care as to diet: no fruit has been touched by anybody this long time.

"Poor Abeken asserts that he is well, and as he is in the active discharge of duty, I trust he will be supported: but it is indeed a hard trial, with weakened health not half recovered, to stand alone in the breach. Lepsius is daily expected, but I write to day to urge his coming here to inhabit Abeken's vacant room, and not risking remaining in Rome, coming as he does fresh from Tuscany. His presence might be a comfort to Abeken, but also an anxiety, for he has no sound constitution to struggle with. Kellermann sent for Abeken at five o'clock in the morning —he was already very bad: Pantaleone came directly, afterwards Dietz (celebrated for successful practice), he wanted no help that could be given, but at one o'clock he had expired. The burial was to take place this morning early.

"The poor people at Monte Caprino are now crowding round Pantaleone, when he comes up to the Capitol, and some have asked for medicine from our Hospital. This is indeed a satisfactory circumstance—and this is after people about Piazza Montanara and the Consolazione had uttered threats to burn the Hospital—the day of the murder of the Englishman Houseal, and when the first report existed, that it was a Prussian who had been seized as a prisoner. I would not write this in my first letter—now the storm may be considered to have blown over. Abeken caused alms to be given to the most distressed about the hill, by Don Felice: but of course could not venture to give

either soup or food. Everything is getting very dear in
Rome. A conspiracy has been discovered, of wretches
who intended to burn and plunder the palaces of such as
they supposed might have deposits of money—Borghese,
Piombino, Banco S. Spirito, &c. Wild stories are told of
a plan of seizing the Pope and changing the government,
probably not true. My Best-Beloved! I will close this
report of death and distress, in thankfulness that we are as
yet personally spared. Were we but re-united!"

To her MOTHER.

" 5 *Sept.*, 1837.—Frascati has as yet been spared the
awful scourge, and though, the season being an unwholesome one, there is much sickness, independent of the
worst: the children have been quite well, and myself also.
Abeken has been fixed in Rome ever since the disorder
was declared to exist, and he is wonderfully supported in
unceasing exertion and anxiety. But we have had a
severe loss in Tommaso, which I have not felt the less,
because I anticipated that he could make no resistance to
the poisoned atmosphere. He has served us ten years, and
never abused the most implicit confidence;—and I need
not tell my Mother that if I knew of twenty people competent for his place (whereas I know not of one) my
sorrow would not be diminished. The 1st September
Kellermann was carried off in eight hours, which Abeken
will not easily get over. He too was close at hand, and
help and remedies were had without delay. A Norwegian
cabinet-maker we knew and valued died in the hospital:
two other cholera patients there have recovered: but all
such of course keep Abeken in continual exertion. In one

person who has taken up much of his time and received much comfort from him, I have taken great interest since I made her acquaintance in May last—Mrs. Vaughan, a young widow, with a fine boy of four years old, who is now an orphan. She was a niece of Mr. Craven who lives at Naples. I never heard the name of her family, but her father had a place in the Mauritius, where she was born and bred. She married at sixteen against the will of her parents, and at nineteen was left a widow immediately after landing at Leghorn among strangers. She however found kind-hearted people to help her, and came on, with an old Scotch lady as a protection, to Florence, where she had a dangerous illness. From Florence I received a letter about her, and since she arrived in Rome I have seen her as often as I could. From a strange irresolution, she staid on in Rome, till she got a dangerous fever: from that she was recovering, when the cholera exhausted the remains of vital strength. Abeken sat by her for hours, many days together, and says the struggle was hard for such youth to part with life: she did at last overcome, and was not only resigned but full of joyful hope. She and Mr. Burlowe the sculptor are the only English who have yet fallen victims to the cholera. Lord Clifford and the English College are said to have exerted themselves to do good to the sufferers in this time of complicated misery: also the Jesuits; Alessandro Torlonia has distinguished himself by increasing the number of his workmen, distributing to the poor, and fearlessly driving out. Almost all other persons of name have shut themselves in their palaces, but they do not shut the cholera out: many individuals of rank were among the first victims, and if they were to be so, it is as well that it was at first, to help to quell the dreadful suspicion among the people, that there was a conspiracy to poison the poor. The Princess Chigi has followed the Massimo, and Monsignor Chigi, for whom the Prince had to borrow the hearse of the Protestants! that he might be taken *con decenza* to the cemetery at S. Lorenzo. The young Duke of Fiano, and Conte Bolognese, husband of the young Brancadoro, are among the dead."

"*Frascati*, 15 *Sept.*, 1837.—Thank God all about me are still well, not only free from the dreadful visitation, but even from the fevers of the season. But, my own Mother, I have received a summons from my husband to follow him with all the children to Berlin, as soon as possible!!— and therefore have more upon my hands than you can quite imagine, or I enumerate. The embarrassment is increased by the present state of Rome, for everybody cautions me against going from the uninfected air into the contagion, until it is more nearly abated, and I can do very little as to preparation till I am on the spot. But the disorder is abating fast, and the season has changed into the finest autumnal weather, and I have hopes that I may speedily remove and set to work, for the time is short to get to Berlin before it is complete winter. From several letters I perceived that plans were in agitation to detain him, although he could not write plainly, under the consciousness that the letters would be opened: nor has he explained anything, but the matter of fact necessary for me to know—that his present post in Rome is continued to him, that a very large sum was to be advanced for his expenses in the removal of his family, besides the continuance of his allowance: which I am soon to receive. His having had a long personal conference with the King, on the business in which he is engaged, was mentioned by the way, and was a very satisfactory circumstance to me. I have always been reminding him, that he could never hope for success, unless he made out that his communications with the King were to be immediate. The whole matter is to appear as if provisional, but I cannot think, that when once over the Alps, we shall return.

"My own dearest Mother, I write, as you see, the most dry unsatisfactory account of this most important crisis, that can be conceived: but I must keep feelings out of the question, that I may if possible continue fit for action. Reflection tells me how highly satisfactory this change is, on the whole,—how highly necessary in short: and I must not set about objecting to some attendant circumstances of hurry and plague, fatigue and responsibility, which if I had a choice should have been otherwise. To have to think of taking leave of these beloved and lovely scenes only so short a time before I leave them, is a great advantage. The children you may suppose, are all spirits—Emilia quite wild. The twins take it the most quietly, tho' Theodore says, 'Je suis bien aise que je vais voir la neige!'"

To ABEKEN (at Rome).

"*Frascati*, 13 *August*, 1837.—When you communicated your intention of passing in solitude the solemn anniversary,* I so fully understood and sympathised in the feeling which prompted you to seek, not uninterrupted indulgence

* Of his wife's death.

of sensation, but undisturbed converse with your own soul and with God, who did not send a warning so awful but for his own purpose of universal good,—that I could not utter one word of objection, feeling as if I should indeed be counteracting great things by insignificant ones, if I sought to withhold you from the *geweihtes Manna lesen** by anxiety for your health : but I have since felt that I ought to urge upon you the duty of circumscribing your stay in Rome, and though I cannot expect of you to give up Tuesday evening, yet at latest on Wednesday morning you should in regard to your health return here. As twelve months ago, at my request, you were induced to leave those remains of what had so recently been life and feeling and intelligence, in order to give your exhausted body the needed rest, for the sake of that affectionate father who has been bereaved of so much, and to whom nothing remains on earth but yourself,—so I hope you will now renounce your intention of remaining in Rome over the funeral anniversary which I have only just learnt to be your purpose.

"Most earnestly do I pray that every blessing you need may attend the season of awful retrospect. Ever yours with maternal affection, F. BUNSEN."

"23 *August*, 1837.—If you could make it possible to see the Platners again, I should be much obliged to you if you will explain that I can contrive seven beds for them, and the *bianchi* and *tavole* for an eighth, and that I have *coperti di lana* for the beds, but not *biancheria*. Change of air would do them more good, than exposure to the air can do evil.

---

* This expression occurs in a hymn of the 17th century.

" Were it not for the fumigating apparatus, I should ask whether you think you can be spared to spend my husband's birthday with us : and yet you must judge yourself whether it is right to be out of the way—perhaps not : the more because if any German should be taken ill, there is nobody to secure his being brought to the hospital if you should be absent. We are all well."

" 24 *August*.—You will be assured of the sympathy with which I have read your truly melancholy accounts, and I should not have hinted even at your coming over here, had I known of there being a case in our hospital. . . . . Yet pray have a regard to your own health and do not go on sitting up all night with patients. I do not complain of your doing so in the first instance :—it was necessary to watch over physician and attendants, as much as the patient : but when you have broken them in, you can economize your own strength, and must do so, if you would not be exhausted."

" *August* 26.—At the gates of Frascati admittance has been refused to the Ciampi family, because a death from cholera (of a blooming daughter) had taken place among them. I cannot therefore help being alarmed lest the Platners should be sent back, because two of the party will look as if recovering from the cholera. It occurs to me that it might be good for Platner to write beforehand to the *Governatore* of Frascati, enclosing a certificate from the physician, that in his house there has been nothing but *febbre intermittente non contagiosa*. He had better also mention that he is coming to inhabit *in casa del Ministro di Prussia a Villa Piccolomini*."

" *August* 27.—I must write, but know not what—except

my most heartfelt thanks for your care of Tommaso. I have no hope of his recovery. How little I can spare him, I scarcely was aware before : I ought not to be so overset —I ought only to be thankful that *as yet* nobody still nearer has been touched. For God's sake take care of yourself. . . . .

" Or if, what I cannot hope, Tommaso should yet be alive when this note arrives, say to him, or let him be told, all he can bear of the shock I have received in the anticipation of his loss,—even to the tears, which I reprove myself for shedding because they can do him no good, and myself only harm : and let Angelina be assured of my most affectionate sympathy, and have a charge to take care of herself all she can."

" 31 *August.*—I have been busy this morning with poor Tommaso's papers, and wish his example may take effect in proportion to the emotion it has occasioned. How it does strike me to see that paper of accounts again, which I had received and returned to him three days before his death, and on which with such admirable exactness, he had, to the last, noted down sums ! It is an example not to forget : for though possessed by the general fear of death, he could have thought as little as any of us that he was not to see the next week.

"The anecdote of Prince Chigi and the hearse is most remarkable ! as is also the confidence of the poor people at Monte Caprino. As to the giving of soup, I should think it was too great a risk, unless to individuals who should make a special request for it, and then as quietly as possible.

"That the body of Monsignor Chigi should have no accompanying clergy, is beyond conception ! "

To ABEKEN (on the news of Kellermann's death).

" 1 *Sept.* 1837.—Alas! what shall I say, when I feel so much! May God support and strengthen you! He does, and He will: that is so entirely my confidence, that, most strangely, as it might seem, I cannot be alarmed about you, altho' the circumstances of danger in which you are placed are for ever present to me:—the will of God is inscrutable! but of His dispensations we see but a part—they must be completed elsewhere, in fulness of justice, and perfection of mercy. ' Ese cuerpo fué depositario de una alma en quien el Cielo puso infinitas partes de sus riquezas:' on this fact let us rest—leaving what we valued to the will of God, who has not created any man ' for nought.' He has but taken that away, which in this mortal state was incompetent to farther progress towards the end and object of moral existence. That we do not know what the divine mercy has in reserve for such as have not complied with the only conditions on which we believe it can be granted— need not distress us: God has ways of helping that we know not of.

" . . . . To walk thus in the valley of the shadow of death is an awful thing! to see the destroying angel almost in visible form, and his shafts flying in every direction—a thousand falling in our sight, and hundreds at our right hand! If indeed *we* at last are spared, should we not look upon ourselves as consecrated by the fiery ordeal to work the work of God in the remainder of life, more especially?

" May God's grace be upon you—better than I can wish —above all I can conceive!"

" *Sept.* 2.—Should Lepsius arrive, will you not offer him to occupy your vacant bed at Villa Piccolomini. Pray assure him of being very welcome to me—and surely after the wholesome air in Tuscany, he should not brave the pestilence in Rome. If you could come for a night, you could get sleep here—but I cannot be of opinion that you ought—I believe you would drive back to Rome more susceptible of poisonous air for having inhaled better. And somebody might, like Kellermann, send to you at five o'clock in the morning! You see how I reckon upon your not wanting Lepsius to stay with you. I think the increase of anxiety would do away with all comfort from his presence, and an occasional hour of solitude must do more good than harm, for in such solitude you can go to Him who alone can give strength for the hour of exertion."

" 5 *Sept.*, 1837.—What you say about the *frische Lebenshauch* that you experienced in the presence of Lepsius, struck me with reference to myself. I am used to inhale nothing *but* that atmosphere of life, and now, unless Lepsius brings it, where should I find it? When my husband is at home, all that lives in his neighbourhood must be *alive*."

" 7 *Sept.*—I was affected indeed by the account of the two deathbeds. What scenes you had to go through! It is self-evident that one has only to thank God for having graciously removed Mrs. Vaughan from a world with which she could not contend : and that we do not equally feel the reasons for thanking Him for the removal of Kellermann, is owing to our short-sightedness."

" 10 *Sept.*—In the first place, I am well—weak to be sure, but already stronger than when I rose this morning, from the delicious air :—the weather was to-day so glorious, the country so beautiful, that it gave a sensation of melancholy—I do not mean quite that, but a sobered and serious consciousness of beauty and splendour not intended for the every-day use of this 'worky-day world.' Secondly, more thanks than I can write for your kindness and anxiety, but you must not distress yourself so much, any more than write yourself dead. Remember the favourite proverb, 'Die Suppe.'* Pray do not let them call you up in the night every time a sick person gets a fancy—*Sie sind auch ein Mensch.* Good night! God bless you!"

" 12 *Sept.*—God support and comfort you! and further, rouse and stimulate you to the fulfilment of all He will have performed by you! of all, for which He granted you the powers and gifts you possess! They were not intended for ornaments, nor playthings.

"Meyer frightens me with accounts of the threats of burning the hospital.—But, God can help."

" 23 *Sept.*—God bless you! do not be in any alarm about me, because I tell you the truth, that I feel neither active nor cheerful."

To her MOTHER.

" 25 *Sept.*, 1837.—On Thursday I went to Rome to make preparations for packing, &c. . . . . I returned quite depressed by the melancholy state of everything—Angelina coming to meet me on the stairs, like a ghost—Tommaso not there, who was always there on previous occasions— Pietro greatly altered by what he has gone through : everybody I saw grieved at our departure, which as far as Angelina is concerned, is really the greatest misfortune,

* A German proverb, "Soup is never eaten so hot as brought on the table."

apparently, that could happen to her, as to which I know not how to offer her consolation."

"*Rome*, 2 *October*, 1837.—Here I have been, my own dearest Mother, since the day before yesterday, and I am, and have been, in such a whirl of business, that only for moments can I be conscious of the sensation of leave-taking. I know as a fact that I have left Villa Piccolomini, probably never to see it again : but having no leisure to dwell on the feelings and reflections called forth by that fact, I have been enabled to avoid all enervating emotion. How I am to give you an account of what I have done, or am likely to do, I know not : for how I am to finish what is to be done in ten days, is beyond my conception. Packing up is the least part. The most necessary part for you to know is that I am well and strong, which is more than I have felt for near a month : just the last four days I have experienced a vast difference, without knowing why or wherefore except that one must never doubt having the strength granted that is necessary, whether of body or mind."

It was after all this that Madame Bunsen heard, and received with equal equanimity, that all was changed, Bunsen was to return to Rome—the departure was in-definitely deferred.

MADAME BUNSEN *to her* MOTHER.

"1 *Nov.*, 1837.—I have read some part of the ' Life of Sir Walter Scott,' with the greatest pleasure and interest : though it is often a very melancholy pleasure ; it is some-thing like watching a boat riding on the smooth surface with swiftness imperceptibly increasing, knowing as we do that a few miles further on is the waterfall, down which the same current will dash, carrying the same frail bark to unavoidable destruction. He was reserved to do bitter penance for the political and literary pique which tempted him to engage in booksellers' speculations, and render his talents mere instruments of trade and profit. I often think, in considering life and biography, of a verse of Göthe, signifying ' Every error finds its retribution on earth.' I firmly believe this to be true, distinguishing error from sin : for sin the Christian dispensation offers an all-sufficient atonement, to those who will become partakers of it, but that atonement applies to another state of existence, and cannot shield us from the consequences, which in the scheme of God's moral government of the world are inseparably annexed to certain courses of feeling and action. It is not often that we can know enough of the history of our fellow-creatures to trace this : but reflection upon our own, when we try to tell ourselves the truth without self-deception, will often reveal the fact, which I think Madame de Staël had in her mind when she wrote—' Vous souffrez longtems, vous prospérez longtems, sans l'avoir mérité, quand tout à coup la scène se change, le mot de votre énigme se révèle ; et le mot, la conscience l'avait bien dit, avant que le destin ne l'eût répété.'

" After tea, Abeken reads to me, and I work cross-stitch on week days, and treat myself to drawing on Sunday evenings. What he reads is generally Niebuhr's ' Roman History,' which he helps me to understand : for though an inexhaustible mine of information to the learned, it is too full of the language of allusion and suggestion to be accessible to the ignorant."

BUNSEN *to* MRS. WADDINGTON.

Berlin, 12, *Oct.* 1837.—Six weeks ago it was almost decided that I was to remain here, as the King's Envoy, but with a special commission for a year. This has been one of the most trying epochs of my life. I *could* not obtain decision *before* the 25th of September, and this was evidently the last time to write to Fanny and bid her come over the Alps with all our treasures. What was to be done? To tell F. to prepare for the *probability*, do everything preparatory for the journey, and still be not disappointed if at last the thing was settled definitively for the contrary. I knew her great soul could bear such an uncertainty, such a trial. No sooner had she received the intimation (without the reasons, for I was not allowed to write them) in the midst of cholera and quarantines, and stoppages and cordons, and all sorts of disorders, vexations, dangers of life, murders, &c., than she settled everything at Frascati and at Rome, packed up, made arrangements for everything, and still did nothing that could commit her, if we did not go. But, what is more admirable still, is that she does not complain any more of the *hardness* of uncertainty, than of the difficulty of overcoming trials which men declare insurmountable. Her letters state every difficulty, but each statement is followed by such expressions as : ' Never mind—*vedremo* and I shall get through it—all will be done that must be done—I feel as high-spirited as ever,' &c."

MADAME BUNSEN *to* BUNSEN.

" 14 *Oct.* 1837.—Lord Clifford has called. He spoke of the dreadful period that Rome had passed through, in which his active benevolence has been universally acknowledged; and said justly, that the death of about ten thousand people who had not the means of living (the whole mortality is estimated by moderate persons at 12,000) is not the calamity : but rather the difficulty of providing for the four thousand orphans left—that there had been an immense sum collected for the sufferers in cholera, and a number of plans made for disposing of it, but not one of those plans executed, and therefore little or no help had been received from it. He related anecdotes proving the sacrifice of lives occasioned by the brutal removal of the sick from their own beds, at a moment when they most required medical treatment, and transporting them to hospitals miles distant, often to one or two in succession, until a vacant bed could be found, which bed received the patient but to expire. In short, the whole substance of his communications proved a state of vicious disorganization everywhere.

"I hear of one Pasquinade, and but one as yet, about the cholera. Pasquino says—'Ma come, Signor Abbate cholera, le abbiamo ricevuto in Roma con tante cerimonie, con illuminazioni, processioni, feste, e lei non ha avuto tanta creanza chi di far visita nè dal Papa, nè dai Cardinali !' The cholera answers ' E vero,—ha mille volte ragione ; per questa volta parto, ma poi *tornerò*, e riparerò il mancamento !' It is a fact that the Pope refused to let his physican, who was shut into the Quirinal, go to a choleric patient."

" 18 *Oct.* 1837.—They now assert here, *in the face of facts*, that the cholera has ceased—having on Sunday sung a Te Deum at Sta. Maria Maggiore, in the

Pope's presence, for the removal of the scourge, and on Monday a Requiem at St. Peter's for those who had died under it. We went to St. Peter's where the *catafalco* was raised in that arm of the cross were the Lavanda takes place, and it had a fine effect: but there were no benches for the Corps Diplomatique, or for anybody but the dignified clergy, and altogether not many people were in the church, the rest of which was decked out in preparation for a Beatification, which is to take place next Sunday. Various miracles of the Beato were painted in the church, with different inscriptions, one of which is that verse of one of the Psalms, with which you have often been edified, and once together with Chateaubriand. I shall write the Latin wrong, but you will recollect it—'quod non cognovi litteras'—*therefore*, I enter into the kingdom of heaven! "*

"23 *Oct.* 1837.—Your dear letter containing so many proofs and expressions of your love, might well make all the amends possible for the tidings of new delay as to your return. May you but be here at Christmas, my Dearest! I thank God for the assistance granted to get us out of our difficulties, but am lost in conjecture *how* you could contrive to obtain it! now that we do not make a journey: but I will be contented in this matter, and so many others, with the fact, until I can get the explanation. What you

---

* A few days after the Polignac Ministry had been established by Charles X., Bunsen was visiting the Sistine Chapel. He had been conversing with one of his colleagues on the most unexpected appointment which had taken place, and the collocutor had just remarked upon Polignac's unfitness and almost entire want of the most ordinary knowledge, when the choir set in. The first Psalm sung contained the words quoted. Bunsen pointed them out to his neighbour, who tried in vain to look serious for the rest of the service!

say of a '*sorgenfreies Leben*' would be a great comfort to
have verified, but unless the *habitual state of things* is to be
placed on a different footing, leaving the circle of receipt
always a little wider than that of expenditure, we shall be
only *ausser Sorgen* for a given time.

"My Best-Beloved, there is nothing more certain than
that, if one did not ungratefully forget the gratifications
one is allowed, a harmless wish is sooner or later gratified,
oftener in life than one is apt to think. How often I have
wished that I could ever be allowed a time to enjoy Rome
in! and regretted never being there at a period when
weather, season, and leisure were together favourable to a
free and comfortable existence. Now this month of
October is of real perfection, the sky clear, the air fresh,
the sun brilliant, no strangers here to take up one's time,
no social trammels to prevent the free disposal of it. So I
go out daily, and every day see something interesting :
there is one great want, that you are not here, but whatever I see, I live in the hope of seeing it again with you.
I was the other day at S. Lorenzo, and after dinner
Abeken read what you have written about it. The aspect
of the burial-ground is comfortless, but yet more shocking
is it to see, that those who have died of cholera are treated
there as excommunicated : a hole broken in the enclosure-
wall, serves as a passage to the open, unenclosed, uneven
field, in which long rough furrows, covered with loose
earth as if by the plough, show where the human seed
divine has been deposited. Tommaso however was laid in
the consecrated ground of the cemetery, intended for those
morti di mali pii, for that is the phrase, to distinguish cholera
as *male impio :*—the heathen had juster notions, for they

thought the special scourge of God had a sanctifying influence. The reason that Tommaso and many others came into the more decent place, was the creditable one that '*quelli bughi per li colerici non erano allora terminati*," and, as you know, the date of his burial was the 28th August, eight days after the existence of cholera was admitted, and four weeks after it had begun. It is a most extraordinary fact, that as far as I can procure information, he was the only sufferer who received decent burial, always excepting the Protestants. Pietro accompanied the funeral procession, and assures me the priests, ten in number, with the Archiprete at their head, followed the corpse to the grave, where the absolution was performed by the Archiprete according to rule; whereas Monsignor Chigi was followed only by two empty carriages, two *torci a vento* being borne by the side of the *borrowed* hearse containing his remains, and not a single priest was there. The impression must have been, that as the Protestants bury their own dead reverently, *you* would expect that your servant should be interred with decency, as it was done at your expense : and Pietro's witnessing the whole probably did much to secure the performance of what was undertaken."

" 26 *Oct.*, 1837.—My Dearest, it has been an event in my life to become acquainted with the tragedies of Sophocles, which Abeken has been reading to me. O! I cannot wonder at the enthusiasm these ancient Greeks inspire, it would only seem as if not half enough had been said of the sublimity of their conceptions. There is an intensity of beauty and grandeur in the two Œdipus-pieces, to which only that of the remains of their sculpture can be compared : with all the interest attending individuality, with all the greatness of abstractions!—all the tenderness for others, of which the human heart is capable, with all the fortitude of self-sacrifice to religious convictions; none of that weakness of feeling, which after all is grounded in selfishness or self-compassion!—the laws of God through-out held paramount to all, no rebellion against eternal, immutable truth! in short, in the real sense of the word, religion, and true religion: although but the dawn, yet awaiting the perfect day. These readings take place after tea, whenever Buch and his satellite Urlichs go to the theatre together."

"22 *Nov.*, 1837.—Yesterday your youngest son, my most particular delight, asked to go up the tower of the Capitol, and your eldest daughter condescended to wish to see a gallery. So we enjoyed ourselves amongst the Corsini pictures, and then walked in the Corsini gardens to the top of the Janiculan, the prospect glorious, the air clear as crystal, the Velino and Leonessa each one mass of snow. I have been lately, with the children and Abeken, in several vigne on the Aventine, from each of which there is a new and beautiful point of view: and enjoy the thought of making Sunday walks thither with you, my Dearest, whenever you are really here again: the time grows more and more tedious, the more the time, please God, approaches."

"25 *Nov.*—Frances and Mary, Theodore and Theodora, with Abeken, have accompanied me to the top of the tower of the Capitol, where we long enjoyed ourselves, basking in the sun, and beholding the prospect. Afterwards we went into the Museum for a short time, and concluded with the garden."

" 27 *Nov.*, 1837.—I have been reading the Life of Walter Scott, in which I have an indescribable interest. But Walter Scott was in a melancholy manner, the *man of his own time*—a time in which men made use of their powers, and gifts, and qualities, to produce effect, attain an end, among their contemporaries, in short, made a gambling speculation with their talents, instead of aiming after an ideal standard, and seeking to satisfy their own conceptions of excellence. Walter Scott did not like his own writings, in particular his own poetry, but he wrote with spirit, as an actor performs a part in which his feelings have no share, enjoying the sympathy and applause of the public : and afterwards reckoning upon that sympathy and applause as a ground of speculation, to help him out of pecuniary difficulties into which he had unnecessarily fallen. Yet his was a fine mind, and his letters, which express his feelings and affections, have an indescribable charm : his liberality of sentiment, and delight in the writings of contemporaries, is most amiable, but he does not appear to have had any more critical judgment than Overbeck as to the works of contemporary painters, and probably for the same reason, supplying by his imagination all that was wanting.

" I have now proceeded with Abeken to the end of Niebuhr, and can conceive what you must feel at the melancholy and sudden break at the end of the third volume : it gives an awful consciousness of what death is, that breaking off in the midst of the fullness of life, when the current of thought seemed setting so strong. But nobody can ever continue that work,—his mind was a magic mirror that reflected the very *form and body* of ancient Roman time; and that magic mirror is broken, and the vision ceases."

" 9 *Dec.*, 1837.—I have nothing to tell, but *das ewige Lied*—will you indeed return? can you return? can you be on the way? The one thought of your being, comparatively speaking, so near, confounds all other thoughts! and yet there is enough to write about besides. The Pope has called a Consistory, and held an Allocution, on the subject of late events: the language of complaint and condemnation is as strong as possible, with the highest praise of the Archbishop of Cologne, and approbation of his sentiments and conduct. But from the tone of the whole, it might be supposed that the question of the mixed marriages was the sole point at issue, and that opposition to the wishes of the King's government on that head was the sole offence of the Archbishop. It is made a great ground of complaint that the intentions of the King's government were not made known here until after they had been executed."

To her SON GEORGE (*at Schulpforte*).

" *Rome*, 9 *Dec.*, 1837.—Your three letters received the same day, by myself, by Abeken and Urlichs, gave, all taken together, a very complete idea of your present situation; and it makes me sad enough to think how little comfort you can have in it. But the object of human existence is not to be as comfortable as possible in every stage of its progress, but to make every advantage possible of the circumstances, whether pleasing or unpleasing, into which the path of life may successively bring you. I can well guess how peculiarly bitter must be the want of sympathy among companions in study and play, who having all to go the same way, and all to combat with the same difficulties, might be supposed willing to show others the kindness they must be conscious of wanting. But a school is the image of life, schoolboys do but show what the natural man is, before he has been worn smooth in some degree by the world's rough billows; or what is not only higher and better, but alone efficient, before the discipline of the cross of Christ, received by a free and willing spirit, has subdued the native powers of hatred and selfishness, which lead the natural man to delight in giving pain rather than pleasure, because he looks upon everything desirable which another enjoys, as stolen from himself. The advantage, however, and an inestimable one, of the foretaste of the world which is experienced in a school, is the being habituated to a steady course of conduct, with responsibility to your own conscience alone : '*fais que dois, advienne que pourra*'—as the old French motto of, I forget what French king says. It is well to have experience early of the uselessness of endeavouring to please the multitude—who ever follow those who do not run after them, but show themselves independent in doing right.

"Dass dieser Aufenthalt Epoche in deinem Leben mache, konntest du nicht verhindern ; dass sie aber deiner werth sei, hängt von dir ab ! '—I trust I shall find my George again, having by God's assistance held fast and improved the notions of right and wrong that he brought from home, and being confirmed in habits of conscientious activity and self-responsibility."

Just before Christmas, Bunsen returned to his family.

It was then hoped that the strong feeling evinced by the Pope against him—as the supposed instigator of the Archbishop of Cologne's arrest—would abate with time, but Gregory XVI. kept his word, he never could be induced to receive Bunsen again. Meantime the letters which Bunsen had written requesting leave of absence had been forwarded to Berlin, though from his strong faith in the King's friendship he did not expect that the permission, which it would have been a mark of confidence to withhold, would really be granted, and when on March 4, Madame Bunsen's birthday, the whole family, surrounded by a band of devoted friends, went to spend the afternoon under the pines of the Villa Pamfili, and returned with "loads of anemones and sweet-scented iris," they little imagined that they had looked upon its loveliness for the last time. But there were those in Berlin who had long been watching for the destruction of Bunsen's court-influence, and who hoped to raise themselves by his ruin.

To her MOTHER.

" 12 *March*, 1838.—I have now to inform you of a plan, which I delight to tell, and you will like to hear: only I beg you, as I charge myself, not to reckon too absolutely upon its execution, that I may not have to blame myself for causing disappointment by a premature communication. Charles has actually written to ask for leave of absence to spend the summer in England! I know not how to believe this while I write !—The prospect of such a summer, passed with my Mother at Llanover, is almost too ideally perfect : Charles would go to London, visit the Puseys and Arnolds, and come back again, and my dear Henry would come to Llanover too, if his grandmother can make room for all.

"O my own Mother, how much I have to tell that there is no time to write! Charles is now in a state of active energy, which is more consonant to his nature than the passive state in which he has spent the last few months : but you would have been pleased with him and proud of him, if you had witnessed all as I have done. And his case is a hard one! to have worked so hard for peace for so many years, to have had his plans defeated by the dilatoriness of his own government (you know when—in allowing the former archbishop to die without having brought the system agreed upon into practice), and now, having done more than the world will ever know or believe to prevent a rupture, to be publicly accused as the principal enemy to peace! But though the case is hard, it might be yet harder, for he has always the comfort of enjoying the confidence of the King and Crown Prince, and of the very Altenstein, who might be jealous of him as his supposed successor, if he was of a little mind : to say nothing of the public applause that has been granted him in Protestant Germany, for having been the cause of rigorous and decisive measures—though that sort of applause he mistrusts too much to overvalue it, being caused in part by a mistaken notion as to his opinions, or as to the system upon which he would act if uncontrolled.

"We have gone on as quietly as before, except one day, when we had here to breakfast the Duke Bernard of Saxe-

Weimar (the same whose travels in America were published), Prince Lieven, and the Count and Countess Panin, who are Russian subjects, but he a Greek, and she a German: after breakfast, which was at half-past twelve, Charles took them a walk to show them the Forum.

"I have always omitted to tell of the Baron de Thile, whom Charles brought back with him from Berlin as attaché, and to succeed the Baron de Buch as Secretary of Legation, in short, to be an efficient labourer in the office. He turns out all that could be wished in application to business, as well as intelligence, and is a most agreeable inmate, full of information and interest in everything worthy to interest an intellectual being.* He is the son of a general officer, whom Charles had known for years, and a very distinguished person; and he has an uncle, another General Thile, who is very kind to Ernest. He said to Charles, on taking leave of him at Berlin—'I give you my boy (being very fond of this nephew) and I take yours in exchange'—and accordingly we have heard that he has the kindness to let Ernest come to him in an evening, with one or two young officers of his own family, when he reads with them the history of some military campaign, with remarks and explanations, that he is highly competent to make interesting as well as instructive."

"2 *April*.—Until we know that our wishes are not to be granted, we may continue to hope they will, but Urlichs has not been sent back from Berlin yet, and we

---

* M. de Thile was afterwards Secretary of Legation to Bunsen at Berne and in London, and later became Under-Secretary of State for Foreign Affairs under Bismarck.

shall know nothing of what is determined there till he does come. . . . . We have been enjoying ourselves at Tivoli : we all went thither on Wednesday morning and returned Thursday to dinner. Emilia was with us, and was conveyed on an ass to see the rocks and cascades, to her great delight; the Baby was there too, and enjoyed her existence, and the sight of the world, as usual. Nothing could be more beautiful than the spring-green, the trees everywhere bursting out, and thus presenting a variety of tints greater than could be furnished at any other time before the autumn ; the dark ever-green oaks, and pines, and cypresses, and the silvery olives, contrasting with the deciduous trees, particularly in the Villa Adriana, which I had never been more struck with. Charles enjoyed himself as usual, in being allowed such an interval of rest from care and trouble, and such an opportunity of air, and exercise, and peace : Abeken and Kestner were there also. We dined by the Temple of the Sybil in the open air, and remained till the sun had set, then went in, and during and after tea read Göthe and Shakspeare—in the latter finishing *Hamlet*, which we have been reading together in an evening occasionally of late."

It was on Easter Monday, as Bunsen and his family were emerging from the Protestant chapel where they had just received the Sacrament, that Urlichs met him with dispatches from Berlin. The news they contained was a practical dismissal, though the lingering kindness of the King caused the notice to be so worded as to give least possible cause for mortification—Bunsen was *permitted* to make use of his oft-requested leave of absence for a journey to England !

Short indeed was the time for which it was possible to stay in the Palazzo Caffarelli—the happy home of twenty-one years—"the dear Capitol, the one idolised spot on earth," as Bunsen called it in a letter to Arnold. On the 28th of April, 1838, he quitted it with firm step and unbroken spirit, saying to his wife, "Come, and let us seek another Capitol elsewhere."

MADAME BUNSEN *to her* SON GEORGE.

"It was impossible for me to go, as feeling would have prompted, to look for the last time at objects of interest without end, endeared by long recollection; only, in the last hour of daylight, two evenings before we set out, I went with your Father, Abeken, and Theodore, to visit the graves of your little brother and sister that lie near the Pyramid of Caius Cestius, where I gathered the first sweet-scented rose of the year; and in the way home we entered the Colosseum: and the very last evening, your Father and I went to take leave of Valentini,* whose grief at parting with us I shall never forget, any more than the faithful friendship he has shown us for so many years. By accident I went into the garden, to look out some pots of flowers to send to Kestner—and felt that it was well that business called me away, and that I had no time to indulge in feelings which can do no good."

To her SON ERNEST.

"We left our beloved Rome, the home of so many

* A Roman Banker acting as Prussian Consul.

years, endeared in so many ways, on the 28th of April, at
half-past 6 in the morning; not having received till Easter
Monday the 16th, through Dr. Urlichs, the requested leave
of absence to go to England. I think you will give us
credit for having got ready in so short a time, considering
that before we got into the carriage everything belonging
to us was packed—not only the comparatively small
mass that we carried with us, but thirty large cases-full:
what remained was either the *Eiserne Bestand* (that
is furniture paid for by the King, and belonging to
the Legation), or set apart to be sold after our departure by
the care of Abeken. The same day that we departed, the
Baron de Buch brought his single person to occupy our
room : poor Angelina remained established as Guardaroba, and Pietruccio as Portiere della Legazione.

"It was the most beautiful, calm, sunny morning on
which we beheld Rome for the last time: and we drove
from that abode, so long our own, but now ours no longer,
a large party; our own open carriage was put into re-
quisition to take Dr. Franz as courier to Berlin, and as we
supposed, your Father with him; a large vetturino-car-
riage, with a French vetturino, was to take me and the
six, with the maid and Caspar, and Dr. Meyer to take care
of us in your Father's stead: and further, Kestner's carriage with our own dear horses and Luigi, went to convey
Abeken and Lepsius, who wished to accompany us as far
as Monterosi, and that we might have an opportunity of
seeing those two friends for the last time, I went in
Kestner's carriage with Abeken, and your Father took
Lepsius, and Dr. Franz went with Meyer in the cabriolet
of the vetturino carriage. At last we parted at Monterosi

with the last remnant of our daily life at Rome—Abeken and Lepsius—but hard as it was, it cost far less than to leave what we shall never see again : we may hope to see *them* again, and we are sure of their affectionate remembrance wherever we are."

With the royal sentence of removal, Bunsen had received a letter from the Crown Prince, written with his wonted kindness, and urging that if Bunsen were to hasten at once to Berlin, and make his personal explanation to the King, all might yet be well. Advice so kindly given, could not be neglected, and Bunsen determined to turn towards Prussia rather than England ; but the desire to linger with his wife on this their first and last journey together into Tuscany, so far overcame his usual promptitude of action, that he did not fairly set out on his journey to Germany till a week after leaving Rome, when he parted with his family at Florence. Thus the precious chance for personally establishing his own justification was lost, for at Munich he was met by what amounted to a prohibition to approach the presence of his sovereign, and was desired "*at once* to make use of his leave of absence for his journey to England."

MADAME BUNSEN *to* ABEKEN.

"*Florence, Saty. Morng., May* 5, 1838.—Not till this moment has it been possible for me to attempt to write, and now the words will be few, and probably the fewer because the world of matter, of thoughts and feelings, threatens to choke utterance. That I should really have left Rome, not to return, is still an idea that I do not compass. I have seen at Siena and here, wonders of ancient art that deserve more days of contemplation than I have had minutes to give them : but general impressions I hope to bring away, and some individual images will not leave me ; in particular of the Chapel of Orcagna in Sta. Maria Novella and some of the pictures in Palazzo Pitti."

" *Sunday*, 8½ P.M.—Here I sit alone—the children gone to bed, and their father gone away :—another event, another parting, in this time of events and strong sensations. I have to be most thankful—may I but feel so as I ought !—for the gift of those eight days spent with him as I have seldom been allowed to spend any—in undisturbed comfort and enjoyment. He has been in perfect health of body and mind, in full energy and calmness, and I rejoice to see what a refreshment this journey has hitherto been to him.

" I cannot thank you now for your letter, nor for all the feelings expressed in it, and in your whole life for some years, towards me. But I am conscious of not being ungrateful, and accept as a free-gift what you confer, wishing that I was what you believe me in excellence, and very sure that my affection *only* is not overrated by you. God bless you ! Be assured, that I cannot pray for my own children, without your being joined in idea with them. Much I could say on the text you start, of not being separated by absence, when habituated to hourly communication of thoughts and sympathy in pleasures. I have often felt during this journey as if you were near, and wondered at the dead silence, when assured of your feeling as I felt at the sight of objects of nature and art."

CHAPTER XI.

THE FIRST RETURN TO ENGLAND.

"Brama assai—poco spera—nulla chiede."

TASSO.

MADAME BUNSEN *to* BUNSEN (after he had set out for Munich).

"*Pianoro*, 18 *May*, 1838.—Before I go to the rest I much need, I must have the satisfaction of addressing a word to my Best-Beloved, and more than ever dear—to thank him in the first place for being what he is, for giving me ever fresh reason to love him, for satisfying my wishes and expectations from him—although they are not trifling;—for my soul demands of him to grow with the occasion, and rise with the opportunity, to bear a moral proportion to the dispensations of Providence he is called upon to pass through: and this he has hitherto done, and may God give his blessing to farther progress! may He give wisdom to meet the conjuncture, and patience to take everything in good part!

"We are happily arrived on the northern side of the Apennines, having crossed them prosperously. Pisa, Lucca, Pistoia, Prato, are all so abundant in objects of interest that it was hard to get away even from the few that we could allow ourselves to look at. The cathedral of Lucca delighted me—grand, simple, the utterance of one idea, not overcharged with decoration.   There I made acquaintance with the sculpture of Matteo Civitali and saw a glorious painting of Fra Bartolommeo.   But in another church of Lucca, St. Frediano, the frescoes of Buonamico, and a painting of Francia, perhaps claim the first notice, and the works of the former will remain with me.   In Pistoia the frieze of the hospital, by Luca della Robbia, is alone worth a journey.   What would I not give that you had seen it, or could see it!   But believe my assurance, that it is the finest of his works that I have seen—finer even than that over the door of the Cathedral of Pistoia.   At Prato we only saw the cathedral, which is in itself a museum, containing the finest of the works of Lippi, and treasures of sculpture : the building also is fine."

"*Rovigo*, 14 *May*.—We had time to see everything well at Bologna : the Raphael, the Francia's, the Perugino, the Timoteo della Vite, are indeed treasures.   At Ferrara, only in the sacristy of S. Andrea did I observe anything that could dwell with me—the painting attributed to Bonifazio, of the Flight to Egypt, and a small piece by an unknown author, representing the Flight on the Nile, the Holy Family in a boat steered by angels, which I never saw but in a drawing of poor Lotsch.   The sculpture over the door of the Duomo is also very fine.   I saw other pictures of merit in the churches of Ferrara, but altogether the best of the Bolognese school appear tame and lifeless, with little variety of composition, though their colouring is fine, and their style sober and dignified ; so that one is gradually screwed down from the heights of Tuscany."

"*Venice*, 18 *May*, 1838.—Your letter is indeed a surprise

to me, in which I try to dwell only on the desirable part, our speedy reunion, for which I am most thankful. As to the cause, whatever it may be, I repeat to myself that being in the ways of Providence, all can but be for the best.

"The quantity of objects of high interest that I have seen and daily see, is so great, that it will be well if I can preserve general impressions clear. I am astonished at the riches of the Venetian School, in which I have made acquaintance with a multitude of painters whose names I never knew before—and the architecture is an unceasing delight."

"*Spresiano*, 21 *May.*—We are advanced into the last portion of our pilgrimage. O how deliciously we floated in the 'heilige Frühe' over the lagune! leaving Venice and its dependent islands behind, and seeing before us, on one side the Alps, on the other the Euganean Hills, rising over the green coast. O why were you not with me! But you were not, because it was not in the way of Providence that you should be, and because nothing is, or ought to be perfect in this world."

To ABEKEN.

"*Venice*, 19 *May*, 1838.—Venice equals any expectations I could have formed, but the general impression is much what I expected : being a work of art, art *can* give an idea of it—not like Naples, the effulgence of which 'Earth, air, and sea,' no hand of man can imitate : but the Canaletti's prepare one for Venice, without lessening the effect of reality. For the riches of art that exist in Venice, I was not prepared : I am astonished at the early Venetian school of painting—a set of names which I for the most part had never heard before. Then the abundance of sculpture, the treasures of architecture: the absence of commonplace in building (for everything is picturesque, everywhere I should be glad to draw), all things contribute together to present a scene of *geistiges Schwelgen*. We were half a day at Padua, where I should have liked to have staid at least a whole day. But Pisa! Lucca! Pistoia! Prato! I had not anticipated such treasures as I found in a mere glimpse at the three latter: and the first-named is beyond all that one could imagine of it.

"A letter received from my husband from Munich gives me the most unexpected intelligence that he will there await my arrival! and that we travel on together. I hope he will have written himself to you or Kestner, and then you will know as much as I. I need not say that I am lost in conjecture: only very decided instructions could have caused such a change of plan. It must be for the best, because Providence would have it so: but you will believe that my satisfaction in the speedy reunion with him is not unclouded."

"*Munich, 3 June.*—I despair of giving an account of Munich, for I am kept in such continual movement and occupation, that I shall esteem myself lucky if I get time enough to pack up before I am called upon to get into the carriage. This has been a time of uninterrupted enjoyment, for which I am very thankful: I have not had a care or an anxiety, the children are well and happy. I met my husband here recovered from his fatigue and exertion, and enjoying as I do the kindness with which we are received by every one with whom we had to do, and the magnificent works of art that are here in progress. I am astonished at the effect which Munich produces, coming to it as I do from the wonders of art in Florence, Pisa, and Venice. I had imagined that all must seem flat, but that is not the case. The Last Judgment by Cornelius gains greatly in the execution, and is a noble work, the greater part finished; other parts of the church are also in rapid progress, under the hands of his scholars, executed after his designs in very different degrees of excellence—those by Hermann are admirable. As for the Basilica, I do not admire it as a whole, for it is heavy and bald. The Allerheiligen Kapelle is so admirable, that all propensity to discover blemishes in it is stifled: I have been there twice, and long together, with increasing admiration of the effect, both in general and in detail; being a work of human skill, I suppose there must be faults in it, but I gladly leave those to other people to discover, and rejoice in the gold ground (which pleased me so much in S. Marco), in the proportion of the figures to the whole, so thoroughly enjoyable, being seen without difficulty: in the selection of subjects, giving a complete view of the Old and New Testaments, in the designs and their execution; in the adaptation of ornaments and subordinate parts—and in short, in the completeness and perfection of taste which pervades the whole :—the merit, as I am told, of Hess, who, as a man of character, controlled the architect in many matters not generally the concern of the painter. The powers of Schnorr have developed most satisfactorily. A great discovery has been made of the method of painting in encaustic, practised by the ancients, and the frieze of the hall of Rudolph of Hapsburg has already been finished according to that method—the effect superior to fresco, as admitting of the employment of all the resources of art, and yet possessing all the advantages of fresco. Hess's designs for a cyclus representing the conversion of Germany to Christianity, are most satisfactory.

"4 *June*.—We were at church twice yesterday,—the sermons very good, Edelmann and Wagner: the effect of the voices of a whole congregation in the singing had a fine effect, which brought tears into my eyes, unused as I am to hear more than our own small handful in the Capitol. The liturgy I missed much, as you will easily believe. To return to the account of things—the painted glass windows are fine in design, arrangement, and colour, and the effect of the Au-kirche—already finer than any of the rest —when they are all put up, will probably annihilate the other churches, with all their merits. The creations of Schwanthaler are everywhere—nothing ever equalled his productiveness, and everything he makes has life and spirit and beauty, although of course his creations are unequal in merit. The head of his colossal Bavaria is worthy of Magna Græcia: as fast as he models, his colossal statues are cast in bronze, by a man full of spirit and intelligence. The effect of the Thron-Saal—columns of white marble, every alternate intercolumniation being filled by a colossal statue of gilded bronze—the ancestors of the royal house, will confound the tinsel splendour of most other royal apartments.

"While I am writing, my husband is closetted with Schelling,* who has been here three hours, and with whom

* F. W. J. Schelling, a metaphysician of great celebrity in Germany, known to English readers of the time through Coleridge's writings,

we are to dine. We were at a supper at Maurer's the other evening, in honour of King Otho's birthday, and met many remarkable persons there. I have great pleasure in the renewal of intercourse with my sister-in-law,* who is in better health than I ever yet saw her. . . . . The children, as well as ourselves, have been received with such eager and animated kindness here, by everybody with whom we have had to do, that I have been inexpressibly gratified, and shall always retain a most cheering recollection of Munich.

"6 *June.*—To-day we have seen the royal apartments—which it would take long to speak of as they deserve. This is truly royal magnificence—all expense being lavished upon works of real art, and real taste, and nothing upon mere upholstery and hangings. The designs of Schnorr, and Kaulbach, and Schwanthaler, are very admirable."

"*Munich,* 1 *July,* 1838.—I have just finished reading your letters by the Verona courier. . . . . To give vent to all the feelings and thoughts they have given rise to, would require the writing of at least as much as I have received, and how am I to manage more than one line per cent.? But luckily in feelings such mechanical admeasurement is impracticable, and I need not distress myself with anything I hate as much as arithmetical calculation : for as you will not even be *thanked,* I can but say I accept most affectionately all you give. Only, whether you will or not,

---

was then in his 63rd year. Bunsen had sat at his feet when very young. He was so fascinated by Schelling's grand attempts and by his manner of unfolding them that he prolonged his stay at Munich chiefly to enjoy his company.

* Christiana Bunsen.

I must thank you, praise you, approve you, what you will —for giving me the details of what you do, whom you see, and where you go—details not only of persons, but of places. How I feel the mention of spots that I have enjoyed, I will not say, because I cannot yet refrain from tears when I think of them, but pray continue to look at them for me, and tell me when you have done so.

"To-day is our wedding-day : we received the Sacrament at the early separate service beginning at half-past eight, and returned later to the principal service at ten, and heard an excellent sermon from Dr. Fuchs. You will not doubt that my thoughts reverted often to Rome, and to the last time of receiving on Easter-Monday—since which so much has happened, both of fact and feeling, and at which time so much evil was apprehended, which it has pleased God to avert. His praises are yet sung upon the Capitol.*

"Pray go soon to Aquila. It is so cool there on the high plain, that you might even make a summer journey of it, though September or October would be better. I am glad your cousin liked it so much. It was a pleasure to me even to read the names of some of the places he had visited, and to think that he had admired the oaks of the Cicolano. But again farewell to the past ! and hail to the present !—to the past χαῖρε. . . . . The beautiful season, and the glorious Tyrol, were a fine introduction to Germany, and nothing could be more pleasing than the first impres-

---

* This refers to a fact which Abeken's letters had disclosed, viz. that the Papal government attempted to close the Protestant German Chapel at Palazzo Caffarelli within a few hours of Bunsen's departure. However, a very decided protest on the part of the chargé d'affaires, Baron de Buch, caused the carabinieri to be withdrawn from the chapel-door.

sion: then Bavaria and the Bavarians do but confirm the prepossession I always had in favour of southern Germany. The aspect of the people here is most refreshing, all seem well off and comfortable in their existence, and when I pass through crowds amusing themselves on a Sunday in the 'English garden,' I delight in the good-humoured, tranquil, cheerful countenances, in the neat and decent clothing, the abundance of blooming, well-cherished children (who seem inseparable from the pleasures of their parents), and in the lower classes the number of pretty faces—not handsome, or beautiful, but *pretty*, and only in the middle or lower classes, for the higher classes are decidedly plain and ungraceful. I have only seen two exceptions, the only daughter of Staats Rath Maurer, and Julie, the youngest daughter of Schelling. You ask me *verfängliche Fragen*, as to the female part of Munich in general, which, in general terms, are not answerable. I am very grateful for the kind reception I have met with everywhere, but I think the only woman I *like* (except those two or three girls) is the wife of Professor Hermann, a droll, original, piquant, kind-hearted, fanciful Bavarian. We all enjoy our existence in Munich, the fresh mountain air and the numerous gardens make amends for not being in the country, and the environs are very attractive, as is the society of the distinguished persons here to my husband, who is very busy, and very much in his element. The dear Baby flourishes, and runs alone, and grows every day fatter and merrier; it was a great gain to her to remain quietly here. . . . . I write now on Sunday evening, after having been at the dwelling-place of Claude Lorraine, Harlaching, and the Nockerschweig, along the elevated bank of the Isar. The afternoon was beautiful, a sky, clouds, and sunset—of Italian brilliancy; wood, meadows, and river—very picturesque; and the steeples of Munich crowning the distance. I can make but one objection to the environs of Munich; the impossibility of being in any pretty spot otherwise than in a crowd and the being able to find something to eat and drink just everywhere. These are recommendations to most people, but to me they would be reasons for not wishing to live here—however I suspect that in many things the South of Germany may be more to my taste than the North. What a contrast is the walk you describe, thro' the vigne of the Aventine! and how many such have I made in Rome! To-day, from old habit, I took with me a drawing-book and the little Dante —but what use could be made of the latter but to show it to Schnorr, who thought of other days—it could not be read in as we sate at one table on the grass, while so many other tables on the grass were filled with company, very quietly and harmlessly amusing themselves with eating and drinking and smoking! But while I communicate this feeling, I admit that it is very unfair, for why should not other people enjoy a pleasant spot as well as I?—but this shows that I have been spoilt, by having what I liked in Italy all to myself.

"I have drawn here and there upon the journey, very little, but still something. The first night's lodging after Innsbruck was a village at the entrance of the Zillerthal: and from thence I have a memorial. On Ascension Day we were at the beautiful Pusterthal, before and after Brunecken: after having slept, for the first time in Germany, at Wälschberg, indescribably caressed and made much of. We read the Collect and Epistle and Gospel of the Church of England, and the exquisite hymn—'Ihr aufgehobenen Segenshände:' and that my thoughts reverted to Rome is most certain. Pray distribute my affectionate remembrance to Kestner, Lepsius, Papencordt, Urlichs, Abekino, Angelina, &c. The children are writing to Abekino—a work of time—and send their kind Grüsse."

The Bunsens proceeded by Ulm to Frankfort, where they had the happiness of spending some days with the sympathising friends of Roman days—Radowitz and Sydow: from Frankfort they followed the Rhine to Rotterdam.

MADAME BUNSEN *to* ABEKEN.

"*Frankfort*, 13 *August*, 1838.—We had good weather at Heidelberg, and thus opportunity of enjoying the views from and of the castle, and certainly, much as I had heard of the beauty of the situation, I think enough has never been said of it. I regretted only that time did not allow of our going up the hills behind the castle. We took Emelia up to it on an ass; and in the two days we spent at Heidelberg, my husband had full opportunity of discussion and explanation with Rothe, much to his satisfaction.

"It is sorely against the grain that I compel myself to write you a lecture, but I have long had the reproaches of my conscience for not doing so. I delayed it for some time, making allowance for the disjointed and shaken state of thought produced by our departure: but three months are past, and the matter does not mend. When I thanked you for mentioning the places you walked to and looked at, because their names recalled to me a world of pleasing images, I did not mean to be accessory to your writing whole pages of description. It is not for my own sake that I complain of the descriptions, because it is one of my sins to be fond of descriptive poetry, and therefore to be able to swallow more descriptive prose than canonical rules will admit of: but they do you nothing but harm, besides consuming time that you know well how to employ. You should, in every sense, besides the highest sense of the word, 'forget those things that are behind, and stretch forward towards those that are before : ' make use of to-day ' while it is called to-day.' You possess gifts that if well employed, will obtain you a hearing : and those who can raise their voices in support of the good cause, are forgetful of their duty if they do not. You have powers to discover and point out to others where the truth lies, and why will you let the right moment go by ? I know, you *will* not, it is not your will that is in fault : but time and moral strength are absorbed in sensation, and I wish you would make it one of the daily points of self-examination what portion of the day you have spent—*prodiguè*—upon sensation or effusion of feeling. I seem to myself in a merciless mood, but I must further protest against confession of sins, and communication of self-reproach ! I *speak by experience*, that no self-reproach serves the purpose, but that which is close bound in rigid silence upon the conscience, admitting no alleviating air to lessen the smart. All oral confession partakes of the evil which the Catholic Church has brought to perfection : we ever practically confound confession with atonement, and feel lightened of our burthen after apparent humiliation, as if we had done great things towards getting rid of our offences, by having admitted their existence.

"Now pray, in your future letters tell me of things *done*, and not *felt*—and inform me of the portion you have accomplished of your projected work. I think your going to Frascati to work in quiet an excellent plan, for in Rome you hardly can be undisturbed : but if you bathe in the lake at sunset, you will soon have the fever of last summer back again. Now I will close my scold.—Ever your affectionate Mother, F. B."

"*Rotterdam*, 20 *August*, 1838.—The banks of the Rhine from Mainz to Bonn, equalled anything that I could have anticipated in beauty and interest; and we had a fine sunset to behold from the roof of the cathedral of Cologne : from whence the picturesque outline of the Siebengebirge announced their volcanic origin, and reminded me, in miniature, of the Euganean hills, as they appear from Venice. Coblentz and Ehrenbreitstein form the brightest passage in the fleeting vision, which I can yet hardly believe I have otherwise enjoyed than in sleep, with such resistless rapidity did the images glide by.

"This steam-travelling is one of the first in the catalogue of necessary evils : it serves the purpose of traversing a large extent of country with a certain economy of time and money, but certainly no economy of strength. I am not ill, but I have never been so tired, and these quiet days in Rotterdam, have not yet rested me. We leave, please God, to-morrow in the Batavier. We met the Geheim Rath v. Voss at Frankfort and had his agreeable company in the steamboat : where we also found Mr. Robert Wil-

berforce, and had much pleasure in making his acquaintance. My husband has just returned from Leyden, whither
he went yesterday, delighted with the Egyptian curiosities.
Good night, God bless you!"

On the 25th of August the family arrived at the
house of Mrs. Hall in London, whence Madame Bunsen
proceeded to Wales with her children. Her mother
and sister met her at Abergavenny, where her arrival
was also eagerly awaited by the venerable Mr. Powell,
always known as "the Vicar," who, himself a man of
remarkable intellectual acquirements, had longed to see
again one whose dawn of excellence had excited his
regard and admiration. At the principal entrance of
Llanover, the avenue was hung with garlands from
tree to tree, and crowds of people, amongst whom many
well-remembered faces greeted Madame Bunsen's return to her early home after an absence of nearly
twenty-one years. The thing which she spoke of as
striking her most in Great Britain, after so many years'
absence, was the smallness of the rivers, after the wide
streams of the continent. " Comme c'est petit! cela
parait un ruisseau," was the remark of the little Theodore upon the Severn at Gloucester, and the Wye and
the Usk near Llanover.

A visit paid to Mrs. Waddington by Lepsius was a
great delight to Bunsen during his stay in South
Wales. The friends used to walk for hours together
upon the hills in eager discussion of Egypt and its

antiquarian records, or to sit in deep converse in the
churchyard of Llanffoist under the yew-tree of a thousand summers. Another of Bunsen's intimate friends
who visited Llanover at this time by Mrs. Waddington's invitation, was Bethmann Hollweg, afterwards
one of the personal and most influential friends of
Frederick William IV. and a member of the liberal
ministry of 1858, 1852, and 1860.*

The children of Madame Bunsen have a vivid recollection of the quiet following winter passed with their
grandmother in the old-fashioned "Upper House"
of Llanover, and the first taste of English country
life and its simple interests and pursuits.

MADAME BUNSEN *to* BUNSEN.

"*Llanover*, 5 *Sept.*, 1838.—We are arrived safely. All
possible pains was taken to welcome me. My sister rode
out to meet me at Abergavenny, and fetched me in her
own carriage with four horses, and my dear mother was
ready to receive me, with her carriage for the children
and maids; the bells rang at Abergavenny and Llanover,
and at the entrance gates were garlands, and musicians,
and people waiting. . . . Yesterday I was greeted with
vaterländische Regen, but to-day it is fine. I have found the
country very beautiful, and the hills higher than I ex-

---

* The father of M. Hollweg took the name of Bethmann—Frank-
fort-fashion—on his marriage with a daughter of the head of the great
Frankfort banking-house. M. Hollweg was Professor of Law in
Berlin and Chancellor of the University of Bonn. With Dr. Wichern,
he was Founder of the Inner Mission. He died at his beautiful castle
of Rheineck on the Rhine, in 1877.

pected, but I am surprised at the narrowness of the spaces, in the haunts of my childhood, which I had supposed much wider. The lowness of the rooms astonishes me, and the smallness of the windows, which are not suited to so cloudy a sky."

To her SON ERNEST.

" 24 *Sept.*, 1838.—In beautiful autumnal weather, this country appears to the greatest advantage, and although I retrace everything as well-known objects, I pass judgment on all things as new, and find this country will show well, even after all the fine scenery I have viewed elsewhere. The works of nature have always such individual attractions, that the sight of one more need never be spoilt by the recollection of another, even though on a greater scale, and of more manifold attraction. I am much struck with the luxury in garden cultivation that is everywhere seen in England, far different from poor Italy, where everything might be in far greater perfection, were nature only a little assisted by industry. It is a most curious sensation to me, to find Henry more at home than myself in my own country, and able as well as willing to help me everywhere. I am sorry, my dear Ernest, to think that another year will end, and another begin without my seeing you ; but I hope and trust the consciousness that your parents are not near enough to you, to exercise an immediate influence to urge or restrain you, will be one stimulus more to induce you to act in all things as they would wish to see you act,—seeking the best things, and the best people, and being in all points actuated by a sense of duty. ' Whatsoever things are just, whatsoever things are pure, whatsoever things are lovely or of good report, wherein there is virtue, wherein there is praise. think of these things, and do these things.' "

To ABEKEN.

"*Llanover*, 17 *October*, 1838.—Although I have millions of things to write, I must spring forward to the present moment, and beg you to fancy us all together with my dearest Mother, Henry included, and Lepsius in addition. In two days Henry must return to Oxford, and in a few days more Lepsius must set out on his southern pilgrimage, and then we shall be reduced to ourselves. Just now our enjoyment is complete, the Cymreigyddion* uproar being past, and the milder autumnal sky having again shown itself, after some threatenings of snow on the 13th, to enable us to see the beautiful country to advantage. I am surprised at the beauty of this neighbourhood, seeing it as a novelty, though so well remembered. Lepsius has won the first place in the heart of my Mother, and has been praised and admired in various degrees by everybody else. The children are all well and are much out of doors. The darling flourishes under the peculiar auspices of the dear grandmamma, whose delight she is.

"Henry came to us in town the 26th August: the 4th September he helped me to convey the whole troop down to Llanover, leaving my husband in London, as he wished to spend some days longer in the British Museum, which we had visited together with admiration and astonishment. But it was otherwise decreed, for a rheumatic pain which had begun in the horrors of the sea-voyage, improved

* A Welsh Society which then met at regular intervals at Abergavenny for the distribution of prizes for Essays and Poetry in Welsh, and for the competition of Welsh harpers.

suddenly into such perfection of sciatica, that he was obliged to take to his bed. On receiving this melancholy account, I set off with Henry, leaving the six children with my dear Mother, and returned to London, where I found my husband up again, but not out of pain. . . . . So he dispatched business, and we saw again the British Museum and Westminster Abbey, and on the 22d September placed ourselves in the steam-carriage, and were transported 80 English miles in four hours and a half, to Rugby, whither the kindest invitations and our own inclinations urged us. Here we spent five days of great enjoyment, rejoicing to find visions realised, and expectations surpassed, in the general impression made by Dr. Arnold, his wife, and family. The 29th September we reached our present home, passing through Worcester and over the Malvern Hills, and I was glad my husband made his approaches to Llanover through so beautiful a country. Jane Arnold, the eldest daughter of our friends, accompanied us, having been invited by my mother and sister, and I was glad to have her longer with us, having a regard for her as a sort of daughter.

"I am afraid Marcus Niebuhr would just miss you at Rome. I never had time to write to you of my meeting with him at Munich, or of the indescribable pleasure I had in what I cannot but call a *renewal* with him, for I have ever thought of him with such interest, that little as can now be traced of the child that I was so fond of, and that was so fond of me, the connection seems not broken; but I have a satisfaction analogous to that of seeing a son grown up in a long absence as wishes might have formed him. Marcus Niebuhr is not as he once was, attractive to the eye, but the mind seems to me of sterling stuff, and to have taken a fine polish, and I should have been very glad to have had the means of knowing more of him through you : for my own opportunity of observation lasted but one morning."

To her SON GEORGE.

" *Llanover*, 24 *Oct.*, 1838.—May God grant his blessing, my dearest George, to the various reflections to which you will be led at your confirmation ! *He* knows indeed that I pray for you in my heart, but you know that well as your parents love you, *He* careth for you with a love of which this human frailty is incapable. May you hold fast that most consoling truth, that God is love, and yourself an object of that love as peculiarly as if you were the sole object. The time may come, my dear George, nay may have been already, when you may be tempted to scepticism, for it is a trial that many have to go through. . . . . In itself there is nothing sinful in an inclination to weigh testimony, and take nothing upon trust, on the contrary, it is praiseworthy, and considered so on the high authority of the inspired historian of the Apostles, who says of the Bereans, ' These were more noble than they of Thessalonica, for they searched the Scriptures daily, whether those things were so—therefore many of them believed,' &c. Doubts or difficulties can never offend the God of light and truth, if accompanied by a sigh after that truth, and a prayer for more of that light. Do you remember, my own boy, the last conversation I had with you and Charles, when we looked at the view from the Capitol for the last time together, in the glorious moonlight of the night

between the 15th and 16th of July, 1837 ? I remember
well telling you how many difficulties in understanding the
ways of God to man may be allowed to weigh upon the
mind for years, but if that mind waits in patience and
unmurmuringly for the moment of being enlightened,
using every honest endeavour, but not rebelling if such
should be ineffectual,—the light will break in, and the
difficulties will be removed, when and in the manner least
expected. ' I am assured that neither death nor life, nor
angels, nor principalities, nor powers, nor height, nor
depth, nor any living creature, hath power to separate us
from the love of God in Christ Jesus ! ' May the comfort of
that assurance, my beloved George, be ever with your spirit.''

To ABEKEN.

    " *Llanover*, 18 *Dec.*, 1838.—To give an account of the
impression that England makes upon me, and to describe
my actual situation and occupations, would be more easy
in ten pages than in the space I can spare. First I will
tell you of the present moment, which is a very satisfactory
point to start from—for we have a sun as bright, an
air as mild, and a sky as clear, as ever yours can be at
this hour—by exception, most certainly; for the standing rule is a sort of wet blanket of sky, letting through
neither sun nor rain, under which the surrounding fluid
which we inhale, whatever you are pleased to call it, gives
no symptom of life in good or evil sense, but is a sort of
negation, moving not, warming not, chilling not. My
husband is just returned in best spirits, better health,
and vehement activity, from his most interesting journey
—of which I *can* only tell you the bubbles ! but those even

the bright of hue, and not the result of the turmoil of cross-currents. Henry is just arrived from Oxford, after a happy and industrious term, disposed for an industrious vacation, and increasing the enjoyment of all about him. Theodore is well and merry, and now at a table with his father and brother, making a practice of Latin declensions with pasteboard letters. The girls are doing examples of arithmetic, to be looked over by Henry. Thus I obtain this writing time, for darling Baby is driving out in her carriage, the picture, or rather reality, of thriving health and gaiety, the delight of the house, the peculiar happiness of her own grandmamma : intelligent as may be, making herself understood by all, but troubling herself little with any language such as other people speak.

"After I received your request for what you call ' ein Wörtchen' on the impression England makes on me, I thought over my answer in a solitary walk of half an hour, and many a page might it occupy. . . . . The time spent with the Arnolds will remain among the brightest in my recollection, and the whole state and order of their house and family, the spirit that moves themselves and their children, that regulates their plans of education and plans of life, is of ideal excellence : it does one good to think that such a family exists, and the pleasure is increased by the thought that we are allowed to call them friends. I believe there are other such families in England, and two or three such my husband has visited—the Harfords near Bristol, the Seymers in Dorsetshire, the Courtenays in Devonshire, and our own Aclands. I hope to inhale an atmosphere of the right sort myself with him at Pusey next month—perhaps too at Lord Harrowby's."

"*Llanover*, 3 *Jan.*, 1839.—Before the Christmas holidays are over, I must accomplish at least the beginning of a letter to you. . . . . My husband and Henry and I remained together to the close of an eventful and important year, and to the beginning of one that can hardly fail to be equally so : the bells of Llanover church showed that a few poor people near us recollected that those hours deserved to be marked, and our thoughts were with many friends at a distance, whose thoughts we were assured of meeting ours. . . . . You wish to know the hour and circumstances under which I write—the hour is the first of the night, and the children are dancing in the room under me to the Welsh harp. On New-Year's Day I gathered two monthly roses in my Mother's garden, not as bright of hue as those you will have gathered, but still existing in the open air : and you can hardly have had a clearer moonlight than we had the last evening of the year. My husband is hard at work, writing and rejoicing in freedom from disturbance. Lepsius was detained at Paris and could not come to spend Christmas with us. Our Christmas tree was accomplished very satisfactorily, and decorated with a Virgin and Child that I had copied in water-colours from a small picture of Overbeck's, in the summer of 1817, when he was with us at Frascati—the only picture of the sort to be found here. The twins have had a happy birthday, the elder girls are well, and Augusta Matilda is one of the happiest and most flourishing of God's creatures, the picture of health and enjoyment, and occupies as great a share of her fellow-creatures' thoughts, affections, and attention, as any little thing ever did.

"We are reading Niebuhr's Letters, without you! but

never without thinking of you: it is in this manner that my husband and Henry and I close the evening, and I am the reader. But there is a sad difference as to the pleasure given by the two volumes: in the greater part of the second Niebuhr is seen in his weakness, as he was before in his strength, and it is plain that the death of his first wife was his death-blow, though he so long survived it. I am continually and painfully reminded of all that was morbid in the mind of Niebuhr, by the letters from Rome: and yet his sister-in-law has without doubt made great and important omissions. I wish she had left out more, but still the work is invaluable. I am sorry indeed that Marcus Niebuhr missed you at Rome: it was one of the things I had reckoned upon, to have heard the impression he made upon you and others. It is a thing that does one's heart good, apart from all considerations of private friendship, to think that a child so prized, so delighted in, should turn out as his parents might well desire to see him. In these Christmas holidays I have nearly read a book, by no means new, which is one of a class that forms an event in my life, from the quantity of matter of thought and edification it furnishes—Southey's 'Life of Wesley.' As a piece of biography it is most valuable, and yet far less in that respect than as an historical picture of the operations of the Spirit of God, when setting powerful though merely human instruments at work to awaken the slumbering church. What will the next year bring forth?—No matter, we know in whose hand it is, and may undisturbedly await it."

" *Llanover*, 6 *Feb.*, 1839.—After an absence of three weeks, just returned to my Mother and my children, having parted at Pusey with my husband,—I give myself leave to take a quarter of an hour from the due time of going to bed to make a beginning of a letter, which would be too full if anything like the multitude of thoughts and feelings could be communicated, to which the packet it is intended to answer gave rise! On Saturday last I was breakfasting for the last time with my husband and our kind friends at Pusey, when the packet came in, and I kept the horses waiting for an hour, to enjoy with my husband part of the contents: the rest addressed to myself, I read in the course of the first solitary stage, after leaving him to go to Oxford with Mr. Pusey. Most deeply was I affected by the passages written on the various festal and devotional occasions, on which we have been almost constantly with you, or near you for many years. You were certainly present to our thoughts and prayers on each and every one, as I hope you never doubted.

"Now I will tell you how the late period has been passed. On the 14th January we set off from hence, my husband and I, with Henry and Frances, and made our first station at the house of Mr. Clifford, near Ross, having spent three hours by the way in seeing antiquities of the Middle Ages, and eating a welcome luncheon, at a finely situated modern Gothic castle of Sir Samuel Meyrick, Goodrich near Ross. A day and a half were passed delightfully in the enjoyment of cordial hospitality, and most agreeable society, Mr. Clifford being perfect as host, and his nieces coming forward to great advantage as hostesses: the country too is beautiful, and the weather was so ideally fine that you could scarcely have had it more brilliant, though it might be warmer in Rome. Mr. Clifford has a fine library, his youngest niece plays surprisingly on the pianoforte, he has Italianized his garden—what would you have more? Gladly would we have stayed longer, but we were expected on the 16th at Gloucester, where a kind welcome awaited us at the Bishop's palace. He is a first cousin and an old friend of mine, and having been among the visitors at Llanover during the *Welsh week*, had already made the acquaintance of my husband, as I had that of his wife. It was a great pleasure to me to see how kindly my husband and my former—playfellow I had almost said (*con rispetto parlando*) took to one another; but the day and a half we passed at Gloucester gave us scarcely any leisure for conversing with the good Bishop, whose mornings are nearly engrossed by the concerns of his diocese. A Bishop in these days sleeps not on roses; but some of the evils attending his position, hemming the usefulness of the best-intentioned—must, one should think, now be remedied, as a prodigious spirit has been aroused for the defence and renovation of the Church of England, in a very considerable and weighty part of the nation, which is at work on various points. The idea of the possibility of your coming to England while we are here, is a very delightful one, and for few things can I answer more certainly, than for my Mother's being very glad to see you. But you must do that which is good and right for yourself, and your own prospects in life, and your own serious occupations, and depend upon it, England would be to you a place of 'geistiges Schwelgen.' "

" *Llanover*, 4 *March*, 1839.—I will not let my birthday pass without addressing some words where my thoughts have often been, well-assured that I have not been forgotten in the beloved home of the best years of my life, but that your thoughts have traced the same path as mine, and your prayers have implored for me all I may need. The sun shone bright upon this day here too, and many flowers had opened to deck out the table covered with gifts, although not anemones and sweet-scented Iris, such as we fetched this day twelve months from the Villa Pamfili— the last time I ever trod that ground, though the enjoyment of it was not marred by any such consciousness. This morning my children and my niece Augusta Charlotte had prepared each something for me, helped and directed by their dear grandmamma; my sister had added a piece of her beautiful embroidery, and her sister-in-law Mrs. Berrington * a painting of an anemone and cyclamen: but what rendered the scene quite original and unlike any other such morning, was a set of humorous verses, concocted by the two last-named ladies, explanatory of the qualities of the gifts, and intentions of the various donors, recited by my sister in the name of each, not omitting Augusta Matilda, who enjoyed bringing me a bag, after all the rest, as much as anybody. Afterwards the twins, Mary, Augusta-Matilda and I, had a drive in an open carriage, and since that I have been out a long time, seeing my Roman ranunculuses planted in my Mother's garden.

"It was on the 18th January that we went to Pusey, where we found our kind friends such as they ever were towards us, and rejoiced to witness the effects of their beneficent and Christian spirit on all around them, as well as to experience those of their good taste in the

---

* Only sister of Sir Benjamin Hall.

selection of society. But I wish there were any means of infusing into that family some of that physical health and vigour which many people know not how to use, but to purposes of evil! they have so much moral soundness and Christian strength of mind, which it is painful to see is only just enough to support them on the defensive against the daily trials of their lives. . . . . Mr. Pusey has a fine new-made Italian garden, with the inherited decoration of noble forest-trees: but that part of England has no beauty, except from fine cultivation. As for the skirts of hilly tracts! like Monmouthshire, not to go farther!—it will be hard to live without seeing barren summits rising over cultivated undulations—*Ma tutto si fa.*

"I made for the first time in my life a journey alone, that is, with Frances and a maid, from Pusey home, and divided it by sleeping at Gloucester, where I stayed over Sunday at the Bishop's, saw my good cousin, in robes, lawn sleeves, and wig, go into the cathedral, and enjoyed the cathedral service in perfection in that magnificent building. The organ was fine, the choir good, and the chaunting left nothing to wish but that it had been (after the fashion of S. Salvatore in Maximis) much slower than the custom retained with too much exactness from Roman-Catholic times. During this visit I had the pleasure of much conversation, and of a very satisfactory renewal of intercourse with the really good and estimable Bishop, who alas! in the prime of life is threatened with blindness, but bears his deprivation with exemplary resignation and cheerfulness. On reaching Llanover I found that the children had all been well and good, under the care of dear grandmamma, and most dutifully put off being ill till I returned, but no sooner was I back, than one after another began to ail."

" *Llanover*, 15 *March*, 1839.—Whether or not there will be any certainty on the point that most interests me,—my husband's going directly to Berlin, or remaining some months longer here, before this letter is sent, I know not. Had he leisure to give you only the rapid view of the passing events of his London life which he sends me—only a list of engagements and interviews and conversations, and of names of his associates— what a a rich treat it would be to you ! It must have been a period of as much interest and high-strained intellectual activity, with enjoyment, as any he ever passed through. The quantity of *work* he has done, besides being on the full stretch of observation, conversation, and locomotion, is beyond my comprehension; even though I know he has accomplished the apparent impossibility in London of early rising. His contribution to the biography of Niebuhr is *one* of the works begun and completed within a few days' time, since he has been in London. He is continually meeting Gladstone, and for hours together. Lady Raffles he often sees, and she remembers you with great affection: she has brought my husband and Mrs. Fry together, and they have had a memorable conversation. His being in England will leave its traces, I believe ! and his reception is such as perhaps no foreigner ever met with before."

Many were the long absences of Bunsen, in London, and on visits to the Aclands, Puseys, and to Mr. Harford of Blaise Castle—to whom he was introduced by Sir Thomas Acland, during the time spent by the

family at Llanover. He was welcomed, both in London and in English country-houses with an enthusiasm,
which could little be anticipated for one who had
arrived, " to all appearance, a man supposed to have no
chance for the future but through the favour of his
own Government, which he seemed to have forfeited."
His simple and ever hopeful nature, gave him a peculiar
charm, which is well indicated in the farewell words of
his Russian friend Joukovsky, who had been much
with him in London—" Conservez toujours votre coeur
d'enfant! vous êtes le premier enfant de cinquante ans
que j'ai jamais rencontré."

During the earlier of her husband's absences Madame
Bunsen remained at Llanover in the happiness of once
more uniting the duties of mother and daughter, but in
May, 1839, she joined Bunsen in London.

To her MOTHER.

" *London,* 19 *May,* 1839.—Endless dinner-parties and
visits : I know not how much I shall be able to collect to
communicate out of the turmoil of my thoughts. Last night
we found a card from Lord Palmerston, inviting the
Chevalier Bunsen to his dinner on the Queen's birthday.
This it is decided must not be declined. I know not what
people mean by pre-supposition of doing what they intend :
we do in general everything *but* what we first intend. I
saw yesterday, besides the old pictures and old friends at
Bridgewater House, a modern picture that astonished me,
by M. de la Roche, a Frenchman : I had not supposed
anything so classical could come out of the present day,

much less out of Paris. . . . . O! I long to be back with you all! I shall breathe next week at Lady Raffles's. This is a strange life to be called amusement."

" *Cambridge*, 22 *May*, 1839.—We had the pleasantest journey possible yesterday in the fly-coach, sat at our ease in the delicious refreshing air, saw on all sides flowers and verdure, and on arriving at Chesterford by way of Epping —all unknown regions, found Mr. Herbert's phaeton waiting for us, which brought us to Ickleton. Here we were received with a kindness which quite touched me. The house is one of those whimsical old ones, added to and modified by successive possessors, which bear all the marks of having been lived in and hallowed by human existence and human feeling : nicely fitted up, much old furniture, and a fine library. This morning we set off early for Cambridge. . . . . In the quadrangle of Trinity we met Mr. Whewell, whom I like very much and who conducted us most kindly till he was called away, and then Mr. Flint brought us to evening service at King's College Chapel. There Mr. Townley had offered to bespeak an anthem such as we should admire, and the choice fell upon Haydn's ' Let there be Light,' with the succeeding air and chorus—a singular and most unsuitable selection as a part of church-service, though in itself beautiful, and sung by very fine voices, accompanied by an exquisite organ. King's Chapel is indeed magnificent; but altogether I am surprised and delighted with the Cambridge buildings, which I think are in general *dénigré*—and such grouping of buildings with fine trees, turf, water, and blossoming shrubs, I do not remember to have seen. Many a point did I long to draw. Mrs. Herbert planned showing us

Audley End, but we must be satisfied with the view from the road, which I was inexpressibly struck with—building, trees, green inequalities, river, and bridge. The river Cam surprised me among other things—a very pretty river, clear, and full up to the green margin."

"*London, Trinity Sunday, 26 May*, 1839.—Many are the people I have seen, and most obliging the recognition I have met with, from many a person where I have not expected it. I wonder at it, considering what the world is. and that I am neither my husband nor my sister. But before I tell any more of our evenings, I must speak of this day, when I went with Charles to Guy's Hospital, to hear Mr. Maurice preach. I cannot describe the refreshment to soul and spirit of this quiet place of worship, the congregation consisting of few besides the sick of the hospital, Mr. Maurice not 'performing the service,' not 'reading the prayers,' as it is generally termed and done—but *praying* with an intensity of seriousness, that would make it hard indeed not to pray with him. His sermon had of course a reference to the Trinity, but instead of being a discussion of abstract orthodoxy, he impressed upon his hearers the all-pervading nature of Divine Love, which as the Father, the Son, and the Holy Ghost—the Creator, Mediator, and Sanctifier, had followed us all, and would follow us, in every stage of existence, as it had accompanied and surrounded our fathers before us. He was calm and persuasive at first, but at the close had a passage of great eloquence, evidently extempore. After church, he and his sister came to ask us to their house, and here again I was met as an old friend. Miss Maurice is a great friend of Mrs. Augustus Hare, and I think a worthy one: she struck me much, as not speaking an insignificant word."

"*Highwood, near Hendon*, 31 *May*, 1839.—A thousand thanks for the detailed accounts of my dear children, after whom every day I long more, and know not how I am to go on much longer without seeing them, and enjoying them. How very kind in my youngest darling to 'want Mamma!' when she never wants for anything that Mamma could give her—neither care, kindness, nor amusement.

"My own Mother, this is a delightful place, and I wish you could witness the dignity, the order, the quiet activity, the calm cheerfulness, with which Lady Raffles rules the house, the day, the conversation. Yesterday we were taken to drive out, and saw the church at Cannons, the place where Handel was so much with the Duke of Chandos, but the fine house has been pulled down since the extinction of the family of the late Duke. The old clergyman showed the grave of the blacksmith from whose harmonious anvil Handel took the hint of the air in that beautiful Clavecin-Lesson."

"*London*, 4 *June*.—The 'Messiah' was glorious, and it was a true enjoyment to hear it with my husband and Lady Raffles, who felt it as I did. Braham performed the opening piece, with the same power as ever! The preservation of his voice is wonderful; but he sung nothing else."

"7 *June*.—Yesterday the effect of sight and sound at St. Paul's was beyond all description that has been given of it —above all was my astonishment great at the accuracy in time and tune of *eight thousand* children: the crash of their voices was thrilling.

" The Seymers are in London and I am often refreshed by the sight of Louisa."

" *Oxford, 10 June,* 1839.—Nothing is like the *absorption* of this place. After breakfast Henry Acland took me to the Christ Church service—wretched music, quite disgraceful—and to his rooms. Then to call on Dr. Buckland, where I could hardly get up the staircase for stuffed animals and fossils. Miss Buckland, aged nine, had been helping her papa to dissect a cat that morning: Mamma tried to prevent its being told, saying it was a shame, but Dr. B. *would* tell. After luncheon we went to Blenheim: the Raphael is alone worth going for. Several people came to dinner, amongst others Mr. Keble the poet. This morning I went to early chapel in an invisible seat, behind not only a grating, but a glass window! that the monastic assembly might not be disturbed by the sight of ladies! Mr. Newman preached, in honour of St. Barnabas' day, but not a word could I understand, so read in the Bible. We went to a breakfast in the beautiful hall at Merton: Mr. Wordsworth was there, grown much older."

" *Claydon, 16 June,* 1839.—I have felt every moment that this is a house I should like to stay in: that I felt too at the Provost of Oriel's, for he and his wife are both good, and kind, and intelligent, and there is no tittle-tattle in the house, and much lively interest in all good things. But *here* there is more freshness of existence: Sir Harry and Lady Verney are both so happy in bodily and mental activity. There is a small, reasonable establishment, no display in anything, but every comfort and rational refinement. . . . . This morning opens beautifully on fine trees, turf, a piece of water, and an old church. I close to go to morning-prayers."

" *Foxhow*, 21 *June*, 1839.—Here I am, my own dearest Mother, at the end of the world! It is so like a dream, that this immense journey should have been performed in so few hours, that I am obliged to recall my thoughts to be sure what the details were. Sure it is that, after luncheon at 12 at Rugby, we walked to the Railway Station, I in state, having one grown-up son to carry my shawl, and another still taller to carry my basket. Not till two did the hissing dragon drag us forth in his tail; but we could have been at Preston much earlier, if it had not been that the dragon got loose, and slid on by itself to Preston, leaving his tail to follow as it could, which it did by means of the impulse already communicated, as long as there was slope downwards, but stopped at last, when, after half an hour's trouble, the dragon was harnessed on again.

" After breakfast yesterday, our immense caravan of twenty-two persons was forwarded in different carriages or by canal-boat. The journey was delicious—and my Mother will guess how it struck me to see that fine Lancaster again, with the noble church and castle on its hill, the fine solid grey-stone buildings, and the broad river and sea : and she will imagine how beautiful the country was, in this season, gradually entering the defiles, and at last coming upon all the beauty of Windermere. At a quarter before five, we reached this beautiful spot, and could sympathise in the joy with which it was greeted by the Arnolds.

" 26 *June*.—I have had a beautiful walk this evening, to drink tea with the Wordsworths, when Mr. Wordsworth took us to see the Rydal waterfalls in Lady Fleming's park. This country is most enjoyable, and I shall ever look back with pleasure to the last week, in which I can only say the impression before made by Dr. and Mrs. Arnold has been deepened, not altered. Their charms stand the test of a journey together, and very close contact in a country-residence : and the good temper, good dispositions, habits of activity and obedience, in the children, deserve all credit."

To ABEKEN.

" 2 *July*, 1839.—I am at present transported about from place to place as if upon the enchanted carpet of the Arabian Nights, and have to reflect where I really am, lest I should write the wrong date. To the best of my judgment and recollection, I am just now at Foxhow, with the Arnolds in full number, and my own George, who has made out his own long way from Schulpforte to Berlin, to Hamburgh, to London, whence after having been received and shown about by Lepsius, Gerhard, the Puseys, and my sister, he was accompanied by Caspar to meet us on the railway between London and Rugby. Henry enjoyed being at Claydon with us, not only because it was a most enjoyable thing in itself, but also because he was glad his Father should see a Whig family in every respect exemplary, and filling every relation to God and man, as completely as any Tory family by which he has been edified since we came to England. We are all of opinion that you did not say a word more than the merits of Lady Verney's talents and agreeable qualities deserve, and Sir Harry pervades his household and family with a spirit of order, harmony, and kindliness, such as can issue from no commonplace mind. He has the immense charge of a large estate (30 English miles square), an enormous mansion, and three villages thickly populated with the poorer orders: nothing is sacrificed to mere show, and there is every sign that the indulgent master not only commands, but directs the whole—another proof of what I have always heard, that military persons always keep up the habits of order and arrangement in their families, whereas naval officers, when once the strict rule of ship-discipline is removed, know not how to keep anything within any bounds whatever. The dear little Lady looks like the elder sister of the three lovely children she so carefully manages. . . . . Claydon is a fine park, with a piece of clear water—artificial, but not appearing so, noble trees, and fine turf, but no other beauty of country. Now I must leave this attractive subject, to tell you of another house in which you are most affectionately remembered—that of Lady Raffles, in which we spent almost five days. She looks down from a height, over green slopes and fine groups of trees, upon a broad and fertile expanse of wood and cultivated ground, bounded by the heights upon which Harrow is situated and which are crowned by its church spire. We had the most delightful weather, and those days, in her society, were perfectly ideal. She ever deepens the first impression she made, and the more opportunity one has of contemplating her on all sides, the more perfect is the effect produced of completeness of grace, dignity, and proportion. Ella is good and pleasing and her head very handsome.

"Of Cambridge, I must say that it is traduced, when people place it so far below Oxford; the general effect is certainly inferior, because the town is shabbier, and

the situation uninteresting : but the fine things of Cambridge are finer than anything in Oxford, and the view
of the principal range of colleges from the gardens and
avenues quite unparalleled.   At Oxford we staid a week—
enjoyed a quiet Sunday, and had time on Monday to go
to Blenheim, and see the Marlborough Raffaelle, before
the Commemoration festivities began.   Of these we only
attended one concert of Sacred Music, besides the grand
day in the Theatre—but daily dinner parties and luncheon
parties kept us on the full stretch, and if Claydon had not
been in itself so delightful, it would have seemed so as
affording rest and quiet.   The Theatre at Oxford was a
grand sight, independent of the extreme interest to
myself of witnessing my husband's reception, with the
loud-repeated and continued plaudits of the university-
public.   Only Wordsworth met with more applause than
he did.   I must try to give an idea of the originality of the
scene.   Imagine the Theatre a fine building, by Sir
Christopher Wren—middle galleries filled with ladies, all
with fine clothes and many with fine faces : upper galleries
filled with under-graduates—*Studenten*, in picturesque black
gowns : ground-floor full of masters of arts, men-strangers,
and a remnant of ladies : raised semicircle of doctors, behind which ladies admitted to posts of distinction—*fra
l'altre, serva sua umilissima :* among the doctors, Sir T.
Acland, Lockhart, and others, sons of the University, and
returning *per il bacia-mano dell' onorata Madre*,—in other
words, making their visit on a gala-day.   Some time
were we assembled, however, before the doctors in procession, headed by the Vice-Chancellors, took their seats : and
that time was employed by the undergraduates in showing

themselves to be at home—cheering 'the Ladies—all the Ladies—the blue bonnets—the pink bonnets,' &c., with deafening clamour, turned afterwards upon public characters, who fared ill or well according to the Tory estimate. When the doctors marched in, our excellent Dr. Arnold was greeted as he deserved—a great triumph in the Tory-university. Having taken their places, the Vice-Chancellor made a Latin speech, proposing the various candidates for honours, and when he had finished, the said candidates entered in procession, headed by Dr. Phillimore, Professor of Civil Law, who spoke himself hoarse in Latin, presenting each person and his merits to the notice of the University. Lord Ripon, Sir J. Herschel, my husband— were the first : then followed others, military, naval, and poetical ; all with uniforms, if they had such, and the scarlet doctor's-gown put on under their epaulettes, enveloping them with the dignity of Rembrandt's Burgomasters. The Vice-Chancellor, after hearing the introductory speech, rose and announced to each favoured person in turn the honour granted, and thereupon that person took his place next to the other doctors. The Vice-Chancellor is a fine-looking man and of graceful deportment. Nobody advanced, bowed, and took his place, with so much dignity and composure as my husband. The new doctors having been admitted, the young men who had obtained prizes recited their poems and essays—one of a sort, Latin and English. This was rather long, for those already fatigued with over-excitement : but the English poem interested me, on the Superstitions of India, and their fall before the Cross—by Ruskin, a young man of promise. They tell me too the Latin was good, by Arthur Stanley, a pupil of Arnold. That Oxford is a wondrous place, and it is indescribably interesting to be there some days, in that college-stillness, surrounded with noble buildings."

To the quiet time of her sojourn at Llanover, belong the following fragments of letters from Madame Bunsen:—

To her AUNT, MRS. RAM.

"I value old friends more than I ever did—for I have, in the last few years, lost so many of those I on all grounds loved;—and at my age, I get no new friends. The younger people are not looking back to those they think are near the close of their course. This is right. It is well that one tie after another should be cut, that we may be the more ready to fly up. It helps us to realize the coming world, when we think of those we loved and valued that are gone before. We know them to be where Death does not separate them from the Love of God, which is in Christ Jesus; and we can say of them, as Jesus said of Abraham, and 'God is not the God of the dead, but of the living.' They live!—that knowledge strengthens our apprehension of the country, to which we are all journeying. And whilst our chief desire should be, to be with Jesus, it is a feeling of the same kind which leads us to hope to be with those beloved ones, who in company with us, joined Jesus here."

"It is in vain to speak against feeling. To lose a person that has ever loved one, during the whole of a long connexion, is always most bitter, however many be the hearts that still remain: but perhaps the bitterest of all sensations, on such occasions of separation by death, is the renewed consciousness of other similar separations,—the rousing of sorrows that slumbered,—and the being reminded how many connexions of friendship and affection belong altogether to the past,—and as far as this world is concerned, are at an end! The sting of grief indeed is taken out by the consideration that those connexions which had an everlasting basis, may well be reckoned upon to endure everlastingly: but the grief itself remains, only He, who was made like unto us in all things, sin only excepted, has sanctified it,—by His sympathy."

END OF VOL. I.

PRINTED BY BALLANTYNE, HANSON AND CO.
EDINBURGH AND LONDON.